Introduction to Social Work Research

MARGARET WILLIAMS
University of Calgary

YVONNE A. UNRAU
Illinois State University

RICHARD M. GRINNELL, JR.
Illinois State University

F.E. Peacock Publishers, Inc.
Itasca, Illinois

Contents

Preface

OUR BOOK is intended for beginning social work students as their first introduction to social work research methodology. We have selected and arranged the contents so that it can be used in a one-semester (or quarter) beginning social work research methods course.

Some of the research instructors that we talked with felt that the hardbound social work research methods book, *Social Work Research and Evaluation: Quantitative and Qualitative Approaches, 5th edition* (i.e., Grinnell, 1997c), was too comprehensive for a one-semester (or quarter) social work research methods course. Thus, the creation of our book—a relatively inexpensive paperback research methods book strictly tailored for beginning generalist social work students.

GOAL AND OBJECTIVES

Our goal has been to produce a "user-friendly," straightforward introduction to social work research methods couched within the quantitative and qualitative research traditions—the two approaches most commonly used to generate relevant social work knowledge.

To accomplish our goal, we strived to meet seven simple objectives:

1 We have written a book for beginning social work students that would comply with the Council on Social Work Education's (Council) research requirements.

2 We included only the core material that is realistically needed in order for the beginning social work student to appreciate and understand the role of research in social work. Our guiding philosophy was to include only research material that beginning social work students realistically need to know to function adequately at entry-level social work positions; information overload was avoided at all costs.

3 We prepare beginning social work students to become beginning critical consumers of the professional research literature. Thus, we do not prepare them with the necessary knowledge and skills to actually conceptualize, operationalize, and carry out a research study—no introductory research methods text can accomplish this.

4 We explain terms with social work examples that students will appreciate. Many of our examples center around women and minorities, in recognition of the need for social workers to be knowledgeable of their special needs and problems. We have given special consideration to the application of research methods to the study of questions concerning these groups.

5 We have written our book in a crisp style using direct language.

6 Our book is easy to teach *from* and *with*.

7 We provide beginning social work students with a solid foundation for more advanced social work research courses and texts (e.g., Grinnell, 1997). Thus, we neither attempt to present an "original" integration of the various ways of knowing nor attempt to "blend" quantitative and qualitative research approaches to form a "unique research continuum" of some kind or another. There are other books on the market that attempt to do this. More importantly, we are of the belief that the breadth and depth of these tasks extend far beyond what beginning social work students need to know, to appreciate, to understand, as well as to become beginning critical consumers of the research literature—the objectives of our book.

Like all introductory social work research books, ours had to include relevant basic research content. Our problem here was not so much what content to include as what to leave out. Every topic that we have touched on in passing *has been* treated in-depth elsewhere. But our elementary book is a primer, an introduction, a beginning. Our aim was to skim the surface of the research enterprise—to put a toe in the water, so to speak, to give beginning social work students a taste of what it might be like to swim.

ORGANIZATION

With the above goal and objectives in mind, we have organized our book to follow the basic phases of the generic research process—from a quantitative perspective (left side of Figure P-1) and from a qualitative perspective (right side). As can be seen in the figure, we begin where every researcher begins—that is, with finding a meaningful problem area to study within a social work context (Chapters 1-2) and developing middle-range theories and initial hypotheses (Chapter 3). We proceed from measuring variables (Chapter 4), selecting samples (Chapter 5), constructing research designs (Chapters 6–9), and collecting (Chapters 10 & 11) and analyzing data (Chapters 12 & 13) through proposal and report writing (Chapters 14 & 15).

Our book is organized in a way that makes good sense in teaching beginning social work research methods. Many other sequences that could be followed would make just as much sense, however. The chapters in our book were consciously planned to be independent of one another. They can be read out of the order in which they are presented, or they can be selectively omitted.

LEARNING FEATURES

We have made an extraordinary effort to make our book inexpensive, esthetically pleasing, and useful for students and instructors alike. In addition, we have incorporated a number of learning features that beginning social work students will find useful:

- Numerous boxes are inserted throughout the book to complement and expand on the chapters; these boxes present interesting research examples, provide additional aids to learning, and offer historical, social, and political contexts of social work research.

- Our book's content is explained in terms of social work examples that students can easily understand. In recognition of the need for us to be knowledgeable of their needs and concerns, many of our examples center around women and minorities. Special consideration has been given to the application of research methods concerning these groups.

- Numerous tables and figures have been used to provide visual representations of the concepts presented in the book.

- A glossary of all key terms contained in the chapters is provided at the end of the text.

We hope that the apparent levity with which we have treated the social work research enterprise will be accepted in the same spirit as it was intended. Our goal was not to diminish research; it was to present the

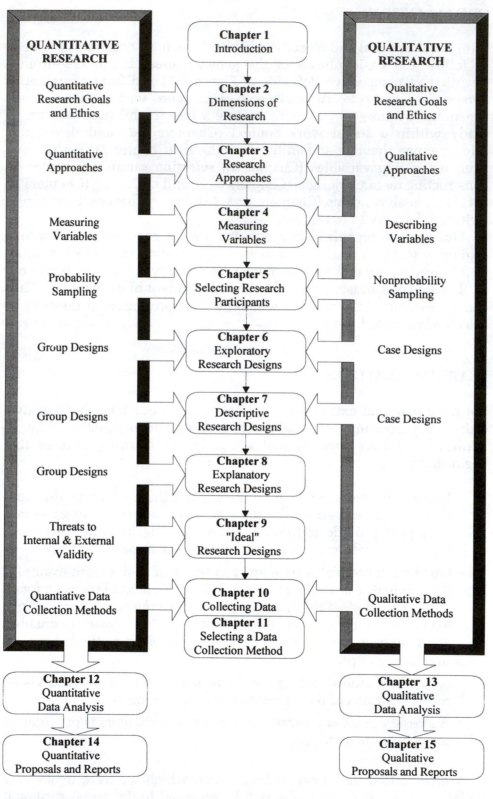

FIGURE P-1   Organization of Book

research process with warmth and humanness so that the student's first experience with it will be a positive one. After all, if wetting your big toe scares you, you'll never learn to swim.

Instructor's Manual and Test Bank Is Available

A complementary copy of an *Instructor's Manual and Test Bank* is available with our book. It was written by Christopher B. Aviles, Ph.D., Department of Social Work at Buffalo State College, Buffalo, New York. The *Instructor's Manual and Test Bank* (including a computer disk) contains numerous true-false and multiple choice questions for each chapter in the book. It was written on a mastery learning model where each question has a parallel version of it (i.e., parallel forms). Thus, research instructors can test two different research sections of the same course without constructing two different exams.

Research instructors who use this book in the classroom can receive a hard copy and computer disk that contains the *Instructor's Manual and Test Bank* by faxing a request on letterhead stationery to Richard M. Grinnell, Jr. (309) 438-5880, or by calling (309) 438-5913. Please state the platform (e.g., IBM, Mac, ASCII) and the word processing language (e.g., WordPerfect, Word) you desire and allow two weeks for shipping.

A LOOK TOWARD THE FUTURE

Research courses in social work education are continuing to grow and develop, and we believe our book will contribute to that growth. A second edition is anticipated, and suggestions for it are more than welcome. Please send your suggestions directly to:

Richard M. Grinnell, Jr.
c/o F.E. Peacock Publishers, Inc.
115 West Orchard Street
Itasca, Illinois 60143-1780
fepeacock@aol.com

OCTOBER 1997

MARGARET WILLIAMS
YVONNE A. UNRAU
RICHARD M. GRINNELL, JR.

Introduction to
Social Work
Research

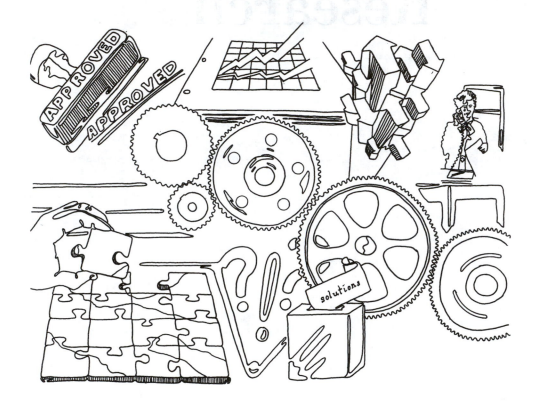

This chapter has been adapted and modified from: Grinnell (1981a, 1985a, 1997a); Grinnell, Rothery, and Thomlison (1993); Grinnell and Siegel (1988); Grinnell and Williams (1990); and Williams, Tutty, and Grinnell (1995)

C h a p t e r 1

Introduction

W E ARE GOING TO BEGIN this book by reintroducing Madame X, a psychic card and palm reader (Grinnell, Rothery, & Thomlison, 1993). She has practiced in our local community for several years and is highly respected. She advertises in the newspaper, claiming:

> With my advice and insight, I will guide and help you to a more successful life. I can help you with such things as love, business, health, and marriage. One visit will convince you that I can solve any of your problems—big or small.

A number of questions should immediately come to mind upon reading Madame X's self-proclaimed expertise: Can she really solve human problems? How does she do it? Is she effective in her problem solving? Is she more (or less) effective than others who also claim to solve such problems? A cynical social worker might even ask: What is my future in social work if Madame X were to establish her practice in my community?

While it is doubtful that any of us would be threatened by Madame X's claims, her advertisement does serve to illustrate how the process and objectives of helping people can mistakenly be reduced to simplicity or, in this case, mysticism. A person who is a true believer in psychic card and palm reading would probably ask very few questions of Madame X.

Most of us, however, would want to know much more about her knowledge base. We would want to ascertain why she feels she can take the complex process of human problem solving and claim to "solve any of your problems—big or small" by reading cards or palms.

It is less likely that similar questions would be addressed to social workers. Society generally makes certain assumptions regarding the extent of our knowledge base, the competency of our practice skills, and the effectiveness of our social service programs. Society is more discriminating about Madame X than it is about social workers because it has greater expectations for the way we develop our knowledge base and practice skills. Social workers—like all professionals (e.g., lawyers, physicians, nurses, architects, police officers)—are expected to have a substantial knowledge base to guide and support their interventions (Grinnell, Rothery, & Thomlison, 1993).

HOW DO WE OBTAIN OUR KNOWLEDGE BASE?

As we know, each of us already has a great deal of knowledge about various things. Some of the things we know stem from tradition because they are commonly thought of as "true" by everyone in our culture. We now "know" that the Earth is round; although, if we had been born a few centuries earlier, we would have "known" that it was flat. Some things we know because someone in authority told us about them: We may have been told that smoking causes cancer, or that when one spouse batters the other it results in a helpless response rather than flight.

Other things we "know" because we have personally experienced them or believe them to be true: We may have found out through experience that knives are sharp the first time we came into contact with one, or that we intuitively believe that the world would be a better place to live if there were no war.

The ways of obtaining knowledge in the above example combined with the research method (the focus of this book) form six ways of developing our knowledge base. These six ways are highly interactive with one another, but for the sake of simplicity, each one is discussed separately. Let us now turn our attention to the first way of obtaining knowledge—tradition.

Tradition

The first way of obtaining knowledge is by following tradition. Most people tend to accept traditional cultural beliefs, for example, without much question. They may doubt some of them and test others for themselves, but, for the most part, they behave and believe as tradition demands. Such conformity has its uses, however. Society could not function if each custom and belief were reexamined by each individual in every generation. On the other hand, unquestioning acceptance of traditional dictates can lead to stagnation and to the perpetuation of wrongs. It would be unfortunate if women had never been allowed to vote because "women had never traditionally voted," or if racial segregation were perpetuated because that was the "way things were done."

Authority

The second way of obtaining knowledge is through the reliance on authority figures. When Galileo looked through his telescope in the year 1610, for example, he saw four satellites circling the planet Jupiter. His discovery presented a problem, as it was truly believed that there were seven heavenly bodies: the Sun, the Moon, and five planets. Seven was a sacred number proclaimed by previous authority figures, but the addition of Jupiter's satellites brought the number to eleven. And there was nothing mystic about the number eleven! It was partly for this reason that professors of philosophy denounced the telescope and refused to believe in the existence of Jupiter's satellites.

In the twentieth century, we may find it incredible that educated people would behave in this way. After all, the doubting professors in Galileo's time had only to look through the telescope in order to see Jupiter's satellites for themselves. Today's "see for yourself" philosophy is based on the belief that "true" knowledge can best be gained through research, which begins with "objective data" about the real world.

In the seventeenth century, obtaining knowledge through the research method was considered a less valid source of knowledge development than tradition and authority (in addition to professional experience and personal intuition, to be discussed shortly). Hence, the professors may not have accepted the "objective data" (in this case, their own personal observations) of their eyes as "*the* truth" if this "new truth" conflicted with traditional beliefs and the established authority of the state or church.

Questioning the Accuracy of Authority Figures

The same dilemma exists with authority as with tradition—the question of the accuracy of the data obtained. Students have a right to expect that data, or information, given to them by their teachers are current and accurate. They will not learn very much if they decide it is essential to verify everything the instructor says. In the same way, the general public trusts that statements made by "experts" will be true. This trust is necessary, since lay people have neither the time nor the energy to evaluate the research studies leading to "scientific discoveries."

Advertisers both use and misuse this necessary reliance on authority figures. Cat foods are promoted by veterinarians, since veterinarians are assumed to be experts on the nutritional needs of cats and it is expected that cat owners will heed their pronouncements. On the other hand, all kinds of products are promoted by movie stars, rock stars, and athletes, whose authority lies not in their specialized knowledge but only in their personal charisma and status in the public eye.

As might be expected, it is advisable to place most trust in experts speaking within their field of expertise and less trust in those who lack expert knowledge. Even experts can be wrong, however, and the consequences can sometimes be disastrous. A social work treatment intervention that was developed several decades ago provides a good example.

The intervention focused on families in which one member suffered from schizophrenia, and primary treatment intervention was an attempt to change the family system. At the time, authority figures in psychoanalysis and family therapy believed that schizophrenia was caused by faulty parenting, so emphasis was placed on such factors as parental discord, excessive familial interdependency, and mothers whose overprotective and domineering behaviors did not allow their children to develop individual identities.

Following this theory, some social workers assumed that all families with a schizophrenic member must be dysfunctional. Because they focused their interventions on changing the family system, they often inadvertently instilled guilt into the parents and increased tensions rather than helping the parents to cope with their child who had been diagnosed as schizophrenic.

Recent research studies have shown that schizophrenia is caused largely by genetic and other biological factors, not by bad parenting. Furthermore, one of the most effective social work interventions is to support the family in providing a nonstressful environment. It is not surprising that, previously, social workers acted on the beliefs of experts in schizophrenia without personally evaluating the research studies that had led to those beliefs. Had they investigated for themselves, and had they been trained in research techniques, they may have found that there was little real objective data to support the bad-parenting theory. Consequently, they may have been more supportive of parents and thus more effective helpers.

While we are in school, our learning is largely structured for us. It is likely that we will spend far more time as practicing social workers than we will in school; and there is an old saying that learning does not really begin until formal education has ended. Out in the field, we will still be required to attend workshops, conferences, and staff training sessions, but most of our learning will come from what we read and from what people tell us.

Our reading material is likely to consist mostly of books and journal articles related to our specific field of practice—whether it be senior citizens, children who have been abused, adolescent offenders, or some other special group. Most of the articles that we read will deal with research studies; many of the books we come across will interpret, synthesize, and comment upon research studies. None of them will explain how research studies ought to be conducted, because it is assumed we learned that in school. With this in mind, we now turn our attention to sorting out "good advice" from advice.

Sorting Out "Good Advice" from Advice

When we first enter a social work agency, as either practicum students or graduate social workers, our supervisors and colleagues will start to show us how the agencies run. We may be given a manual detailing agency policies and procedures: everything from staff holidays, to locking up client files at night, to standard techniques for interviewing children who have been physically and emotionally abused. Informally, we will be told other things: how much it costs to join the coffee club, whom to ask when we want a favor, whom to phone for certain kinds of information, and what form to complete to be put on the waiting list for a parking space.

In addition to this practical information, we may also receive advice about how to help clients. Colleagues may offer opinions about the most effective treatment intervention strategies. If we work in a child sexual abuse treatment agency, for example, it may be suggested to us that the nonoffending mother of a child who has been sexually abused does not need to address her own history of abuse in therapy in order to empathize with and protect her daughter.

Such a view would support the belief that the best interventive approach is a behavioral/learning one, perhaps helping the mother learn better communication skills in her relationship with her daughter. Conversely, the suggestion may be that the mother's personal exploration is essential and that, therefore, the intervention should be of a psychodynamic nature.

Whatever the suggestion, it is likely that we, as beginning social workers, will accept it, along with the information about the coffee club and the parking space. We will want to fit in, to be a member of the team. If this is the first client for whom we have really been responsible, we may also be privately relieved that the intervention decision has been made for us. We may rightfully believe that colleagues, after all, have more professional experience than we and they should surely know best.

Perhaps they do know best. At the same time, it is important to remember that they also were once beginning social workers and they formed their opinions in the same way as we are presently forming ours. They too once trusted in their supervisors' knowledge bases and the experiences of their colleagues. In other words, much of what we will initially be told is based upon tradition and authority.

Box 1.1

JANE AND HER PHYSICIAN

Suppose one day Jane goes to a physician for a medical checkup because she has been feeling tired and depressed. After talking with her for a few minutes, the physician concludes that she has high blood pressure and gives her hypertension medication. Following the physician's advice, Jane takes the medication for a few months and begins to feel better. Since she is now feeling better, she phones the physician and asks if it is all right to stop taking the medication. The physician says yes.

At no time did the physician take her blood pressure, either to confirm the initial diagnostic hunch or to determine the effects of the medication. Hence, it was entirely possible that she was taking a drug for which she had no need, or a drug that could actually harm her, or that she stopped taking the medication that was helping her. The point here is that the physician made crucial decisions to begin and end intervention (treatment) without gathering all the necessary data.

Ethical social workers do *not* do what the physician did in the preceding two paragraphs. Just as the wrong medication has the potential to harm, so does the wrong social work intervention. In the past, some studies have shown that the recipients of social work services fare worse, or no better, than people who do not receive our services. Thus, we have a responsibility always to evaluate the impact of our interventions.

We must fully realize that we have no business intervening in other peoples' lives simply on the assumption that our *good* intentions lead to *good* client outcomes. Although we may mean well, our good intentions alone do not ensure that we really "help" our clients. Research and evaluation must be integrated within our practice so we can measure the effects of our helping efforts. We have a moral obligation to do this—even more so when clients have not asked for our services. Truly professional social workers never rely solely on their good intentions, intu-

itions, subjective judgments, and practice wisdoms. They use the research process to *guide* their interventions and assess their effectiveness.

Despite the compelling ethical reason for using research and evaluation in social work practice, a few social workers still continue to rely only on their intuitions, informed judgments, and practice wisdoms to assess, monitor, and "evaluate" their practice activities. These workers usually argue that they simply lack the expertise, time, money, and inclination to gather the data needed to determine whether their clients have improved at all. These workers believe that trying to measure the effects of their practices is like trying to catch a sunbeam. They maintain that what social workers do is an art that cannot be measured and guided by the research method. Additionally, they *feel* that important changes in their clients' lives are not measurable in the first place.

These social workers are making a serious mistake. They are ignoring four important problems inherent in their sole reliance on intuition: (1) intuition and reality do not always mesh, (2) intuitive judgments may lead to superstitious behavior and complacency, (3) intuitive judgments vary dramatically from person to person, and (4) intuition is susceptible to bias.

INTUITION AND REALITY
DO NOT ALWAYS MESH

The first problem that is inherent when we use *only* intuition in assessing, monitoring, and evaluating our practices is that intuition and reality do not always mesh. It is deceptively easy to underestimate the impact of our practice efforts on our clients. For example, if we fail to recognize our clients' growth and change when growth and change have in fact occurred, several unfortunate consequences are possible. The clients may be deprived of the reinforcement that strengthens their

Box 1.1 Continued

future efforts and encourages further movement.

In addition, we may suffer unnecessary feelings of defeat and impotence. Such feelings may contribute to burnout or simply diminish our effectiveness, since effective helpers must have faith in their own abilities as change agents and belief in their clients' ability to self-actualize. Further, our profession is deprived of knowledge about the effectiveness of a particular intervention with a particular client system.

On the other hand, we may overestimate the extent of our client's growth and change. Such overestimation may result in loss of opportunity for the client to progress in further problem resolution; reinforcement of the client's ineffective coping efforts; misapplication by the worker of similarly ineffective interventions in future cases; and wasted time and money for the client, the worker, and the agency.

INTUITIVE JUDGMENTS MAY LEAD TO SUPERSTITIOUS BEHAVIOR

A second limitation of intuition is that an erroneous intuited judgment may lead to a superstitious behavior and complacency. A social worker may, for example, use certain interventions assuming that they are effective when they are in fact useless. This is akin to the people who wear a rabbit's foot around their necks in order to keep vampires away. They are certain that the charm works because vampires have never appeared. A knowledge-based social worker knows that this same fallacious kind of logic can lead to equally superstitious behaviors in our profession.

INTUITIVE JUDGMENTS VARY DRAMATICALLY

A third limitation of intuition is that intuitive subjective judgments vary dramatically from person to person. Obviously, one social worker's intuition is not necessarily the same as another's. Two people who observe the same phenomenon can easily come to very different conclusions about what was seen. So, for example, in the absence of valid and reliable data documenting client change over the course of an intervention, there is no basis to support the assertions of either the worker who maintains that "little change" has occurred or the worker who asserts that "much change" has occurred.

INTUITION IS SUSCEPTIBLE TO BIAS

Finally, intuition is notoriously susceptible to bias. Workers who believe it is important to uncover early childhood experiences in order to unleash pent-up rage and grief, for example, may consider the client's newfound tears as indicators of forward "movement." The client, on the other hand, may be horrified at falling apart. Is the client growing or decompensating? This is a question that intuition alone cannot answer.

Or, consider a director of residential institutions for juveniles who have committed violent crimes. The director may view a child whose only offense is truancy to be less in need of help than other children because he or she compares the child with the other youths at the institution. Health planners who come from a mental health background may see mental illness as the most compelling community health problem to be addressed simply because, in their own work, they are confronted by it daily, even when other public health issues may in fact be more widespread or intense. In short, our individual biases color our intuitions and thus our intuitions are not necessarily valid indicators of reality.

Source: Grinnell and Siegel (1988)

Like all knowledge derived from these two sources, the practice recommendations offered by our colleagues allow us to learn from the achievements and mistakes of those who have tried to do our job before us. We do not have to "reinvent the wheel." We are being given a head start.

On the other hand, knowledge derived from tradition and authority has the disadvantage that it can become too comfortable. We know that the traditional approaches to client problems practiced in our agency are effective because everyone says they are; we know that certain intervention strategies work because they have worked for years. And armed with this comfortable and certain knowledge, we may not look for better ways of helping our clients.

In addition, we may not wish to test the intervention methods presently employed to see if they work as well as our colleagues say. We may even be inclined to reject out-of-hand evidence that our present interventions are ineffective or that there is a better way. And if we do happen to seek and find new interventions, we may discover that our colleagues are unreceptive or even hostile. Tradition dies hard, and authority is not so easily relinquished.

In summary, authority is one of the many ways of knowing, and it is sometimes confused with the use of professional practice experience and personal intuition as two additional ways of knowing. We now turn our attention to how professional experience and personal intuition are used in the generation of social work knowledge.

Professional Experience and Personal Intuition

The third and fourth ways of obtaining knowledge are through professional experience and personal intuition. Learning from professional experience is great—no one will ever deny this. Relying solely on personal intuition, sometimes referred to as *common sense,* however, is another matter. There are many reasons why we should not rely solely on personal intuitions when working with clients. Box 1.1, contained on the previous two pages, illustrates this point further by using a simple example we all can relate to—our own personal intuition.

Media Myths

The fifth way of obtaining knowledge is by watching television shows and movies in addition to reading newspapers and magazine articles. These four forms of communication provide rich information (right and wrong) about the social life of individuals and society in general. Most people, for example, who have had no contact with criminals learn about crime by these forms of communication. However, as we know too well, the media can easily perpetuate the myths of any given culture (Neuman, 1997):

. . . The media show that most people who receive welfare are African American (most are actually non-African American), that most people who are mentally ill are violent and dangerous (only a small percentage actually are), and that most people who are elderly are senile and in nursing homes (a tiny minority are).

Also, a selected emphasis on an issue by the media can change public thinking about it. For example, television repeatedly shows low-income, inner-city African-American youth using illegal drugs. Eventually, most people "know" that urban African Americans use illegal drugs at a much higher rate than other groups in the United States, even though this notion is false. (p. 4)

The Research Method

This sixth method of obtaining knowledge is the research method, sometimes referred to as the *problem-solving method* or the *scientific method*. We highlight this method throughout this book, as it is today's primary way of obtaining knowledge in contemporary social work research. However, we emphasize that the other five forms of knowledge development are also of some importance in the knowledge-building enterprise.

On a very general level, and in the simplest of terms, the research method utilizes four generic highly interrelated phases:

Phase 1 Observing (or measuring) a person, an object, or an event

Phase 2 Making an assumption on the basis of the observation (or measurement)

Phase 3 Testing the assumption to see to what extent it is true

Phase 4 Revising the assumption on the basis of the test

The research method is *one* way of knowing, one method of approaching truth. As we know, there are five other ways. We may *know* a thing is true because everyone says it is true; for example, men are better at math than women. Or we may *know* it is true because it has always been held to be true—lightning never strikes the same place twice. Or we may *know* it is true because it follows logically from that which is obviously true, such as the fact that all men are created equal and are therefore treated equally in all respects.

Now, all men may be equal in the sight of God but, in the sight of other men they are short, fat, intelligent, cowardly, good-natured, strong, influential, or rich. More often than not, they are treated according to their attributes. In addition, God now sees women who may also be short, fat, intelligent, and so forth. Sometimes these women are professors of mathematics. Sometimes, even, these women professors of mathematics have trees in their backyards that are continually struck by lightning.

As we have stated above, the research method begins with some kind of an observation or measurement. Suppose, for example, we observe that when a certain kind of seed is planted in the ground, it grows into a petunia. This might be a coincidence but, if we plant thirty-seven more identical seeds and all of them become petunias, we might assume that the seeds have something to do with the petunias. We have now reached the second phase in the research method; we have made an assumption based on our observations.

The third phase is to test our assumption and this is done by planting yet another seed in the same way as before. If this seed, too, becomes a petunia, we will be more certain that the seed has something to do with the petunia. On the other hand, if it grows into a cabbage, we will begin to wonder if our original assumption was wrong.

It is possible, of course, that we are quite mad and we only imagined those thirty-seven petunias. The research method is a *public method of knowing,* and imagination and divine visions do not constitute scientific knowledge. We would be more certain of the real existence of those petunias if someone else had seen them as well. The more people who had seen them, the surer we would become.

Even then, there might be some doubt. Perhaps the world does not exist at all or; if it does exist, it cannot be known or; if it can be known, it cannot be known through our senses. Perhaps nothing in truth is related to anything else and all that we think we see is an illusion in the mind of a mad god.

Life is too short for such dismal philosophies. The research method of knowing holds that, in most cases, something exists if we can observe or measure it. To guard against objects that are seen without existing, such as cool pools of water observed by people dying of thirst in deserts, the research method has taken the premise one step further. A thing exists if, and only if, we can *observe and measure* it. The cool pools of water that we *observed,* for example, probably could not be *measured* by a thermometer and a depth gauge. Things that have always occurred in sequence, such as summer and fall, probably will continue to occur in sequence. In all likelihood, rivers will flow downhill, water will freeze at zero degrees centigrade, and crops will grow if planted in the spring.

But nothing is certain; nothing is absolute. It is a matter of slowly acquiring knowledge by making observations or measurement, deriving theories from those observations, and testing the theories by making more observations or measurements. Even the best-tested theory is held to be true only until another observation comes along to disprove it. Nothing is forever. It is all a matter of probabilities.

Let us say that you have lived your whole life all alone in a log cabin in the middle of a large forest. You have never ventured as much as a hundred yards from your cabin and have had no access to the outside world. You have observed for your entire life that all of the ducks that flew over your land were white. You have never seen a different-colored duck. Thus, you theorize, and rightfully so, that all ducks are white. You would only have to see one nonwhite duck fly over your land to disprove your theory: Nothing is certain no matter how long you "objectively observed" it.

Beside the comfortable certainty of tradition and authority, the research method is a prickly bedfellow. But, of all the possible ways of knowing, we have discovered that the research method has brought us farthest in terms of food, clothing, shelter, and freedom from diseases. Mystic numbers do not predict earthquakes; authoritative statements do not provide food; herbal remedies do not cure appendicitis. The research method can do all these things once we have translated the body of knowledge acquired through it into machines, instruments, and tools; in other words, when we have transformed the research method into technology.

The Research Method and Technology

Technology is the child of the research method. It has enabled us to fly through the air and walk on the moon. It helps us to talk with our friends over long distances, to build bombs and bridges, to construct cities, and to create gardens in the midst of desolation. It has given us power over our environment and over each other; it has provided us with weapons and with tools.

First, we will consider weapons. There was doubtless a time in the dawn of history when one caveman (we will not involve women in such an indelicacy) clubbed another caveman over the head and stole his hunk of mammoth. Probably the assembled clan did not greet this with cries of moral outrage. More than likely, they eyed the victor with fear and admiration; they followed him in the hunt and offered him other hunks of mammoth. The more mammoth he had, the more their admiration grew. The vanquished starved, unmourned, in bat-infested caves.

This is a scene that is still being played. On a general level, people tend to be more interested in the triumphs of the victor than in the agonies of the vanquished. They have a sneaking suspicion that those who finish in gutters were of a lesser moral fiber to begin with than those who finish in boardrooms. They believe that victors have the right to as many hunks of mammoth as they can capture.

On the other hand, we now do our best to rescue people from bat-infested caves. We do this because seeing other people suffer makes us uncomfortable and we want to do something about it. Perhaps we also do it, as Karl Marx argued, not to aid the starving but to stop them from storming the boardrooms. If we let them grow hungrier and more miserable, they may finally revolt and profit from the revolution. People such as social workers, therefore, who throw them crumbs, are contributing to their misery and helping to preserve the status quo.

Whatever we personally feel about Marx and revolutions, it is well to ponder upon this idea so that we understand our role as social workers in the light of our own value systems. Should we be helping Mrs. Jones adapt to her environment or should we try to adapt the environment to Mrs. Jones? If we choose the latter, what unexpected nasty thunderbolts will we encounter? Can we do both at the same time? Is that a contradiction in terms? Are we agents of social change or social control? And where does the research method and technology fit into all of this philosophical stuff anyway?

First, technological revolution has produced societal change which, in turn, has created additional social problems. In preindustrial society, for example, the task of caring for an elderly parent or relative, such as Uncle Fred, would have fallen to the extended family. However, we live in an industrialized society. This society demands mobility; we cannot drag our arthritic Uncle Fred with us from job to job or from city to city. The extended family has therefore been replaced by the nuclear family and the task of caring for Uncle Fred has fallen upon the government.

Second, technology has endowed us with more subtle and effective clubs. The vanquished are no longer quite sure how they were clubbed, by whom, or whether they were clubbed at all. Therefore, they are more likely to believe that their misery stems from their own shortcomings and thus will experience guilt rather than rage. Guilt is an easier emotion to deal with in terms of social control.

Third, technology has granted us more effective tools, if only we can learn to use them properly. We want to know how best to care for Uncle Fred, how to evaluate the social service program that cared for Mrs. Jones, and what we should do to help Johnny. We could decide these things on the basis of personal experiences or from what a colleague tells us. We could even follow an intuition. The most effective way to decide the answer to these questions, however, is on the basis of research studies, conducted via the research method. This is more difficult than following a hunch, since now we have to understand the research method well enough to either use it ourselves or to evaluate how other people used it. In short, we have to know how the steps within the research method are related to acquiring "objective knowledge."

Steps Within the Research Method

As we know, there are four highly interrelated phases of the research method. With this in mind, we will now turn our attention to the six steps (and the chapters within this book that discuss each step) that the research method follows in order to obtain knowledge that is as "error free" and "objective" as possible. These six steps are:

Step 1 Choosing a general research topic This step will be discussed in Chapter 2.

Step 2 Focusing the topic into a research question This step will be discussed in Chapter 2.

Step 3 Designing the research study This step will be discussed in Chapters 4–9.

Step 4 Collecting the data This step will be discussed in Chapters 10 and 11.

Step 5 Analyzing and interpreting the data This step will be discussed in Chapters 12 and 13.

Step 6 Writing the report This step will be discussed in Chapters 14 and 15.

Now that we know the six generic steps of doing research, via the research method, it is important to see how they are translated into doing a cross-cultural research study, as illustrated in Box 1.2.

The Research Attitude

The six steps of the research method, or "scientific method" if you will, described above refer to the many ideas, rules, techniques, and approaches that we—the research community—use. The research attitude, on the other hand, is simply a way that we view the world. It is an attitude that highly values craftsmanship, with pride in creativity, high-quality standards, and hard work. These traits must be incorporated into each one of the six steps within the research method in order for the findings generated from research studies to be appropriately utilized within our profession's knowledge base. As Grinnell (1987) states:

> Most people learn about the "scientific method" rather than about the scientific attitude. While the "scientific method" is an ideal construct, the scientific attitude is the way people have of looking at the world. Doing science includes many methods: what makes them scientific is their acceptance by the scientific collective. (p. 125)

Before we go on to discuss the three research roles that social workers can take in reference to advancing the knowledge base of our profession, it is necessary to point out that all social work researchers must be aware of their biases and insensitivities when engaging in any type of research, as illustrated in Box 1.3.

THE SOCIAL WORKER'S ROLES IN RESEARCH

Armed with the knowledge of how our profession's knowledge base is obtained—especially through the use of the research method—we will now explore how we can perform three complementary research-related roles (Garvin, 1981): (1) the research consumer, (2) the creator and disseminator of knowledge, and (3) the contributing partner.

The Research Consumer

The first research role that social workers can perform is that of research consumer. As we have said, social workers deal with people's lives. We have a responsibility to evaluate the effectiveness of our interventions before we use them with clients; and we must also ensure that the interventions we select are the best possible ones, given the limits of social work knowledge. In other words, we must keep up with advances in our

Box 1.2

STEPS IN CONDUCTING A CROSS-CULTURAL RESEARCH STUDY

Step 1 Defining the Research Participants

1a Use labels such as race, nationality, ethnicity, religion correctly.
1b Be familiar with the cultural labels used to describe the group of interest.
1c Determine whether the group of interest has shown a preference for or resentment of any particular label.
1d Ask research participants to indicate national origin or ancestry.

Step 2 Avoiding Previous Pitfalls

2a Consider multiculturalism versus social deficit or pathology framework to guide cross-cultural research.
2b Review Pedersen's (1987, 1988) ten assumptions that can contribute to cultural encapsulation.
2c Explore reasonable opposites to biased assumptions.
2d Use cultural relativity to conceptualize behavior.
2e Use concepts that are culturally relevant with the group of interest.
2f If feasible, become immersed in the target group's culture.
2g Procure cultural data through consultation with the group of interest.
2h Attend to between- and within-group differences and similarities such as race, gender, class, nationality, historical background, and language.
2i Factor in relevant variables to reduce confusion about whether differences are cultural or socioeconomic.

Step 3 Knowing Cultural Variables

3a *Collectivism Versus Individualism*. If the group of interest demonstrates collectivistic tendencies, consider a personal rather than impersonal approach. For example, send a personal invitation to participate, conduct interviews, do case studies.
3b *Communication Styles*. If the group of interest uses a nonverbal and indirect communication style, consider personal contact, development of rapport and trust with research participants, mutual respect, and the use of culturally similar research aides.
3c *Time Orientation*. If the group of interest is present-oriented, understand and accept differences in time orientation and be flexible with respect to time lines and scheduling.

Step 4 Using Measuring Instruments

4a Make sure the the cultural concepts are relevant.
4b Use a measuring instrument that employs the same language, that is, one that takes into account language, dialect, fluency, and socioeconomic variables, of the group of interest.
4c Use a simple translation process that includes minority cultural information gained through consultation or collaboration and testing.

Step 5 Gathering Data

5a Find out about the culture of interest through consultation or collaboration.
5b Use the personal rather than the impersonal approach to gather data.
5c Use culturally similar research assistants.
5d Engender trust.
5e Speak the language and know the culture of the research participant.

Step 6 Becoming a Good Researcher

6a Become familiar with cultural sensitivity and white racial and minority identity development models.
6b Know your own developmental stage.
6c Participate in activities that can promote movement toward the integration stage in which diversity is recognized, valued, and respected.

Source: Wilkinson and McNeil (1997)

Box 1.3

BIAS AND INSENSITIVITY REGARDING GENDER AND CULTURE

In this book you will encounter examples of how gender and cultural bias and insensitivity can hinder the methodological quality of a study and therefore the validity of its findings. Much has been written about these problems in recent years, and some have suggested that when researchers conduct studies in a sexist or culturally insensitive manner, they are not only committing methodological errors, but they are also going awry ethically.

The question of ethics arises because some studies are perceived to perpetuate harm to women and minorities. Feminist and minority scholars have suggested a number of ways that such harm can be done. Interviewers who are culturally insensitive can offend minority respondents. If they conduct their studies in culturally insensitive ways, their findings may yield implications for action that ignore the needs and realities of minorities, may incorrectly (and perhaps stereotypically) portray minorities, or may inappropriately generalize in an unhelpful way. By the same token, studies with gender bias or insensitivity may be seen as perpetuating a male-dominated world or failing to consider the potentially different implications for men and women in one's research.

Various authors have recommended ways to try to avoid cultural and gender bias and insensitivity in one's research. We will cover some of these recommendations in greater depth in later chapters on methodology, but we will mention them here as well, in light of their potential ethical relevance. Commonly recommended guidelines regarding research on minorities are the following:

- Spend some time immersing yourself directly in the culture of the minority group(s) that will be included in your study (e.g., using participant observation methods before finalizing your research design).
- Engage minorities in the formulation of the research problem and in all the stages of the study to ensure that the study is responsive to the needs and perspectives of minorities.
- Involve minority groups who will be studied in the development of the research design and measurement instruments.
- Do not automatically assume that instruments successfully used in prior studies of whites can yield valid information when applied to minorities.
- Use culturally sensitive language in your measures.
- Pretest your measures to correct problematic language and flaws in translation.
- Use bilingual interviewers when necessary.
- Be alert to the potential need to use minority interviewers instead of nonminorities to interview minority respondents.
- In analyzing your data, look for ways in which the findings may differ among different categories of ethnicity.
- Avoid an unwarranted focus exclusively on the deficits of minorities; perhaps focus primarily on their strengths.

Margrit Eichler (1988) recommends the following feminist guidelines to avoid gender bias and insensitivity in one's research:

- If a study is done on only one sex, make that clear in the title and the narrative and do not generalize the finding to the other sex.
- Do not use sexist language or concepts (i.e., males referred to as head of household, while females referred to as spouses).
- Do not use a double standard in framing the research question (such as looking at the work-parenthood conflict for mothers but not for fathers).
- Do not overemphasize male-dominated activities in research instruments (such as by assessing social functioning primarily in terms of career activities and neglecting activities in homemaking).
- Look for ways in which the study's findings may differ for men and women.
- Do not assume that measurement instruments that have been used successfully with males are valid for women.
- Report the proportion of males and females in your study sample.

Source: Rubin and Babbie (1993)

field, as doctors, lawyers, and other professionals do. We must acquaint ourselves with the findings from the latest research studies and decide which findings are important, which might possibly be useful, and which should be ignored.

Sometimes, social workers want to conduct their own research studies, particularly when they have read about findings that come into the "possibly useful" category. Nevertheless, every new intervention must be tried once for the first time, and a social worker who wants to build a repertoire of interventions will experience a number of "first times." It is particularly important to understand how others have implemented the intervention—if others have—and to monitor the client's progress carefully.

Social workers contemplating larger research studies will obviously need to be well acquainted with previous studies. However, it is a mistake to believe that only those who "do research" read research studies. The purpose of a research study is to collect objective data, which are combined with other objective data to generate knowledge. The purpose of generating knowledge, in social work, is to pass the knowledge to social workers, who will accomplish the primary purpose of the profession—helping clients to help themselves.

Consuming research findings—reading with understanding in order to utilize the findings—is the most important research role a social worker can play.

The Creator and Disseminator of Knowledge

The second research role that social workers can undertake is that of knowledge creator and disseminator. Social workers who conduct their own research studies, for example, are helping to create knowledge—provided that they inform others about their findings. Many social workers try something new from time to time. However, comparatively few social workers use the research method of testing their new interventions in an effort to gather evidence about how well these interventions work with different clients in various situations. Even fewer share their findings—or even their interventions—with their colleagues; and fewer still disseminate the information to the profession as a whole by writing manuscripts to submit to professional journals for possible publication.

The consequence, as previously mentioned, is that most of the best work accomplished by social work professionals is never recorded and never used by anyone but its creator. Clients who could be helped derive no benefit, because a social worker in Chicago does not know that the problem has already been solved by a colleague in Boston.

The Contributing Partner

The third research role that social workers undertake is that of contributing partner. We have said that researchers conducting a large study are often dependent on agency staff for help and advice, and many studies can succeed only if staff and researchers form a team. Different staff members can contribute their own various talents to the team effort. One member may be particularly acute and accurate when it comes to observing client behavior; another may have practical and innovative ideas about how to solve a problem; a third may act as a liaison between researcher and client, or between one agency and another. All may be asked to help in testing and designing measuring instruments and gathering or providing data.

It is a rare social worker who is not involved in one research study or another. Some social workers are cooperative, some less so, depending on their attitudes toward research. The ones who know most about research methods tend to be the most cooperative, and also the most useful. Hence, the greater the number of social workers who understand research principles, the more likely it is that relevant studies will be successfully completed and social work knowledge will be increased.

Integrating the Three Research Roles

The three research roles are not independent of one another. They must be integrated if research is to accomplish its goals of increasing our profession's knowledge base and improving the effectiveness of our interventions with clients.

The issue is not whether social workers should consume research findings, produce and disseminate research results, or become contributing partners in research studies. Rather it is whether they can engage the full spectrum of available knowledge and skills in the continual improvement of their practices. Social workers who adopt only one or two research roles are shortchanging themselves and their clients (Reid & Smith, 1989):

> . . . If research is to be used to full advantage to advance the goals of social work, the profession needs to develop a climate in which both doing and consuming research are normal professional activities. By this we do not mean that all social workers should necessarily do research or that all practice should be based on the results of research, but rather that an ability to carry out studies at some level and the facility in using scientifically based knowledge should be an integral part of the skills that social workers have and use. (p. ix)

There are economic as well as ethical reasons for our profession's commitment to research and evaluation. It was once believed that perhaps throwing money at social problems would solve them. Today, funding sources demand evidence that social service agencies are accomplishing their intended goals and objectives. Anecdotal case studies alone are lame when unaccompanied by valid and reliable data of the agency's effectiveness. In the competitive scramble of social service agencies for limited funds, the agencies that can demonstrate their effectiveness and efficiency will prevail. Hence, learning how to integrate practice activities with the research process is a matter of survival in our profession.

Expanding our research/practice base is also a way of enabling our profession to assert its place in the community of human service professionals. It is a way of carving out a niche of respectability, of challenging the insidious stereotype that, although social workers have their hearts in the right place, they are uninformed and ineffective.

Any profession (and especially ours) that bases its credibility on faith or ideology alone will have a hard time surviving. Although a research base to our profession will not guarantee us public acceptance, the absence of such a base and the lack of vigorous research efforts to expand it will—in the long run—undoubtedly erode our credibility.

SUMMING UP AND LOOKING AHEAD

Knowledge is essential to human survival. Over the course of history, there have been many ways of knowing, from divine revelation to tradition and the authority of elders. By the beginning of the seventeenth century, people began to rely on a different way of knowing—the research method, sometimes referred to as the problem-solving method.

Social workers derive their knowledge from tradition, authority, professional experience, personal intuition, and media, as well as from findings derived from research studies—which differ in important ways from the other five methods.

Social workers engage in three research roles. They can consume research findings by using the findings of others in their day-to-day practices, they can produce and disseminate research results for others to use, and they can participate in research studies in a variety of ways.

Now that we have briefly explored the place of research in social work, in the following chapter we will turn to the various dimensions of the research enterprise.

REVIEW QUESTIONS

1 Before you entered your social work program and before you read the chapter, how did you think our profession obtained its knowledge base?

2 Discuss in detail the six ways our profession obtains its knowledge base. Compare and contrast your answer to your response in Question 1.

3 List and discuss the four reasons why we should never exclusively rely on our intuitions when making practice decisions. When is it necessary to make practice decisions based solely on intuition? Explain and discuss in detail using a social work example.

4 What is "the research method?" How is this "method of knowing" more "objective" than the other five ways of knowing?

5 List and discuss in detail the four basic phases that the research method uses to obtain knowledge in our profession. Provide a social work example throughout your response.

6 List and discuss in detail the three research roles social workers can take to generate knowledge for our profession.

7 In groups of four, discuss the possible problems you feel could surface between social work researchers and social work practitioners. Discuss how the research method of knowing—*one* of the six ways of knowing—can be used to highlight the similarities rather than the differences between the two. How can the integration of the three research roles assist in diminishing potential problems? What other solutions can your group suggest to bridge the gap? Present your findings, in point form, to your entire class.

8 In groups of four, agree on one social work–related problem area (and a specific research question) and briefly discuss how each one of the six ways of knowing could be used to answer the research question. What is the overall goal of your study? Present your findings to the entire class.

This chapter has been adapted and modified from: Grinnell (1997a); Grinnell, Rothery, and Thomlison (1993); Grinnell and Williams (1990); Rothery (1993a, b); and Williams, Tutty, and Grinnell (1995)

C h a p t e r   2

Dimensions of Research

BEFORE WE DISCUSS the various forms that social work research studies can take, let us begin this chapter by briefly examining what motivates us to do research studies in the first place. Two articles from Canadian newspapers will be used as examples (Grinnell, Rothery, & Thomlison, 1993). The newspaper article reproduced in Box 2.1 is concerned with the attempted abduction of a child in an elementary school at Innisfail, Alberta, and the newspaper article in Box 2.2 remarks on the unusual lack of stereotyping of Native Indians in a Canadian television program. Both newspaper articles can be applied equally to the problems of child abuse (Box 2.1) and racism (Box 2.2) throughout the world.

WHAT MOTIVATES RESEARCHERS TO DO RESEARCH STUDIES?

One way to answer this question is by examining possible reactions to the articles reproduced in Boxes 2.1 and 2.2. Our discussion (pages 23–26) on what motivates researchers to do research studies has been adapted from Grinnell, Rothery, and Thomlison (1993).

Box 2.1

ANOTHER KIDNAP BID HAS PARENTS NERVOUS

INNISFAIL—Anxious parents are uniting to protect their kids after the fifth child abduction incident since June in this normally peaceful town.

And teachers are on red alert for strangers.

The drastic precautions have been forced on them by the latest kidnap bid—the attempted abduction last Friday of a seven-year-old girl inside the town's only elementary school.

As John Wilson Elementary School ended its day Tuesday, the parking lot was jammed with parents, big brothers, big sisters, friends and neighbors.

"Now, everybody's coming to the school to pick up their kids—or other people's kids. Even parents that never used to come and get their kids are walking them to school every day now," said Jeanette Clark, waiting for her daughter.

"We have to make sure every child gets home safely now.

"This last abduction was really serious because the guy went right into the school," she said.

The culprit, described as a 50-year-old white male with brown hair and a moustache, walked into the school, grabbed the girl, who was just coming out of the bathroom, and demanded: "Come with me."

But the girl bit his arm and ran for help.

Laurie Moore, mother of a Grade 3 girl, said she and her friends with children are emphasizing "stay away from strangers" warnings.

"I tell my daughter not to talk to anyone, and if anyone comes near her she has to scream and run. It really is sad that we all have to go through this," she said.

School Principal Bill Hoppins has created a volunteer program where parents can help each other by supervising kids on the play-ground during the morning.

Tim Belbin, whose daughter attends Grade 2, said he's willing to offer his time to watch his and other children.

"I find this all really disturbing . . . really scary."

The abduction attempt has also prompted teachers to supervise all the students in their classes as they leave the school grounds and make sure they can identify all adults in the area.

"If we don't know them, we have to go up and ask them, even if they don't like it," said Hoppins.

And Hoppins said that when students are absent without a parental notification, their homes are called immediately. "There have been a number of precautions taken here since the last abduction attempt. And we are working together with the parents."

Source: Calgary Herald (1991b)

Readers will have different reactions to the story about the kidnaped child. Parents of young children, for example, may feel fear and anxiety about the safety of their children because they may be reminded that in their communities there are those who could harm them. They and others may experience anger toward those who victimize children and a desire to see them caught, restrained, or punished. They may feel concern for the abducted seven-year-old, mixed with feelings of relief that she was returned to her family.

An adult who was victimized as a child may be likely to have more complex and strong emotional reactions than a person who was not

Box 2.2

SHOW IGNORES NATIVE STEREOTYPE

GIBSONS, B.C. (CP)—Native actress Marianne Jones had to fight to keep from laughing when a script once called for her to utter the line: "Him shot six times."

"It was really a difficult thing to say," recalls Jones, who now plays Laurel on CBC's Beachcombers.

That, she says, is typical of the way natives are portrayed on TV and films.

And that, she says, is what's different about Beachcombers.

"It's one of the only shows that portray native people on a day-to-day basis," says Jones.

"No other series has that sort of exposure. When you think of how many native people there are in the country, it's amazing that there isn't more."

Television's portrayal of natives touches a nerve in Jones.

The striking actress with shoulder-length raven hair cherishes her Haida heritage. She identifies her birthplace as "Haida Gwaii—that's the Queen Charlotte Islands, the real name."

The natives are depicted as people rather than stereotypes.

"I've done a lot of other shows and they sort of want to put you in a slot: You're a noble savage, you know, the Hollywood stereotypes that have been perpetuated forever."

She admits that natives are struggling with their identity these days; wrestling with tradition and the attractions of the 20th century.

"We're all weighing the traditional life, the spirituality, against being human . . . . We're living today."

"Everybody has a fridge, so to speak," she adds with a raspy laugh.

Jones is doing her part by venturing into video production, starting with a documentary on a Haida artist.

"For a long time, native people have not been allowed or able to define their own images."

"We need to take control to get rid of those Hollywood stereotypes, and to change native people on television to real people."

Source: Calgary Herald (1991a)

---

victimized as a child. Teachers, social workers, and police officers whose jobs entail responsibility for such situations may experience professional curiosity.

With the second newspaper article (Box 2.2), a reader may react with admiration for Marianne Jones, who has overcome the barriers imposed by racism to establish herself in a difficult career. Those of you who are members of a minority group may well applaud more enthusiastically than those of you who are not; you may even share her success in some way.

An administrator in a school system that serves minority students, for example, may sense an opportunity—a chance to do a meaningful research study into what images of minorities are perpetuated through the educational system and what impact this has on the students. Some readers may have little or no reaction, however. If nothing in their past history or current involvements is linked to the issues of child abuse or racism, they may merely glance and pass them over quickly.

A great variety of responses to these two news items is possible, each shaped by the reader's history and circumstances. It is in reactions such as these that research projects are born. We may be drawn into research projects simply because they are there—support is available to conduct a particular study, or our careers will benefit from seizing the opportunities.

Nevertheless, a research project would not be initiated without someone, somewhere, sometime confronting a situation or event and finding it relevant. Potential researchers begin with the sense (often vaguely formulated) that there is more to be known about a problem area; a question exists that is important enough to justify investing time and other resources in the search for an answer.

The most important thing to know before doing any research study is what implications the study's findings might produce that will advance the knowledge base of social work practice, education, and policy.

PURPOSES OF SOCIAL WORK RESEARCH

In general, research studies fall into three broad categories: exploration, description, and explanation. If little is known about the general problem area we want to study and we wish to simply explore and gather facts, an *exploratory* research study will be in order. Such a study will not provide data that can be relied upon with any certainty nor can its results be generalized to other individuals with similar experiences who were not included in the study. The purpose of exploratory research studies is largely to prepare the ground for later, more intensive work.

When some knowledge has been obtained through exploratory research studies, the next task may be to describe a specific aspect of the problem area in greater detail, in either words or numbers. This will entail a *descriptive* research study.

After descriptive studies have provided a substantial knowledge base in the problem area, we will be in a position to ask very specific and complex questions that hopefully will explain the facts that were previously gathered. These *explanatory* research studies are needed in order to confirm or reject the possible explanations that were proposed in the descriptive study.

As shown in Figure 2.1, the three types of research studies lie on a knowledge-level continuum:

- **Exploratory research studies**, at the left end of the continuum, begin with very little knowledge in our problem area and produce knowledge at only a low level of certainty.
- **Descriptive research studies**, at the center of the continuum, begin with more knowledge and produce knowledge at a higher level of certainty.
- **Explanatory research studies**, at the right end of the continuum, begin with quite a lot of knowledge and produce the most certain results.

- **Knowledge-Level Continuum:**

  Exploratory   →   Descriptive   →   Explanatory

- **Knowledge Prior to the Study:**

  Very Little   →   Some   →   Substantial   →   Very Substantial

- **Knowledge Resulting from the Study:**

  Uncertain   →   Certain   →   More Certain   →   Highly Certain

FIGURE 2.1   The Knowledge-Generation Enterprise

It should be stressed that the knowledge-building continuum is just that—it is a *continuum*. Neither the level of knowledge possessed prior to the *research* study nor the level of knowledge attained by the study can be assigned to discrete sections labeled exploratory, descriptive, and explanatory. Such a distinction is totally arbitrary. Despite the arbitrary nature of the labels, exploratory, descriptive, and explanatory studies do differ considerably with respect to the way a research study is designed and the nature of the research question asked.

Exploratory Research Studies

Exploratory studies are most useful when the problem area is relatively new. In the United States during the 1970s, for example, the development of new drugs to control the symptoms of mental illness, together with new federal funding for small community-based mental health centers, resulted in a massive discharge of people from large state-based mental health institutions.

Some of us applauded this move as restoring the civil liberties of these people; others were concerned that inadequate community facilities would result in harm to them and community members alike. Social workers active in the 1970s were anxious to explore the results of the new movement, some with an eye to influencing local, state, and federal social policy. Others were interested in developing social service programs to serve these people and their families.

The general problem area here is very broad: What are the consequences of a massive discharge of people who were psychiatrically challenged and who were once institutionalized? Many widely different research questions pertaining to this situation can be asked. Where are these recently discharged people living? Alone? In halfway houses? With their families? On the streets? Are they receiving proper medication and nutrition? What are their financial situations? What stresses are they imposing on family members and the communities in which they now reside? Do neighbors ridicule or help them? How do they spend their time? What work and leisure activities are appropriate for them? How do local authorities respond to them?

These kinds of questions are exploratory and attempt to gather facts in a hitherto unmapped general problem area. No single research study can answer all of them. We must decide what specific aspect of the general research problem the study will address, always in light of the use that will be made of the data derived from the study.

For example, we may consider setting up community support groups for the families of these discharged people. In this case, a relevant research question might be: What types of community support (if any) would most benefit families trying to care for them? Alternatively, we may try to determine their needs in order to develop various sorts of community-based social support facilities such as halfway houses. Relevant research questions here might be: What type of previously institutionalized person would benefit the most from a halfway house?

These two different, but related, questions will involve attention to different factors. In the first case, our study would focus on the needs of the families with respect to the provision of community services. In the second case, our focus would be on the discharged people in relation to the services provided by halfway houses.

In each situation, the underlying purpose of our study would be to explore the problem of a massive discharge of people who were psychiatrically challenged and were once institutionalized, by asking more specific questions related to the problem area. The broad, vague, general problem area is gradually being refined until it is small enough and specific enough to be the subject of a feasible research study.

So, for example, at an exploratory level, we might interview these previously institutionalized people in an attempt to identify meaningful themes or issues that may characterize them. These themes may raise further, more specific questions about the initial broad problem area. In response to the current question of what happens to these people after discharge, interviews with them may reveal a central theme, or issue: Because of difficulty finding housing, many return home to live with their parents. This situation then leads to emotional turmoil for some, but support for others. Having identified this trend to move home, we might then decide to pursue further inquiry focused on a descriptive question such as, "How many families are supportive to them and how many are not?"

The process of sifting a feasible research question from the broad mass of a problem area is like putting the problem through a series of successively finer sieves. Much of the larger problem will be temporarily set aside as topics for other studies. Only the small, definitive question surviving the final sieve will be addressed in the present study. In a nutshell, the goals of exploratory research studies are (Neuman, 1997):

- Become familiar with the basic facts, people, and concerns involved.
- Develop a well-grounded mental picture of what is occurring.
- Generate many ideas and develop tentative theories and conjectures.
- Determine the feasibility of doing additional research.
- Formulate questions and refine issues for more systematic inquiry.
- Develop techniques and a sense of direction for future research.

Descriptive Research Studies

The same sifting process applies to all three types of research studies. A descriptive study can describe one factor within a problem area, or it may describe the ways in which one factor is related to a second factor. Taking the previous example, we may decide to investigate not only how many of these previously institutionalized people return home to live with their families, but also how many of the families are supportive and how many are not. We could hypothesize that those families who are not supportive tend to have negative views about their offspring and to communicate these nonverbally, through exasperated sighs and angry confrontations.

Such negative reactions in response to family members diagnosed with a mental illness have been labeled "expressed emotion." We may decide to do a research study to determine which families appear supportive to see whether, in fact, they show high levels of expressed emotion. The purpose of doing a descriptive research study is to gather facts. No attempts are made to explain *why* some families are more supportive than others, or *why* some families have high expressed emotion while others do not. The *why* belongs to an explanatory study. A descriptive study only determines the *what*. In a nutshell, the goals of descriptive research studies are (Neuman, 1997):

- Provide an accurate profile of a group.
- Describe a process, mechanism, or relationship.
- Give a verbal or numerical picture (e.g., percentages).
- Find information to stimulate new explanations.
- Create a set of categories or classify types.
- Clarify a sequence, set of stages, or steps.
- Document information that contradicts prior beliefs about a subject.

Explanatory Research Studies

Suppose a descriptive study has determined that the families who are perceived as supportive to their previously institutionalized children show low levels of expressed emotion, while those perceived as nonsupportive show high levels. An explanatory study may be undertaken to determine why this is so.

If we hypothesize that high levels of expressed emotion are found when families do not know how to communicate clearly, we may wonder whether a psycho-educational group treatment intervention aimed at improving communication in families would resolve the amount of support perceived by their children.

We may also look at the problem from many different angles. We might want to know whether involving these previously institutionalized people in a supportive network of peers could improve their self-independence so that they have less need of support from their parents. Again, these different questions will involve attention to different factors. One study may be concerned with family interaction and another with peer support. The research question finally selected determines the basic concepts around which the study will be designed. In a nutshell, the goals of descriptive research studies are (Neuman, 1997):

- Determine the accuracy of a principle or theory.
- Find out which competing explanation is better.
- Link different issues or topics under a common general statement.
- Build and elaborate a theory so it becomes more complete.
- Extend a theory or principle into new areas or issues.
- Provide evidence to support or refute an explanation.

PURE AND APPLIED RESEARCH STUDIES

Social work research studies can be described as pure or applied. The goal of pure research studies is to develop theory and expand the social work knowledge base. The goal of applied studies is to develop solutions for problems and applications in practice. The distinction between theoretical results and practical results marks the principal difference between pure and applied research studies (Grinnell, Rothery, & Thomlison, 1993). Box 2.3 clearly illustrates the differences between pure and applied research studies.

APPROACHES TO THE RESEARCH METHOD

Our discussion on research approaches (pages 30–34) has been adapted from Grinnell (1997) and Grinnell, Rothery, and Thomlison (1993). The research method of knowing contains two complementary research approaches—the quantitative research approach and the qualitative research approach. Quantitative research studies rely on quantification in collecting and analyzing data and sometimes use statistics to test hypotheses established at the outset of the study

On the other hand, qualitative studies rely on qualitative and descriptive methods of data collection and generate hypotheses and

Box 2.3_____

PURE VERSUS APPLIED RESEARCH STUDIES

PURE RESEARCH STUDIES

Pure research studies are motivated primarily by a researcher's curiosity. The questions they address are considered important because they can produce results that improve our ability to describe or explain phenomena. Successfully answering a pure research question advances theory.

Social workers with a sociological background may be interested, for example, in the organizational patterns that evolve in a social system such as the John Wilson Elementary School when an intruder threatens children (Box 2.1). What are the specific processes whereby the teachers formulate a coherent response to the threat? How are parents, often relatively marginal members of the school community, drawn into more central positions and made effective partners in the effort to maintain a defense? What differentiates this school, where the children reportedly cope with danger while maintaining good morale, from other schools where similar stress would have more debilitating effects?

Social workers with a psychological background also would be interested in responses to stress, but from a different perspective. If their focus is on the development of personality, they may attempt to identify traits that allow some children to cope more effectively with danger than others. If they focus on the perpetrators, they may try to learn what it is about such people that could explain why they behave in ways that are repellent to most other people.

All of these potential research questions are motivated by a desire to increase or improve the knowledge base of our profession. The questions have a theoretical relevance, and the purpose in seeking to answer them is to advance basic knowledge about how social systems organize themselves or how personality develops.

APPLIED RESEARCH STUDIES

The advantage of applied research over pure research is pointed up in a defense of "useful" rather than "useless" facts presented by Sherlock Holmes to his companion, Dr. Watson, in Conan Doyle's story titled, *A Study in Scarlet*:

> "You see," he explained, "I consider that a man's brain originally is like a little empty attic, and you have to stock it with such furniture as you choose. . . . It is a mistake to think that the little room has elastic walls and can distend to any extent. . . . There comes a time when for every addition of knowledge you forget something that you knew before. It is of the highest importance, therefore, not to have useless facts elbowing out the useful ones."
>
> "But the Solar System!" I protested.
>
> "What the deuce is it to me?" he interrupted impatiently: "You say that we go around the sun. If we went around the moon it would not make a pennyworth of difference to me or to my work." (Doyle, 1901/1955, p. 11)

A worker with professional responsibilities for knowing how to be helpful in circumstances like those at Innisfail's Elementary School may have some sympathy for Holmes's position. Theory about the dynamics of social organizations or the development of personality is fine for those who have time to invest in such issues.

For an applied researcher, there is reason to be interested in the young girl who bit her assailant and ran for help, for example. How did she know so clearly what to do that she could handle the attack against herself with such competence? Can anything be learned from her history that would help parents or teachers prepare other children to be equally effective should the need arise?

A researcher could also be interested in how the principal of the school handled the situation. Are there generalizable

Box 2.3 Continued

guidelines that can be extracted from the principal's approach to mobilizing teachers and parents? Should other professionals be informed about what the principal did to enable the children to keep their spirits up, while at the same time alerting them to the danger?

Many practicing social workers would be interested in the long-term effects of this kind of experience on the children. Some children will certainly be more deeply affected than others, and it is important to know how they are affected and what kinds of attention to their emotional needs will help them cope adaptively with the experience and its aftermath.

These questions are motivated in part by curiosity, as pure research questions are, but there is another need operating as well, and that is mastery. In a nutshell, the goal of an applied research study is more practical than theoretical.

PURE VERSUS APPLIED RESEARCH STUDIES

The distinction between pure and applied research studies is emphasized in many research texts, and academics and funding bodies often use this distinction as one of several criteria for assessing the "value" of a research study. There is some merit to this. If a research project is intended to accomplish nothing more than to determine whether a particular social work intervention has a given effect, its use is limited. It is fair to suggest that this type of research study is less important in the long run than one that adds permanently to the body of theoretical knowledge that would help us understand why our interventions and their outcomes are related.

In practice, however, the goals of pure and applied research studies overlap to some degree. This is why the research questions asked in both cases are not totally dissimilar. Many supposedly pure research findings (especially in the area of human relations) have practical implications. Conversely, most applied research findings have implications for knowledge development.

Pure and applied research studies complement each other. They both have a place in the generation of our knowledge base. With a little forethought, we could easily design a single research study that could include a "pure" component and an "applied" component.

Source: Grinnell, Rothery, and Thomlison (1993)

---

generalizations as a part of the research process. Their unique characteristics and contributions to the knowledge base of social work are examined in the following chapter. Which approach is to be taken is determined by the research question or hypothesis, or by the philosophical inclination of the researcher. As we have discussed, pure and applied research studies further the goals of social work research and they both complement each other. The quantitative and qualitative research approaches also complement each other and are equally important in the generation and testing of social work knowledge.

The Quantitative Research Approach

A quantitative research study follows the general steps of the generic research process in a more-or-less straightforward manner. First, a

TABLE 2.1   Quantitative Style versus Qualitative Style

Quantitative Style	Qualitative Style
Measure objective facts	Construct social reality, cultural meaning
Focus on variables	Focus on interactive processes, events
Reliability is key	Authenticity is key
Value-free	Values are present and explicit
Independent of context	Situationally constrained
Many cases	Few cases
Statistical analysis	Thematic analysis
Researcher is detached	Researcher is involved

problem area is chosen and a relevant researchable question (or specific hypothesis) is specified. Second, relevant variables within the research question (or hypothesis) are delineated. Third, a plan is developed for measuring the variables within the research question (or hypothesis). Fourth, relevant data are gathered for each variable and then analyzed to determine what they mean. Fifth, on the basis of the data generated, conclusions are drawn regarding the research question (or hypothesis). Finally, a report is written giving the study's findings, conclusions, and recommendations.

The study may then be evaluated by others and perhaps replicated (or repeated) to support or repudiate the application of the study's findings. More will be said about the quantitative research approach in the following chapter.

The Qualitative Research Approach

Qualitative research studies are also driven by meaningful problem areas. However, their direct relationship to the research process is somewhat different. In a quantitative study, conceptual clarity about the research question (or hypothesis) usually precedes the collection and analysis of data. In contrast to the quantitative approach, researchers doing qualitative studies do not use the data collection and analysis process simply to answer questions (or to test hypotheses).

Qualitative research studies are used first to discover what the most important questions are, and then to refine and answer questions (or test hypotheses) that are increasingly more specific. The process is one of moving back and forth between facts and their interpretation, between answers to questions and the development of social work theory. More will also be said about the qualitative research approach in the following chapter.

Now that we know that the goal of the research method is to generate pure and applied knowledge that is as value-free and objective as possible, via the quantitative and qualitative research approaches (see Table 2.1 on the previous page), let us turn to a brief *definition* of social work research.

DEFINITION OF SOCIAL WORK RESEARCH

Armed with the knowledge of the previous chapter and the contents discussed so far in this one, we now turn our attention to defining *research*, which is composed of two syllables, *re* and *search*. Dictionaries define the former syllable as a prefix meaning "again," "anew," or "over again," and the latter as a verb meaning "to examine closely and carefully, to test and try, or to probe." Together, these syllables form a noun describing a careful and systematic study in some field of knowledge, undertaken to establish facts or principles. Thus,

> Social work research is a structured inquiry that utilizes acceptable quantitative and qualitative methodologies to solve human problems and creates new exploratory, descriptive, and explanatory knowledge for the profession.

While we obtain much of our knowledge base from the findings derived from research studies, all research studies have built-in biases and limitations that create errors and keep us from being absolutely certain about the studies' outcomes.

This text helps us to understand these limitations and to take them into account in the interpretation of our research findings, and it helps us avoid making errors or obtaining wrong answers. As we know, one of the principal products of a research study is obtaining "objective" data—via the research method—about reality as it is, "unbiased" and "error-free."

FACTORS AFFECTING RESEARCH STUDIES

We will continue our discussion of the research method by presenting the contexts in which research studies take place. No social work research study is conducted in a vacuum. People engaged in all kind of social work research studies work with colleagues and research participants (who are often clients), frequently in a social work agency whose operation is affected by social and political factors. In addition, and most importantly, we must follow strict ethical procedures when carrying out our studies.

On a general level, there are four highly interrelated factors that have a major impact on the way a research study is conducted. For the sake of clarity, they will be presented separately although in reality they always act in combination. These factors are: (1) the social work profession and researcher, (2) the social work agency, (3) the social work practitioner, and (4) professional ethics.

The Social Work Profession and Researcher

The first factor affecting all social work research studies is the social work profession itself. Research in a real-life social work practice setting is vastly different from research in a scientific, sterile laboratory. A part of this difference deals with ethics, which we will touch on later in this chapter. We cannot, for example, manipulate clients like we can manipulate chemicals in a chemistry experiment.

Suppose, for example, we are serious about evaluating Professor Barsky's treatment intervention for people who are depressed. A good way would be to take a large group of similar clients (e.g., depressed people) and assign each client at random to one of two groups. One group would receive Professor Barsky's treatment intervention and the other would not.

Regarding a specific client, however—Uncle Fred—we might consider that one intervention (e.g., behavior modification) would benefit him more than another (e.g., Professor Barsky's inspiration-driven treatment) and, on this ground, we would oppose having him randomly assigned to groups. If we cannot randomly assign Uncle Fred, we cannot conduct our study in a "scientific manner." Research scientists who work with inanimate objects do not face the same kind of limitation.

Research scientists do face the limitation, however, of working in close association with their colleagues—other scientists. In any professional organization, there are certain accepted ways of doing things, which we ignore at our peril; that is, *customary* ways of performing research studies, *customary* ways of reporting research findings, *customary* ways of selecting what to study, and even *customary* ways of writing social work research books like the one you are now reading.

As we know, Galileo, for example, was eventually hauled before the inquisitional tribunal and forced to recant his various sinful opinions. Social workers who hold sinful opinions are rarely threatened with the rack but there is, nevertheless, such a thing as a social worker holding a sinful opinion.

In our day, it is sinful to believe that African Americans are inferior to non–African Americans; indeed, that anybody is inferior to anybody else. In the past when the white British empire ruled blacks, it was sinful to believe that blacks were equal to nonblacks because such a belief might have cast doubt on the morality of the white British empire. Sinful beliefs, in our civilized era, tend to be punished subtly; that is, in the form of research papers and books that are never accepted for publication, invitations to present research papers at conferences that are never offered, and academic appointments that are never given.

Punishment may also be delivered in the form of research proposals that are not funded. Doing a social work research study can become an extremely expensive endeavor. If a funding body cannot be found that has faith in our talents and shares our research interests sufficiently to grant the needed money, then our study cannot be accomplished. Our talents are one thing; our interests are entirely something else. Funding bodies tend either to be governments or to be influenced by government policies so that their interests are molded by the prevailing political climate.

There are some political climates in which the vanquished are rescued from their bat-infested caves because we feel sorry for them. These feelings of sympathy, passed down from on high, can also lead our research endeavors in certain definite directions. We study the many ways of improving social services, for example, and better designs for public housing.

In other political climates, as stated previously, the vanquished are rescued to prevent them from storming the boardrooms—or possibly because we want our public image to show kindness to the less fortunate. Public image motives do not lead us to study ways of improving social services; instead they lead us to study ways of increasing our efficiency. There is often a keen interest in evaluating social service programs, for example, that may tend to be viewed as inefficient. The topics that we *are able to study* are thus dictated to a large extent by current political and social realities. It is also true that the topics we *decide to study* are dictated by these same realities. Researchers are as interested as anyone else in money, recognition, and professional advancement. They therefore may be tempted to choose research topics that are likely to be funded.

It is important to remember, though, that many research studies can be easily conducted without the aid of government money. When our own practices are evaluated, for example, no extra funding is usually necessary; indeed, evaluation should be an integral part of social work practice. When we evaluate a social service agency, funding is needed for sure, but it does not have to be *government* funding. We will learn more about evaluating our practices and social service agencies in Chapters 6–9.

Along with political and social realities, there are also fads, fashions, and fancies. Minority groups might suddenly come into prominence (e.g., refugees) for whom it will become stylish to provide various kinds of social service. Perhaps Professor Barsky's first disciple, Professor Anderson, will leap to the fore as the founder of a brand new treatment intervention designed to aid persons fleeing from tyrannical governments. Perhaps research studies will be funded to investigate the very real trauma of leaving one's home under desperate circumstances. In recent years, however; our profession has finally grown more tolerant of research studies and is even starting to demand them. The reasons for this are twofold: (1) money, and (2) the professionalization of social work.

Money and Social Problems

We no longer believe that throwing money at social problems will solve them in the end. Our faith was lost at about the same time as cuts in funding were experienced. In a similar vein, lacking both faith and funding, we are obliged to turn to "science" to tell us how best to employ the money we have. Should we concentrate on casework, for example, or is group work cheaper per capita—just as effective? Is Professor Barsky's successor's treatment intervention really effective for refugees? These are vital questions that can only be resolved through research and then more research.

Is our money being used properly? Are there ways in which it could be used better? Are publicly funded social service programs actually doing what they are supposed to be doing? And, is there a way in which they could do it less expensively? In other words, we are now required to justify our procedures to funding bodies and to society in general. Funding bodies are not willing to take our word that Uncle Fred is coming along quite nicely. They want to know how far he has come, how fast, and by what method of propulsion; they want charts, statistics, tables, and graphs. They are not really concerned about Uncle Fred as an individual person. They want to know *how many* Uncle Freds were served and *how much* it cost.

The Professionalization of Social Work

The second reason for research's sudden respectability is the professionalization of social work. Social work has always been something of a poor cousin among the social sciences—borrowing bits from sociology and psychology, pieces from political science and economics, and never really being able to stand up and say, "I am a profession." This may be partly because we, as professionals, are identified with our clients who are sometimes not regarded as "productive" people. It may also be because we deal in vague concepts such as self-actualization, which may sound a little odd to people who are unfamiliar with social work jargon.

Mostly it is because a profession that strives to be respectable must be "research based." It is difficult to define precisely what is meant by *respectable* but the idea involves committees, commissions, conventions, and corporations, with a flavor of well-dressed matrons and a suggestion of well-aged port. Behind the facade lies power, prestige, authority—a position in the hierarchy of the professions. To some degree, it is a question of the more research the more authority because research *is* authority. It symbolizes power; it has become the modern god. It is apparent, therefore, that if the social work profession wishes to crawl its way up the ladder of respectability, its driving force must be research: terminology, numbers! All of the paraphernalia and something at least of the essence.

We must never forget that it is not all a facade. As previously stated, the research method is *one* way of knowing. It can help us to know what we are doing so that the selected intervention to be tried on Uncle Fred is based on more than faith and hope.

The Social Work Agency

The second factor affecting social work research is the social work agency. Most of us are employed in a social service program that is housed within an agency. It is usually within the confines of the program that our research studies take place. The word *confines* is used advisedly since we need our program to support, or at least to tolerate, our activity before any research study can be accomplished. Some social service programs are extremely interested in research endeavors; others shiver at the merest mention. There are so many different social service programs that it is difficult to generalize, but there are some things that all of them have in common. The first of these is worry.

Program administrators have very little money. They worry that in the coming year they may have even less money. They worry that their programs will be terminated or at least drastically cut, that clients will suffer, and that staff will follow programs into oblivion. Anything that even looks as if it might be related to research tends to be regarded with suspicion. The main thing is that all research studies have evaluative potential. All programs, like all people, have flaws and weaknesses. All researchers are in a splendid position to embarrass everyone by making wrong statements too soon, right ones too late, and both to the wrong people.

Some social service programs have more flaws than others and fear evaluation because they are, in fact, a blot upon the fair face of social work. Most programs, however, struggle along being effective and ineffective in an inefficient sort of way and doing their genuine best in trying to help clients like Uncle Fred. They know that they are inefficient, that is, by business standards. They know that their effectiveness is open to doubt by the public sector. They simply believe that a crumb here and there is better than no bread at all.

Sometimes program administrators have been through this research battle before. They have seen disaster flow in the wake of glint-eyed researchers who only wanted to look at some aspect of their program and they will not, under any circumstances, let another glint-eyed researcher anywhere close. They will divert neither staff nor money from direct client service to some esoteric research project that will do them no good at all and may well hurt them. They will not read another one of those final research reports that are comprehensible only to Einstein and the author and Einstein's understanding is in doubt.

On the other hand, positive evaluations are very useful in the area of public relations. All social work programs are interested in maintaining good public relations. Some programs are valued within their community and wish to remain that way. Others are regarded with resentment and labeled as places where public money is dispensed to the "idle" and criminals are "rehabilitated" instead of being where they ought to be— locked up. Anything, therefore, that will improve a program's image in the community is of value, and that includes research.

Another purpose in doing a research study is that it might arrive at a genuinely practical way in which a social service program could improve its services to clients or do what it does more efficiently. Most programs are interested in improving their effectiveness and efficiency, but they are so involved with the daily struggle that they have neither the time nor the money to learn how to do the needed studies. A research project—a *discreet* research project—carried out by a worker who is close-mouthed rather than glint-eyed and uses an absolute minimum of the program's resources might possibly, just might, be acceptable.

But there is something else to consider. As we will see later in this book, we do not always collect original data when we conduct a research study. Often existing data are used such as those contained in client files and the commonly collected statistics that programs routinely gather. Client files are necessarily confidential, however, and it is these confidential files that we wish to tap. Our program administrator is caught, as usual, between a rock and a hard place. Disaster will undoubtedly follow if client confidentiality is breached and data are released to a questionable authority. On the other hand, disaster will also follow if data are denied to an appropriate authority. The problem now is: As potential researchers, are we appropriate or questionable authorities?

Suppose that we are finally deemed to be appropriate. Client files are released in the presence of a program staff member who knows which box to look for in the basement or how to get the computer running. Glancing through the client files, we see that they were not arranged with "research" in mind. They consist of a general mishmash of everything but recipes, some of it typed, some of it written in a rapid scrawl. It is not even the same scrawl! Some of the files have been kept by four or more different workers who have contributed their own perceptions of the client, as well as those of the previous worker; and there are occasional gems that make no sense at all.

Some files, typewritten and bland, have probably been read by the client and are more soothing than accurate. Some of the files, prepared for the supervisor, are neither soothing nor accurate. It is probable that much the social workers knew was not recorded at all. We look at our client files and wonder, quite seriously, if it would not be better to collect new data.

The Social Work Practitioner

The third factor affecting social work research is the social worker. At every stage in the research process there are decisions to be made based on our own knowledge and value systems. It might be more advantageous, for example, to ignore the existing client files and collect original data. If we are investigating poverty and believe that poverty results from deficiencies in the poor, we might study treatment interventions designed to overcome these deficiencies (with Professor Barsky's second disciple, Professor Smith). If we believe that ghettos are a factor, we might prefer to focus on environmental causes. In other words, the question we choose to study is determined by our own value systems as well as by the social and political realities of the hour.

We should remember that our beliefs about the causes of poverty are only that—our beliefs. There is some evidence to suggest that such beliefs form a system with other beliefs and lead to a political allegiance. Conservatives, for example, are more likely to blame an individual's deficiencies, whereas liberals/radicals put the blame on the individual's environment. Be that as it may, we cannot know anything about the factors that contribute to poverty until the appropriate research studies have been conducted.

Another factor in the study of poverty would be our definition of *poor.* How much should we not have in order to be categorized as poor? There was once a movie in which the family to whom the audience was supposed to relate was having a tennis court built in their backyard. On this scale, most of us could probably be thought of as poor. On the other hand, there are people living in shacks who think of themselves as being rich.

When concluding our report on poverty, we might be expected to make recommendations for change based on our study's findings. These recommendations, too, will depend on our personal value systems, which in turn will be modified by certain other considerations. It might not be feasible to recommend, for example, that we spearhead a revolution. Neither would we recommend that all persons on welfare be gathered together and shot. Between these two extremes there is a great deal of room for practical suggestions that will arise both from what we find in our study and from what we believe to be right.

When evaluating a social service program, for example, our personal value systems are much in evidence. We have said before that most programs are inefficient according to business standards. Some of them are also ineffective, not because the workers are incompetent but because of the nature of their clients' problems. For example, think of our "long-term success rate" when we counsel the terminally ill. Perhaps programs in which dying people are counseled ought to be terminated. Maybe it would be advisable to spend the money on some other type of social service program.

Our decision in matters like this, and in our evaluation of such programs, will depend on our estimation of our clients' worth. On the other hand, it is only of late that we have had the opportunity to evaluate programs at all. Evaluation of social service programs used to be carried out by nonsocial workers who were skilled in such techniques as planning, programming, and budget systems (PPBS to the initiated) but who knew nothing about social work practice and even less about poor old Uncle Fred.

Social work administrators, who generally preferred the Uncle Freds to PPBS, quivered at the very word *evaluation* and grumbled about using cost efficiency to measure the worth of human services. A business, they said, is supposed to make a profit; a social service program, on the other hand, is supposed to rescue Uncle Freds.

If we are not careful, said the administrators, social service programs will end up being evaluated according to business criteria. Furthermore, with all this talk about efficiency, what is the meaning of *efficient*? Efficient in terms of time, money, labor, suffering, human rights, or what? Eventually the grumblings were heard. Program evaluations are now starting to be conducted by social workers who strive to reach a compromise between PPBS efficiency and Uncle Fred.

Many of us are more concerned with helping Uncle Freds than with doing research and program evaluations. This is the reason we went into social work—to help other people help themselves. If we wanted to do research, we would have majored in sociology or psychology instead. It must not be forgotten, however, that in order to help people help themselves, we need to draw our helping interventions from a knowledge base. The only way to obtain this knowledge base, and to add to it, is through the research method, which includes evaluation. It is hard work, but as Crocodile Dundee has wisely said, "Someone's got to do it, mate."

In real-life social work practice situations, we often labor under a difficulty in that we cannot say to our distressed client, "Hold on a moment while I look it up." Even if we could look it up, we would probably be unable to find it. Social work abounds with treatment interventions but few of them have been thoroughly evaluated. More often than not, we are left to stumble our way through day-to-day practice situations, desperately hoping that what we are doing turns out to be right.

Often, as social work practitioners, we will do what somebody taught us to do, for example, Professor Barsky, who instructed us in his own particular treatment intervention. We should not underestimate Professor Barsky. He was a man of presence and passion (as prophets often are). He gave us, along with his intervention, the very thing denied to us by science—the certainty that we are right.

Endowed with this certainty, we were probably able to help a number of clients since certainty on the part of the practitioner tends to be translated into certainty on the part of the client, and certainty on the part of the client generally meets with reward. Success followed success and, with each success, we became more certain of the infallibility of Professor Barsky's treatment intervention. We became skilled at it; we wrote papers about it; we were expert and respected. We resisted to the last ditch the idea that it should be evaluated.

However, if we have managed somehow to avoid Professor Barsky, we may be quite interested in various research studies so long as the aim of the studies is to help us with helping Uncle Fred. We may be interested, that is, until we discover precisely what will be involved. Suppose that the researcher wants to be present during our interviews with Uncle Fred to see what we do and to see if we actually do what we think and say we do. We chew thoughtfully on our bottom lip and try to explain to the researcher why no one can be present at the interviews with Uncle Fred.

The reasons are it will mess up the relationship, we will never help Uncle Fred if we mess up the relationship, and "Uncle Fred" comes before "research."

The researcher, who has met resistant people before and knows when arguments are useless, suggests a video recorder in place of a physical presence. We shake our heads no. It is too disruptive. Uncle Fred would not be at ease in the presence of a video recorder. What about an audio recorder? We shake our heads no again (sorrowfully because we really are trying to be cooperative) and the researcher goes away to evaluate some other treatment intervention. Meanwhile, we continue to practice as before and, after a while, we become comfortable with our method as well as skilled at it. We write papers about the method and are respected because of it. Once again, we resist the idea that it should be evaluated.

Social work research is thus affected by our beliefs about practice. Many of us believe that "objective observers" and recorders are disruptive to practice even though experience has shown that, after a few curious glances, Uncle Fred will ignore both of them. Our belief in disruption, however, will lead us to be disrupted and we will never be able to have our treatment intervention evaluated.

Some of us seem to believe that there is a sort of aura surrounding practice relationships that is shattered by measuring instruments, to be discussed in Chapter 4. To a certain extent it is true that the act of making a measurement alters the thing being measured, but we should not fear that contact with a measuring instrument will turn Uncle Fred instantly from a self-assured citizen into a quivering wreck. It may reveal that Uncle Fred is not so self-assured as we thought. It may reveal that our treatment intervention is not so effective as we hoped.

But usually it is not from fear of having our weaknesses revealed that measuring instruments are avoided. We feel that measuring instruments are unlikely to know as much about Uncle Fred as we do and we are afraid that introducing them will destroy the healing magic. Witch doctors, who use dance as a prelude to the hypodermic needle, tend to have more sense.

Professional Ethics

The last important factor affecting social work research directly is professional ethics. Our discussion on ethics (pages 42–50) has been mostly adapted from Grinnell and Williams (1990) and supplemented from Williams, Tutty, and Grinnell (1995). Physical scientists are by no means exempt from ethical considerations. Consider Robert Oppenheimer and other atomic scientists, who learned too late that their scientific findings about splitting the atom were used to create an atomic bomb—a purpose the scientists themselves opposed. A physical scientist who wishes to run tests on water samples, however, does not have to consider the feelings of the water samples or worry about harming them.

For people engaged in social work research studies, the ethical issues are far more pervasive and complex. A fundamental principle of social work research is that increased knowledge, while much to be desired, must never be obtained at the expense of human beings. Since many of our research activities revolve directly around human beings, safeguards must be put in place to ensure that our research participants are never harmed, either physically or psychologically.

An American committee known as the National Commission for the Protection of Human Subjects of Biomedical and Behavioral Research is only one of several professional organizations and lay groups that focus on protecting the rights of research participants. (Most research participants have never heard of any of them.) Clients participating in studies do not put their trust in committees; they trust the individual practitioners who involve them in the studies. It is therefore incumbent upon all of us to be familiar with ethical principles so that our clients' trust will never be betrayed.

Essentially, there are three precautionary ethical measures that must be taken before beginning any research study. These are: (1) obtaining the participant's informed consent, (2) designing the study in an ethical manner, and (3) ensuring that others will be properly told about the study's findings.

Obtaining Informed Consent

The most important consideration in any research study is to obtain the participants' *informed* consent. The word "informed" means that each participant fully understands what is going to happen in the course of the study, why it is going to happen, and what its effect will be on him or her. If the participant is psychiatrically challenged, mentally delayed, or in any other way incapable of full understanding, our study must be fully and adequately explained to someone else—perhaps a parent, guardian, social worker, or spouse, or someone to whom the participant's welfare is important.

It is clear that no research participant may be bribed, threatened, deceived, or in any way coerced into participating. Questions must be encouraged, both initially and throughout the course of the study. People who believe they understand may have misinterpreted our explanation or understood it only in part. They may say they understand, when they do not, in an effort to avoid appearing foolish. They may even sign documents they do not understand to confirm their supposed understanding, and it is our responsibility to ensure that their understanding is real and complete.

It is particularly important for participants to know that they are not signing away their rights when they sign a consent form. They may decide at any time to withdraw from the study *without penalty*, without so much as a reproachful glance. The results of the study will be made available to them as soon as the study has been completed. No promise will be made to them that cannot be fulfilled. Figure 2.2 contains an example of a simple consent form that was used by a research department within a child welfare agency. The purpose of the study was to obtain the line-level practitioners' views on burnout.

A promise that is of particular concern to many research participants is that of anonymity. A drug offender, for example, may be very afraid of being identified; a person on welfare may be concerned whether anyone else might learn that he or she is on welfare. Also, there is often some confusion between the terms "anonymity" and "confidentiality."

Some studies are designed so that no one, not even the person doing the study, knows which research participant gave what response. An example is a mailed survey form, bearing no identifying mark and asking the respondent not to give a name. In a study like this, the respondent is *anonymous*. It is more often the case, however, that we do know how a particular participant responded and have agreed not to divulge the information to anyone else. In such cases, the information is *confidential*. Part of our explanation to a potential research participant must include a clear statement of what information will be shared with whom.

All this seems reasonable in theory, but ethical obligations are often difficult to fulfill in practice. There are times when it is very difficult to remove coercive influences because these influences are inherent in the situation. A woman awaiting an abortion may agree to provide private data about herself and her partner because she believes that, if she does not, she will be denied the abortion. It is of no use to tell her that this is not true: She feels she is not in a position to take any chances.

There are captive populations of people in prisons, schools, or institutions who may agree out of sheer boredom to take part in a research study. Or, they may participate in return for certain privileges, or because they fear some penalty or reprisal. There may be people who agree because they are pressured into it by family members, or they want to please the social worker, or they need some service or payment that they believe depends on their cooperation. Often, situations like this cannot be changed, but at least we can be aware of them and try to deal with them in an ethical manner.

A written consent form should be only part of the process of informing research participants of their roles in the study and their rights as volunteers. It should give participants a basic description of the purpose of the study, the study's procedures, and their rights as voluntary participants. All information should be provided in plain and simple language, without jargon.

A consent form should be no longer than two pages of single-spaced copy, and it should be given to all research participants. Survey questionnaires may have a simple introductory letter containing the required information, with the written statement that the completion of the questionnaire is the person's agreement to participate. In telephone surveys, the information will need to be given verbally and must be standardized

[AGENCY LETTERHEAD]

Ms. Blackburn, MSW
Intake Worker II
City Social Services
Dallas, Texas 75712

Dear Ms. Blackburn:

As discussed on the phone, burnout among child protection workers is an issue of concern not only to child protection workers like yourself but to management alike. Research Services is asking you to voluntarily participate in our study. We will need this signed informed consent form before our interview can begin. We are deeply appreciative of your willingness to voluntarily participate in the department's research project.

Our interview will be held in your office and should last no more than one hour. Our objective is to elicit your views on the nature of the stresses (if any) that you face on a day-to-day basis. We may be discussing politically sensitive issues from time to time, and you have our assurance that we will maintain absolute confidentiality with respect to views expressed by you.

We will be asking you to complete a standardized measuring instrument that assesses a worker's degree of burnout before our interview begins. This task should take no more than ten minutes. All research materials will be kept in a locked file, and the identity of all workers interviewed for this study will be safeguarded by assigning each a number, so that names do not appear on any written materials.

With respect to any research or academic publications resulting from this study, specific views and/or opinions will not be ascribed either to you or to your organization without your prior written consent.

Your signature below indicates that you have understood to your satisfaction the information regarding your participation in our research project. Should you decide not to participate for whatever reason, or should you wish to withdraw at a later date, this will in no way affect your position in the agency. If you have any further questions about our study, please contact Research Services and we will address them as quickly as possible.

Sincerely,
Beulah Wright, MSW
Director, Research Services

YES: I AM WILLING TO PARTICIPATE IN THE PROJECT

Signature_____   Today's Date:_____

FIGURE 2.2   Example of a Simple Consent Form

across all calls. A written consent form should contain the following items, recognizing that the relevancy of this information and the amount required will vary with each research project:

1 A brief description of the purpose of the research study, as well as the value of the study to the general/scientific social work community (probability and nature of direct and indirect benefits) and to the participants and/or others.

2 An explanation as to how and/or why participants were selected and a statement that participation is completely voluntary.

3 A description of experimental conditions and/or procedures. Some points that should be covered are:

   a The frequency with which the participants will be contacted.

   b The time commitment required by the participants.

   c The physical effort required and/or protection from overexertion.

   d Emotionally sensitive issues that might be exposed and/or follow-up resources that are available if required.

   e Location of participation (e.g., need for travel/commuting).

   f Information that will be recorded and how it will be recorded (e.g., on paper, by photographs, by videotape, by audiotape).

4 Description of the likelihood of any discomforts and inconveniences associated with participation, and of known or suspected short- and long-term risks.

5 Explanation of who will have access to the collected data and to the identity of the participants (i.e., level of anonymity or confidentiality of each person's participation and information) and how long the data will be stored.

6 Description of how the data will be made public (e.g., scholarly presentation, printed publication). An additional consent is required for publication of photographs, audiotapes, and/or videotapes.

7 Description of other projects or other people who may use the data.

8 Explanation of the participants' rights:

   a That they may terminate or withdraw from the study at any point.

   b That they may ask for clarification or more information throughout the study.

   c That they may contact the appropriate administrative body if they have any questions about the conduct of the people doing the study or the study's procedures.

Designing an Ethical Study

A second necessary precaution before beginning a research study is to ensure that the study is designed in an ethical manner. One of the more useful research designs, presented in Chapters 8 and 9, involves separating participants into control and experimental groups, and providing a treatment to the experimental group but not to the control group.

The essential dilemma here is whether or not it is ethical to withhold a treatment, assumed to be beneficial, from participants in the control group. Even if control group participants are on a waiting list and will receive the treatment at a later date, is it right to delay service in order to conduct the study?

Proponents of this research design argue that people on a waiting list will not receive treatment any faster whether they are involved in the research study or not. Furthermore, it is only *assumed* that the treatment

Box 2.4

OBSERVING HUMAN OBEDIENCE

One of the more unsettling cliches to come out of World War II was the German soldier's common excuse for atrocities: "I was only following orders." From the point of view that gave rise to this comment, any behavior—no matter how reprehensible—could be justified if someone else could be assigned responsibility for it. If a superior officer ordered a soldier to kill a baby, the fact of the *order* was said to exempt the soldier from personal responsibility for the action.

Although the military tribunals that tried the war crime cases did not accept the excuse, social scientists and others have recognized the extent to which this point of view pervades social life. Very often people seem willing to do things they know would be considered wrong by others, *if* they can cite some higher authority as ordering them to do it. Such was the pattern of justification in the My Lai tragedy of Vietnam, and it appears less dramatically in day-to-day civilian life. Few would disagree that this reliance on authority exists, yet Stanley Milgram's study (1963, 1974) of the topic provoked considerable controversy.

To observe people's willingness to harm others when following orders, Milgram brought 40 adult men—from many different walks of life—into a laboratory setting designed to create the phenomenon under study. If you had been a subject in the experiment, you would have had something like the following experience.

You would have been informed that you and another subject were about to participate in a learning experiment. Through a draw of lots, you would have been assigned the job of "teacher" and your fellow subject the job of "pupil." He would have then been led into another room, strapped into a chair, and had an electrode attached to his wrist. As the teacher, you would have been seated in front of an impressive electrical control panel covered with dials, gauges, and switches. You would have noticed that each switch had a label giving a different number of volts, ranging from 15 to 315. The switches would have had other labels, too, some with the ominous phrases, such as, "Extreme-Intensity Shock," "Danger—Severe Shock," and "XXX."

The experiment would run like this. You would read a list of word pairs to the learner and then test his ability to match them up. Since you couldn't see him, a light on your control panel would indicate his answer. Whenever the learner made a mistake, you would be instructed by the experimenter to throw one of the switches—beginning with the mildest—and administer a shock to your pupil. Through an open door between the two rooms, you'd hear your pupil's response to the shock. Then you'd read another list of word pairs and test him again.

As the experiment progressed, you'd be administering ever more intense shocks, until your pupil was screaming for mercy and begging for the experiment to end. You'd be instructed to administer the next shock anyway. After a while, your pupil would begin kicking the wall between the two rooms and screaming. You'd be told to give the next shock. Finally, you'd read a list and ask for the pupil's answer—and there would be no reply whatever, only silence from the other room. The experimenter would inform you that no answer was considered an error and instruct you to administer the next higher shock. This would continue up to the "XXX" shock at the end of the series.

What do you suppose you would have done when the pupil first began screaming? Or when he became totally silent and gave no indication of life? You'd refuse to continue giving shocks, right? Of the first 40 adult men Milgram tested, nobody refused to administer the shocks until the pupil began kicking the wall between the two rooms. Of the 40, 5 did so then. Two-thirds of the subjects, 26 of the 40, continued doing as they were told through the entire series—up to and including the

Box 2.4 Continued_____

administration of the highest shock. As you've probably guessed the shocks were phoney, and the "pupil" was another experimenter.

Only the "teacher" was a real subject in the experiment. You wouldn't have been hurting another person, even though you would have been led to think you were. The experiment was designed to test your *willingness* to follow orders, to the point of presumably killing someone.

Milgram's experiments have been criticized both methodologically and ethically. On the ethical side, critics particularly cited the effects of the experiment on the subjects. Many seem to have

personally experienced about as much pain as they thought they were administering to someone else. They pleaded with the experimenter to let them stop giving the shocks. They became extremely upset and nervous. Some had uncontrollable seizures.

How do you feel about this research study? Do you think the topic was important enough to justify such measures? Can you think of other ways in which the researcher might have examined obedience?

_____

Source: Rubin and Babbie (1993)

is beneficial; if its effects were known for sure, there would be no need to do the study. Surely, we have an ethical responsibility to test such assumptions through research studies before we continue with treatments that may be ineffective or even harmful.

The same kind of controversy arises around a research design in which clients are randomly assigned to two different groups whereby each group receives a different treatment intervention. Proponents of this research design argue that no one is sure which treatment is better—that is what the research study is trying to discover—and so it is absurd to assert that a client in one group is being harmed by being denied the treatment offered to the other group.

Social workers, however, tend to have their own ideas about which treatment is better. Ms. Gomez's worker may believe that she will derive more benefit from behavioral than from existential therapy, for example, and that it will be harmful to her if random assignment happens to put her in the existential group.

Controversy also exists around the ethics of deception when the study's results will not be valid without the deception. We may wish to study the prevalence of abuse and neglect of adolescents who are psychiatrically challenged and live in residential institutions, for example. Staff in institutions are unlikely to abuse or neglect residents while being directly watched, but a person who poses as a new staff member may be able to document mistreatment (if any). Some of us may consider that such a deception is justified in order to protect the adolescents. Others may argue that it is unethical to spy on people, no matter how noble the cause.

Consider the ethical implications of Stanley Milgram's 1963 study, presented in Box 2.4. Milgram's study may be judged to be unethical for a number of reasons, but he did not consider it unethical or he would not have performed it. Ethics, like politics, hinges on points of view, values, ideologies, cultural beliefs, and perspectives. People disagree about the political aspects of research studies just as they do about ethics.

Informing Others About Findings

A third important ethical consideration in a research study is the manner in which the findings are reported. It may be tempting, for example, to give great weight to positive findings while playing down or ignoring altogether negative or disappointing findings. There is no doubt that positive findings tend to be more enthusiastically received, often by journal editors who should know better; but it is obviously just as important to know that two things are not related as to know that they are.

All studies have limitations, because practical considerations make it difficult to use the costly and complex research designs that yield the most certain results. Since studies with more limitations yield less trustworthy findings, it is important to be honest about our studies' limitations and for other social workers to be able to understand what the limitations imply.

Finally, there are issues concerned with giving proper credit to colleagues and ensuring that results are shared in an appropriate manner. With the exception of single-case designs, presented in Chapters 6–8, where one social worker may do all the work, research studies are normally conducted by teams. The principal person, whose name is usually listed first on the report, must be sure that all team members are given recognition and all research participants are apprised of the results.

Sometimes, the sharing of results will be a delicate matter. Staff may be reluctant to hear that the program is less effective than they thought. It will also be difficult, and often inadvisable, for us to share with research participants results that show them in an unfavorable light. It may be honest to tell Mr. Yen, for example, that he scored high on an anxiety scale of some kind, but it may also be extremely damaging to him. Practitioners wrestle every day with the problems of whom to tell, as well as how, when, and how much. The same difficulties arise in social work research.

To summarize, the National Association of Social Workers (1980) has published a code of ethics in which scholarship and research are addressed in six ethical guidelines:

E **Scholarship and Research** The social worker engaged in study and research should be guided by the conventions of scholarly inquiry.

1 The social worker engaged in research should consider carefully its possible consequences for human beings.

2 The social worker engaged in research should ascertain that the consent of participants is voluntary and informed, without any implied deprivation or penalty for refusal to participate, and with due regard for participants' privacy and dignity.

3 The social worker engaged in research should protect participants from unwarranted physical or mental discomfort, distress, harm, danger, or deprivation.

4 The social worker who engages in the evaluation of services or cases should discuss them only for professional purposes and only with persons directly and professionally concerned with them.

5 Information obtained about participants in research should be treated as confidential.

6 The social worker should take credit only for work actually done in connection with scholarly and research endeavors and should credit contributions made by others.

SUMMING UP AND LOOKING AHEAD

There are two basic complementary research approaches—quantitative and qualitative. They obtain and use data differently, and each approach has utility in the generation of relevant social work knowledge.

There are two main goals of social work research—pure and applied. The purpose of a pure research study is to develop theory and expand the social work knowledge base. The purpose of an applied study is to develop solutions for problems and relevant applications for social work practice. Both goals complement each other.

There are four factors that affect all social work research studies that are highly interrelated with one another: the social work profession and researcher; the social work agency: the social work practitioner: and professional ethics. These factors need to be taken into consideration when discussing the two main complementary approaches to social work research, the topic of the following chapter.

REVIEW QUESTIONS

1 List and discuss in detail the four factors that affect social work research studies. Provide a social work example throughout your entire discussion.

2 Discuss how the four factors mentioned above are highly interrelated with one another. Provide a social work example throughout your entire discussion.

3 Explain why social work research studies must follow strict ethical guidelines.

4 In groups of four, discuss the importance of ethics in social work. How do ethical considerations affect social work research? Discuss the dangers of conducting research in an unethical manner. As a class, discuss the eight ethical guidelines for research as outlined in the chapter and any problems that might arise from adhering to or ignoring these guidelines.

5 In groups of four, create a hypothetical research study that would require the participation of social work clients. Decide on the study's purpose and the research methodology. Discuss how you would protect the participants from harm, ensure confidentiality, provide adequate information about the study, and encourage voluntary participation. Draft an informed consent statement that would address

your ethical concerns. Read the statement to the class.

6 In groups of four, read and discuss the contents of Box 2.4. Have each member of the group answer the questions contained in the last paragraph. Present your results to the entire class.

7 At this very beginning point in your social work course, and in groups of four, design a qualitative research study that proposes to answer a social work–related research question of your choice. With the same research question, design a quantitative research study. Compare the advantages and disadvantages of using both research approaches when it comes to

gaining the permission for someone to become a research participant. Present your results to the entire class.

8 In groups of four, discuss in detail how you would go about gaining a client's permission to participate in an "applied" research study and in a "pure" research study. What are the main differences between getting a client to participate in a "pure" study verses an "applied" study?

9 At your university library, search the key words of *ethics* and *social work* on any computerized information retrieval system. Prepare a brief statement of the number and types of references you located.

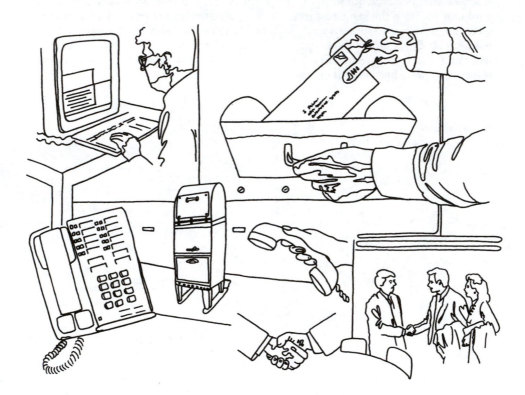

C h a p t e r   3

Research Approaches

As WE KNOW FROM CHAPTER 1, there are two research approaches that we can use in social work research—quantitative and qualitative. As we have stressed in the previous two chapters, they both complement one another. The quantitative research approach has typically been associated with research studies in disciplines such as medicine, education, psychology, and sociology, while the qualitative research approach has been associated with disciplines such as anthropology and ethology. Social work's long historical ties to the medical model and its reliance on psychology and sociology for theories of human behavior can explain, in part, why quantitative research studies have had such a commanding role in the social work profession—until now, that is.

As the years go by, our profession is becoming more appreciative of the qualitative research approach and how it can be used in actual social work research situations. The research methods associated with qualitative "ways of knowing" have filled a much-needed research gap within our profession. With both quantitative and qualitative research approaches at our disposal, we are now better equipped to learn more about complex social problems through their use.

PHILOSOPHICAL DIFFERENCES

It is important to note at this point that the quantitative and qualitative research approaches have different philosophical underpinnings. Let us briefly compare the differences between the two approaches in relation to how each one perceives reality, how it relates to the ways of knowing, how it uses its value base, and how it is applied (Jordan & Franklin, 1995):

Perceptions of Reality

- **Quantitative**   One reality exists and it can only be separated and studied in parts; the reality is "objective."
- **Qualitative**   Multiple realities exist and they are studied holistically; the reality is "subjective."

Ways of "Knowing"

- **Quantitative**   Knowledge is generated through a process of strict logic and reason; knowledge is generated primarily through a deductive process.
- **Qualitative**   Knowledge is personally constructed and contextually bound; knowledge is generated primarily through an inductive process.

Value Bases

- **Quantitative**   The research process is "value-free" and "unbiased." The researcher is separate and independent from the research participants and data analyses.
- **Qualitative**   The research process is "value-bound." The researcher and research participant mutually enter a "research partnership" to produce data.

Applications

- **Quantitative**   Research results are generalized across time, people, places, and contexts. Data exist separate and apart from the research participants who provided them.
- **Qualitative**   Research results provide a richer understanding of a particular person, problem, or event. Data are "expressions" of the research participants who provide them.

By comparing these four features and the philosophical underpinnings of quantitative and qualitative research approaches, we can more fully appreciate their important differences. Each approach offers us a unique method to studying a social work-related problem; and any research problem can be studied using either approach.

Suppose, for example, we are interested in a broad social problem such as, racial discrimination. In particular, let us say we are interested in studying the social problem of racial discrimination within public social service agencies. Let us revisit the differences between quantitative and qualitative research approaches and see how our research problem, racial discrimination, could be studied under both approaches.

Perceptions of Reality

- **Quantitative** Ethnic minorities share similar experiences within the public social service system. These experiences can be described objectively; that is, reality exists outside any one person.

- **Qualitative** Individual and ethnic group experiences within the public social service system are unique. Their experiences can only be described subjectively; that is, reality exists within each person.

Ways of "Knowing"

- **Quantitative** The experience of ethnic minorities within public social services is made known by closely examining specific parts of their experiences. Scientific principles, rules, and tests of sound reasoning are used to guide the research process.

- **Qualitative** The experience of ethnic minorities within public social services is made known by capturing the whole experiences of a few cases. Parts of their experiences are considered only in relation to the whole of it. Sources of knowledge are illustrated through stories, diagrams, and pictures that are shared by the people with their unique life experiences.

Value Bases

- **Quantitative** The researchers suspend all their values related to ethnic minorities and social services from the steps taken within the research study. The research participant "deposits" data, which are screened, organized, and analyzed by the researchers who do not attribute any personal meaning to the research participants or to the data they provide.

- **Qualitative** The researcher *is* the research process, and any personal values, beliefs, and experiences of the researcher will influence the research process. The researcher learns from the research participants, and their interaction is mutual.

Applications

- **Quantitative** Research results are generalized to the population from which the sample was drawn (e.g., other minority groups, other social services agencies). The research findings tell us, on the average, the experience that ethnic minorities have within the public social service system.

- **Qualitative** Research results tell a story of one individual's or one group's experience within the public social service system. The research findings give us an in-depth understanding of a few people. The life context of each research participant is key to understanding the stories he or she tells.

SIMILAR FEATURES

So far we have been focusing on the differences between the quantitative and qualitative research approaches. They also have many similarities. First, they both use careful and diligent research processes in an effort to discover and interpret knowledge. They both are guided by systematic procedures and orderly plans.

Second, both approaches can be used to study any particular social problem. The quantitative approach is more effective than the qualitative approach in reaching a specific and precise understanding of one aspect (or part) of an already well-defined social problem. The quantitative approach seeks to answer research questions that ask about quantity, such as:

1 Are women more depressed than men?

2 Does low income predict one's level of self-concept?

3 Do child sexual abuse investigation teams reduce the number of times an alleged victim is questioned by professionals?

4 Is degree of aggression related to severity of crimes committed among inmates?

A qualitative research approach, on other hand, aims to answer research questions that provide us with a more comprehensive understanding of a social problem from an intensive study of a few people. This approach is usually conducted within the context of the research participants' natural environments (Rubin & Babbie, 1997b). Research questions that would be relevant to the qualitative research approach might include:

1 How do women experience depression as compared to men?

2 How do individuals with low income define their self-concept?

3 How do professionals on child sexual abuse investigation teams work together to make decisions?

4 How do federal inmates describe their own aggression in relation to the crimes they have committed?

Not only can both approaches be used to study the same social problem, they both can be used to study the same research question. Chapter 10 presents how one research question can be answered by either research approach. Whether a quantitative or qualitative research approach is used clearly has impact on the type of findings produced to answer a research question (or to test a research hypothesis).

Regardless of the research approach we use to answer any given research question, we know from Chapter 1 that there are six steps that are common to both approaches: (1) choosing a general research topic, (2) focusing the topic into a research question, (3) designing the research study, (4) collecting the data, (5) analyzing and interpreting the data, and (6) writing the report. As we will see, each research approach is played out a bit differently in relation to each one of these research steps.

THE QUANTITATIVE RESEARCH APPROACH

The quantitative research approach is a "tried and tested" method of scientific inquiry. It has been used for centuries. Its process is depicted in

Figure 3.1. As can be seen, it is front-end loaded; that is, all of the critical decisions to be made in a quantitative study (e.g., conceptualization, sample selection, operationalization of variables, data collection procedures, data analysis procedures) occur *before* the study is ever started.

This means that the researcher is well aware of all the study's limitations before a single speck of datum is ever collected. It is possible, therefore, for a researcher to decide that a quantitative study has simply too many limitations and eventually decides not to carry it out. Regardless of whether a proposed quantitative study is ever carried out or not, the process always begins with choosing a research topic and focusing the research question.

Steps 1 and 2: Choosing a General Research Topic and Focusing the Topic into a Research Question

Box 3.1 presents some useful hints in choosing research questions. Quantitative research studies are usually deductive processes; that is, they usually begin with a broad and general query about a social problem and then pare it down to a specific research question. For instance, our general research problem previously introduced may have started out with a general curiosity about racial discrimination within the public social service agencies.

We may have noticed through our professional practices, for example, that many of our clients who are from ethnic minorities have high

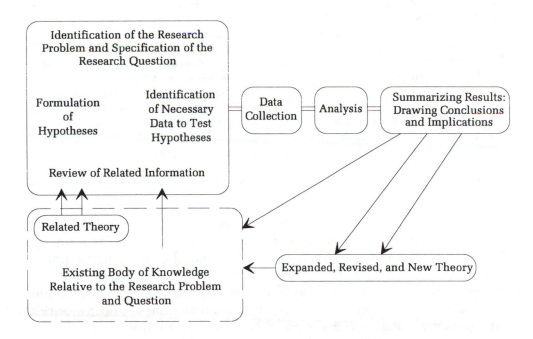

FIGURE 3.1   Hypothesis Construction and the Research Process

Box 3.1

HINTS FOR SELECTING A RESEARCH AREA

Perhaps your research teacher is requiring you to conduct a research project for this course. Here are some hints, in case you're having trouble coming up with a good idea. Your problem probably will become selecting one idea from many possibilities, rather than locating a single idea.

1 Pick a social work theory that interests you. Your introductory social work textbook may be a good source to remind you of a variety of social work theories. Find a few research studies that have been done to test this theory. Perhaps you can replicate or modify one of them. Design your own study to test the accuracy of this theory or to demonstrate its applicability to some issue.

2 Think of some familiar phrase, such as "A stitch in time saves nine" or "Absence makes the heart grow fonder." Consider stereotypes. Do women actually talk more than men? Are children's cartoons really violent? Perhaps you could design a simple research study to analyze the accuracy of one of these stereotypes.

3 Don't be afraid to test your own intuition. Perhaps you've always believed that attractive people are more popular than unattractive people or that teachers give higher grades to typed papers than to handwritten papers. You could design a study to test your intuitive conclusions.

4 Spend some time in a public place observing people. What do you see? How do you explain it? Can you test your theory? For example, you might notice that people tend to face the door in elevators. Maybe you can develop and test a theory that explains this behavior.

5 Scan some journals and read a few articles that interest you. Perhaps you could replicate one of the studies described, or part of it. Do the articles end with suggestions for further research or a discussion of limitations that you could explore?

6 Pick an issue that is important to you. Are you interested in affirmative action, AIDS, study skills, or alcoholism? Do some reading to find out what is already known about this area, and design a study that replicates previous research studies or that makes use of procedures or materials that have already been developed.

7 Ask a practical question and design a study to answer it. For example, you might be interested in how students can learn to study better, and you might decide to conduct an exploratory study contrasting students with high grades and students with low grades.

8 Don't lose track of the purpose of this assignment. The goal of this assignment is for you to practice conducting a study. You are not expected to invent a new theory that applies to all human behaviors. Keep your study simple. You will discover that even simple studies involve a series of tough decisions.

Source: Allen (1995)

---

unemployment rates, have a large proportion of their members living under the poverty level, and have low levels of educational attainment; three conditions that may increase the likelihood of their using public social services.

Yet, at the same time, we may have also observed that our clients who are Caucasian far outnumber our clients who come from ethnic minorities. Our personal observations may then lead us to question whether discrimination of ethic minorities exists within the public social service system. We can easily test the possibility of such a relationship between the two concepts by using the quantitative research approach.

The next step in focusing our research question would be to visit the library and review the literature related to our two concepts:

- Discrimination within social service agencies (Concept 1)
- Access to social service (Concept 2)

We would want to read theoretical and empirical literature related to the two main concepts within our research question—racial discrimination within social service agencies, and access to social services. We would want to learn about how various theories explain both of our main concepts in order to arrive at a meaningful research question. It may be, for example, that many ethnic minority cultures are unlikely to ask "strangers" for help with life's personal difficulties.

Furthermore, we may learn that most social service agencies are organized using bureaucratic structures, which require new clients to talk to several strangers (e.g., telephone receptionist, waiting-room clerk, intake worker) before they are able to access social services. Given that we know that ethnic minorities do not like talking with strangers about their personal problems, and that social services is set up for clients to deal with a series of strangers, we could ask a very simple quantitative research question:

Research Question:
Do clients who come from an ethnic minority have difficulty in accessing social services?

Our simple straightforward research question has become more specific as a result of our literature review. Our literature review also played a key role in determining which concepts we are going to include in our study. In our research question, for example, we have identified client ethnicity and access to social services as our two concepts of interest. We must always remember the four characteristics of the quantitative research approach while formulating our research question in addition to defining our concepts and variables, as outlined in Box 3.2.

Our next step in the quantitative research process is to redefine our concepts into variables. To make a very long story short, the main difference between a concept and a variable is that a variable can be measured and a concept cannot. That is, the two variables within our research question are operationalized so we can determine if they exist or not.

Take our concept of client ethnicity, for example. Suppose we develop the following conceptual definition of client ethnicity:

Conceptual Definition of Client Ethnicity:
Racial groups of people who can be differentiated by common customs, traits, and language

Box 3.2_____

CHARACTERISTICS OF THE
QUANTITATIVE RESEARCH APPROACH

The quantitative research approach strives for: (1) measurability, (2) objectivity, (3) reducing uncertainty, (4) duplication, and (5) standardized procedures.

STRIVING TOWARD MEASURABILITY

The quantitative research approach tries to study only those variables that can be objectively measured. That is, knowledge gained through this research approach is based on "objective measurements" of the real world, not on someone's opinions, beliefs, or past experiences. Conversely, knowledge gained through tradition or authority *depends* on people's opinions and beliefs. Entities that cannot be measured, or even seen, such as id, ego, or superego, are not amenable to a quantitative study but rather rely on tradition and authority.

In short, the phenomena we believe to exist must be measurable. However, at this point in our discussion, it is useful to remember that quantitative researchers believe that practically everything in life is measurable.

STRIVING TOWARD OBJECTIVITY

The second characteristic of the quantitative research approach is that it strives to be as *objective* as possible. The direct measurements of the real world that comprise *empirical data* must not be affected in any way by the person doing the observing, or measuring. Physical scientists have observed inanimate matter for centuries, confident in the belief that objects do not change as a result of being observed. In the subworld of the atom, however, physicists are beginning to learn what social workers have always known. Things *do* change when they are observed. People think, feel, and behave very differently as a result of being observed. Not only do they change, they change in different ways

depending on who is doing the observing.

There is yet another problem. Observed behavior is open to interpretation by the observer. To illustrate this point, let us take a simple example of a client we are seeing, named Ron, who is severely withdrawn. He may behave in one way in our office in individual treatment sessions, and in quite another way when his mother joins the interviews. We may think that Ron is unduly silent, while his mother remarks on how much he is talking. If his mother *wants* him to talk, perhaps as a sign that he is emerging from his withdrawal, she may perceive him to be talking more than he really is.

Researchers go to great lengths to ensure that their own hopes, fears, beliefs, and biases do not affect their research results, and that the biases of others do not affect them either. Nevertheless, as discussed in later chapters, complete objectivity is rarely possible in social work despite the many strategies we have developed in our efforts to achieve it.

Suppose, for example, that a social worker is trying to help a mother interact more positively with her child. The worker, together with a colleague, may first observe the child and mother in a playroom setting, recording how many times the mother makes eye contact with the child, hugs the child, criticizes the child, makes encouraging comments, and so forth on a three-point scale (i.e., $-1 =$ discouraging, $0 =$ neutral, $1 =$ encouraging). The social worker may perceive a remark that the mother has made to the child as "neutral," while the colleague thinks it was "encouraging."

In such a situation, it is impossible to resolve the disagreement. If there were six objective observers, however, five opting for "neutral" and only one for "encouraging," the one observer is more likely to be wrong than the five, and it is very likely that the mother's remark was "neutral." As more people agree on what they have observed, the less likely it becomes that

Box 3.2 Continued

the observation was distorted by bias; and the more likely it is that the agreement reached is "objectively true."

As should be obvious by now, objectivity is largely a matter of agreement. There are some things—usually physical phenomena—about which most people agree. Most people agree, for example, that objects fall when dropped, water turns to steam at a certain temperature, sea water contains salt, and so forth. However, there are other things—mostly to do with values, attitudes, and feelings—about which agreement is far more rare.

An argument about whether Beethoven is a better composer than Bach, for example, cannot be "objectively" resolved. Neither can a dispute about the rightness of capital punishment, euthanasia, or abortion. It is not surprising, therefore, that physical researchers, who work with physical phenomena, are able to be more "objective" than social work researchers, who work with human beings.

STRIVING TOWARD REDUCING UNCERTAINTY

The quantitative research approach tries to rule out uncertainty. Since all observations in both the physical and social sciences are made by human beings, personal bias cannot be entirely eliminated, and there is always the possibility that an observation is in error, no matter how many people agree about what they saw. There is also the possibility that the conclusions drawn from even an accurate observation will be wrong.

A number of people may agree that an object in the sky is a UFO when in fact it is a meteor. Even if they agree that it is a meteor, they may come to the conclusion—probably erroneously—that the meteor is a warning from an angry extraterrestrial person.

In the twentieth century, most people do not believe that natural phenomena have anything to do with extraterrestrial people. They prefer the explanations that modern researchers have proposed. Nevertheless, no researcher would say—or at least be quoted as saying—that meteors and extraterrestrial beings are not related for certain. When utilizing the research method of knowledge development, nothing is certain. Even the best-tested theory is only tentative, accepted as true until newly discovered evidence shows it to be untrue or only partly true. All knowledge gained through the research method (whether quantitative or qualitative) is thus provisional. Everything presently accepted as true is true only with varying degrees of probability.

Let us suppose we have lived all alone in the middle of a large forest. We have never ventured as much as a hundred yards from our cabin and have had no access to the outside world. We have observed for our entire life that all of the ducks that flew over our land were white. We have never seen a different-colored duck. Thus, we theorize, and rightfully so, that all ducks are white. We would only have to see one nonwhite duck fly over our land to disprove our theory: Nothing is certain no matter how long we "objectively observed" it.

STRIVING TOWARD DUPLICATION

The quantitative research approach tries to do research studies in such a way that they can be duplicated. Unlike qualitative studies, if quantitative studies cannot be duplicated, they are not really quantitative endeavors. As we have said before, the quantitative research approach, and to some extent, the qualitative approach as well, is a public method of knowing.

Evidence for the relationship between students' grade point average and their future abilities as good social workers must be open to public inspection if it is to be believed. Furthermore, belief is more likely if a second researcher can produce the same findings by using the same research methods.

In scientific laboratories, the word "replication" refers to the same experiment conducted more than once in the same way, at approximately the same time, by the same person. A person testing

Box 3.2 Continued

a city's water supply for pollutants, for example, will take several samples of the water and test them simultaneously under identical conditions, expecting to obtain close to identical results. If the water needs to be retested for some reason, further samples will be taken and the same procedures followed, but now another person may do the work and the test conditions may be very slightly different: A recent downpour of rain may have flushed some of the pollutants out of the reservoir, for example. The second set of tests are then said to be *duplicates* of the first. Social workers are not able to replicate research studies, because no person, situation, or event is identical to any other. Therefore, despite the fact that most texts use the word "replicate" in reference to repeating studies, we will use the word "duplicate" instead.

Example of Duplication   Suppose we are running a 12-week intervention program to help fathers who have abused their children to manage their anger without resorting to physical violence. We have put a great deal of effort into designing this program, and believe that our intervention (the program) is more effective than other interventions currently used in other anger-management programs. We develop a method of measuring the degree to which the fathers in our group have learned to dissipate their anger in nondamaging ways and we find that, indeed, the group shows marked improvement.

Improvement shown by one group of fathers is not convincing evidence for the effectiveness of our program. Perhaps our measurements were in error and the improvement was not as great as we hoped for. Perhaps the improvement was a coincidence, and the fathers' behavior changed because they had joined a health club and each had vented his fury on a punching bag. In order to be more certain, we duplicate our program and measuring procedures with a second group of fathers: In other words, we duplicate our study.

After we have used the same procedures with a number of groups and ob-

tained similar results each time, we might expect that other social workers will eagerly adopt our methods. As presented in Chapter 1, tradition dies hard. Other social workers have a vested interest in *their* interventions, and they may suggest that we found the results we did only because we *wanted* to find them.

In order to counter any suggestion of bias, we ask another, independent social worker to use the same anger-management program and measuring methods with other groups of fathers. If the results are the same as before, our colleagues in the field of anger management may choose to adopt our intervention method (the program). Tradition does not merely die hard, however. It dies with enormous difficulty, and we should not be surprised if our colleagues choose, instead, to continue using the familiar interventions they have always used.

Whatever our colleagues decide, we are excited about our newfound program. We wonder if our methods would work as well with women as they do with men, with adolescents as well as with adults, with Native Americans, Asians, or African Americans as well as with Caucasians, with mixed groups, larger groups, or groups in different settings. In fact, we have identified a lifetime project, since we will have to apply our program and measuring procedures repeatedly to all these different groups.

STRIVING TOWARD THE USE OF STANDARDIZED PROCEDURES

Finally, the quantitative research approach tries to use, if at all possible, well-accepted standardized procedures. For quantitative research studies to be credible, and before others can accept our results, they must be satisfied that our study was conducted according to accepted scientific standardized procedures. The allegation that our work lacks "objectivity" is only one of the criticisms they might bring. In addition, they might suggest that the group of fathers we worked with was not typical of abusive fathers in

Box 3.2 Continued_____

general, and that our results are not there-fore applicable to other groups of abusive fathers. It might be alleged that we did not make proper measurements, or we measured the wrong thing, or we did not take enough measurements, or we did not analyze our data correctly, and so on.

In order to negate these kinds of criticisms, social work researchers have agreed on a set of standard procedures and techniques that are thought most likely to produce "true and unbiased" knowledge—which is what this book is all about. Certain steps must be performed in a certain order. Foreseeable errors must be guarded against. Ethical behavior with research participants and colleagues must be maintained. These procedures must be followed if our study is both to generate usable results and to be accepted as useful by other social workers.

_____

Source: Adapted and modified from: Krysik and Grinnell (1997); Williams, Tutty, and Grinnell (1995)

In order to measure our conceptual definition above, we need to operationalize it by creating a variable (called *client ethnicity*), which we operationally define by using existing meaningful "ethnicity categories," such as:

What is your ethnicity (check one category below)?
- Aboriginal
- African American
- Asian
- British
- Dutch
- German
- Hispanic
- Italian
- Native American
- Other_____

We can be as specific—or broad—as would be meaningful to our research question. We could, for example, operationally define our ethnicity variable by using only two "ethnicity categories," such as:

What is your ethnicity (check one category below)?
- Ethnic Minority
- Non–Ethnic Minority

We defined these two broad categories by "collapsing" our nine more specific categories. That is, we may have assigned our Aboriginal, African American, Asian, Hispanic, and Native American categories to a single category called "ethnic minority." Likewise, we could group our British, Dutch, German, and Italian categories into a single category called "non–ethnic minority." We would simply ask all of our clients to check off one of the two categories that they felt pertained to them.

Our second variable, difficulty in assessing social services, also has to be measured. Like our oversimplified two-category ethnicity variable above, we could also operationalize this variable in a variety of ways. We have chosen to operationalize it once again in a simple "yes-no" format. We could ask all of our clients, for example:

> Did you have difficulty in accessing any form of social services over the last 12-month period *(check one category below)*?
>
> • Yes
>
> • No

So far in our quantitative research study we have refined both variables so that each one can be easily measured. Both variables are two-category variables in that a client can only be in one category for each variable. For example, a client can only be:

- **An ethnic minority** and **had difficulty** in accessing social services
- An ethnic minority and **did not have difficulty** in accessing social services
- **A non–ethnic minority** and **had difficulty** in accessing social services
- **A non–ethnic minority** and **did not have difficulty** in accessing social services

Research Hypotheses

We can focus our research question even further by formulating a research hypothesis, in which we make an educated guess about the relationship between our two variables. Box 3.3 presents a few criteria for evaluating research hypotheses, in which there are two types: (1) nondirectional, and (2) directional.

Nondirectional Research Hypotheses   A nondirectional research hypothesis (also called a two-tailed hypothesis), is simply a statement that says we expect to find a relationship between our two variables. We are not willing, however, to "stick our necks out" as to the specific relationship between them. A nondirectional hypothesis for our research question could be, for example:

> *Nondirectional Research Hypothesis:*
> *Ethnic minorities have different levels of difficulty in accessing social services, compared to non–ethnic minorities.*

Notice that the above nondirectional research hypothesis does not propose that ethnic minorities have any more (or less) difficulty in accessing social services than non–ethnic minorities.

Box 3.3_____

EVALUATING A RESEARCH HYPOTHESIS

As we know by now, a hypothesis is derived from the research question, which is derived from the research problem area.

There are four criteria that can used to differentiate a good, useful hypothesis from one that is not so good or useful. They are: (1) relevance, (2) completeness, (3) specificity, and (4) potential for testing.

RELEVANCE

It is hardly necessary to stress that a useful hypothesis is one that contributes to our knowledge base. Nevertheless, some social work problem areas are enormously complex, and it is common for people to get so sidetracked in reading the professional literature that they develop very interesting hypotheses totally unrelated to the original problem area they wanted to investigate in the first place.

The relevancy criterion is a reminder that, to repeat, the research hypothesis must be directly related to the research question, which in turn must be directly related to the general research problem area.

COMPLETENESS

A hypothesis should be a complete statement that expresses our intended meaning in its entirety. The reader should not be left with the impression that some word or phrase is missing. "Moral values are declining" is one example of an incomplete hypothesis.

Other examples include a whole range of comparative statements without a reference point. The statement, "Males are more aggressive," for example, may be assumed to mean "Men are more aggressive than women," but someone investigating the social life of animals may have meant, "Male humans are more aggressive than male gorillas."

SPECIFICITY

A hypothesis must be unambiguous. The reader should be able to understand what each variable contained in the hypothesis means and what relationship, if any, is hypothesized to exist between them. Consider, for example, the hypothesis, "Badly timed family therapy affects success." Badly timed family therapy may refer to therapy offered too soon or too late for the family to benefit; or to the social worker or family being late for therapy sessions; or to sessions that are too long or too short to be effective. Similarly, "success" may mean resolution of the family's problems as determined by objective measurement, or it may mean the family's—or the social worker's—degree of satisfaction with therapy, or any combination of these.

With regard to the relationship between the two variables, the reader may assume that we are hypothesizing a negative correlation: That is, the more badly timed the therapy, the less success will be achieved. On the other hand, perhaps we are only hypothesizing an association: Bad timing will invariably coexist with lack of success.

Be that as it may, the reader should not be left to guess at what we mean by a hypothesis. If we are trying to be both complete and specific, we may hypothesize, for example:

> Family therapy that is undertaken *after* the male perpetrator has accepted responsibility for the sexual abuse of his child is more likely to succeed in reuniting the family than family therapy undertaken *before* the male perpetrator has accepted responsibility for the sexual abuse.

This hypothesis is complete and specific. It leaves the reader in no doubt as to what we mean, but it is also somewhat wordy and clumsy. One of the difficulties in writing a good hypothesis is that specific statements need more words than inspecific, or ambiguous statements.

Box 3.3 Continued_____

POTENTIAL FOR TESTING

The last criterion for judging whether a hypothesis is good and useful is the ease with which the truth of the hypothesis can be verified. Some statements cannot be verified at all with presently available measurement techniques.

"Telepathic communication exists between identical twins," is one such statement. Moreover, much of Emile Durkheim's work on suicide was formulated in such a way that it was not testable by the data-gathering techniques available in the 1960s.

A hypothesis of sufficient importance will often generate new data-gathering techniques, which will enable it to be eventually tested. Nevertheless, as a general rule, it is best to limit hypotheses to statements that can be tested immediately by available measurement methods in current use.

_____

Source: Adapted and modified from: Williams, Tutty, and Grinnell (1995)

Directional Research Hypotheses   A directional research hypothesis (also called a one-tailed hypothesis) specifically indicates the "predicted" direction of the relationship between the two variables. The direction stated is based on an existing body of knowledge related to our research question. Let us return to what we learned from our literature review. We may find out, for example, that clients who are from ethnic minorities may be less likely to seek help from strangers than clients who do not come from ethnic minorities. And, since social service agencies are full of strangers, we might develop the following directional research hypothesis:

Directional Research Hypothesis:
Ethnic minorities have more difficulty in accessing social services than non–ethnic minorities.

Rival Hypotheses

Another kind of hypothesis to be aware of is the rival hypothesis. This hypothesis states that there is something that exists apart from our research hypothesis (i.e., nondirectional, directional); it takes into consideration other variables that are not a part of our nondirectional or directional research hypothesis. Take another look at the directional research hypothesis above. It only identifies ethnicity (independent variable) as a variable that affects access to social services (dependent variable). There are many other variables that could also affect our dependent variable but are not a part of our research study. Variables such as available transportation, amount of family support, and location of residence are a few of the many examples that might explain why clients have difficulties in accessing social services—regardless of their ethnicity.

These other variables are known as competing variables, or rival variables, and could be formulated into a statement that "rivals" our nondirectional or directional research hypothesis. Rival hypotheses are not statistically tested and no data are usually collected in relation to them. Rather, they are simply statements that demonstrate the thought we have given to the variables that are extraneous to our research hypothesis.

Step 3: Designing the Research Study

Having focused our research question, and if appropriate, developed a research hypothesis, we enter into the next phase of our study—designing the study. We begin with a word about sampling. One of the major objectives of the quantitative research approach is to generate knowledge that can be generalized beyond our study's sample. For now, it is useful to know that the "ideal" sample for a quantitative study is one that has been randomly selected from a carefully defined population. The topic of sampling will be discussed much more fully in Chapter 5.

As we shall see in the following chapter, most research questions have at least one independent variable and one dependent variable. As indicated above, the independent variable in our study is client ethnicity (i.e., ethnic minority, non–ethnic minority) and the dependent variable is difficulty in accessing social services (i.e., yes, no). We organize our variables in this way because we are expecting that our clients' ethnicity is somehow related to their difficulty in accessing social services. It would be absurd to say the opposite—that the degree of difficulty that potential clients have in accessing social services influences their ethnicity.

Having set out our hypothesis in this way, we can plainly see that our research design will compare two groups (i.e., ethnic minorities, non–ethnic minorities) in terms of whether or not (i.e., yes, no) each group had difficulty accessing a social service of some kind. Our research design is the "blueprint" for our study. It is a basic guide to deciding how, where, and when data will be collected. How data are collected and where they are collected from is determined by the data collection method we choose (Chapter 10). *When* data are collected is dictated by the specific research design we select (Chapters 6–9). Clearly, there are many things for us to consider when developing our research design.

All quantitative research designs are not created equal. Chapters 6–9 discuss three groups of research designs (i.e., exploratory, descriptive, explanatory) and how each varies in terms of the knowledge it produces. Exploratory type research designs are the most simple. These research designs are useful for describing variables but do not have anything to say about the relationships (that may or may not exist) between and among them. An exploratory design can answer questions such as:

1 How many smokers have cancer?

2 What is the amount of study time logged by students with high grades?

3 How many clients who are ethnic minorities have experienced difficulty in accessing social services?

Descriptive research designs establish whether or not two or more variables are related to one another. They tell us whether a change in the first variable predictably varies with a change in the second variable. We could ask, for example:

1 Are people who smoke more likely to be diagnosed with cancer, compared to people who do not smoke?
2 Is studying related to achieving higher grades for students?
3 Are clients who are ethnic minorities more or less likely to experience difficulty accessing social services than clients who are not ethnic minorities?

"Cause-effect" type quantitative research designs are at the explanatory level. They can help us determine whether a causal relationship existed between the two variables within our research hypothesis:

1 Does smoking *cause* cancer?
2 Does studying *cause* good grades?
3 Does being a client from an ethnic minority *cause* people to experience more difficulty in accessing social services?

Establishing causal relationships between variables such as those above, however, requires sophisticated research designs that are usually not feasible in social work.

Step 4: Collecting the Data

As we know, data collection is one phase within any research design. It is the phase, however, that is important in and of itself. Data collection is where we truly test out the operational definitions of our study's variables. There are three features of data collection that are key to all quantitative research studies:

1 **All of our variables must be measurable** This means that we must precisely record the variable's frequency, its duration, or its magnitude (intensity). Think about our ethnic minority independent variable for a minute. As noted earlier, we simply operationalized this variable into two categories: ethnic minority and non–ethnic minority. Here we are simply measuring the presence (ethnic minority) or absence (non-ethnic minority) of a trait for each participant within our study.

   We also needed to operationalize our dependent variable, difficulty in accessing social services. One again, we could have operationalized this variable in a number of ways. We chose, however to operationalize it where each client could produce a simple response to a simple question: Did you have difficulty (i.e., yes, no) in accessing any form of social services over the last 12-month period?"

2 **All of our data collection procedures must be objective** That is, the data are meant to reflect a condition in the *real* world and should not be biased by the person collecting the data in any way. In our study, the clients produced the data—not the researcher. That is, the researcher only recorded the data that each client individually provided for both variables:

- "Ethnic Minority" **or** "Non–Ethnic Minority" for the independent variable
- "Yes" **or** "No" for the dependent variable

3 **All of our data collection procedures must be able to be duplicated**   In other words, our data collection procedures that we used to measure our independent and dependent variables must be clear and straightforward enough that other researchers could use them in their research studies.

The three features of measurability, objectivity, and duplication within a quantitative research study are accomplished by using a series of standardized uniform steps that are applied consistently throughout a study's implementation. We want to ensure that all of our research participants are measured the same way—in reference to their ethnicity and whether they had any difficulty in accessing social services within the last 12 months, that is.

Step 5: Analyzing and Interpreting the Data

There are two major types of quantitative data analyses: (1) descriptive statistics, and (2) inferential statistics.

Descriptive Statistics

Descriptive statistics describe our study's sample or population. Consider our ethnicity variable for a moment. We can easily describe our research participants in relation to their ethnicity by stating how many of them fell into each category of the variable. Suppose, for example, that 50 percent of our sample were in the ethnic minority category and the remaining 50 percent were in the non–ethnic minority category as illustrated below:

Variable Categories:
- Ethnic Minority............. 50%
- Non–Ethnic Minority..... 50%

The above two percentages give us a "picture" of what our sample looked like in relation to their ethnicity. A different picture could be produced where 10 percent of our sample are ethnic minorities and 90 percent are not as illustrated below:

Variable Categories:
- Ethnic Minority............. 10%
- Non–Ethnic Minority..... 90%

The above describes only one variable—client ethnicity, or our independent variable. A more detailed picture is given when data about an independent variable and a dependent variable are displayed at the same time. Suppose, for example, that 60 percent of our clients who are ethnic minorities reported that they had difficulty in accessing social services, compared to 20 percent of our clients who are non–ethnic minorities:

	Dependent Variable	
Independent Variable	Yes	No
• Ethnic Minority	60%	40%
• Non–Ethnic Minority	20%	80%

Other descriptive information about our research participants could include variables such as average age, percentages of males and females, average income, and so on. Much more will be said about descriptive statistics in Chapter 12.

Inferential Statistics

Inferential statistics determine the probability that a relationship between the two variables within our sample also exists within the population from which it was drawn. Suppose in our study, for example, we find a statistically significant relationship between our clients' ethnicity and whether they successfully accessed social services. The use of inferential statistics permits us to say whether or not the relationship detected in our sample exists in the larger population (i.e., the population from which our sample was drawn) and the exact probability that our finding is in error.

Clearly, a basic understanding of mathematics is needed to analyze quantitative data. With advances in computerized software packages, however, we also need to be sure that we understand the functions performed by the computer so that we can accurately interpret any computer output. Much more will also be said about inferential statistics in Chapter 12.

Interpreting the Findings

Interpreting quantitative findings is not as straightforward as it first may appear. We must be careful in our interpretations at two levels. First, we must be aware that expert interpretation of data is required at the level of statistical analysis. Second, interpretation of findings is greatly influenced by the case or group design selected.

Statistical Interpretation   Just because a number appears in a computer printout does not mean that it is meaningful. Working with numbers in statistics takes considerable "know how." Remember that the purpose of a statistic is to describe a variable or the relationship between two or more variables. It is important to realize that all statistical tests are based on the notion of probability—or chance of error. In a nutshell, every relationship we test using a statistical test has associated with it the possibility or probability that we are wrong in our conclusion. The entire process of statistics is checking to see if the "right" conditions exist for a particular statistic so that we may have confidence in our study's results.

Research Design Selected   Interpretation of quantitative data also is affected by the particular research design we select. Specifically, the interpretation of findings relates to the internal and external validity of our research design (Chapter 9).

Step 6: Writing the Report

Quantitative research findings are easily summarized in tables, figures, and graphs. When data are disseminated to lay people, we usually rely on straightforward graphs and charts to illustrate our findings.

THE QUALITATIVE RESEARCH APPROACH

The qualitative research approach is akin to exploring a "social problem maze" that has multiple entry points and paths. We have no way of knowing whether the maze will lead us to a place of importance or not but we enter into it out of our own curiosity and, perhaps, even conviction. We enter the maze without a map or a guide; we have only ourselves to rely on and a notebook to record important events, observations, conversations, and impressions along the way.

We begin our journey of qualitative inquiry by stepping into one entrance and forging ahead. We move cautiously forward, using all of our senses in an effort to pinpoint our location and what surrounds us at any one time. We may enter into dead-end rooms within the maze and have to backtrack. We may also encounter paths that we did not think possible.

Steps 1 and 2: Choosing a General Research Topic and
   ## Focusing the Topic into a Research Question

Qualitative studies are generally inductive and can be categorized into three types as illustrated in Figure 3.2. They require us to reason in such

---

VAN MAANEN'S TAXONOMY OF TALES

John Van Maanen has classified qualitative research reports into three types, which he describes as different categories of tales. Each uses a distinctive type of literary exposition.

Realist Tales   A single author narrates the outcome of the study in a dispassionate, third-person voice. According to Van Maanen, "Perhaps the most striking characteristic of ethnographic realism is the almost complete absence of the author from most segments of the finished text. Only what members of the studied culture say and do and, presumably, think are visible."

Confessional Tales   The author attempts to demystify fieldwork or participant observation by showing how the technique is practiced in the field. Such accounts are in the first person, seldom are dispassionate, and unfold over time. Fieldwork is narrated as a series of events leading to certain conclusions or results. The narrator-hero is typically beset along the way by troubles, uncertainty, and doubt.

Impressionist Tales   The author provides vivid, memorable stories, reconstructing in dramatic detail the "facts" of an episode or life. Such yarns are often incorporated into "realist" writing.

FIGURE 3.2   Types of Qualitative Reports

---

a way that we move from a part to a whole or from a particular instance to a general conclusion. Box 3.4 illustrates the similarities among all qualitative research studies.

Let us return to our research problem introduced at the beginning of this chapter—discrimination within the social services. We begin the qualitative research process, once again, from our observations—ethnic minorities are among the highest groups for unemployment, poverty, and low education; Caucasian clients outnumber ethnic minority clients within agencies providing social services.

We can focus our qualitative research question by identifying the key concepts in our question. These key concepts set the parameters of our research study—they are the "outside" boundaries of our maze. As in the quantitative research approach, we would want to visit the library and review the literature related to our key concepts. Our literature review, however, takes on a very different purpose. Rather than pinpointing "exact" variables to study, we review the literature to see how our key concepts are generally described and defined by previous researchers.

Going with the maze example for the moment, we might learn whether our maze will have rounded or perpendicular corners, or whether it will have multiple levels. The knowledge we glean from the literature assists us with ways of thinking that we hope will help us move through the maze in a way that we will arrive at a meaningful understanding of the

Box 3.4_____

WHAT DO QUALITATIVE RESEARCH STUDIES LOOK LIKE?

Below are a few characteristics that most qualitative research studies have in common:

- Research studies that are conducted primarily in the natural settings where the research participants carry out their day-to-day business in a "nonresearch" atmosphere

- Research studies where variables cannot be controlled and experimentally manipulated (though changes in variables and their effect on other variables can certainly be observed)

- Research studies in which the questions to be asked are not always completely conceptualized and operationally defined at the outset (though they can be)

- Research studies in which the data collected are heavily influenced by the experiences and priorities of the research participants, rather than being collected by predetermined and/or highly structured and/or standardized measurement instruments

- Research studies in which meanings are drawn from the data (and presented to others) using processes that are more natural and familiar than those used in the quantitative method. The data need not be reduced to numbers and statistically analyzed (though counting and statistics can be employed if they are thought useful).

_____

Source: Rothery, Tutty, and Grinnell (1996)

---

problem it represents. Because we may never have been in the maze before, we must also be prepared to abandon what we "think we know" and accept new experiences presented to us along the way.

Let us revisit our research question presented earlier—*Do clients who come from an ethnic minority have difficulty in accessing social services?* In our literature review, we would want to focus on definitions and theories related to discrimination within the social services. In the quantitative research approach, we reviewed the literature to search for meaningful variables that could be measured. We do not want, however, to rely on the literature to define key variables in our study. Rather, we will rely upon the qualitative research process itself to identify key variables and how they relate to one another.

Hypotheses can also be used in a qualitative study. They can focus our research question even further. A hypothesis in a qualitative study is less likely to be outright "accepted" or "rejected," as is the case in a quantitative study. Rather, the hypothesis is refined over time as new data are collected. Our hypothesis is changed throughout the qualitative research process based on the reasoning of the researcher—not on a statistical test.

Step 3: Designing the Study

We can enter into a qualitative research study with general research questions or specific hypotheses but we are far less concerned about honing-in on specific variables. Because qualitative research studies are inductive processes, we do not want to constrain ourselves with preconceived ideas about how concepts or variables will relate. Thus, while we will have a list of key concepts, and perhaps variables, we want to remain open to the possibilities of how they are defined by our research participants and any relationships that our research participants may draw. Box 3.5 lists the common characteristics of what researchers actually do when they design qualitative research studies.

A qualitative study is aimed at an in-depth understanding of a few cases, rather than a general understanding of many cases, or people. In other words, the number of research participants in a qualitative study is much smaller than a quantitative one. Sampling, therefore, is a process of selecting the "best-fitting" people to provide data for our study. Nonprobability sampling strategies are designed for this task because they purposely seek out potential research participants. More will be discussed about nonprobability sampling strategies in Chapter 5.

The qualitative research approach is about studying a social phenomenon within its natural context. As such, the case study is a major qualitative research design. A case can be a person, a group, a community, an organization, or an event.

It is possible to ask exploratory, descriptive, or explanatory level research questions within a case. In the quantitative research approach, each level of research question is accompanied by a particular case or group design. This is not true for the qualitative research approach. Instead, the level of question being pursued guides the continued focusing of the research question and helps us to know when our study should end.

Let us revisit our research problem related to discrimination within the public social service system. At an exploratory level, we may ask questions to see whether other people have noted the same observations as we. We could identify various colleagues who work in social services and ask them about their observations of the clients who are from an ethnic minority. Our questions can reach a descriptive level if we begin to ask our research participant to describe any relationship between clients who are from an ethnic minority and their access to social services. At the explanatory level, our questions are even more specific. Are clients who are from an ethnic minority more likely to experience barriers to accessing social services?

Any case study design can be guided by different qualitative research methods. Grounded theory is a method that guides us in a "back and forth" process between the literature and the data we collect. Using grounded theory, we can look to the literature for new ideas and linkages between ideas that can bring meaning to our data. In turn, our data may nudge us to read in areas that we might not have previously considered.

Box 3.5_____

WHAT DO QUALITATIVE RESEARCHERS DO?

Now that we know what qualitative research studies look like (from Box 3.4), we can now describe what some of our roles and responsibilities would be if we actually carried out a qualitative research study. Below is a helpful summary of what would be required to do a qualitative investigation. The qualitative researcher:

- Observes ordinary events and activities as they happen in natural settings, in addition to any unusual occurrences.

- Is directly involved with the people being studied and personally experiences the process of daily social life in the field setting.

- Acquires an insider's point of view while maintaining the analytic perspective or distance of an outsider.

- Uses a variety of techniques and social skills in a flexible manner as the situation demands.

- Produces data in the form of extensive written notes, as well as diagrams, maps, or pictures to provide very detailed descriptions.

- Sees events holistically (e.g., as a whole unit, not in pieces) and individually in their social context.

- Understands and develops empathy for members in a field setting, and does not just record "cold" objective facts.

- Notices both explicit and tacit aspects of culture.

- Observes ongoing social processes without upsetting, disrupting, or imposing an outside point of view.

- Is capable of coping with high levels of personal stress, uncertainty, ethical dilemmas, and ambiguity.

Many of the above roles and activities are not only carried out in qualitative research studies but are required for good social work practice as well.

_____

Source: Neuman (1997)

Ethnography is a branch of qualitative research that emphasizes the study of a culture from the perspective of the people who live the culture. With our research example, we would be interested in studying the culture of social services, particularly with respect to how ethnic minorities experience it.

Phenomenology is another branch of qualitative research. "It is used to emphasize a focus on people's subjective experiences and interpretations of the world" (Rubin & Babbie, 1993). These subjective experiences include those of the researcher, as well as of the research participants. As researchers in our discrimination study, we would want to keep a careful account of our reactions and questions to the events we observe and the stories we hear. Our task is to search for meaningful patterns within the volumes of data (e.g., text, drawings, pictures, video recordings).

Step 4: Collecting the Data

"Qualitative researchers are the principal instruments of data collection." (Franklin & Jordan, 1997). This means that data collected are somehow "processed" through the person collecting them. Interviewing, for example, is a common data collection method that produces text data. Data collection in the interview is interactive, where we can check out our understanding and interpretation as researchers through dialogue with our research participants.

To collect meaningful data, we want to be immersed into the context or setting of the study. We want to have some understanding, for example, of what it is like to be a client of social services before we launch into a dialogue with clients about their experiences of discrimination, if any, within the social services. If we do not have a grasp of the setting in which we are about to participate, then we run the risk of misinterpreting what is told to us.

Given that our general research question or specific hypothesis evolves in a qualitative study, the data collection process is particularly vulnerable to biases of the data collector. There are several principles to guide us in data collection. First, we want to make every effort to be aware of our own biases. In fact, our own notes on reactions and biases to what we are studying are used as sources of data later on, when we interpret the data.

Second, data collection is a two-way street. The research participants tell their stories to the researcher and, in turn, the researcher tells the research participant his or her understanding or interpretation of the stories. It is a process of check and balance. Third, qualitative data collection typically involves multiple data sources and multiple data collection methods. In our study, we may see clients, workers, and supervisors as potential data sources. We may collect data from each of these groups using interviews, observation, and existing documentation.

Step 5: Analyzing and Interpreting the Data

Collecting, analyzing, and interpreting qualitative data are intermingled. Let us say that, in our first round of data collection, we interview a number of clients who come from ethnic minorities about discrimination in social services. Suppose they consistently tell us that to be a client of social services, they must give up many of their cultural values. We could then develop more specific research questions for a second round of interviews in an effort to gain more of an in-depth understanding of the relationship between cultural values and being a social service client.

Overall, the process of analyzing data is an iterative one. This means that we must read and reread the volumes of data that we collected. We simply look for patterns and themes that help to capture how our research participants are experiencing the social problem we are studying.

The ultimate goal is to interpret data in such a way that the true expressions of research participants are revealed. We want to explain meaning according to the beliefs and experiences of those who provided the data. The aim is to "walk the walk" and "talk the talk" of research participants and not to impose "outside" meaning to the data they provided. Box 3.6 illustrates how qualitative research studies, when the text data have been analyzed correctly, can add to our profession's knowledge base. Much more will be said about analyzing and interpreting qualitative data in Chapter 13.

Step 6: Writing the Report

Qualitative research reports are lengthier than quantitative ones. It is not possible to strip the context of a qualitative study and present only the study's findings. The knowledge gained from a qualitative endeavor is nested within the context from which it was derived. Furthermore, text data are more awkward and clumsy to summarize. We cannot rely on a simple figure to indicate a finding. Instead, we display text usually in the form of quotes or summary notes to support our conclusions.

USING BOTH APPROACHES IN ONE STUDY

Given the seemingly contradictory philosophical beliefs associated with quantitative and qualitative research studies, it is difficult to imagine how they could exist together in one research study. As is stands, most research studies incorporate only one approach. The reason may, in part, relate to philosophy, but practical considerations of cost, time, and resources are also factors.

It is not unusual, however, to see numerical data in a qualitative study or text data in a quantitative study. Just think that, if we were to use a quantitative approach, there is no reason why we could not ask research participants a few open-ended questions to more fully explain their experience. In this instance, our quantitative research report would contain some pieces of text data to help bring meaning to the study's findings.

Let us say we want to proceed with a qualitative research study to examine our research question about discrimination within the public social service system. Surely, we would want to identify how many research participants were included, as well as important defining characteristics such as their average age, the number who had difficulty accessing social services, or the number who were satisfied with the services they received.

While it is possible to incorporate qualitative research activity into a quantitative study (and quantitative research activity into a qualitative study) the approach we use is guided by our purpose for conducting the study. Ultimately, research—quantitative or qualitative—is about the pursuit of knowledge. Just what kind of knowledge we are after is up to us.

Box 3.6_____

IS QUALITATIVE RESEARCH GOOD RESEARCH?

There are a few general criticisms leveled against the qualitative research approach when it is directly compared to the quantitative approach. Some people claim that it is too subjective, its procedures are so vague they cannot be replicated, sweeping conclusions are made on the basis of too few cases, and often there is no way to tell if the conclusions are really supported by the data. As Taylor (1993) so aptly points out:

> There is also confusion between the terms empiricist and empirical. Empiricist refers to the teaching of the twentieth-century philosophy of science known as logical empiricism or logical positivism. The qualitative research approach does not follow this school, so qualitative research is nonempiricist. Empirical, on the other hand, refers to data or knowledge derived from observation, experience, or experiment. All science therefore is empirical, and qualitative research is about as empirical as anything can be.
>
> Confusion also arises because some qualitative research studies are not intended to be "science." The aim of science is to produce robust generalizations (capable of standing up to further research) about the real world. Some qualitative studies aim instead to broaden awareness of the human condition and perhaps to move the reader to empathy, indignation, or action. Such studies, which are not much different from good journalism or investigative reporting, are usually described as ideographic. Their aims are worthy, but they are not the aims of science.
>
> What should be asked of any research approach that claims to be "objective"? Four requirements apply:
>
> 1 If someone else examines the data a researcher has collected and applies the same analytic procedures, the exact same results should be obtained.
> 2 If a second researcher collects data from the same kinds of sources, under similar circumstances, and using comparable methods of data elicitation and coding, then similar results should be obtained. If the second researcher's findings differ, the data were probably not much good in the first place.
> 3 The conclusions drawn from the data should be clearly supported by those data. Data that seem contradictory to the conclusions should be fully reported, and it must be demonstrated that the data do not negate the conclusions.
> 4 If researchers generalize their findings and claim that the results they have obtained from X_1 will also hold for $X_2, X_3. \ldots X_n$, their claims should be clearly supported by the data, and the rationale for the conclusions should be clear and compelling.
>
> These four requirements are no more than common sense. They are also the general standards of science. In traditional research terms, the first requirement speaks to the reliability of measurement methods, the second to the replicability of findings, the third to the internal validity of conclusions, and the fourth to the external validity of results. These concepts are discussed later on in this text. There is no inherent reason why qualitative studies cannot meet all four requirements, although practical realities sometimes stand in the way.
>
> Simple checks on the reliability of coding procedures take care of the first requirement, but the second requirement is not so cut and dried. Many qualitative studies cannot be replicated even in part: the cost is too high, the interest too low, or the setting too difficult. Cultures and groups

Box 3.6 Continued

change; today's observations are to-morrow's history. However, a researcher can often test the replicability of findings using several methods. In Hanson's (1989) study of families with chronic mental patients, for example, he used his interview findings as the basis for a brief mail-back questionnaire and obtained comparable results from this larger sample.

The third requirement—that any conclusion should be in accord with the empirical findings—has to do with the care with which the analysis has been done. Has the researcher systematically examined all relevant data to support the conclusions, or simply picked some convenient piece of text to illustrate them, without searching for counterexamples? Are counterexamples adequately explained? Does any other evidence bear on the conclusions? And beyond the data is the argument itself; useful data can be nullified by shoddy thinking. Does the researcher make a good case for the conclusions? Are the concepts clear and well enough defined so that another person could judge their fit to the data, or are "weasel words" used that sound profound but have unclear referents? Is the reasoning straightforward?

The fourth requirement, concerning generalization to other groups, places, or times, also primarily rests on logic. Hanson, for example, found that the families all described similar issues, whether they were old or young, in a rural or urban community, poor or rich. Nor did the findings vary for different institutions and centers. He had chosen his informants by purposive sampling in order to maximize diversity. Since, nevertheless the informants agreed, then other informants probably would also. By this logic, the conclusions could be generalized.

Source: Adapted and modified from: Taylor (1993); Franklin and Jordan (1997)

SUMMING UP AND LOOKING AHEAD

This chapter briefly discussed the differences and similarities between the quantitative and qualitative research approach. These two complementary and respected research approaches are divergent in terms of their philosophical principles. Yet, they share six common steps: choosing a general research topic, focusing the topic into a research question, designing the research study, collecting the data, analyzing and interpreting the data, and writing the report.

REVIEW QUESTIONS

1 In your own words, discuss what is meant by the quantitative research approach to knowledge generation.

2 Discuss the characteristics of quantitative research studies as opposed to the characteristics of obtaining knowledge via tradition, authority, intuition, and practice wisdom methods.

3 Discuss the process of selecting problem areas and formulating research questions within quantitative studies.

4 Discuss all of the steps of doing a quantitative research study. Use an example throughout your entire response.

5 What is the main difference between a concept and a variable?

6 Discuss the advantages and disadvantages of the quantitative research approach to knowledge generation. Use one common example throughout your discussion.

7 At this very beginning point in your social work research course, in groups of four, discuss the various cultural factors that you feel need to be taken into account when doing a quantitative social work research study. Do you feel any of these factors are different for doing an "applied" study verses a "pure" one? Discuss in detail and provide one common social work example in your discussion. Report back to the entire class what your group found.

8 At this very beginning point in your social work course, and in groups of four, design a quantitative research study that proposes to answer a social work–related research question of your choice. Describe in detail how you could incorporate both an "applied" research component and a "pure" research component in the same quantitative study. Present your results to the entire class.

9 At your university library, locate a social work–related journal article that used a quantitative research approach. Using what you know about quantitative research, answer the following nine questions: (a) What was the problem area and research question? What were the study's concepts, independent variables, dependent variables, and operational definitions? (b) What were the hypotheses (if any)? (c) What were the extraneous variables (if any)? (d) Evaluate the study's research hypothesis in relation to the criteria as outlined in the chapter. (e) Was the hypothesis one- or two-tailed? (f) What were some rival hypotheses that the

study could have contained? (g) How did the author overcome the four primary limitations of doing a quantitative study? (h) Did the author question any collective subjective beliefs? If so, what were they? (i) Did the quantitative study incorporate "human concern" for the client with effective social work practice? Explain, providing examples from the study.

10 At your university library, locate a quantitative social work–related journal article. Comment on how well it strived toward:

- Measurability
- Objectivity
- Reducing uncertainty
- Duplication
- Using standardized procedures

11 Using the article above, comment on how well its author(s):

- Selected a problem area
- Conceptualized variables
- Operationalized variables
- Identified constants and labeled variables
- Formulated a research hypothesis
- Developed a sampling plan
- Selected a data collection method
- Analyzed the data

12 Discuss the process of selecting problem areas and formulating research questions within qualitative research studies. Compare and contrast your response to quantitative research studies.

13 Discuss all of the steps in doing a qualitative research study. Use a social work example throughout your entire response.

14 Discuss the advantages and disadvantages of the qualitative research approach to knowledge generation. Use one common example throughout your discussion.

15 Describe in the four types of interview questions that can be used when doing qualitative research.

16 In groups of four, discuss what qualitative researchers do that quantitative researchers do not. What "research skills" do qualitative researchers have to have that quantitative researchers do not? Present your findings to the entire class.

17 At your university library, locate a social work–related journal article that used a qualitative research approach. Using what you know about qualitative research, answer the following five questions: (a) What was the problem area and research question? (b) What were the study's concepts, independent variables, dependent variables, and operational definitions? (c) How did the author overcome the limitations of doing a qualitative study? (d) Did the author question any collective subjective beliefs? If so, what were they? (e) Did the qualitative study incorporate "human concern" for the client with effective social work practice? Explain, providing examples from the study.

18 Using the above journal article, comment on how well its author(s):

• Selected a problem area

• Selected research participants

• Selected a site or setting

• Gained permission and access to the field

• Entered the field and identified key informants

• Selected a research design and data collection method

• Recorded, logged, and analyzed the data

This chapter has been adapted and modified from: Grinnell and Williams (1990)

C h a p t e r   4

Measuring Variables

IN THE PREVIOUS CHAPTER we discussed how the quantitative and qualitative research approaches are utilized to develop knowledge for our profession. As we know, both research approaches eventually deal with variables in some form or another—which in turn, have to be eventually measured in some from or another. In this chapter, we will briefly discuss how measuring instruments are used to measure these variables. Technically speaking, the measurement of variables within any research study is known as *operationalization.* Box 4.1 presents an interesting discussion of how the operationalization of variables can be a tricky business in the "hard" *and* "soft" sciences, and Box 4.2 discusses the importance of naming variables correctly.

In a nutshell, there are a large number of measuring instruments, short and long, simple and complex, and probably better and worse. Not only are there lots of them around in professional journals, they also can be found through publishing houses.

Box 4.1

OPERATIONALIZATION ACROSS THE SCIENCES

One aspect of the stereotype of science shared by many educated persons is that it invariably involves precise measurements with instruments that are accurate to several decimal places. Indeed, this is seen as a crucial difference between the so-called hard sciences, such as chemistry and physics (more accurately called the natural or physical sciences), and the soft sciences, such as psychology, sociology, and anthropology (most of which are social sciences).

Of course, the hard–soft distinction is not meant to be flattering to that which is considered soft; and many natural scientists, who misunderstand the nature of social measurement, believe that the social sciences do not constitute science at all. According to biologist Jared Diamond (1987), however, this criticism misses two crucial points. First, all scientists, natural or social, face the step of operationalizing concepts. As Diamond says," To compare evidence with theory requires that you measure the ingredients of your theory." Second, the "step of operationalizing is inevitably more difficult and less exact in the [social] sciences, because there are so many uncontrolled variables."

Diamond illustrates operationalization with examples drawn from both the natural and social sciences. Learning how various scientists go about this should help your understanding and appreciation of the measurement process. The first example comes from mathematics. As Diamond says,

> I'd guess that mathematics arose long ago when two cave women couldn't operationalize their intuitive concept of "many." One cave woman said, "Let's pick this tree over here, because it has many bananas." The other cave woman argued, "No, let's pick that tree over there, because it has more bananas." Without a number system to operationalize the concept of "many," the two cave women could never prove to each other which tree offered better pickings. (p. 38)

Diamond's second example comes from another "hard" science, analytical chemistry, which generally seeks to measure the properties of substances.

> When my colleagues and I were studying the physiology of hummingbirds, we knew that the little guys liked to drink sweet nectar, but we would have argued indefinitely about how sweet it was if we hadn't operationalized the concept by measuring sugar concentrations. The method we used was to treat a glucose solution with an enzyme that liberates hydrogen peroxide, which reacts (with the help of another enzyme) with another substance called dianisidine to make it turn brown, whereupon we measured the brown color's intensity with an instrument called a spectrophotometer. A pointer's deflection on the spectrophotometer dial let us read off a number that provided an operational definition of sweet. (p. 38)

One of Diamond's "soft" science examples is taken from the field of clinical psychology, specifically his wife Marie Cohen's work with cancer patients and their families. Cohen was interested in how doctors reveal the diagnosis of cancer. What determines how frank they are and how much information they withold? She guessed that this

> might be related to differences in doctors' attitudes toward things like death, cancer, and medical treatment. But how on earth was she to operationalize and measure such . . . ? . . . Part of Marie's solution was to use a questionnaire that other scientists had developed by extracting statements from sources like tape-recorded doctors' meetings and then asking other doctors to express their degree of agreement with each statement. It turned out that each doctor's responses tended to cluster in several groups, in such a way that his [or her] responses to one statement in a cluster were correlated with his [or her] responses to other statements in the same cluster.
>
> One cluster proved to consist of expressions of attitudes toward death, a second cluster consisted of expressions of attitudes toward treatment and diagnosis,

Box 4.1 Continued

and a third cluster consisted of statements about patients' ability to cope with cancer. The responses were then employed to define attitude scales, which were further validated in other ways, like testing the scales on doctors at different stages in their careers (hence likely to have different attitudes). By thus operationalizing doctors' attitudes, Marie discovered (among other things) that doctors most convinced about the value of early diagnosis and aggressive treatment of cancer are the ones most likely to be frank with their patients. (p. 39)

Notice how the problem (finding and creating ways of operationalizing one's intuitive concepts) is the same in each case. Notice also how operationalization can be very indirect, as in both the chemistry and clinical psychology examples, irrespective of the accuracy of the measurement. Finally, these examples might suggest, as Diamond (p. 39) concludes, that the "ingrained labels 'soft science' and 'hard science' could be replaced by hard (i.e., difficult) science and easy science, respectively" For the social sciences "are much more difficult and [to some] intellectually challenging than mathematics and chemistry."

Source: Singleton, Straits, and Miller Straits (1993)

QUESTIONS TO ASK BEFORE MEASURING

What we want is some method of making a selection from the huge array of measuring instruments that exists. There are six questions we can ask ourselves to help us make our choice. When we have answered these six questions, we will be able to distinguish the kind of instrument we need from the kind we do not need; hopefully, this will eliminate a large number of all those instruments lying in wait in the library. Let us take a simple example to illustrate how the use of measuring instruments can be used in the research process. Let us say we want to know if there is a relationship between the two variables: depression and sleep patterns.

Why Do We Want to Make the Measurement?

The first question is: *Why do we want to make the measurement?* At first glance, this does not seem too difficult. We just want to measure, or operationalize, depression and sleep patterns in order to study the relationship between the two variables, if any. But things are not quite as simple as they appear. There are three general reasons for using measuring instruments, and we need to select the one that applies to our study.

The first of these reasons is *assessment and diagnosis.* We are not really assessing or diagnosing anyone, as we might be in clinical practice, so this reason can be eliminated. The second reason is *evaluation of practice effectiveness,* and we are not doing that either. The last reason is *applied research.* Determining relationships between two variables certainly counts as research and we hope to eventually apply it to our practice, so we will select that one.

Box 4.2

THE IMPORTANCE OF VARIABLE NAMES

Operationalization is one of those things that are easier said than done. It is quite simple to explain to someone the purpose and importance of operational definitions for variables, and even to describe how operationalization typically takes place. However, until you've tried to operationalize a rather complex variable, you may not appreciate some of the subtle difficulties involved. Of considerable importance to the operationalization effort is the particular name that you have chosen for a variable. Let's consider an example from the field of Urban Planning.

A variable of interest to planners is citizen participation. Planners are convinced that participation in the planning process by citizens is important to the success of plan implementation. Citizen participation is an aid to planners' understanding of the real and perceived needs of a community, and such involvement by citizens tends to enhance their cooperation with and support for planning efforts. Although many different conceptual definitions might be offered by different planners, there would be little misunderstanding over what is *meant* by citizen participation. The name of the variable seems adequate.

However, if we asked different planners to provide very simple operational measures for citizen participation, we are likely to find a variety among their responses that does generate confusion. One planner might keep a tally of attendance by private citizens at city commission and other local government meetings; another might maintain a record of the different topics addressed by private citizens at

similar meetings; while a third might record the number of local government meeting attendees, as well as letters and phone calls received by the mayor and other pubic officials during a particular time period.

As skilled researchers, we can readily see that each planner would be measuring (in a very simplistic fashion) a different *dimension* of citizen participation: extent of citizen participation, issues prompting citizen participation, and form of citizen participation. Therefore, the original *naming* of our variable, citizen participation, which was quite satisfactory from a conceptual point of view, proved inadequate for purposes of operationalization.

The precise and exact naming of variables is important in research. It is both essential to and a result of good operationalization. Variable names quite often evolve from an iterative process of forming a conceptual definition, then an operational definition, then renaming the concept to better match what can or will be measured.

This looping process continues (our example above illustrates only one iteration), resulting in a gradual refinement of the variable name and its measurement until a reasonable fit is obtained. Sometimes the concept of the variable that you end up with is a bit different from the original one that you started with, but at least you are measuring what you are talking about, if only because you are talking about what you are measuring!

Source: Rubin and Babbie (1993)

The point of making this selection is to discover how accurate we need the instrument to be. If our measurement is going to affect someone's life, for example, it has to be as accurate as we can possibly make it. We might be doing an assessment that will be used in making decisions about treatment interventions, referrals, placements, and so forth. On the other hand, if our measurement will not affect anyone's life directly, we can afford to be a little less rigid in our requirements. How much less rigid depends on what we are doing.

If this is to be a beginning research study (e.g., exploratory) in a relatively unexplored field, the result will only be a tentative suggestion that some variable is possibly related to some other variable; for instance, sleep patterns are related to depression. A little inaccuracy in measurement in this case is not the end of the world. When a little more is known in our subject area (e.g., descriptive, explanatory), we might be able to formulate a more specific hypothesis; for example, depressed people spend less time in delta-wave NREM sleep than nondepressed people.

In this case, we obviously should be able to measure sleep patterns accurately enough to distinguish between delta-wave NREM sleep and other kinds of sleep. All in all, then, how accurate our measurement needs to be depends on our purpose. Because we are only doing a beginning study, we can afford to be relatively inaccurate. We have now answered the first question: *Why do we want to make the measurement?*

What Do We Want to Measure?

The second question is: *What do we want to measure?* We know the answer to that one also; we want to measure depression and sleep patterns. Or, to put it another way, we want to operationalize depression and sleep patterns. But here again, it is not so simple as it seems. Not only are measuring instruments more accurate or less accurate, they can be *wideband* or *narrowband*.

Wideband instruments measure a broad trait or characteristic. A trait is pretty much the same thing as a characteristic and it means some aspect of character such as bravery, gaiety, or depression. Logically enough, *narrowband* instruments measure just a particular aspect of a particular trait. A narrowband instrument, for example, might tell us how Uncle Fred feels about his daughter moving to Moose Jaw but it will not give us an overall picture of Uncle Fred's depression.

A wideband instrument, on the other hand, will give an overall picture of Uncle Fred's depression but it will not tell us how he feels about his daughter moving to Moose Jaw. In our particular study, we are not interested too much in how Uncle Fred feels about his daughter moving to Moose Jaw. If he is one of our research participants, we just want to know about his overall depression so that we can relate it to his sleep patterns. We need a wideband instrument then, which does not have to be absolutely smack-on accurate.

Who Will Make the Measurement?

The third question asks: *Who will make the measurement?* Well, we will—that seems obvious enough. However, it is not always social workers who make measurements, sometimes clients make them. In our study, it will be the people who participate in the study who will fill out the instrument to measure depression. Sometimes family members make the measurements, or then again, teachers, specially trained outside observers, or the staff members in an institution make them.

The point is that different kinds of people require different kinds of measuring instruments. An instrument that could be completed easily and accurately by a trained social worker might prove too difficult for Uncle Fred, who has arthritis and cataracts and a reading level of around the fourth grade. In our simple research study, we will have to take care that the instrument we choose is easy for our research participants to understand. So far, then, we need a wideband instrument, easy to complete, and not necessarily smack-on accurate.

What Format Do We Require?

The fourth question is: *What format do we require?* A format is the way our questions will look on the page. They may appear in the form of an inventory, such as:

List below the things that make you feel depressed.

_____

_____

Or a checklist such as:

Check below all the things that you sometimes feel:
_____ My mother gets on my nerves.
_____ My father does not understand me.
_____ I do not get along very well with my sister.
_____ I think I hate my family sometimes.

Or a scale such as:

How satisfied are you with your life? (Circle one number below.)
1 Very unsatisfied
2 Somewhat satisfied
3 Satisfied
4 More than satisfied
5 Very satisfied

More often than not, measuring instruments contain a number of items, or questions, that when totaled, yield more accurate results than just asking one question. These measuring instruments are called summative scales. Figures 4.1 and 4.2 present two examples of popular summative scales.

After careful thought, we decide that a wideband, easy-to-complete, not-smack-on-accurate summative scale would do the job. However, we have not finished yet. Instruments may be unidimensional or multidimensional. A unidimensional instrument only measures one variable, for example, self-esteem (e.g., Figure 4.1). On the other hand, a multidimensional instrument measures a number of variables at the same time (e.g., Figure 4.2). A multidimensional instrument is nothing more than a number of unidimensional instruments stuck together.

For example, Figure 4.2 is a multidimensional instrument that contains three unidimensional instruments: (1) relevance of received social services (Items 1–11), (2) the extent to which the services reduced the problem (Items 12–21), and (3) the extent to which services enhanced the client's self-esteem and contributed to a sense of power and integrity (Items 22–34).

Where Will the Measurement Be Made?

Question five asks: *Where will the measurement be made?* Well, probably in our good friend's sleep laboratory. At first glance, it may seem that it does not matter where the measurement is made but, in fact, it matters a great deal. For example, we might have a child who throws temper tantrums mostly in school. In this case, measurements dealing with temper tantrums should obviously be made at school. Or we might have a man who is particularly depressed in railway stations because they remind him of his dead wife. And so the examples go on.

We can see that an instrument that is to be completed in a railway station might differ from an instrument that is to be used in the comparative serenity of our office. It should be shorter, say, and simpler, possibly printed on paper that glows in the dark so that if it gets torn out of our hands, we can chase after it more easily. We decide that our research participants will probably be equally depressed everywhere, more or less, and the measurements will take place in the laboratory.

When Will the Measurement Be Made?

Our last question, question six, is: *When will the measurement be made?* Probably some time in August if it all goes well. But no, the month of the year is not what is meant by *when. When* refers to the time or times during the study when a measurement is made.

There are certain research designs in which we measure a client's problem, do something to change the problem, and then measure the problem again to see if we have changed it. This involves two measurements, the first and second measurements of the problem. In research

INDEX OF SELF-ESTEEM

Name: _____   Today's Date:_____

Context: _____

This questionnaire is designed to measure how you see yourself. It is not a test, so there are no right or wrong answers. Please answer each item as carefully and as accurately as you can by placing a number beside each one as follows:

1 = None of the time
2 = Very rarely
3 = A little of the time
4 = Some of the time
5 = A good part of the time
6 = Most of the time
7 = All of the time

1. _____ I feel that people would not like me if they really knew me well.
2. _____ I feel that others get along much better than I do.
3. _____ I feel that I am a beautiful person.
4. _____ When I am with others I feel they are glad I am with them.
5. _____ I feel that people really like to talk with me.
6. _____ I feel that I am a very competent person.
7. _____ I think I make a good impression on others.
8. _____ I feel that I need more self-confidence.
9. _____ When I am with strangers I am very nervous.
10. _____ I think that I am a dull person.
11. _____ I feel ugly.
12. _____ I feel that others have more fun than I do.
13. _____ I feel that I bore people.
14. _____ I think my friends find me interesting.
15. _____ I think I have a good sense of humor.
16. _____ I feel very self-conscious when I am with strangers.
17. _____ I feel that if I could be more like other people I would have it made.
18. _____ I feel that people have a good time when they are with me.
19. _____ I feel like a wallflower when I go out.
20. _____ I feel I get pushed around more than others.
21. _____ I think I am a rather nice person.
22. _____ I feel that people really like me very much.
23. _____ I feel that I am a likeable person.
24. _____ I am afraid I will appear foolish to others.
25. _____ My friends think very highly of me.

3, 4, 5, 6, 7, 14, 15, 18, 21, 22, 23, 25.

FIGURE 4.1   Hudson's Index of Self-Esteem

Using the scale from one to five described below, please indicate on the line to the left of each item the number that comes closest to how you feel.

1 Strongly agree
2 Agree
3 Undecided
4 Disagree
5 Strongly disagree

_____ 1   The social worker took my problems very seriously.
_____ 2   If I had been the social worker, I would have dealt with my problems in just the same way.
_____ 3   The worker I had could never understand anyone like me.
_____ 4   Overall the agency has been very helpful to me.
_____ 5   If friends of mine had similar problems I would tell them to go to the agency.
_____ 6   The social worker asks a lot of embarrassing questions.
_____ 7   I can always count on the worker to help if I'm in trouble.
_____ 8   The agency will help me as much as it can.
_____ 9   I don't think the agency has the power to really help me.
_____ 10   The social worker tries hard but usually isn't too helpful.
_____ 11   The problem the agency tried to help me with is one of the most important in my life.
_____ 12   Things have gotten better since I've been going to the agency.
_____ 13   Since I've been using the agency my life is more messed up than ever.
_____ 14   The agency is always available when I need it.
_____ 15   I got from the agency exactly what I wanted.
_____ 16   The social worker loves to talk but won't really do anything for me.
_____ 17   Sometimes I just tell the social worker what I think she wants to hear.
_____ 18   The social worker is usually in a hurry when I see her.
_____ 19   No one should have any trouble getting some help from this agency.
_____ 20   The worker sometimes says things I don't understand.
_____ 21   The social worker is always explaining things carefully.
_____ 22   I never looked forward to my visits to the agency.
_____ 23   I hope I'll never have to go back to the agency for help.
_____ 24   Everytime I talk to my worker I feel relieved.
_____ 25   I can tell the social worker the truth without worrying.
_____ 26   I usually feel nervous when I talk to my worker.
_____ 27   The social worker is always looking for lies in what I tell her.
_____ 28   It takes a lot of courage to go to the agency.
_____ 29   When I enter the agency I feel very small and insignificant.
_____ 30   The agency is very demanding.
_____ 31   The social worker will sometimes lie to me.
_____ 32   Generally the social worker is an honest person.
_____ 33   I have the feeling that the worker talks to other people about me.
_____ 34   I always feel well treated when I leave the agency.

FIGURE 4.2   Reid-Gundlach Social Service Satisfaction Scale

jargon we represent these measurements as Os (*O* stands for Observation). Whatever we do to change the problem—usually a social work treatment of some kind—is represented by *X*. In short, in research designs we represent the:

Dependent variables by: *O*s

Independent variables by: *X*s

If our research design is such that we make an initial measurement of the dependent variable (O_1); introduce an independent variable (X); and then measure the same dependent variable again (O_2) our design would look like:

$$O_1 \quad X \quad O_2$$

Where:

O_1 = First measurement of the dependent variable
X = Independent variable, the intervention
O_2 = Second measurement of the dependent variable

Then there are other research designs in which a whole string of measurements of the dependent variable are made:

$$X \quad O_1 \quad O_2 \quad O_3 \ldots$$

Where:

X = Independent variable
O_1 = First measurement of the dependent variable
O_2 = Second measurement of the dependent variable
O_3 = Third measurement of the dependent variable

If we make the measurement more than once, the accuracy of the results may be threatened. In short, the physical act of completing the measuring instrument may cause a change in the feeling or behavior being measured. For example, we remember, during that bleak period of trying to quit smoking, there was one horrible morning when we sat in our office and counted the cigarette butts. We mentally translated all those butts into blackened lungs, and the vision was so disturbing that we smoked more cigarettes in that hour than in the whole of the previous day.

The process of measuring, or operationalizing, our smoking behavior by counting butts most definitely affected our smoking behavior. An instrument that affects behavior in this way is known as *reactive*. On the other hand, an instrument that does not affect the variable being measured is known as *nonreactive*. Obviously, we do not want a reactive measuring instrument.

In addition to the above, the scores on a subsequent administration of a measuring instrument may be affected by changes in the respondent such as memory, or fatigue, or annoyance. In other words, the second or third time you fill out the same measuring instrument, you might remember and repeat what you said the first time or you might become so irritated with the whole procedure that you start to make rude remarks.

The trouble is that, in our study of the relationship between depression and sleep patterns, we had intended to measure the depression levels just before bedtime on the same nights as we measured the sleep patterns. This would result in lots of measurements close together. Some instruments, it appears, are more stable over time, possibly because the questions contained within the instrument are less irritating and less likely to be remembered. We would need a stable instrument then.

We have now considered all six questions. Glancing back through our answers, we came up with a wideband scale, easy to complete, not necessarily smack-on accurate, stable, and nonreactive. All we have to do now is to look through the professional literature and the publishing house lists until we find one. In final analysis, however, we need to be able to select one from the many that exist. This selection process requires the skills of evaluating them.

HOW WE EVALUATE INSTRUMENTS

Suppose that we have found five similar measuring instruments that we think will meet our needs. The next step is to evaluate them so that we can select just one. There are four criteria to consider when we are evaluating a measuring instrument: sample, practicality, validity, and reliability. First, let us look at the sample that the people who designed the instrument used to formulate and test it.

Sample

People who design measuring instruments have to test them out on someone to ensure that they work the way they are supposed to. At first glance, it is difficult to see what the testing procedure has to do with us; we only want to *use* the instrument. But suppose, for example, that a year ago we designed an instrument to measure depression in Native Americans. We included in our instrument questions that we thought would be understandable to Native Americans, given their particular cultural background.

Then, we tested the instrument to make sure that those questions did, in fact, make sense to Native Americans. We could not contact every Native American in the country to make our measurement; there are too many of them and the measurement would be too expensive and difficult to administer. We just used a few of them, that is, a sample, and we hoped that the sample we used was representative of the total Native-American population from which our sample was drawn. In fact, we did more than hope. Using one of the sampling methods, to be presented in the next chapter, we selected the sample carefully so that it *was* representative of the total population of Native Americans as nearly as possible.

Now, faced with measuring depression in our present study, we go burrowing in the basement to find the instrument we designed a year ago. But, even if we find it, we will not be able to use it because this particular instrument was designed for Native Americans and tested on a sample of Native Americans. It may be quite accurate for Native Americans but perhaps it will not be accurate at all if used on our present population of Caucasians. We must make sure that any instrument we use to measure depression in Caucasians was designed for and tested on Caucasians.

It turns out that all of the instruments we are evaluating were tested on a Caucasian population, so we cannot eliminate any of them on that account. Now, we will proceed to the next criterion in evaluating an instrument.

Practicality

The first practical consideration we have to examine is whether our research participants will complete the instrument. There are three factors that influence this: (1) how long the instrument is, (2) whether the research participants understand it, and (3) whether the participants like the look of it.

If the instrument is long, it is usually more accurate but also less likely to be completed. We contemplate our five instruments and imagine Uncle Fred in his pajamas squinting bleary-eyed at the seventy-second question while the night draws on and around him the other research participants snore. It is guaranteed to play havoc with his sleep patterns. And Uncle Fred, though slow, is at least willing. Suppose, for a moment, that we were in a different situation where we had to administer this instrument to a resentful, involuntary research participant who would rather be anywhere else than here. It would not work.

Provided it does not have to be smack-on accurate (ours does not), shorter is definitely better. Particularly if it has to be completed more than once. One of the five instruments we are evaluating has seventy-five questions; the remaining four have twenty-five each. Scratch the first instrument—it is too long. We are now down to four, each with twenty-five questions, or items, apiece.

The second factor affecting completion of the instrument is whether the research participants understand it. For example, the fifth question on one of the remaining four instruments is:

> **5** I feel blue: (Circle one letter below.)
>
> **a** Strongly agree
>
> **b** Agree
>
> **c** Unsure
>
> **d** Disagree
>
> **e** Strongly disagree

Surely, even Uncle Fred could cope with that; the instructions seem clear enough. But then, we remember administering an instrument some time ago to a woman named Maria—abundantly fleshed, with bleached blonde hair, a seductive grin, and a cigarette bouncing on her scarlet lower lip. The third question in that instrument stated:

> **3** What is your marital status? (Circle one letter below.)
>
> **a** Married
>
> **b** Separated
>
> **c** Widowed
>
> **d** Divorced
>
> **e** Single

Maria circled the first four letters but not the fifth (single). When we asked her about it, she said, "Well ducks, there was Albert—see he was me first—and I separated from him and then he went and snuffed it. So that's separated *and* widowed, right there ducks, and then there was George and we was divorced and now I'm married to Harry." She beamed broadly and we beamed back. Before administering the instrument again, we changed, "What is your marital status?" to "What is your *present* marital status?" (But even that might not have done it for Maria.)

Another point about "I feel blue" is that, in a way, it is a slang expression. Slang expressions should be avoided since they might be unfamiliar to some of us. Surely, "I feel blue" is such a common expression that it would be familiar to everyone but, then again, maybe it would not. The only way to find out is to ask as many different people as possible. Asking as many people as possible is called a *pretest*. Before using an instrument in a real research study, we pretest it, preferably on people similar to those who will eventually complete it. They tell us what they did not understand, what they were not sure about, and what they disliked. Then, we correct those things and try the instrument on other people until we have it right.

We note that all of our four remaining instruments have been pre-tested. Sometimes you can pretest over and over and still miss gems like Maria. Fortunately, we will be with Uncle Fred and the others when they complete their instruments, so we will be able to clear up any mysteries immediately. It does not look as if we can eliminate any of the four remaining instruments because our research participants will not understand them.

The third factor affecting completion of the instrument is whether or not the research participants like the look of it. If it is offensive or insulting, it will not be completed, of course, but not too many instruments are offensive or insulting. Certainly, none of our four are. Some instruments, though, do seem to be irrelevant. That is, they do not appear to the people completing them to be asking sensible questions related to the issue at hand.

Suppose, for example, that we tried to examine BSW social work students on their knowledge of social work administration by giving them a test originally designed for business students. The administrative principles involved might in fact be the same and the test might be an adequate measure of the social work students' knowledge. But it would not appear to the students to be an adequate measure because the questions involved business situations rather than social work. The students would probably score worse on this test than they would on the same test rephrased in terms of social work situations.

As far as we can see, all four of our instruments would appear relevant to Uncle Fred. So now we are about to pass on to another issue concerned with practicality; that is, how easy it is to interpret the instrument's scores. Interpretation is easiest when the instrument has utility, provides direct measurement, is nonreactive, is sensitive to small changes, and is easy to score.

First, an instrument has utility if the results provide some useful data. Obviously, we are not going to use an instrument if it does not provide useful data.

The second point concerns direct measurement. Interpretation of scores is usually easiest when the instrument measures the variable directly. A variable, as already noted, is something that varies, such as age, weight, or depression level. Anything that can have more than one value is a variable. Some variables can be measured directly. Mostly, these are physical variables such as gender, height, weight, or age

Other variables, such as depression, can only be measured indirectly through some feeling or thought that we believe to be associated with the variable. If you want to know how heavy you are, for example, you hop on a scale. If you want to know how depressed you are, on the other hand, you first have to decide what depression is, a miserable feeling or a change in eating habits, and measure *that*. Generally, direct measures are more suitable for research purposes than indirect measures because we do not have that intermediate step.

The third point is that the instrument should be nonreactive. *Nonreactive* means, as discussed above, that the act of completing the instrument *does not* affect the variable being measured. *Reactive* means that the act of measuring *does* affect the variable being measured, as counting cigarette butts affects smoking behavior, for example. Well, so far as we know, Uncle Fred will not be more depressed or less depressed when he finishes our instrument than he was at the beginning. Since completing the instrument should not take more than five minutes, there really will not be time.

Fourth, the instrument should be sensitive to small changes. That would certainly be nice because, for all we know, a small change in depression level might correspond to slightly different sleep patterns. In fact, an instrument that is sensitive to small changes is important in any study where the purpose is to measure client change.

The fifth point is that the instrument should be easy to score. Most certainly, yes, since we have to score it. We look at our remaining four instruments, trying to figure out how difficult they would be to score and how much time they would take. Two of them seem to be more or less just a question of addition and we can probably handle addition. The other two are more complex—you have to add things on here and subtract other things there, a bit like the Federal Income Tax Form. We do not want to do anything that reminds us of income tax. Happily, we ditch the two more complex instruments.

We now have two instruments left to evaluate. Of the four criteria we use for evaluation (i.e., sampling, practicality, validity, and reliability) we have covered sampling and practicality. That leaves only validity and reliability.

Validity

A measuring instrument is valid when it measures what it is supposed to measure. For example, an instrument designed to measure depression is valid if it measures depression and invalid if it measures something else, such as self-esteem. But there is more to validity than that. In order to be valid, the instrument must also measure depression *accurately.*

One of the main things to remember is that we must think not in terms of validity but in terms of validities. An instrument is valid only if it fulfills the purpose for which it was designed, and an instrument may have several purposes. There are therefore several kinds of validity, of which we will consider only three: (1) content, (2) face, and (3) criterion.

Content Validity

The first kind of validity to consider is content validity. Here, we ask whether the instrument is really measuring the variable it was designed to measure. If it is supposed to measure depression, for example, is it really measuring depression, or is it measuring something else, like self-esteem, or is it just producing a meaningless score?

In order to decide whether an instrument is really measuring, say, self-esteem, we first have to be able to conceptualize what self-esteem is. That is, we have to be able to define self-esteem in terms of feelings and/or behaviors that can be measured. For example, what is it that makes people think highly of themselves? Is it whether they think they are physically attractive, whether they feel other people like them, or whether they feel they have a good sense of humor? Probably, it is all of these and a great many more.

In order to have a valid measure of self-esteem, we have to include in our instrument at least one question for each of the feelings and behaviors that go to make up self-esteem; that is *all* of them. If we include everything except for feelings of competence, our instrument is not totally content valid. If we include competence and omit a sense of humor, our instrument still is not content valid. We may well wonder how anyone can cram all of those things into an instrument short enough for Uncle Fred to complete in his lifetime.

The trouble with including all of the factors that go to make up self-esteem is that we have to *know* all of them. Since experts are human, they often disagree as to what precisely constitutes all of them and whether they have all been included in the instrument. An instrument may be content valid to one expert, therefore, and not to another. It is strictly a matter of personal judgment. In fact, no instrument of a practical length can possibly contain all the factors that go to make up a complex variable such as self-esteem, even if all these factors can be known. No instrument therefore can be perfectly content valid. But it can be more content valid or less valid depending on what factors are selected for inclusion by the person who constructs it.

Face Validity

The second kind of validity to be considered is face validity. Face validity is concerned not with what an instrument *measures* but with what it *appears to measure*. We have come across this before when we were discussing factors that affected whether or not the instrument was completed. Thinking back, one of those factors was whether or not the research participants liked the look of the instrument; not so much whether the instrument was offensive, because not many instruments are, but whether the questions included in the instrument seemed relevant to the research participants.

We talked about testing BSW social work students on their knowledge of social work administration by giving them a test designed for business students; the conclusion was that most social work students would not do very well on this test because the questions did not seem to apply to social work. In other words, the test, or measuring instrument, had no *face validity.*

Criterion Validity

The third kind of validity is called criterion validity. One way to establish the validity of an instrument is to compare it with another instrument that is supposed to measure the same variable. If both instruments give the same results, then we can assume that both have criterion validity. If they give different results, then one of them is wrong and we have to use a third instrument to discover which it is.

Suppose, for example, that we want to establish the criterion validity of an instrument that is supposed to predict the success of students in a BSW program. To do this, we administer the instrument to students entering the BSW program; then, four years later, we look at the grade point averages of those same students as they leave the program. If the instrument successfully predicted which students would have a high grade point average and which students would have a low grade point average, we can say that the instrument has criterion validity.

Of course, in this example, we have operationally defined, or measured, success in terms of grade point averages. We could have operationally defined success differently either in terms of good practicum work as reported by the students' field instructors or simply as graduation from the BSW program. In this case the instrument has criterion validity if it predicts which students will do good practicum work or which students will graduate. If it fails to make these predictions accurately, it has no criterion validity.

In the above paragraph, we used the phrase "operationally defined" knowing already that a variable is operationally defined when it is defined in terms that can be measured. Success is an abstract sort of concept but grade point averages are definitely measurable, and so is graduation.

Criterion validity is often divided into two categories: (1) concurrent validity, and (2) predictive validity.

Concurrent Validity   Concurrent validity deals with the present. Suppose, for example, we have an instrument that is supposed to distinguish between children who need remedial reading services and children who do not. We can validate the instrument by asking the children's teacher to tell which children need the services. If the teacher and the instrument name the same children, the teacher is probably right and the instrument has concurrent validity. If they disagree, then we can bring in another test of reading skills or the visiting social work educational consultant. The point is that we validate the instrument by comparing it with a different measure of the same thing.

Predictive Validity   Unlike concurrent validity, predictive validity deals with the future. Suppose we have an instrument designed to predict which children will need remedial reading services in six months' time, on the basis of their present performance. The only way we can validate this instrument is to wait six months to discover which children are then in need of remedial reading services. But again, in six months, we will still have to ask the teacher which children need services in order to find out whether the instrument's prediction was right. And, if teacher and instrument disagree, we will still have to bring in another teacher or another instrument. We still validate our instrument by comparing it with some other measure of the same variable.

Table 4.1 summarizes the three major methods in which the validity of a measuring instrument can be assessed and the various types of research questions that can be answered.

Reliability

The fourth criterion used when evaluating an instrument is reliability. In order to be reliable, an instrument must be able to measure the same variable over and over again and arrive at the same conclusion. It must be stable; it must be consistent. There is no guarantee, though, that the variable it measures so consistently is the one it is supposed to measure. We could go along happily measuring Uncle Fred's depression, get perfectly consistent, reliable results, and realize some time later that we had not been measuring depression at all; we had been measuring self-esteem. In this case, the instrument would be perfectly reliable but, since it was not measuring the variable it was supposed to measure, it would not be valid. In this way, if we are sufficiently silly, we can have reliability without validity.

If an instrument is valid, as already learned, it measures what it is supposed to measure and measures it accurately. If the measurement is different each time we make it (i.e., if the instrument is unreliable), we can hardly say that we have made an accurate measurement. In other words, an instrument has to be reliable before it can be valid. There are several procedures for establishing the reliability of an instrument and we will look at only three of them: (1) the test-retest method, (2) the alternate-form method, and (3) the split-half method.

Test-Retest Method

The first method for establishing reliability is the test-retest method. Very simply, this means that if we administer the same instrument to Uncle Fred on two or more occasions, the results will be the same if the instrument is temporally stable, or temporarily reliable. They will not be exactly the same. There are always small differences due to the fact that

TABLE 4.1   Types of Measurement Validity
and Questions Addressed by Each

Type	Question Addressed
Content Validity	Does the measuring instrument adequately measure the major dimensions of the variable under consideration?
Face Validity	Does the measuring instrument appear to measure the subject matter under consideration?
Criterion Validity	Does the individual's measuring instrument score predict the probable behavior on a second variable (criterion-related measure)?

Uncle Fred had a bad night, a pneumatic drill is tearing up the pavement outside our office, or another cut in social security payments has been announced by the president. But the results should be more or less the same. The more reliable an instrument is, in fact, the less the results are affected by such incidentals as conditions in our office and Uncle Fred's mood.

To a certain extent though, Uncle Fred's mood is what we are measuring. How can we know whether a difference in the results from one measure to the next is because of something trivial such as a bad night or a genuine change in the level of Uncle Fred's depression? In order to answer this question, we must first consider the possibility that the first measure affected the second. For example, Uncle Fred is a patient soul but he might get tired of being asked if he is feeling blue. Irritation might cause him to fill in the blanks at random rather than taking the time to actually read the questions. Or he might remember what he wrote the last time and answer the questions differently just to enliven the proceedings.

There is also the possibility that taking the measure will actually change the variable being measured. When that variable is Uncle Fred's depression, the possibility is smaller; depression is not usually affected by filling out a form. But other variables (e.g., attitudes) are much more easily affected.

Suppose, for a moment, we took a poll among the residents of a senior citizen's complex to see how they felt about being allowed to keep pets. The poll might raise certain questions in the minds of the residents. Mrs. Hannelberry, say, might become convinced that, if she got a parrot, Mrs. Dodd next door would get a cat to spite her. If we then did a second poll, Mrs. Hannelberry might change her answer from "don't know" to "strongly disagree" whereas Mrs. Dodd, in love with a pet store kitten, might switch to "strongly agree." It was the original poll itself that awoke paranoia in Mrs. Hannelberry and kitten love in Mrs. Dodd, so influencing their answers in the second poll.

We want to be sure, in our study, that Uncle Fred's depression can be measured again and again without one measurement affecting either another measurement or his depression. Whether or not one measurement affects the next depends to a large extent on how much time there is between them. If it is a short time, the likelihood is higher that the first measurement will affect the second; if it is a long time, a real change might have occurred in the level of Uncle Fred's depression. If these measures are being done in order to establish the test-retest reliability of our instrument, what we need is some kind of compromise—not so short a time that one measure affects the next; not so long a time that the level of Uncle Fred's depression changes. Two to four weeks is generally considered a reasonable interval for most psychological measures.

Alternate-Form Method

The second method of establishing the reliability of a measuring instrument is the alternate-form method. An alternate form of an instrument, as the name suggests, is a second instrument that is as similar as possible to the original except that the actual questions have been changed. Because the actual questions, or items, are not the same, Uncle Fred will not be able to remember what he said the first time and might change his answers just to be difficult.

It might be necessary to use the alternate form of an instrument if, for example, we are giving an exam to a large number of students who cannot all write it at the same time. Thus, we have decided to have half of them write it on Tuesday and the other half on Wednesday. It cannot be exactly the same exam in case the group on Tuesday talk about it to the Wednesday group, but it has to be at least equivalent to be fair to all students. To make certain that the two exams are equivalent, we have an entirely different set of students write both exams with an hour's break between them. The hour's break is merely a lunch and bathroom break.

It may seem that to have one set of students write two equivalent exams is definitely a matter for the ethics committee. But let us take another example. This time, suppose that we are going to conduct a four-week educational program in a certain community to improve attitudes toward racial minorities. First we administer a measure to find out what the community's attitudes are to begin with. Then we conduct the program. Then, we administer the measurement again to see if the program has been effective. As we know, we can write this in research jargon as:

$$\boxed{O_1 \quad X \quad O_2}$$

Where:

O_1 = First measurement of the community's attitudes
X = Introduction of the educational program
O_2 = Second measurement of the community's attitudes

There have been four weeks between the first measurement and the second—a short enough time, possibly, for individuals like Uncle Fred to remember what they said in the first measurement. If the first measurement affects the second, we will not get a 100 percent accurate measure of the effectiveness of our educational program.

In order to foil Uncle Fred and persons like him, we do not give the original measure on the second occasion; we give an alternate form of the measure. Before we can do this, though, we must take care to ensure that both forms of the measure are really equivalent and that they are equivalent across a four-week interval. We can find out if the two forms of the measure are equivalent by having a group of people—probably another set of students—complete both measures, with a four-week break between them instead of an hour. The reliability of alternate-form instruments is always tested over the same time interval as will be used in the actual study for which the instruments are needed.

The trouble with alternate forms of the same instrument is that there are two of them. Consequently, we must make sure that the two instruments are valid and reliable, both when they are used together and when they are used as entirely separate instruments. Then, we have to consider that there are certain kinds of problems that, once solved, can always be solved again using the same method. If we were trying to construct two alternate forms of the same intelligence test, for example, we would have to remember that a person who learned from the first test might do a lot better on the second one, even though the questions were different. For these reasons, we need a different way of establishing reliability.

Spilt-Half Method

The third method of establishing reliability is known as the split-half method. This involves splitting one instrument in half so that it becomes two instruments. The point of doing this is to prove that our instrument is the same all the way through, or internally consistent. In some cases, for example, we do not want an instrument in which the questions at the end take longer to complete than those at the beginning. Neither do we want harder questions at the end, or even different kinds of questions; we just want the instrument to be homogeneous all the way through.

One way to test this is to split the instrument in half and have the students complete both halves to see if the two sets of scores compare. The big question is, how do we make the split? Usually, all the even numbered questions are used to make up one half and all the odd numbered

TABLE 4.2   Types of Measurement Reliability
                       and Questions Addressed by Each

Type	Question Addressed
Test-Retest Method	Does an individual respond to a measuring instrument in the same general way when the instrument is administered twice?
Alternate-Forms Method	When two forms of an instrument that are equivalent in their degree of validity are given to the same individual, is there a strong convergence in how that person responds?
Split-Half Method	Are the scores on one half of the measuring instrument similar to those obtained on the other half?

questions to make up the second half. If the students' scores are very similar for both halves, it can be said that our instrument is the same all the way through, that is, homogeneous.

Table 4.2 summarizes the three major methods in which the reliability of a measuring instrument can be assessed and the various types of research questions that can be answered.

We have now finished with ways of establishing the reliability of instruments. After a brief summary of validity and reliability, we will discuss measurement errors.

Validity and Reliability Revisited

A valid instrument measures what it is supposed to measure and measures it accurately. A reliable instrument yields the same result (or almost the same result) when it is administered repeatedly under the same conditions. That is, a reliable instrument has stability; it is not influenced unduly by such incidental hazards as bad nights and pneumatic drills. The stability of a measuring instrument can be established by the test-retest method.

A reliable instrument also yields the same, or almost the same, results as a second instrument that is equivalent to it when both are administered under the same conditions. That is, an individual who completes two equivalent instruments will obtain similar scores from each if both are reliable. The equivalence of a measuring instrument can be established by the alternate-form method. A reliable instrument is also homogeneous or internally consistent. Homogeneity can be established using the split-half method.

It is already known that nothing can be valid if it is not also reliable; that is, it cannot be said that accurate measurements are being made if different ones are made each time. But it is perfectly possible to have a reliable instrument that is not accurate and therefore is not valid. Instruments, as well as poor students, can be reliably wrong, for example. Watches can be consistently and reliably half an hour slow; people can be consistently and reliably half an hour late. Then, of course, we can have instruments that are both valid and reliable as well as instruments that are both invalid and unreliable.

The relationship between validity and reliability can be illustrated with a simple analogy of firing five rounds from a rifle at three different targets as illustrated in Figure 4.3. This analogy illustrates an instrument that is both unreliable and invalid (Figure 4.3a); here, the bullet holes are all scattered. After adjustment, the instrument is reliable but not valid (Figure 4.3b); here, all the bullet holes are in the same place but not in the right place. After still further adjustment, the instrument is both reliable and valid (Figure 4.3c); finally, we have managed to consistently hit the bull's eye.

MEASUREMENT ERROR

Measurement error is a variation in measurement that has nothing to do with the variable being measured and which is not wanted. As the error increases, the instrument becomes less reliable and less valid. Obviously, we want to reduce this error as much as possible but before we can do that, we must discover where the error originates. Measurement errors spring from an infinite variety of sources but most can be categorized as: (1) constant errors, or (2) random errors.

Constant Errors

The first type of measurement error is constant errors. Constant errors are those that remain with us throughout a study. They remain with us because they come from an unvarying source, such as the intelligence, education, socioeconomic status, race, culture, or religion of our research participants. Suppose, for example, that we have a number of students waiting to be assigned to different research courses and, in order to assign them, we want to measure their knowledge of research.

We give them all the same research test, but it turns out that they are of various nationalities and some of them have a poor understanding of English. In this situation, we would not be measuring just their knowledge of research but also their ability to read and write English. It would not be possible to tell whether they failed to answer a question because they did not know the research content or because they did not understand the question. The varying standard of English of the research participants constitutes a constant error.

Constant errors can also be due to the personal style of the research participants. These errors include acquiescence (a tendency to agree with

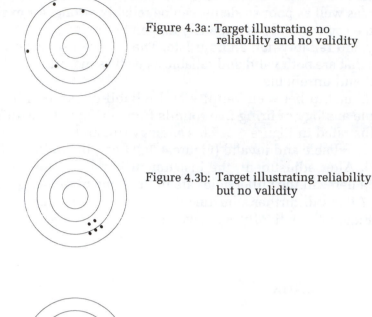

Figure 4.3a: Target illustrating no
reliability and no validity

Figure 4.3b: Target illustrating reliability
but no validity

Figure 4.3c: Target illustrating both
reliability and validity

FIGURE 4.3   Validity and Reliability Relationship

anything, regardless of what it is); social desirability (a tendency to give answers that make one look good); and deviation (a tendency to give unusual responses). We think of Uncle Fred, who is a harmless soul but does like to be a little bit different.

It is not only research participants who can introduce error into measurement. Observers can as well. These are the people who complete instruments about other individuals' behavior; for example, parents counting a child's nightmares or the staff in a nursing home counting how many hours each resident spends alone. Observers can commit various sins in a constant fashion, for example:

1 **Contrast Error**—to rate others as opposite to oneself with respect to a particular characteristic.

2 **Halo Effect**—to think that someone is altogether wonderful or terrible because of one good or bad trait. Or to think that the trait being observed must be good or bad because the person is altogether wonderful or terrible.

3 **Error of Leniency**—to always give a good report.

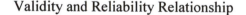

> **4 Error of Severity**—to always give a bad report.
>
> **5 Error of Central Tendency**—to stay comfortably in the middle and avoid both ends.

Since the five errors are constant (i.e., they are present throughout the study), we often notice them and are able to do something about them. Another observer might be used, for example, or allowances might be made for Uncle Fred's tendency to be different. Errors that are not constant, that is, random errors, are harder to find and to make allowances for.

Random Errors

The second type of measurement error is random errors. Random errors spring out of the dark, wreak temporary havoc, and then go back into hiding. It has been suggested that eventually they cancel each other out and, ultimately, they probably do cancel each other. The only problem is that, during our particular study, they might not cancel each other; they might band together and wreck our study. There are three types of random errors: (1) transient qualities of the individual, (2) situational factors, and (3) administrative factors:

- **Transient qualities of the individual** include things such as Uncle Fred's bad night, or boredom or fatigue or anything temporary that might affect the way that he fills out the measurement instrument.
- **Situational factors** include the pneumatic drill outside our office window, the weather, the news, or anything that might affect the way Uncle Fred fills out the measuring instrument.
- **Administrative factors** include anything relating to the way in which the instrument is administered. For example, interviewers who are supposed to ask people questions and fill in the answers on a sheet can affect the answers by the way they look, talk, dress, or wink when asking the question.

People administering an instrument that the research participants complete do not have quite as much influence but even they can sometimes affect the responses; for example, they might glare at Uncle Fred across the room, whistle through their teeth, or read out the wrong set of instructions.

SUMMING UP AND LOOKING AHEAD

Measurement serves as a bridge between theory and reality. Our variables must be operationalized in such a way that they can be measured. Which measuring instrument we select will depend on why we need to make the measurement and under what circumstances it will be done. Provided that a number of instruments can be found that seem to meet our needs, the next step is to evaluate them. Measurement error refers to variations in instrument scores that cannot be attributed to the variable being measured. Basically, all measurement errors can be categorized as constant errors or random errors.

Of the four criteria used to evaluate measuring instruments, the only one not discussed in detail is sampling. Therefore, in the next chapter, sampling will be considered in detail.

REVIEW QUESTIONS

1   Discuss why measurement is fundamental to social work research. Discuss the common components of the definitions of measurement as outlined in the chapter. Discuss how the measurement process is different from, and similar to, the quantitative and qualitative research approaches.

2   List and discuss the functions of measurement in the social work research process as outlined in the chapter. Discuss how measurement functions are different from, and similar to, the quantitative and qualitative research approaches.

3   Discuss what is meant by measurement validity. Provide an example of measurement validity via a social work example. Discuss how measurement validity is different from, and similar to, the quantitative and qualitative research approaches.

4   Discuss what is meant by measurement reliability. Provide an example of measurement reliability via a social work example. Discuss how measurement reliability is different from, and similar to, the quantitative and qualitative research approaches.

5   Discuss the relationship between measurement validity and measurement reliability as presented in this chapter. Provide a quantitative and qualitative social work example throughout your discussion.

6   Discuss how a measuring instrument is assessed for its content validity. How can you tell if an instrument is content valid?

7   What is face validity? What is the difference between content validity and face validity? Provide a social work example throughout your discussion.

8   What is the difference between concurrent validity and predictive validity? Describe a situation in which you would use an instrument that has concurrent validity. Describe a situation in which you would use an instrument that has predictive validity. Discuss how concurrent validity and predictive validity are different from, and similar to, the quantitative and qualitative research approaches.

9   What does the test-retest method of reliability determine? Provide a social work example of how it could be used.

10   What is the alternate-form method of reliability? Discuss how it could be determined in a social work situation.

11   What is the split-half method of reliability? Discuss how it could be determined in a social work situation.

12   Discuss the various cultural factors that you feel need to be taken into account when it comes to the measurement process in social work research.

13   In groups of four, construct a 10-item self-administered questionnaire that measures a variable of your choice. What difficulties, if any, did you have with the construction of the questionnaire? As a class, discuss each questionnaire and the problems associated with its construction.

14   Choose one of the questionnaires developed in the above exercise and have the entire class fill it out. What were some of the problems encountered? Was the questionnaire understandable and answerable? Using Figure 4.2, explain if the questionnaire was both valid and reliable. What methods would you use to improve the validity and the reliability of this self-administered questionnaire?

15   In groups of four, discuss how the process of measurement is different in a quantitative study when compared to a qualitative one.

16   At your university library, locate a social work–related article that makes use of a measuring instrument. If the measuring instrument is not included in the article, find a copy of the instrument. Using what you know about measuring instruments, answer the following two questions: (a) How were the validity and reliability of the instrument demonstrated? (b) Were any measurement errors mentioned? How were these errors compensated for or corrected?

This chapter has been adapted and modified from: Grinnell and Williams (1990)

C h a p t e r 5

Selecting Research Participants

IN THE PREVIOUS CHAPTER, measuring instruments were presented—how to select them, where to find them, and how to evaluate them. In this chapter, we are going to discuss who will fill them out. In short, we will discuss how to select the actual people, or research participants, who will take part in our quantitative and/or qualitative research study?

Suppose we are still trying to discover whether there is a relationship between two variables—depression and sleep patterns. At this point, it is obviously necessary to find a few people so we can measure their depression levels (Variable 1) and sleep patterns (Variable 2). One way of doing this is to phone our trusty social worker friend, Ken, who works with people who are depressed and ask if he will please find us some clients, or research participants, who do not mind sleeping in a laboratory once a week with wires attached to their heads. "Certainly," says Ken crisply. "How many do you want?" "Er . . ." we say, ..."how many have you got?" "Oh, lots," says Ken with cheer. "Now, do you want them young or old, male or female, rich or poor, acute or chronic, severely or mildly depressed . . . ?" "Oh and by the way," he adds, "all of them are refugees from Outer Ganglinshan."

We decide that we need to think about this some more. Suppose that the sleep patterns of Outer Ganglinshanians who are depressed, for example, are different from the sleep patterns of Bostonians who are depressed. Suppose even further, that males who are depressed have different sleep patterns from females who are depressed, adolescents who are depressed from seniors who are depressed, or Anabaptists who are depressed from Theosophists who are depressed. The list of possibilities is endless. We had hoped to find out only if there was a relationship between sleep patterns and depressed *people.*

One solution, of course, would be to assemble all the people who are depressed in the Western Hemisphere in the hope that Anabaptists and Theosophists and so forth were properly represented. This leaves out the Eastern Hemisphere, but we have to eliminate something since our sleep laboratory has only ten beds.

There is another difficulty too. Not only are we restricted to ten sleeping people but, on our limited budget, we will be hard pressed to pay them bus fare from their homes to our lab. This being the case, we have to forget about the Western Hemisphere and concentrate on the area served by the city transit, within which there are probably very few Anabaptists who are depressed and no Theosophists at all to speak of. How are we going to select ten people from this small area and still be fair to the Theosophist population? The answer is simple: We do this through the use of sampling frames.

DEFINING A POPULATION

A *population* is the totality of persons or objects with which our research study is concerned. If, for example, we are interested in all the people who are depressed in the Western Hemisphere, then our population is all the people who are depressed in the Western Hemisphere. If we decide to restrict our study to all the people who are depressed in the area served by city transit, then our population is all the people who are depressed in the area served by city transit. However we decide to define our population, the results of our study will apply only to that population from which our sample was drawn.

We cannot do our study within the confines of city transit and then apply the results to the whole of the Western Hemisphere. When our population has been defined, the next step is to make a list of all the people included in that population. Such a list is called a *sampling frame.* For example, if our population is to be all the people who are depressed in the area served by city transit, then we must create a list, or sampling frame, of all the people who are depressed in the area served by city transit. Obtaining a sampling frame is often one of the hardest parts of a research study. We probably will not be able to generate a list of all the people who are depressed in the area served by city transit since there is not a single person or social service agency who knows about all of them.

It might be better to restrict our study to all the depressed people treated by Ken—or some other source of people who are depressed who will provide us with a list.

Suppose, then, that we have decided to restrict our study to all the people who are depressed treated by Ken. We may think that "all the people who are depressed treated by Ken" is a reasonable definition of our population. But a population has to be defined exactly. "All the people who are depressed treated by Ken" is possibly not very exact, especially when we consider that Ken has been treating them for over twenty years. The ones treated eighteen and nineteen years ago have doubtless disappeared by now over the far horizon; indeed, the fates of those treated a mere year ago might be equally veiled in mystery. Perhaps we should redefine our population as "all the people who are depressed treated by Ken over the last three months" or; better yet, as "all the people who are depressed treated by Ken from January 1 to April 1, 1998."

SAMPLING PROCEDURES

If we can make a list of all the people who are depressed treated by Ken from January 1 to April 1, 1998, we have our sampling frame. The next thing is to use it to select our sample. This process is called *sampling* and the people (or other units such as case files) picked out make up a *sample*. There are two main ways of selecting samples: (1) *probability* sampling, which requires a sampling frame, and (2) *nonprobability* sampling, which does not require a sampling frame.

Probability Sampling

The first main category of sampling procedures is probability sampling. A *probability sample* is one in which all the people (or units in the sampling frame) have the same known probability of being selected for the sample. By probability, we mean chance, such as the probability of winning a lottery. The selection is based on some form of random procedure of which there are four main types: (1) simple random sampling, (2) systematic random sampling, (3) stratified random sampling, and (4) cluster random sampling.

Simple Random Sampling

The first type of probability sampling is simple random sampling. Suppose now that there are 100 names in our sampling frame; that is, Ken has seen 100 different clients who are depressed during the last three months. We assign each one of these clients a number; the first one on the list will be 001, the second 002, and so on until 100 is reached.

TABLE 5.1   One Page of a Random Numbers Table

02584	75844	50162	44269	76402	33228	96152	76777
66791	44653	90947	61934	79627	81621	74744	98758
44306	88222	30967	57776	90533	01276	30525	66914
01471	15131	38577	03362	54825	27705	60680	97083
65995	81864	19184	61585	19111	08641	47653	27267
45567	79547	89025	70767	25307	33151	00375	17564
27340	30215	28376	47390	11039	39458	67489	48547
02584	75844	56012	44269	76402	33228	96152	76777
66791	44653	90497	61934	79627	81621	74744	98758
44306	80722	30317	57776	90533	01276	30525	66914
65995	**81864**	19184	61585	19131	08641	47653	27267
45567	79547	89025	70767	25307	33151	00375	17564
27340	30215	23456	47390	11039	39458	67489	48547
02471	10721	30577	03362	54825	27705	60680	97083
60791	40453	90227	61934	79627	81621	74744	98758
43316	87212	36967	57576	90533	01276	30525	66914

Then, we take a book of random numbers, open the book at random, and pick a digit on the page also at random. The first half page of such a table is shown in Table 5.1.

Suppose the digit we happen to pick on is 1, the second digit in the number in the fifth row from the bottom in the second column from the left. (That whole number is **81864** and is highlighted in bold.) The two digits immediately to the right of 1 are 8 and 6; thus, we have 186. We take three digits in total because 100, the highest number on our sampling frame, has three digits. The number 186 is more than 100 so we ignore it. Going down the column, 954 is also more than 100 so we ignore it also. The next one, 021, is less than 100, so we can say that we have selected number 021 on our sampling frame to take part in our study. After 072 and 045 there are no more numbers less than 100 in the second column (middle three digits) so we go to the third column (middle three digits). Here we discover seven more people (i.e., 016, 094, 096, 049, 031, 057, 022).

We go down the columns, picking out numbers, until it occurs to us that we do not really know how many numbers should be selected. Our sleep laboratory has accommodation for ten but then, if we do a different ten each night of the week, that is seventy. Sundays off, to keep us sane, is sixty. Union hours, and we are looking at closer to thirty-five. There has to be a better way than union hours to figure out sample size; but, before looking at sample size, we should examine three more probability sampling procedures.

Systematic Random Sampling

The second type of probability sampling is systematic random sampling. Here, the size of our population is divided by the desired sample size to give us our sampling interval *k*. To state it more simply, if we only want half the population to be in the sample, we select every other person. If only a third of the population is needed to be in the sample, we pick every third person; a quarter, every fourth person; a fifth, every fifth person; and so on.

The problem with this is that we need to know our sample size in order to do it. We will not really know what our sample size ought to be until later in this chapter; at this point, we can only make a guess. Let us assume that we will work at our sleep lab every weeknight. Ten sleepers every night for five nights gives us a sample size of five nights times ten sleepers equals fifty.

The idea of a sampling interval can be expressed mathematically in the following way: Suppose that our population size is 100 and we have set our sample size—the number of people taking part in our study—at fifty. Then, dividing the former by the later (100/50 = 2) provides the size of the sampling interval, which in this case is two.

If our sample was only going to be one-fourth of the population instead of one-half, our sampling interval would be four instead of two. We might start at the fourth person on our sampling frame and pick out, as well, the eighth, twelfth, sixteenth persons, and so on.

The problem with this method is that everyone does not have the same chance of being selected. If we are selecting every other person, starting with the second person, we select the fourth, sixth, and so on. But this means that the third and the fifth never get a chance to be chosen. This procedure introduces a potential bias that calls for caution.

Suppose, for example, we have applied for a credit card and the credit card company examines our bank account every thirtieth day. Suppose, further, that the thirtieth day falls regularly on the day after we pay this month's rent and on the day before we receive last month's paycheck. In other words, our bank account, while miserable at all times, is particularly low every thirtieth day. This is hardly fair because we never get a chance to show them how rich we are on days other than the thirtieth.

If we do not have to worry about this sort of bias, then a systematic sample is largely the same as a simple random sample. The selection is just a bit easier because we do not have to bother with random numbers as given in Table 5.1.

Stratified Random Sampling

The third type of probability sampling is stratified random sampling. If, for example, our study of depression and sleeping patterns is also concerned with religious affiliation, we can look at our population and

TABLE 5.2   Stratified Random Sampling Example

Category	Number	1/10 Proportionate Sample	Number and (Disproportionate Sampling Fractions) for a Sample of 1 per Category
Jews	40	4.0	1(1/40)
Christians	19	1.9	1(1/19)
Muslims	10	1.0	1(1/10)
Buddhists	10	1.0	1(1/10)
Hindus	10	1.0	1(1/10)
Sikhs	10	1.0	1(1/10)
Theosophists	1	.1	1(1)
Totals	100	10.0	7

count how many of them are Christians, Jews, Muslims, Buddhists, Hindus, Theosophists, and so forth. Suppose that, in our population of 100, we found 40 Jews, 19 Christians, 10 Muslims, 10 Buddhists, 10 Hindus, 10 Sikhs, and 1 lone Theosophist. Now, we can sample our religious categories, or strata, either proportionally or disproportionally. If we sample our population proportionally, we will choose, say, one-tenth of each category to make up our sample; that is, we will randomly select 4 Jews, 1.9 Christians, 1 Muslim, 1 Buddhist, 1 Hindu, 1 Sikh, and .1 of a Theosophist. This comprises a total sample of 10, as illustrated in Table 5.2.

However; the 1.9 Christians and the .1 of a Theosophist present a difficulty. In this case, it is necessary to sample disproportionately. For example, it may be preferable to choose one member of each religious affiliation for a total sample of seven. In this case, the sampling fraction is not the same for each category; it is 1/40 for Jews, 1/19 for Christians, 1/10 for Muslims, Buddhists, Hindus, and Sikhs, and 1 for Theosophists. A total sample of only seven is not a good idea for reasons that will be discussed shortly.

Our population is divided into religious categories only if we believe that religious affiliation will affect either depression or sleep patterns.; that is, if we really believe that Buddhists who are depressed have different sleep patterns than Muslims who are depressed, everything else being equal. However, we must admit that we do not believe this. There is nothing in the literature or our past experience to indicate anything of the sort. And anyway, our friend's clients who are depressed, from whom the sample will be drawn, will not include anything so interesting as Buddhists and Muslims. Probably the best we can hope for is a few odd sects and the town atheist.

This method, though, could be used to look at the sleep patterns of different age groups. Our population could be divided quite sensibly into eight categories: those aged 10 to 20, 21 to 30, 31 to 40, and so on until we reach 81 to 90. We might then sample proportionately by randomly selecting one-tenth of the people in each category. Or we might sample disproportionately by selecting, say, six people from each category, regardless of the number of people in the category.

It might be preferable to sample disproportionately, for example, because there are a small number of people in the 71 to 80 and 81 to 90 categories, but it is our belief that advanced age significantly affects sleep patterns. Therefore, we want to include in our sample more than the one or two elderly people who would be included if we took one-tenth of each category.

Categorizing people in terms of age is fairly straightforward. They have only one age and they usually know what it is. Other types of categories, though, are more complex. Psychological labels, for instance, can be uncertain so that people fall into more than one category and the categories themselves are not homogeneous; that is, the categories are not made up of people who are all alike. There is no point in using stratified random sampling unless the categories are both homogeneous and different from each other.

In theory, the more homogeneous the categories are, the fewer people will be needed from each category to make up our sample. Suppose, for example, we had invented robots that were designed to perform various tasks. Those robots designed to be electricians were all identical and so were all the plumbers, doctors, lawyers, and so forth. Of course, each kind of robot was different from every other kind. If we then wanted to make some comparison between all lawyer and all doctor robots, we would only need one of each since same-kind robots were all the same; or; in other words, the robot categories were completely homogeneous. People categories are never completely homogeneous, but the more homogeneous they are, the fewer we need from each category to make comparisons. The fewer we need, the less our study will cost.

However, we must take care not to spend the money we save in this manner on the process of categorization. If people already are in categories, as they might be in a hospital, very good. If they are easy to categorize, say by age, very good too. If they are not already categorized and are difficult to categorize, it might be more appropriate to use another sampling method.

There is one more point to be considered. The more variables we are looking at, the harder it is to create homogeneous strata. It is easy enough, or example, to categorize people as Buddhists or Hindus, or as aged between 21 and 30 or 31 and 40. It is not nearly so easy if they have to be, say, between 21 and 30 *and* Buddhist.

Cluster Random Sampling

The fourth type of probability sampling is cluster random sampling. This is useful if there is difficulty creating our sampling frame. Suppose, for a moment, we want to survey all the people in the area served by city transit to see if they are satisfied with the transit system. We do not have a list of all these people to provide a sampling frame. There is a list, however, of all the communities in the city served by the transit system and we can use this list as an alternative sampling frame.

First, we randomly select a community, or cluster, and survey every person living there. We will be certain what this community thinks about the transit system as we talked to every member of it. But there is still the possibility that this community, in which there are a large number of families with children, has a different opinion from that of a second community, which consists largely of senior citizens. Perhaps we ought to survey the second community as well. Then there is a third community inhabited largely by penniless writers, artists, and social work students who might have yet a different opinion. Each community is reasonably homogeneous; that is, the people in the community are very much like each other. But the communities themselves are totally unlike; that is, they are heterogeneous with respect to each other.

One of the problems here is that we may not be able to afford to survey everyone in the three clusters. But we could compromise. Perhaps we could survey not every street in each cluster but only some streets taken at random—and not every house on our chosen streets, but only some houses, also taken at random. This way, we survey more clusters but fewer people in each cluster.

The only difficulty here is that, since we are not surveying everyone in the community, we might happen to select people who do not give us a true picture of that community. In a community of people with small children, for example, we might randomly select a couple who does not have children and does not intend to, and whose home was demolished, moreover, to make way for the transit line. Such untypical people introduce an error into our results that is due to our sampling procedure and is therefore called a sampling error.

Box 5.1 graphically presents how a random sample was selected for a nationwide survey that was conducted by the Survey Research Center at the University of Michigan. We will now turn our attention to the next category of sampling procedures—nonprobability sampling.

Nonprobability Sampling

In nonprobability sampling, not all the people in the population have the same probability of being included in the sample and, for each one of them, the probability of inclusion is unknown. As will be seen in Chapter 6, this form of sampling is often used in exploratory studies where the purpose of the study is just to collect as much data as possible. There are four types of nonprobability sampling procedures: (1) availability sampling, (2) quota sampling, (3) purposive sampling, and (4) snowball sampling.

Availability Sampling

The first type of nonprobability sampling is availability sampling. It is the simplest of the four nonprobability sampling procedures and is sometimes called *accidental sampling*. As its name suggests, it involves selecting for our sample the first people or units who make themselves available to us. We might survey people, for example, who pass us in a shopping mall. Or we might base our study on the caseload of a particular social worker. Or we might just seize upon the first fifty of Ken's clients who are depressed who agree to sleep in our lab with wires attached to their heads.

Quota Sampling

The second type of nonprobability sampling is quota sampling. In this type of sampling, we decide, on the basis of theory, that we should include in our sample so many of a certain type of person. Suppose we wanted to relate the sleep patterns of people who are depressed to body weight and age. We might decide to look at extremes; for example, fat and

Box 5.1_____

SAMPLING DESIGN FOR A NATIONWIDE SURVEY

Survey organizations such as the Survey Research Center (SRC) at the University of Michigan use multistage cluster sampling to conduct nationwide surveys. The steps involved in selecting the SRC's national sample in the 1970s are roughly diagramed in the accompanying figure. The steps are numbered and labeled according to the type of unit selected.

Step 1 The United States is divided into *primary areas* consisting of counties, groups of counties, or metropolitan areas. These areas are stratified by region and a proportionate stratified sample of seventy-four areas is selected.

Step 2 The seventy-four areas are divided into *locations* such as towns, cities, and residual areas. After these have been identified and stratified by population size, a proportionate stratified sample of locations is drawn within each area.

Step 3 All sample locations are divided into *chunks*. A chunk is a geographic area with identifiable boundaries such as city streets, roads, streams, and county lines. After division into chunks, a random sample of chunks is drawn.

Step 4 Interviewers scout each sample chunk and record addresses and estimates of the number of housing units at each address. They then divide the chunks into smaller units called *segments*, and a random sample of segments is selected.

Step 5 Within each sample segment either all or a sample of the housing units, usually about four, are chosen for a given study. Finally, for every housing unit in the sample, interviewers randomly choose one respondent from among those eligible, which ordinarily consists of all U.S. citizens 18 years of age or older.

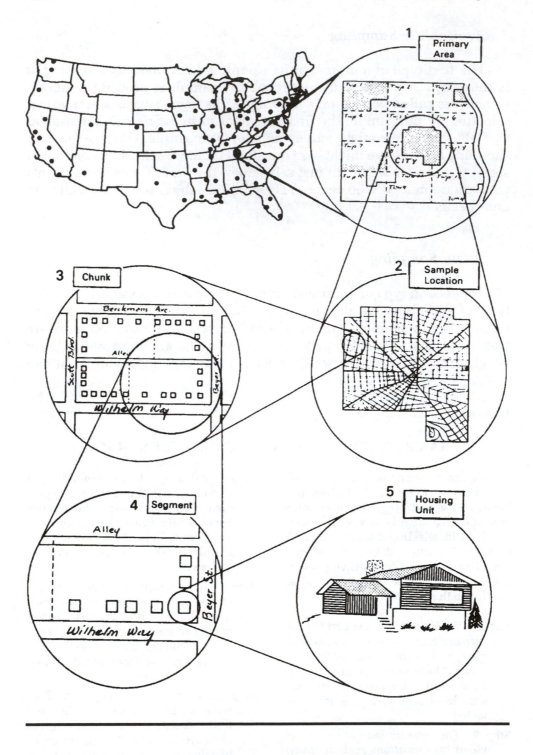

young, thin and young, fat and old, and thin and old. This gives us four categories (i.e., *A, B, C, D*) as illustrated in Table 5.3.

We might want, for example, fifteen people in each category or, for some reason, we might need more elderly people than young. In this case,

TABLE 5.3   Quota Sampling Matrix of Body Weight by Age

| | Body Weight | |
Age	Fat	Thin
Young.............	*Category A* Fat/Young	*Category B* Thin/Young
Old..................	*Category C* Fat/Old	*Category D* Thin/Old

we may decide on ten people in each of Categories A and B and twenty people in each of Categories C and D. Whatever quotas we decide on, we only have to find enough people to fill them who satisfy the two conditions of age and weight. We might discover all the heavy people at a weight loss clinic, for example, or all the young, thin ones at a clinic for anorexics. It does not matter where or how we find them so long as we do.

Purposive Sampling

The third type of nonprobability sampling is purposive sampling. This type is used when we want to purposely choose a particular sample. For example, if we are testing a questionnaire that must be comprehensible to less well-educated people while not offending the intelligence of better-educated people, we might present it both to doctoral candidates and to people who left school cheerfully as soon as they could. In other words, we purposely choose the doctoral candidates and the happy school leavers to be in our two subsamples. There is nothing random about it. In the same way, if we know from previous studies that there is more family violence in the city than in the country, we might restrict our sample to those families who live in cities.

Snowball Sampling

The fourth type of nonprobability sampling is snowball sampling. If a follow-up study is to be conducted on a self-help group that broke up two years ago, for example, we might find one member of the group and ask that member to help us locate other members. The other members will then find other members and so on until the whole group has been located. The process is a bit like telling one person a secret, with strict instructions not to tell it to anyone else. Snowball sampling is commonly used in qualitative research studies. Box 5.2 presents some interesting ethical dilemmas in reference to sampling.

Box 5.2

WELFARE STUDY WITHHOLDS BENEFITS FROM 800 TEXANS

The preceding front-page headline greeted readers of the Sunday, February 11, 1990, edition of the *Dallas Morning News*. On the next line they read:

Thousands of poor people in Texas and several other states are unwitting subjects in a federal experiment that denies some government help to a portion of them to see how well they live without it.

This was pretty strong stuff, and soon the story was covered on one of the national TV networks. Let's examine it further for another illustration of research ethics:

The Texas Department of Human Services received federal money to test the effectiveness of a pilot program designed to wean people from the welfare rolls. The program was targeted to welfare recipients who found jobs or job training. *Before* the new program was implemented, these recipients received four months of free medical care and some child care after they left the welfare rolls. The new program extended these benefits to one year of Medicaid coverage and subsidized child care. The theory was that extending the duration of the benefits would encourage recipients to accept and keep entry-level jobs that were unlikely to offer immediate medical insurance or child care.

The federal agency granting the money attached an important condition. States receiving grants were required to conduct a scientifically rigorous experiment to measure the program's effectiveness in attaining its goal of weaning people from welfare. Some federal officials insisted that this requirement entailed randomly assigning some people to a control group that would be denied the new (extended) program and instead kept on the old program of only four months of benefits.

The point of this was to maximize the likelihood that the recipient group (the experimental group) and the nonrecipient (control) group were equivalent in all relevant ways except for the receipt of the new program. If they were, and if the recipient group was weaned from welfare to a greater extent that the nonrecipient group, then it could be safely inferred that the new program, and not something else, caused the successful outcome. (We will examine this logic further in Chapters 8 and 9.)

If you have read many journal articles reporting on experimental studies, you are probably aware that many of them randomly assign about one-half of their research participants to the experimental group and the other half to the control group. Thus, this routine procedure denies the experimental condition to about one-half of the participants. The Texas experiment was designed to include all eligible welfare recipients statewide, assigning 90 percent of them to the experimental group and 10 percent to the control group. Thus, only 10 percent of the research participants, which in this study amounted to 800 people, would be denied the new benefits if they found jobs.

Although this seems more humane than denying benefits to 50 percent of the research participants, the newspaper account characterized the 800 people in the control group as "unlucky Texans" who seemed to be unfairly left out of a program that was extending benefits to everyone else who was eligible statewide, who numbered in the many thousands. Moreover, the newspaper report noted that the 800 control research participants would be denied the new program for two years in order to provide ample time to compare outcomes between the two groups. To boot, these 800 "unlucky Texans" were not to be informed of the new program or of the experiment. They were to be told of only the normal four-month coverage.

Advocates of the experiment defended this design, arguing that the control group would not be denied benefits. They would receive routine benefits, and the

Box 5.2 Continued

new benefits would not have been available for anyone in the first place unless a small group was randomly assigned to the routine policy. In other words, the whole point of the new benefits was to test a new welfare policy, not merely to implement one.

They further argued that the research design was justified by the need to test for unintended negative effects of the new program, such as the possibility that some businesses might drop their child care or insurance coverage for employees, knowing that the new program was extending these benefits. That, in turn, they argued, could impel low-paid employees in those businesses to quit their jobs and go on welfare. By going on welfare and then getting new jobs, they would become eligible for the government's extended benefits, and this would make the welfare program more expensive.

Critics of the study, on the other hand, argued that it violated federal ethics standards such as voluntary participation and informed consent. Anyone in the study must be informed about it and all its consequences and must have the option to refuse to participate. One national think tank expert on ethics likened the experiment to the Tuskegee syphilis study, saying, "It's really not that different." He further asserted, "People ought not to be treated like things, even if what you get is good information."

In the aftermath of such criticism, Texas state officials decided to try to convince the federal government to rescind the control group requirement so that they could extend the new benefits to the 800 people in the control group. Instead of using a control group design, they wanted to extend benefits to everyone and find statistical procedures that would help ferret out program defects (a design that might have value, but which would be less conclusive as to what really causes

what, as we will see in later chapters). They also decided to send a letter to the control group members explaining their special status.

Two days after the *Dallas Morning News* broke this story, it published a follow-up article reporting that the secretary of the U.S. Department of Health and Human Services, in response to the first news accounts, instructed his staff to cooperate with Texas welfare officials so that the project design would no longer deny the new program to the 800 control group members. Do you agree with his decision? Did the potential benefits of this experiment justify its controversial ethical practices?

It probably would not have been possible to form a control group had recipients been given the right to refuse to participate. Who would want to be denied extended free medical and child care benefits? Assuming it were possible, however, would that influence your opinion of the justification for denying them the new program? Do you agree with the expert who claimed that this study, in its original design, was not that different from the Tuskegee syphilis study?

What if, instead of assigning 90 percent of the research participants to the experimental group, the study assigned only 10 percent to it? That way, the 800 assigned to the experimental group may have been deemed "lucky Texans," and the rest might not have been perceived as a small group of unlucky souls being discriminated against. In other words, perhaps there would have been fewer objections if the state had merely a small amount of funds to test out a new program on a lucky few. Do you think that would have changed the reaction? Would that influence your perception of the ethical justification for the experiment?

Source: Rubin and Babbie (1993)

SAMPLE SIZE

Before our sample can be selected, we obviously have to decide on how many people are needed to take part in our study; in other words, we have to decide on our sample size. The correct sample size depends on both our population and research question. If we are dealing with a limited population, for example, such as the victims of some rare disease, we might include the whole population in our study. Then, we would not take a sample. Usually, however, the population is large enough that we do need to take a sample, the general rule being, the larger the sample, the better.

As far as a minimal sample size is concerned, experts differ. Some say that a sample of 30 will allow us to perform basic statistical procedures, while others would advise a minimum sample size of 100. In fact, sample size depends on how homogeneous our population is with respect to the variables we are studying. Recalling all those categories of robot doctors, lawyers, and so forth considered awhile back, if our population of robot doctors is all the same, that is, homogeneous, we only need one robot doctor in our sample. On the other hand, if the factory messed up and our robot doctors have emerged with a wide range of medical skills, we will need a large sample to tell us anything about the medical skills of the entire robot doctor population. In this case, of course, medical skill is the variable we are studying.

Sample size must also be considered in relation to the number of categories required. If the sample size is too small, there may be only one or two people in a particular category; for example 1.9 Christians and .1 of a Theosophist. This should be anticipated and the sample size adjusted. The situation can also be handled using the disproportionate stratified random sampling procedure. This procedure is the one where we selected one person from each religious category, thus neatly avoiding our 1.9 Christians and .1 of a Theosophist. In addition, Box 5.3 presents and interesting discussion on sex bias and sampling.

There are many formulas available for calculating sample size but they are complicated and difficult to use. Usually, a sample size of one-tenth of the population is considered sufficient to provide reasonable control over sampling error. The same one-tenth convention also applies to categories of the population; we can include one-tenth of each category in our sample.

SUMMING UP AND LOOKING AHEAD

In the course of a research study, the entire population that we are interested in is usually too big to work with and, in any case, we rarely have enough money to include everyone. For these reasons, it is necessary to draw a sample. The idea is that the sample represents the population from which it was drawn; that is, the sample is identical to the population with

Box 5.3

SEX BIAS AND SAMPLING

Feminists have been sensitizing us to the relationship of women's issues to research. All aspects of the research process can be affected by sex bias, and sampling is one area where such bias can be particularly problematic. Even probability sampling can be affected by sex bias, for example, when we inappropriately decide to exclude a particular gender from our sampling frame.

Perhaps the most commonly encountered sex bias problem in sampling is the unwarranted generalization of research findings to the population as a whole when one gender is not adequately represented in the research sample. (The same type of problem, by the way, is encountered when certain minority groups are inadequately represented in the sample but generalizations are made to the entire population.)

Campbell (1983) reviewed the occurrence of sex biases in the sex-role research literature and identified a number of illustrations of this problem. For example, she cited studies on achievement motivation and on management and careers whose samples included only white, middle-class male subjects but whose conclusions did not specify that their generalizations were limited to individuals with those attributes. She was particularly critical of life-cycle research, as follows (p. 206):

> Nowhere is the effect of bias on sampling more evident than in the popular and growing field of the life cycle or stages. Beginning with Erikson's . . . work on the "Eight Stages of Man" to Levinson's *Seasons of a Man's Life* . . . the study of life cycles has focused on male subjects. When women are examined, it is in terms of how they fit or don't fit the male model. Without empirical verification, women are said to go through the same cycles as men . . . or are said to go through cycles that are antithetical to men's . . . Based on a survey of the literature on life cycles, Sangiuliano . . . concluded that "Mostly we (researchers) persist in seeing her (woman) in the reflected light of men". . .

The inadequate representation of a particular gender in a sample can be much subtler than just excluding them entirely or including an insufficient proportion of them. It could also occur due to biased data-collection procedures, even when the number of individuals of a particular sex is not the issue. For example, Campbell notes that the Gallup poll interviews male subjects beginning at 6:00 PM, while conducting most interviews with females between 4:00 and 6:00 PM. Thus, Campbell argues that most professional women would not be home before 6:00 PM and are not adequately represented in the sample. If she is correct, then even if the overall proportion of women in the Gallup poll seems to be sufficient, the views expressed by the women in the sample are not adequately representative of the views of the population of women.

As another example, if we wanted to generalize about gender-related differences in job satisfaction, we would not want to select our sample only from those work settings where professional or managerial positions go predominately to men and where semiprofessional jobs go predominately to women.

There may instances, however, when the exclusion of a particular gender from a study's sample is warranted or inescapable—instances where only one gender is relevant and where generalizations will be restricted to that gender. Thus, only one gender would be included in the sample of a survey of client satisfaction in a program whose clientele all happen to be of the same gender. For example, perhaps it is a group support program for battered women or for rape victims.

But we must be on guard not to let any sex-role biases improperly influence us to deem a particular gender irrelevant for a given study. For example, we should not be predisposed to restrict our samples to men when we study things like aggression, management, unemployment, or criminal behavior and to women when we study things like parenting, nurturing, or housekeeping.

Source: Rubin and Babbie (1993)

respect to every variable that we are interested in. When the sample is truly representative of the population, we can generalize the results received from the sample back to the population from which it was drawn. No sample is ever totally representative of the population from which it was drawn.

Now that we know how to draw a sample from a population, we will turn our attention to the use of exploratory research designs, the topic of the next chapter.

REVIEW QUESTIONS

1   Discuss how sampling theory assists in the process of social work research.

2   Discuss the purpose and the use of sampling frames in social work research.

3   Discuss the issue of generalizability in social work research.

4   Discuss the differences between probability and nonprobability sampling. What are their comparative advantages and disadvantages? Justify your answer by using the points as outlined in the chapter.

5   List and discuss the different types of probability sampling procedures.

6   Discuss the procedure of generating a random sample. Explain how the use of Table 5.1 could be used to generate a random sample.

7   List and briefly discuss the different types of nonprobability sampling procedures.

8   Discuss how sampling errors vary with the size of the sample.

9   Suppose you wanted the students in your class to participate in a research study. In groups of four, discuss what random sampling procedures could be used. Using Table 5.1, decide on a procedure, discuss how you would collect the data, and explain your decisions to the class. How does your study compare with those of the other groups? Discuss the problems associated with random sampling and possible solutions to the problems.

10   Suppose you design a research project that concerns all of the students of your university. In groups of four, decide on a sample size and discuss how you could use the four nonprobability sampling methods. Discuss the potential problems and possible solutions to the problems.

11   At your university library, locate a social work–related research study that used a *probability* sampling procedure. Answer the following five questions: (a) What sampling procedure was used? (b) From what general population was the sample drawn? (c) Do you believe that the sample was representative of the population from which it was drawn? Why or why not? (d) What other sampling procedure could have been used? What would be the implications if this sampling method were used? (e) What changes could you suggest that would make the study more rigorous in terms of sampling procedures and/or controlling for nonsampling errors? Discuss in detail.

12   At your university library, locate a social work–related research study that used a *nonprobability* sampling procedure. Answer the following three questions: (a) What sampling procedure was used? (b) Could the author have used a different nonprobability sampling procedure? If so, which one? (c) In your opinion, does probability sampling or do nonprobability sampling procedures produce a more rigorous study? Justify your answer.

This chapter has been adapted and modified from: Grinnell (1993a); Grinnell and Unrau (1997); Grinnell and Williams (1990); Grinnell, Williams, and Tutty (1997); and Williams, Tutty, and Grinnell (1995)

C h a p t e r   6

Exploratory Research Designs

NOW THAT WE KNOW how to draw samples for qualitative and quantitative studies, we turn our attention to the various designs that studies can take. The two most important factors in determining what research design to use in a specific study are:

- What the research question is
- How much knowledge about the problem area is available

As we know from Chapter 1, if there is already a substantial knowledge base in the area, we will be in a position to address very specific research questions, the answers to which could add to the explanation of previously gathered data (Chapters 8 & 9). If less is known about the problem area, our research questions will have to be of a more general, descriptive nature (Chapter 7). If very little is known about the problem area, our questions will have to be even more general, at an exploratory level—the topic of this chapter.

It is totally impossible to fit a specific research question to a specific knowledge level, however. Rather than existing as separate categories, therefore, research knowledge levels are arrayed along a continuum, from exploratory at the lowest end to explanatory at the highest.

Because research knowledge levels are viewed this way, the assignment of the level of knowledge accumulated in a problem area prior to a study, as well as the level that might be attained by the study, is totally arbitrary.

At the lowest level are the exploratory designs, also called pre-experimental or nonexperimental designs, which explore only the research question or problem area. These designs do not produce statistically sound data or conclusive results; they are not intended to. Their purpose is to build a foundation of general ideas and tentative theories, which can be explored later with more precise and hence more complex designs, and their corresponding data-gathering techniques.

While, in a particular case, a design may need to be complex to accomplish the purpose of the study, a design that is unnecessarily complex costs more, takes more time, and probably will not serve its purpose nearly as well as a simpler one. In choosing a research design, therefore, the principle of parsimony must be applied: The simplest and most economical route to the objective is the best choice.

EXPLORATORY GROUP-LEVEL DESIGNS

The four examples of exploratory group-level designs given in this section do not use pretests; they simply measure the dependent variable only after the independent variable has been introduced. Therefore, they cannot be used to determine whether any changes took place in the study's research participants.

There does not necessarily have to be an independent variable in a study, however; we may just want to measure some variable in a particular population such as the number of people who receive AFDC benefits over a ten-year period. In this situation, there is no independent or dependent variable. There are four exploratory group-level designs: (1) one-group posttest-only design, (2) multigourp posttest-only design, (3) longitudinal case study design, and (4) longitudinal survey design.

One-Group Posttest-Only Design

The first exploratory group-level design is the one-group posttest-only design. It is sometimes called the one-shot case study or cross-sectional case study design. It is the simplest of all the exploratory group-level designs. Box 6.1 contains a discussion of how case studies have been used on split-brain patients.

Suppose in a particular community, Rome, Wisconsin, there are numerous parents who are physically abusive toward their children (Williams, Tutty, & Grinnell, 1995). The city decides to hire a school

Box 6.1_____

CASE STUDIES OF SPLIT-BRAIN PATIENTS

Roger Sperry (1968) joined two neurosurgeons, Philip Vogel and Joseph Bogen, to evaluate the psychological characteristics of split-brain patients. The brain is divided into two major hemispheres that are in constant communication through connective tissue, the corpus callosum. The corpus callosum can be surgically severed, isolating the two hemispheres. This has been done to eliminate debilitating seizures in patients with severe epilepsy that could not be controlled with medication.

Their first analyses were done on one split-brain patient, but eventually more than a dozen were studied. The first patient was a middle-aged veteran who had been struck in the head repeatedly in a concentration camp, leading to severe, uncontrollable seizures that occurred a dozen or more times a day.

Sperry and his colleagues flashed visual stimuli on a screen. Subjects were asked to fixate their eyes on a central dot, and two words were flashed, such as KEY on the left and CASE on the right. KEY was transmitted to the right brain, and CASE was transmitted to the left brain. The left hemisphere, which specializes in language, would report that the word CASE was read; but if the subject was asked to use the left hand (directed by the right hemisphere) to pick up the designated object, a key would be picked up.

Split-brain patients had split minds. Some reported anecdotes confirmed this conclusion, such as buttoning a shirt with the left hand, followed immediately by the right hand unbuttoning it.

Sperry and his colleagues also found that the two brains can have different memories. When a group of objects were shown to the left brain, these objects were recognized if displayed again to the left brain, but were viewed as if for the first time if shown to the right brain. Sensations of touch also were not communicated. An object held in the right hand could be named easily by the left hemisphere. An object in the left hand could not be named by the right hemisphere, but could be recognized if touched again by the left hand. (The right brain knew what it felt, but it could not name the object.)

An object held in the left hand could not be recognized by the touch of the right hand. Subjects were given an object to hold in each hand, then were asked to find them by touch among a group of objects. The two hands moved independently, each searching for its own object, unaware of the other hand's goal.

Were the split-brain patients running into walls, tripping over their own feet, or having trouble feeding themselves? Not at all. The carefully controlled laboratory conditions prohibited shared information in the two hemispheres by flashing stimuli into one hemisphere or by allowing objects to be manipulated by one hand hidden from view.

Under normal circumstance, the two hemispheres are exposed to the same information, so they operate on shared information. Patients also developed tricks to compensate for their split minds, such as "talking to themselves." The left brain would talk out loud to the right brain, and the right brain would point at objects with the left hand to direct the left brain's attention. The left brain controlled language, but the right brain demonstrated its own skills, such as facial recognition.

Sperry's research earned him a Nobel prize in physiology and medicine in 1981. His case studies demonstrated that split brains can produce split minds and that people can adapt to compensate for this bizarre condition (Schwartz, 1986).

_____

Source: Allen (1995)

---

social worker, Antonia, to implement a program that is supposed to reduce the number of parents who physically abuse their children. She conceptualizes a 12-week child abuse prevention program (the intervention) and offers it to parents who have children in her school who wish to participate on a voluntary basis. A simple research study is then conducted to answer the question, "Did the parents who completed the program stop physically abusing their children?" The answer to this question will determine the success of the intervention.

There are many different ways in which this program can be evaluated. For now, and to make matters as simple as possible, we are going to evaluate it by simply counting how many parents stopped physically abusing their children after they attended the program.

At the simplest level, the program could be evaluated with a one-group posttest-only design. The basic elements of this design can be written as follows:

$$X \quad O_1$$

Where:

X = Independent variable (Child Abuse Prevention Program, the intervention) (see Box 6.2)

O_1 = First and only measurement of the dependent variable (number of parents who stopped physically abusing their children, the program's outcome, or program objective)

All that this design provides is a single measure (O_1) of what happens when one group of people is subjected to one treatment or experience (X). The program's participants were not randomly selected from any particular population, and, thus, the results of the findings cannot be generalized to any other group or population.

It is safe to assume, however, that all the members within the program had physically abused their children before they enrolled, since people who do not have this problem would not enroll in such a program. But, even if the value of O_1 indicates that some of the parents did stop being violent with their children after the program, it cannot be determined whether they quit because of the intervention (the program) or because of some other factors, or rival hypotheses.

Perhaps a law was passed that made it mandatory for the police to arrest anyone who behaves violently toward his or her child, or perhaps the local television station started to report such incidents on the nightly news, complete with pictures of the abusive parent. These other extraneous variables may have been more important in persuading the parents to cease their abusive behavior toward their children than their voluntary participation in the program.

Box 6.2_____

TREATMENT: A VARIABLE OR A CONSTANT?

For instructional purposes, group designs are displayed using symbols where X is the independent variable (treatment) and O is the measure of the dependent variable. This presentation is accurate when studies are designed with two or more groups.

When one-group designs are used, however, this interpretation does not hold. In one-group designs, the treatment, or program, cannot truly vary because all research participants have experienced the same event; that is, they all have experienced the program.

Without a comparison or control group, treatment is considered a constant because it is a quality shared by all members in the research study. In short, *time* is the independent variable.

_____

Source: Grinnell and Unrau (1997)

Cross-Sectional Survey Design

Let us take another example of a one-group posttest-only design that *does not* have an independent or dependent variable. In survey research, this kind of a group-level designs is called a cross-sectional survey design.

In doing a cross-sectional survey, we survey *only once* a cross-section of some particular population. In addition to Antonia's child abuse prevention program geared for abusive parents, she may also want to start another program geared for all the children in the school (whether they come from abusive families or not)—a child abuse educational program taught to children in the school (Williams, Tutty, & Grinnell, 1995).

Before Antonia starts the program geared for the children, however, she wants to know what parents think about the idea. She may send out questionnaires to all the parents or she may decide to personally telephone every second parent, or every fifth, or tenth, depending on how much time and money she has. The results of her survey constitute a single measurement, or observation, of the parents' opinions of her second proposed program (the one for the children) and may be written as:

The symbol O_1 represents the entire cross-sectional survey design since such a design involves making only a single observation, or measurement, at one time period. Note that there is no X, as there is really no independent variable. Antonia only wants to ascertain the parents' attitudes toward her proposed program—nothing more, nothing less.

Multigroup Posttest-Only Design

The second exploratory group-level design is the multigroup posttest-only design. It is nothing more than an elaboration of the one-group posttest-only design in which more than one group is used. To check a bit further into the effectiveness of Antonia's program for parents who have been physically abusive toward their children, for example, she might decide to locate several more groups of parents who had completed her program and see how many of them had stopped abusing their children—and so on, with any number of groups. This design can be written in symbols as follows:

Experimental Group 1: X O_1
Experimental Group 2: X O_1
Experimental Group 3: X O_1
Experimental Group 4: X O_1

Where:

X = Independent variable (Child Abuse Prevention Program, the intervention) (see Box 6.2)

O_1 = First and only measurement of the dependent variable (number of parents who stopped physically abusing their children, the program's outcome, or program objective)

With the multigroup design it cannot be assumed that all four Xs (the independent variables) are equivalent because the four programs might not be exactly the same; one group might have had a different facilitator, the program might have been presented differently, or the material could have varied in important respects.

In addition, nothing is known about whether any of the research participants would have stopped being violent anyway, even without the program. It certainly cannot be assumed that any of the groups were representative of the larger population.

Longitudinal Case Study Design

The third exploratory group-level design is the longitudinal case study design. It is exactly like the one-group posttest-only design, except that it provides for more measurements of the dependent variable (Os). This design can be written in symbols as follows:

$$X \quad O_1 \quad O_2 \quad O_3 \ldots$$

Where:

X = Independent variable (Child Abuse Prevention Program, the intervention) (see Box 6.2)

O_1 = First measurement of the dependent variable (number of parents who stopped physically abusing their children, the program's outcome, or program objective)

O_2 = Second measurement of the dependent variable (number of parents who stopped physically abusing their children, the program's outcome, or program objective)

O_3 = Third measurement of the dependent variable (number of parents who stopped physically abusing their children, the program's outcome, or program objective)

Suppose that, in our example, Antonia is interested in the long-term effects of the child abuse prevention program. Perhaps the program was effective in helping some people to stop physically abusing their children, but will they continue to refrain from abusing their children? One way to find out is to measure the number of parents who physically abuse their children at intervals—say at the end of the program, the first three months after the program, then the next three months after that, and every three months for the next two years.

Longitudinal Survey Design

The fourth exploratory group-level design is the longitudinal survey design. Unlike cross-sectional surveys, where the variable of interest (usually the dependent variable) is measured only once, longitudinal surveys provide data at various points so that changes can be monitored over time. Longitudinal survey designs can be written as:

$$O_1 \quad O_2 \quad O_3$$

Where:

O_1 = First measurement of some variable
O_2 = Second measurement of some variable
O_3 = Third measurement of some variable

Longitudinal survey designs usually have no independent and dependent variables and can broken down into three types: (1) trend studies, (2) cohort studies, and (3) panel studies.

Trend Studies

A trend study is used to find out how a population, or sample, changes over time (Williams, Tutty, & Grinnell, 1995). Antonia, the school social worker mentioned previously, may want to know if parents of young children enroled in her school are becoming more receptive to the idea of the school teaching their children child abuse prevention education in the second grade. She may survey all the parents of Grade 2 children this year, all the parents of the new complement of Grade 2 children next year, and so on until she thinks she has sufficient data.

Each year the parents surveyed will be different, but they will all be parents of Grade 2 children. In this way, Antonia will be able to determine whether parents are becoming more receptive to the idea of introducing child abuse prevention material to their children as early as Grade 2. In other words, she will be able to measure any attitudinal trend that is, or is not, occurring. The design can still be written:

$$O_1 \quad O_2 \quad O_3$$

Where:

O_1 = First measurement of some variable for a sample
O_2 = Second measurement of some variable for a different sample
O_3 = Third measurement of some variable for yet another different sample

Cohort Studies

Cohort studies are used over time to follow a group of people who have shared a similar experience—for example, AIDS survivors, sexual abuse survivors, or parents of grade-school children (Williams, Tutty, & Grinnell, 1995). Perhaps Antonia is interested in knowing whether parents' attitudes toward the school offering abuse prevention education to second-grade students change as their children grow older. She may survey a sample of the Grade 2 parents who attend a Parent Night this year, and survey a different sample of parents who attend a similar meeting from the same parents next year, when their children are in Grade 3.

The following year, when the children are in Grade 4, she will take another, different sample of those parents who attend Parent Night. Although different parents are being surveyed every year, they all belong to the same population of parents whose children are progressing through the grades together. The selection of the samples was not random, though, because parents who take the time to attend Parent Night may be different from those who stay at home. The design may be written:

$$O_1 \quad O_2 \quad O_3$$

Where:

O_1 = First measurement of some variable for a sample drawn from some population

O_2 = Second measurement of some variable for a different sample drawn from the same population one year later

O_3 = Third measurement of some variable for a still different sample, drawn from the same population after two years

Panel Studies

In a panel study, the *same individuals* are followed over a period of time (Williams, Tutty, & Grinnell, 1995). Antonia might select one particular sample of parents, for example, and measure their attitudes toward child abuse prevention education in successive years. Again, the design can be written:

$$O_1 \quad O_2 \quad O_3$$

Where:

O_1 = First measurement of some variable for a sample of individuals

O_2 = Second measurement of some variable for the same sample of individuals one year later

O_3 = Third measurement of some variable for the same sample of individuals after two years

A trend study is interested in broad trends over time, whereas a cohort study provides data about people who have shared similar experiences. In neither case do we know anything about *individual* contributions to the changes that are being measured. A panel study provides data that we can use to look at change over time as experienced by particular individuals.

EXPLORATORY CASE-LEVEL DESIGNS

Our discussion of exploratory case-level designs (pages 138–148) has been adapted and modified from three sources: Grinnell and Williams (1990); Grinnell, Williams, and Tutty (1997); and Williams, Tutty, and Grinnell (1995). On a very general level, case-level designs are more "practice orientated" than group-level designs. That is, they are used more by social work "practitioners" than by social work "researchers." Research studies conducted to evaluate treatment interventions with social work clients are called case-level designs. They are also called *single-subject designs, single-case experimentations*, or *idiographic research*.

They are used to fulfil the major purpose of social work practice: to improve the situation of a client system—*an* individual client, *a* couple, *a* family, *a* group, *an* organization, or *a* community. Any of these client configurations can be studied with a case-level design. In short, they are used to study *one* individual or *one* group intensively, as opposed to studies that use two or more groups of research participants.

Case-level designs can provide information about how well a treatment intervention is working, so that alternative or complementary interventive strategies can be adopted if necessary. They can also indicate when a client's problem has been resolved. Single-case studies can be used to monitor client progress up to, and sometimes beyond, the point of termination.

They can also be used to evaluate the effectiveness of a social work program as a whole by aggregating or compiling the results obtained by numerous social workers serving their individual clients within the program. A family therapy program might be evaluated, for example, by combining family outcomes on a number of families that have been seen by different social workers.

Requirements

In order to carry out a single-case study, the client's problem must be identified, the desired objective to be achieved must be decided upon, the intervention that is most likely to eliminate the client's problem must be selected, the intervention must be implemented, and the client's progress must be continually monitored to see if the client's problem has been resolved, or at least reduced. If practitioners are careful to organize, measure, and record what they do, single-case studies will naturally take shape in the clients' files, and the results can be used to guide future interventive efforts. Only three things are required when doing a single-case study:

1 setting client objectives that are measurable
2 selecting valid and reliable outcome measures
3 graphically displaying the results of the outcome measures

Setting Measurable Client Objectives

One of the first tasks a worker does when initially seeing a client is to establish the purpose of why they are together. Why has the client approached the worker? Or, in many nonvoluntary situations, such as in probation and parole or child abuse situations, why has the worker approached the client? The two need to formulate objectives for their mutual working relationship. A specific, measurable, client desired outcome objective is known as a *client target problem*. Client target problems are feelings, knowledge levels, or behaviors that need to be changed.

Many times clients do not have just one target problem, they have many. They sometimes have a number of interrelated problems and, even if there is only one that is more important than the rest, they may not know what it is. Nevertheless, they may be quite clear about the desired outcome of their involvement with social work services. They may want to "fix" their lives so that, "Johnny listens when I ask him to do something," or "My partner pays more attention to me," or "I feel better about myself at work." Unfortunately, many clients express their desired target problems in vague, ambiguous terms, possibly because they do not know themselves exactly what they want to change; they only know that something should be different. If a worker can establish (with the guidance of the client) what should be changed, why it should be changed, how it should be changed, and to what degree it should be changed, the solution to the problem will not be far away.

Consider Heather, for example, who wants her partner, Ben, to pay more attention to her. Heather may mean sexual attention, in which case the couple's sexual relations may be the target problem. On the other hand, Heather may mean that she and Ben do not socialize enough with friends, or that Ben brings work home from the office too often, or has hobbies she does not share, or any of a host of things.

Establishing clearly what the desired change would look like is the first step in developing the target problem. Without this, the worker and client could wander around forever through the problem maze, never knowing what, if anything, needs to be solved. Desired change cannot occur if no one knows what change is desired. It is, therefore, very important that the target problem to be solved be precisely stated as early as possible in the client–social worker relationship.

Continuing with the above example of Heather and Ben, and after a great deal of exploration, the worker agrees that Heather and Ben have many target problems to work on, such as improving their child discipline strategies, improving their budgeting skills, improving their communication skills, and many other issues that, when dealt with, can lead to a successful marriage. For now, however, they agree to work on one target problem of increasing the amount of time they spend together with friends. To do this, the worker, Heather, and Ben must conceptualize and operationalize the term "increasing the amount of time they spend together with friends." As we know, a variable is conceptualized by defining it in a way that is relevant to the situation and operationalized in such a way that its indicators can be measured.

Heather may say that she wishes she and Ben could visit friends together more often. The target problem has now become a little more specific: It has narrowed from "increasing the amount of time they spend together with friends" to "Heather and Ben visiting friends more often.""Visiting friends more often with Ben," however, is still an ambiguous term. It may mean once a month or every night, and the achievement of the target problem's solution cannot be known until the meaning of "more often" has been clarified.

If Heather agrees that she would be happy to visit friends with Ben once a week, the ambiguous objective may be restated as a specific, measurable objective—"to visit friends with Ben once a week." The social worker may discover later that "friends" is also an ambiguous term. Heather may have meant "her friends," while Ben may have meant "his friends," and the social worker may have imagined that "the friends" were mutual.

The disagreement about who is to be regarded as a friend may not become evident until the worker has monitored their progress for a month or so and found that no improvement was occurring. In some cases, poor progress may be due to the selection of an inappropriate interventive strategy. In other cases, it may mean that the target problem itself is not as specific, complete, and clear as it should be. Before deciding that the interventive strategy needs to be changed, it is always necessary to clarify with the client exactly what it is that specifically needs to be achieved.

Selecting Valid and Reliable Outcome Measures

A target problem cannot really be said to be measurable until it is decided how it will be operationalized, or measured. Can Heather and Ben, who wanted to visit friends more often, be trusted to report truthfully on whether the friends were visited? Suppose she says they were not visited and he says they were? Social workers must always be very conscious of what measurement methods are both available and feasible when formulating a target problem with a client. It may be quite possible for the social worker to telephone the friends and ask if they were visited; but, if the worker is not prepared to get involved with Heather's and Ben's friends, this measurement method will not be feasible. If this is the case, and if Heather and/or Ben cannot be trusted to report accurately and truthfully, there is little point in setting the target problem.

Heather's and Ben's target problem can be easily observed and measured. However, quite often, a client's target problem involves feelings, attitudes, knowledge levels, or events that are known only to the client and cannot be easily observed and/or measured.

Consider Bob, a client who comes to a social worker because he is depressed. The worker's efforts may be simply to lessen his target problem, depression, but how will the worker and/or Bob know when his depression has been alleviated or reduced? Perhaps he will say that he feels better, or his partner may say that Bob cries less, or the worker may note that he spends less time in therapy staring at his feet. All these are indicators that his depression is lessening, but they are not very valid and reliable indicators.

What is needed is a more "scientific method" of measuring depression. Fortunately, a number of paper-and-pencil standardized measuring instruments have been developed that can be filled out by the client in a relatively short period of time, can be easily scored, and can provide a fairly accurate picture of the client's condition. One such widely used instrument that measures depression is the General Contentment Scale (*GCS*). Since higher scores indicate higher levels of depression, and lower scores indicate lower levels of depression, the target problem in Bob's case would be to reduce his score on the *GCS* to a level at which he can adequately function (a score of 30 or less).

People who are not depressed will still not score zero on the *GCS*. Everyone occasionally feels blue (Item 2) or downhearted (Item 10). There is a clinical cutting score that differentiates a clinically significant problem level from a nonclinically significant problem level, and it will often be this score that the client aims to achieve. If the target problem is, "to reduce Bob's score on the *GCS* to or below the clinical cutting score of 30," the worker will know not only what the target problem is, but precisely how Bob's success is to be measured.

Usually, client success, sometimes referred to as client outcome, can be measured in a variety of ways. Bob's partner, Maria, for example, may be asked to record the frequency of his crying spells, and the target problem here may be to reduce the frequency of these spells to once a week or less. Again, it would be important to further operationalize the term "crying spell" so that Maria knows exactly what it was she has to measure. Perhaps "crying spell" would be operationally defined as ten minutes or more of continuous crying, and a gap of at least ten minutes without crying would define the difference between one "spell" and another.

There are now two independent and complementary indicators of Bob's level of depression: the *GCS* as rated by Bob, and the number of his ten-minute crying spells per day as rated by Maria. If future scores on both indicators display improvement (that is, they both go down), the worker can be reasonably certain that Bob's depression is lessening and the intervention is effective.

If the two indicators do not agree, the worker will need to find out why. Perhaps Bob wishes to appear more depressed than he really is, and this is an area that needs to be explored. Or perhaps Maria is not sufficiently concerned to keep an accurate recording of the number of Bob's ten-minute crying spells per day; and it may be Maria's attitude that has caused Bob's crying in the first place. Accurate measurements made over time can do more than reveal the degree of a client's improvement. They can cast light on the problem itself and suggest new avenues to be explored, possibly resulting in the utilization of different interventive strategies.

Be that as it may, a client's target problem cannot be dealt with until it has been expressed in specific measurable indicators. These indicators cannot be said to be measurable until it has been decided how they will be measured. Specification of the target problem will, therefore, often include mention of an instrument that will be used to measure it. It will also include who is to do the measuring, and under what circumstances.

It may be decided, for example, that Bob will rate himself on the *GCS* daily after dinner, or once a week on Saturday morning, or that Maria will make a daily record of all crying spells that occurred in the late afternoon after he returned home from work. The physical record itself is very important, both as an aid to memory and to track Bob's progress. In a single-case study, progress is always monitored by displaying the measurements made in the form of graphs.

Graphically Displaying Data

As we know from Chapter 4, the word *measurement* can be simply defined as the process of assigning a number or value to a variable. If the variable, or target problem, being considered is depression as rated by the *GCS,* and if Bob scores, say 72, then 72 is the number assigned to Bob's initial level of depression. The worker will try to reduce his initial score of 72 to at least 30—the desired *minimum* score. The worker can then select and implement an intervention and ask Bob to complete the *GCS* again, say once a week, until the score of 30 has been reached. Bob's depression levels can be plotted (over a 12-week period) on a graph, such as the one shown in Figure 6.1.

In the graph, Bob's depression level for each week is plotted on the *y*-axis, while time, in weeks, is plotted on the *x*-axis. There is a reason for this. Obviously, the social worker is hoping that the selected intervention will result in lowering Bob's level of depression, over time, as measured

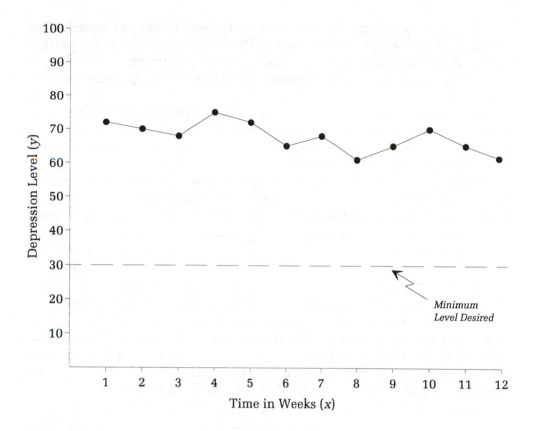

FIGURE 6.1   Bob's Depression Level Over Time

by the *GCS*. In other words, the worker is hypothesizing that: If Intervention *A* is implemented, Bob's depression will decrease. In research terminology, the independent variable in this hypothesis is the intervention (*X*) and the dependent variable (*Y*) is Bob's depression level. The frequency of Bob's ten-minute crying spells per day, as recorded by Maria, could also be graphed.

KINDS OF EXPLORATORY CASE-LEVEL DESIGNS

We will briefly discuss three kinds of exploratory case-level designs: (1) the *B* design, (2) the *BC* design, and (3) the *BCD* design.

The *B* Design

The first type of exploratory case-level design is the *B* design, which is the simplest of all case-level designs. The italicized letter *B* refers to the fact that an intervention of some kind has been introduced. Let us take a simple example of how a *B* design works.

A couple, David and Donna, have had a long history of interrupting one another while the other is talking. They have tried to stop the pattern of this destructive behavior, to no avail. They have finally decided to do something about this and have sought out the services of a social worker. After some exploration, it becomes apparent that the couple need to concentrate on their interruptive behaviors. In short, the worker wishes to reduce the frequency with which David and Donna interrupt each other while conversing. This could be observed and measured by having them talk to each other while in weekly, one-hour sessions.

The worker teaches basic communication skills (the intervention) to the couple and has them practice these skills during each weekly session while other marital relationship issues are being addressed. Each week during therapy, while the couple is engaged in conversation, the worker makes a record of how many times each partner interrupts the other. Thus, in this situation, the worker is trying to reduce the number of interruptions—the target problem. For now, suppose that the data for David and Donna over a 12-week period look like those displayed in Figure 6.2.

Figure 6.2 shows that the number of times interruptions occurred decreased gradually over the 12-week period until it reached zero in the twelfth week—that is, until the goal of therapy had been achieved. Even so, the worker could continue to record the level of the target problem for a longer period of time to ensure that success was being maintained.

In this case, the worker hypothesized that if the intervention—teaching communication skills—were implemented, then the number of times the couple interrupted each other while conversing during therapy sessions would be reduced. Figure 6.2 shows that the target problem was achieved for both partners, but it does not show that the worker's hypothesis was in fact correct. Perhaps teaching communication skills had nothing to do with reducing the couple's interruptions.

The interruptions may have been reduced because of something else the worker did (besides the communication skills training), or something the couple did, or something a friend did. There is even the possibility that their interruptions would have ceased if no one had done anything at all. Be that as it may, extraneous variables have not been controlled for. Thus, we cannot know how effective this particular intervention is in solving this particular target problem for this particular couple.

If we use the same interventive strategy with a second couple experiencing the same target problem and achieve the same results, it becomes more likely that the intervention produced the results. If the same results follow the same intervention with a third similar couple, it becomes more likely still. Thus, we can become more certain that an intervention causes a result the more times the intervention is successfully used with similar target problems.

However, if an intervention is used only once, as is the case with the exploratory *B* design, no evidence for causation can be inferred. All that can be gleaned from Figure 6.2 is that, for whatever reason, David's and Donna's target problem was reduced: or, if a graph such as Figure 6.3 is

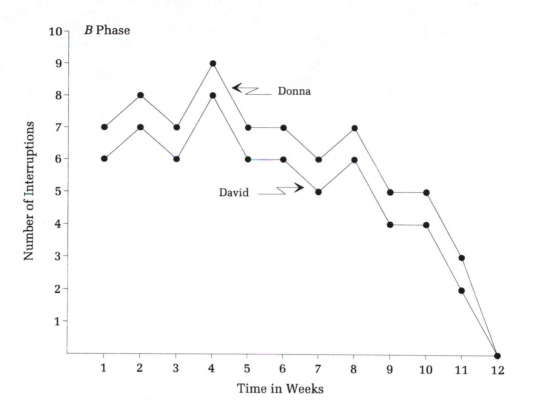

FIGURE 6.2   *B* Design: Frequency of Interruptions for a Couple During One Intervention, Indicating an Improvement

obtained instead, this indicates that the problem has not been resolved, or has been only partly resolved. If David and Donna continued to interrupt each other, week after week, a graph like the one shown in Figure 6.3 would be produced.

The data from graphs, such as the data presented in Figures 6.2 and 6.3, are extremely useful since a worker will be better able to judge whether the intervention should be continued, modified, or abandoned in favor of a different interventive strategy. In the simplest of terms, the *B* design only monitors the effectiveness of an intervention over time and indicates when the desired level of the target problem has been reached.

The *BC* and *BCD* Designs

The second and third types of exploratory case-level designs are the *BC* and *BCD* designs. In the *B* design previously described, the italicized letter *B* represents a single interventive strategy. Suppose now that a *B* intervention, such as communication skills training, is implemented with David and Donna, and a graph like the one shown in Figure 6.4 is

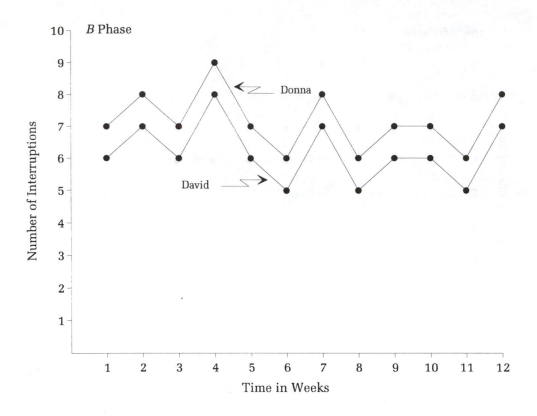

FIGURE 6.3   *B* Design: Frequency of Interruptions for a Couple
                       During One Intervention, Indicating No
                       Improvement

obtained. The left side of the graph shows that the problem is not being
resolved with the implementation of the *B* intervention, and the social
worker may feel that it is time to change the intervention, so a *C* intervention is tried starting the fifth week. Four weeks, for example, may have
been as long as the worker was prepared to wait for the hoped-for change
to occur for the *B* intervention to work.

As can be seen in Figure 6.4, the worker implemented a second
different intervention, *C*, starting the fifth week and measured the target
problem in the same way as before, by making weekly recordings of the
number of times that each partner interrupts the other during the course
of therapy sessions. These measurements are graphed as before, plotting
the level of the client's target problem along the *y*-axis and the time in
weeks along the *x*-axis. The data are shown in the *C* phase of Figure 6.4.

Figure 6.4 shows that no change occurred in the target problem after
Intervention *B* was implemented, but the target problem was resolved
following the implementation of Intervention *C*. As before, extraneous
variables have not been considered, and Figure 6.4 does not show that
Intervention *C* caused the problem to be resolved: It shows only that
success occurred during Intervention *C* but not during Intervention *B*.

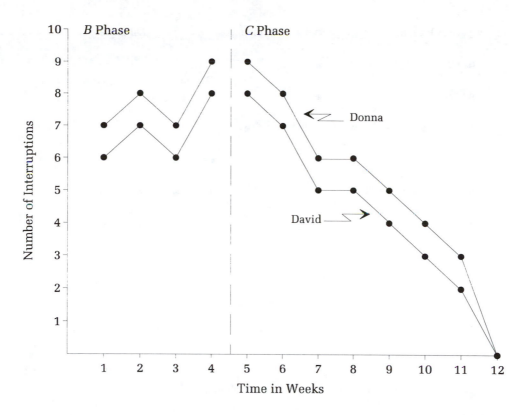

FIGURE 6.4   *BC* Design: Frequency of Interruptions for a Couple After Two Interventions, Indicating an Improvement with the Second Intervention

In order to demonstrate causation, the worker would have to obtain successful results with Intervention *C* on a number of occasions with different couples experiencing the exact same target problem. Similarly, the inherent uselessness of Intervention *B* could be shown only if it was implemented unsuccessfully with other couples—an unlikely event since the most hopeful intervention surely would be implemented first.

If Intervention *C* does not work either, the worker will have to try yet another intervention (Intervention *D*). Combined graphs may be produced, as in Figure 6.5, illustrating the results of the entire *BCD* case-level design.

Since the *BC* and *BCD* designs involve successive, different interventions, they are sometimes known as successive interventions designs. It is conceivable that an *E* intervention might be necessary, forming a *BCDE* design, and even an *F*, forming a *BCDEF* design. Multiple-treatment interference, discussed in Chapters 8 and 9, is a major threat to the external validity of successive intervention designs.

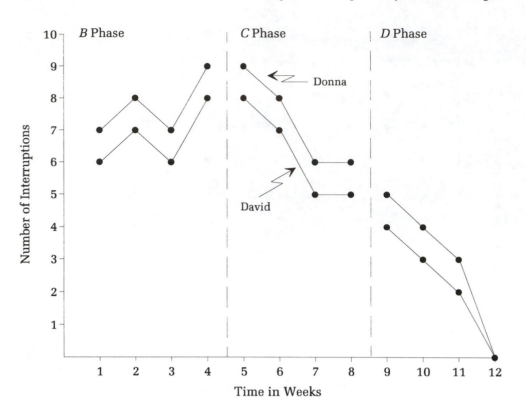

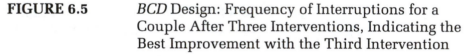

FIGURE 6.5   *BCD* Design: Frequency of Interruptions for a
Couple After Three Interventions, Indicating the
Best Improvement with the Third Intervention

SUMMING UP AND LOOKING AHEAD

Exploratory designs are used when little is known about the field of study
and data are gathered in an effort to find out "what's out there." These
ideas are then used to generate hypotheses that can be verified using more
rigorous designs. No design is inherently inferior or superior to the others.
Each has advantages and disadvantages in terms of time, cost, and the data
that can be obtained. Those of us who are familiar with all the exploratory
designs will be equipped to select the one that is most appropriate to a
particular research or practice question. In the following chapter we will
turn our attention away from exploratory designs and concentrate on
descriptive designs.

REVIEW QUESTIONS

1 Discuss the differences among trend
studies, cohort studies, and panel
studies. Use a social work example
throughout your discussion.

2 Out of all the exploratory group-
level designs presented in this chapter, which one do you think is used
most often in social work research?

Why? Justify your answer. Which one do you think is least utilized? Why? Justify your answer.

3 In groups of four, decide on a social work–related problem area. Design hypothetical studies using each one of the exploratory group-level designs. For each study determine what data need to be gathered. Provide the graphic representation of the study detailing the Rs, Os, and Xs. Present the four designs to the entire class with a detailed explanation of the population and the sampling procedures.

4 In groups of four, decide on a social work–related problem area. Design hypothetical studies using each one of the exploratory case-level designs. For each study determine what data need to be gathered. Provide the graphic representation of the study detailing the Bs, Cs, and Ds. Present the designs to the entire class with a detailed explanation of the population and the sampling procedures.

5 At your university library, find a social work article that reports on a research study that used an *exploratory* group-level design. Comment on how well the study was done.

6 At your university library, find a social work article that reports on a research study that used an *exploratory* case-level design. Comment on how well the study was done.

7 Discuss in your own words the purpose of exploratory case-level designs. Use a social work example throughout your discussion.

8 List and discuss in detail the requirements that all case-level designs must have in order for them to be useful to social work practitioners and researchers. Use a social work example throughout your discussion.

9 In your own words, discuss the similarities and differences between exploratory case-level designs and exploratory group-level designs. Use a social work example throughout your discussion.

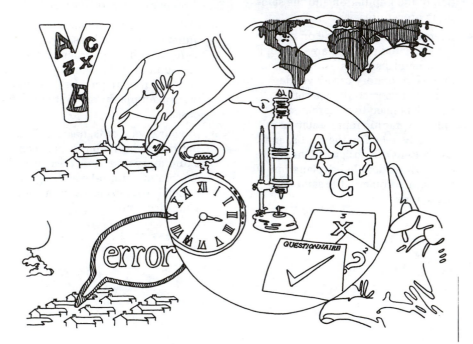

This chapter has been adapted and modified from: Grinnell (1993a); Grinnell and Unrau (1997); Grinnell and Williams (1990); Grinnell, Williams, and Tutty (1997); and Williams, Tutty, and Grinnell (1995)

C h a p t e r   7

Descriptive Research Designs

THE LAST CHAPTER discussed exploratory research designs that can be used with quantitative and qualitative studies. As we know, exploratory designs are on the far left of the knowledge-building continuum as illustrated in Figure 2.1. Thus, they are primarily used in qualitative studies. At the midpoint of the knowledge continuum are descriptive designs, which have some but not all of the requirements of explanatory research designs—to be discussed in the following chapter.

As we will see in the next chapter, explanatory designs make an effort to randomly assign research participants to either an experimental or control group. However, more often than not, the groups we are studying are already in existence; sometimes ethical issues are involved. It would be unethical, for example, to assign clients who need immediate help to two random groups, where only one of the groups (i.e., experimental) is to receive the intervention.

The previous chapter presented exploratory designs by breaking them into two categories, group-level designs and case-level designs. We will discuss descriptive designs in the same way.

DESCRIPTIVE GROUP-LEVEL DESIGNS

There are six kinds of descriptive group-level research designs:: (1) randomized one-group posttest-only design, (2) randomized cross-sectional and longitudinal survey design, (3) one-group pretest-posttest design, (4) comparison group posttest-only design, (5) comparison group pretest-posttest design, and (6) interrupted time-series design.

Randomized One-Group Posttest-Only Design

The first descriptive group-level design is the randomized one-group posttest-only design. Its distinguishing feature is that members of the group are randomly selected for it. Otherwise, this design is identical to the exploratory one-group posttest-only design mentioned in the previous chapter. It is written as follows:

$$R \quad X \quad O_1$$

Where:

R = Random selection from a population
X = Independent variable (see Box 6.2)
O_1 = First and only measurement of the dependent variable

We will continue to use the example of the child abuse prevention program mentioned in the previous chapter to illustrate how the randomized one-group posttest-only design can be used. The difference between this design and the one-group posttest-only design, mentioned in the previous chapter, is that the group does not accidentally assemble itself by including anyone who happened to be interested in volunteering for the program. Instead, group members are randomly selected from a population, say, of all the 400 parents who were reported to child welfare authorities for having physically abused a child and who wish to receive voluntary treatment in Rome, Wisconsin, in 1998. These 400 parents comprise the population of all the physically abusive parents who wish to receive treatment in Rome, Wisconsin.

The sampling frame of 400 people is used to select a simple random sample of 40 physically abusive parents who voluntarily wish to receive treatment. The program (X) is administered to these 40 people, and the number of parents who stopped being abusive toward their children after the program is determined (O_1). The design can be written as:

$$R \quad X \quad O_1$$

Where:

R = Random selection of 40 people from the population of physically abusive parents who voluntarily wish to receive treatment in Rome, Wisconsin

X = Child Abuse Prevention Program (see Box 6.2)

O_1 = Number of parents in the program who stopped being physically abusive to their children

Say that the program fails to have the desired effect, and 39 of the 40 people continue to physically harm their children after participating in the program. Because the program was ineffective for the sample and the sample was randomly selected, it can be concluded that it would be ineffective for the physically abusive parent population of Rome, Wisconsin—the other 360 who did not go through the program. In other words, because a representative random sample was selected, it is possible to generalize the program's results to the population from which the sample was drawn.

Since no change in the dependent variable occurred, it is not sensible to consider the control of rival hypotheses. Antonia need not wonder what might have caused the change—X, her program, or an alternative explanation. If her program had been successful, however, it would not be possible to ascribe her success solely to the program.

Randomized Cross-Sectional and Longitudinal Survey Design

The second descriptive group-level design is the randomized cross-sectional and longitudinal survey design. As discussed in the previous chapter, a cross-sectional survey obtains data only once from a sample of a particular population. If the sample is a random sample—that is, if it represents the population from which it was drawn—then the data obtained from the sample can be generalized to the entire population from which the sample was drawn. Thus, a simple cross-sectional survey design using a random sample can be written:

$$R \quad O_1$$

Where:

R = Random sample drawn from a population
O_1 = Only measurement of the dependent variable (see Box 6.2)

One-Group Pretest-Posttest Design

The third descriptive group-level design is the one-group pretest-posttest design. It is also referred to as a before-after design because it includes a pretest of the dependent variable, which can be used as a basis of comparison with the posttest results. It is written as:

$$O_1 \quad X \quad O_2$$

Where:

O_1 = First measurement of the dependent variable
X = Independent variable, the intervention (see Box 6.2)
O_2 = Second measurement of the dependent variable

The one-group pretest-posttest design, in which a pretest precedes the introduction of the independent variable and a posttest follows it, can be used to determine precisely how the independent variable affects a particular group. The design is used often in social work decision making—far too often, in fact, because it does not control for many rival hypotheses. The difference between O_1 and O_2, on which these decisions are based, therefore, could be due to many other factors rather than the independent variable.

Comparison Group Posttest-Only Design

The fourth descriptive group-level design is the comparison group posttest-only design. It improves on the exploratory one-group and multi-group posttest-only designs by introducing a comparison group that does not receive the independent variable, but is subject to the same posttest as those who do (the experimental group).

A group used for purposes of comparison is usually referred to as a comparison group in an exploratory or descriptive design and as a control group in an explanatory design. While a control group is always randomly assigned, a comparison group is not. The basic elements of the comparison group posttest-only design are as follows:

Experimental Group: X O_1
Comparison Group: O_1

Where:

X = Independent variable, the intervention
O_1 = First and only measurement of the dependent variable

In Antonia's child abuse prevention program, if the January, April, and August sections are scheduled but the August sessions are canceled for some reason, those who would have been participants in that section could be used as a comparison group. If the values of O_1 on the measuring instrument were similar for the experimental and comparison groups, it could be concluded that the program was of little use, since those who had experienced it (those receiving X) were not much better or worse off than those who had not.

Comparison Group Pretest-Posttest Design

The fifth descriptive group-level design is the comparison group pretest-posttest design. It elaborates on the one-group pretest-posttest design by adding a comparison group. This second group receives both the pretest (O_1) and the posttest (O_2) at the same time as the experimental group, but it does not receive the independent variable. This design is written as follows:

Experimental Group: O_1 X O_2
Comparison Group: O_1 O_2

Where:

O_1 = First measurement of the dependent variable, the parents' scores on the measuring instrument

X = Independent variable, the intervention

O_2 = Second measurement of the dependent variable, the parents' scores on the measuring instrument

The experimental and comparison groups formed under this design will probably not be equivalent, because members are not randomly assigned to them. The pretest scores, however, will indicate the extent of their differences.

Interrupted Time-Series Design

The sixth descriptive group-level design is the interrupted time-series design. It is a series of pretests and posttests that are conducted on a group of research participants over time, both before and after the independent variable is introduced. The basic elements of this design are illustrated as follows:

$$O_1 \quad O_2 \quad O_3 \quad X \quad O_4 \quad O_5 \quad O_6$$

Where:

Os = Measurements of the dependent variable

X = Independent variable (see Box 6.2)

This design takes care of the major weakness in the descriptive one-group pretest-posttest design, which does not control for rival hypotheses. Suppose, for example, that a new policy is to be introduced into an agency whereby all promotions and raises are to be tied to the number of educational credits acquired by social workers. Since there is a strong feeling among some workers that years of experience should count for more than educational credits, the agency's management decides to examine the effect of the new policy on morale.

Because agency morale is affected by many things and varies normally from month to month, it is necessary to ensure that these normal fluctuations are not confused with the results of the new policy. Therefore, a baseline is first established for morale by conducting a number of pretests over, say, a six-month period before the policy is introduced. Then, a similar number of posttests is conducted over the six months following the introduction of the policy. This design would be written as follows:

$$O_1 \quad O_2 \quad O_3 \quad O_4 \quad O_5 \quad O_6 \quad X \quad O_7 \quad O_8 \quad O_9 \quad O_{10} \quad O_{11} \quad O_{12}$$

The same type of time-series design can be used to evaluate the result of a treatment intervention with a client or client system, as will be discussed in the next section on descriptive case-level designs.

DESCRIPTIVE CASE-LEVEL DESIGNS

Our discussion of descriptive case-level designs (pages 157–162) has been adapted and modified from three sources: Grinnell and Williams (1990); Grinnell, Williams, and Tutty (1997); and Williams, Tutty, and Grinnell (1995). One of the difficulties with the three exploratory case-level designs (i.e., *B*, *BC*, and *BCD*) discussed in the previous chapter is that they provide no data about the level of the client's target problem *before* the intervention was introduced. Bob, for example, might show himself to be severely depressed according to his initial score of 72 (Figure 6.1) on the *GCS*. Perhaps the cause of his depression, however, is the recent death of his 20-year-old cat, Teddy; and the problem will resolve itself naturally as he recovers from Teddy's loss.

Or perhaps he was more depressed on the day that he approached the worker than he usually is. Thus, it would have been useful if we had had an accurate measure of Bob's depression levels over time *before* he received social work services. Descriptive case-level designs provide such a procedure. We will briefly discuss two types: (1) the *AB* design, and (2) the *ABC* design. We will now turn our attention to the *AB* design.

The *AB* Design

The first descriptive case-level design is the *AB* design. An *AB* design is useful when a worker can afford to monitor a client's target problem for a short time *before* implementing an intervention. Suppose a social worker is seeing Juan, who experiences a great deal of anxiety in social situations, for example. He is nervous when he speaks to his teacher or boss or when he meets people for the first time, and the prospect of speaking in public appalls him.

The worker could decide that progress for Juan's target problem might be measured in two ways: first, he will complete the Interaction and Audience Anxiousness Scale (*IAAS*) that measures social anxiety. For the first four weeks, the worker will not intervene at all. The purpose of the worker's contact, in these weeks, will be merely to gather data on the initial level of Juan's anxiety—that is, to gather baseline data.

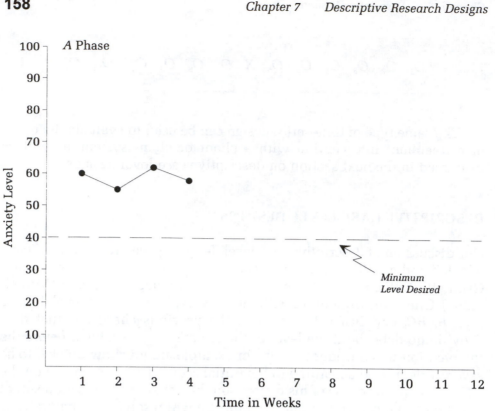

FIGURE 7.1   Magnitude of Juan's Anxiety Level Before an Intervention, Indicating a Stable Baseline

The period in which initial data are being gathered is known as the *A* phase of the study. The italicized letter *A* symbolizes no intervention—in the same way as the letters *B, C,* and *D* symbolize the first, second, and third interventive strategies, respectively. Suppose, now, that Juan scores 60 on the *IAAS* the first week he is assessed, 55 the second week, 62 the third, and 58 on the fourth. Juan's anxiety scores for this four-week period before an intervention was introduced can be graphed as shown in Figure 7.1.

Taken together, the four scores in Figure 7.1 show that Juan's anxiety level is reasonably stable at about an average of 59. Since it has remained relatively stable over a four-week period, the likelihood is that it will continue to remain at the same level if a social worker does not intervene: That is, Juan's problem will not solve itself. The worker would be even more justified to intervene immediately if Juan achieved anxiety scores as illustrated in Figure 7.2. Here, Juan's anxiety level is rising: his anxiety problem is growing worse.

Conversely, if he achieved the four scores shown in Figure 7.3, the worker might be reluctant to intervene, because Juan's anxiety level is decreasing anyway. If the worker did intervene, however, and his anxiety level continued to decrease, we would never know if the worker's

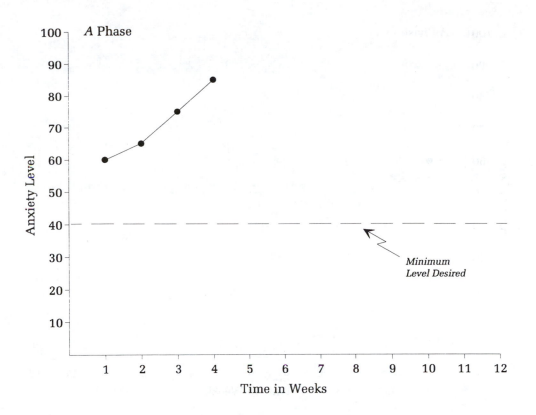

FIGURE 7.2   Magnitude of Juan's Anxiety Level Before an
Intervention, Indicating a Deteriorating Baseline

intervention had a positive effect or if the same result would have been
achieved without it.

The four scores shown in Figure 7.4 vary to such an extent that it is
not possible to tell how anxious Juan really is. Again, we would be
reluctant to intervene because there would be no way of knowing whether
Juan was making progress or not, and whether the intervention was
helpful or not. In order to conduct an *AB* single-case research study—and
in order to be helpful to a client—the level of the target problem must be
stable (e.g., Figure 7.1), or getting worse (e.g., Figure 7.2) in the *A* phase.

Suppose that it has been established that Juan's target problem level
is stable, as illustrated in Figure 7.1. An objective may then be set: to
reduce Juan's social anxiety level to 40. Forty has been selected because
people who suffer from social anxiety at a clinically significant level tend
to score *above* 40 on the *IAAS*, while people whose social anxiety is not
clinically significant score *below* 40. It will not really matter whether the
objective is precisely met. If Juan becomes more confident in social
situations, feels more ready to meet people, and only reaches a score of 45,
this may be good enough to warrant termination of services.

Having produced a baseline graph and established a target problem,
the worker can now implement an intervention package that could

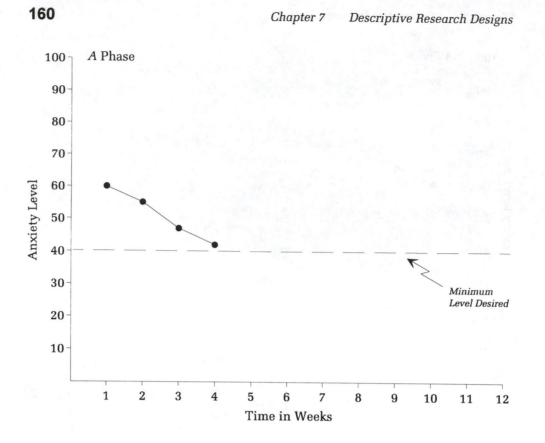

FIGURE 7.3   Magnitude of Juan's Anxiety Level Before an
Intervention, Indicating an Improving Baseline

include such activities as role-playing through anxiety-producing situations and coping strategies. Whatever the intervention package, it is important that a record of its process is made so that another worker will know, in the future, exactly what the specific intervention was.

Once the baseline, or *A* phase, has been established, the *B* phase will proceed as in the three exploratory *B* designs discussed in the last chapter. Juan will complete the *IAAS* weekly, or every two weeks, or however often is appropriate, and the scores will be graphed.

The worker could continue to monitor the level of Juan's target problem after it has been achieved in order to ensure that progress is being maintained. We cannot adequately judge the usefulness of an intervention until it is known not only that it works, but that it continues to work when it is no longer the focus of our attention. It is, therefore, essential to make follow-up measurements whenever possible, perhaps a month, six months, and a year after the client's target problem appears to have been resolved. The actual number and frequency of follow-up measurements will depend on the type of problem and the client's situation.

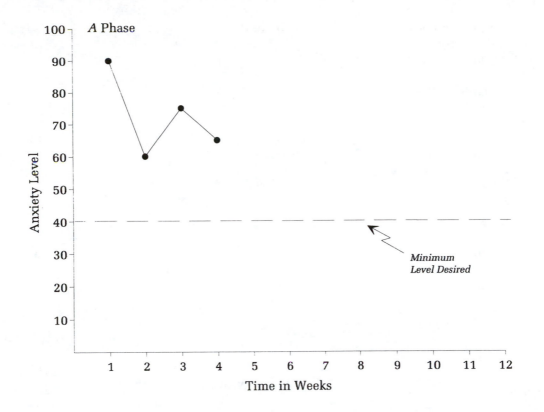

FIGURE 7.4   Magnitude of Juan's Anxiety Level Before an Intervention, Indicating a Fluctuating Baseline

The *ABC* Design

The second descriptive case-level design is the *ABC* design. Figure 7.5 shows the same *A* phase as in Figure 7.1, but now the *B* phase indicates that Juan's problem is not being satisfactorily resolved. In this case, his worker will probably want to change the *B* intervention, initiating a *C* intervention. Juan's problem level will be continually measured over time and may progress to the level set in the objective. On the other hand, if there is still no improvement, or an insufficient improvement, a *D* intervention may need to be implemented.

As with the exploratory *BC* and *BCD* designs presented in the previous chapter, descriptive *ABC* and *ABCD* case-level designs involve trying successive interventions until the target problem level is reached, or almost reached. However, exploratory designs only enable workers to compare the progress made in each new phase with progress in the previous phase or phases. Look at Phase *B* in Figure 7.6. Juan's *B*-phase scores are slightly lower than his *A*-phase scores. Some improvement has occurred, although a worker may not have been able to judge that from the *B*-phase if baseline scores were not established. When the results are not clear-cut, it is the *A*

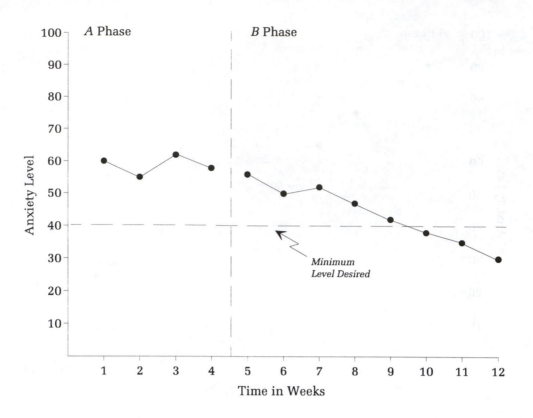

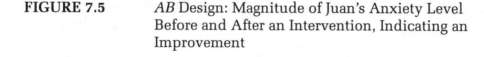

FIGURE 7.5   *AB* Design: Magnitude of Juan's Anxiety Level
Before and After an Intervention, Indicating an
Improvement

phase that enables us to see whether there has been a little progress from
the initial problem level, no progress at all, or perhaps even a regression.

When a new intervention is initiated in the *C* phase, the social worker
is not really starting again from the beginning. The worker is starting from
where the problem level was at the end of the *B* phase. If the *C* intervention is successful in resolving the problem, it is impossible to tell, without
further studies, whether the *C* intervention would have worked alone or
whether it was the combination of *B* and *C* that did the trick. If a *D*
intervention is employed as well, the various effects of *B*, *C*, and *D* grow
even more intertwined, so that we cannot know which intervention had
what effect—even supposing that a given intervention had any effect.

SUMMING UP AND LOOKING AHEAD

When we use a descriptive research design, we might be trying to
determine whether two or more variables are associated. Often, descriptive
designs are employed when we are unable, for practical reasons, to use the
more rigorous explanatory designs.

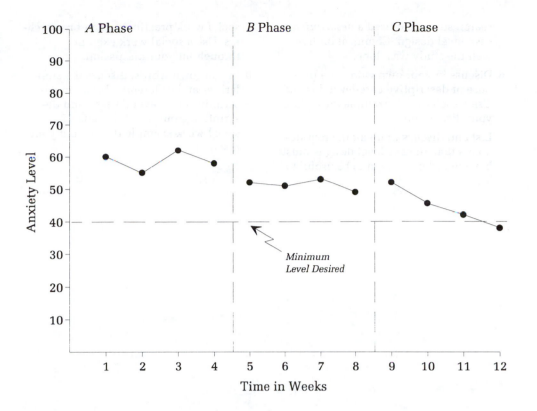

FIGURE 7.6   *ABC* Design: Magnitude of Juan's Anxiety Level Before and After Two Interventions, Indicating an Improvement with the *C* Intervention

REVIEW QUESTIONS

1 Out of all the descriptive group-level designs presented in this chapter, which one do you think is used most often in social work research? Why? Justify your answer. Which one do you think is least utilized? Why? Justify your answer.

2 In groups of four, decide on a social work–related problem area. Design hypothetical studies using each one of the descriptive group-level designs. For each study determine what data need to be gathered. Provide the graphic representation of the study detailing the *R*s, *O*s, and *X*s. Present the four designs to the entire class with a detailed explanation of the population and the sampling procedures.

3 In groups of four, decide on a social work–related problem area. Design hypothetical studies using each one of the descriptive case-level designs. For each study determine what data need to be gathered. Provide the graphic representation of the study detailing the *B*s, *C*s, and *D*s. Present the designs to the entire class with a detailed explanation of the population and the sampling procedures.

4 At your university library, find a social work article that reports on a research study that used a *descriptive* group-level design. Comment on how well the study was done.

5 At your university library, find a social work article that reports on a research study that used a *descriptive* case-level design. Comment on how well the study was done.

6 Discuss in your own words the purpose of descriptive case-level designs. Use a social work example throughout your discussion.

7 List and discuss in detail the requirements that all case-level designs must have in order for them to be useful to social work practitioners and researchers. Use a social work example throughout your discussion.

8 In your own words, discuss the similarities and differences between descriptive case-level designs and descriptive group-level designs. Use a social work example throughout your discussion.

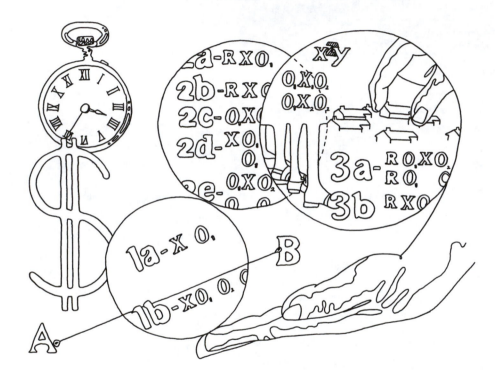

This chapter has been adapted and modified from: Grinnell (1993a); Grinnell and Unrau (1997); Grinnell and Williams (1990); Grinnell, Williams, and Tutty (1997); and Williams, Tutty, and Grinnell (1995)

Chapter 8

Explanatory Research Designs

T HE LAST CHAPTER discussed descriptive research designs that can be used with quantitative and qualitative studies. As we know, descriptive designs are in the middle of the knowledge-building continuum as illustrated in Figure 2.1. At the far right of the knowledge continuum are explanatory designs, the topic of this chapter. As we will see in the following chapter, explanatory designs approach the "ideal research study" most closely (which incidently, does not exist). They are at the highest level of the knowledge continuum, have the most rigid requirements, and are most able to produce results that can be generalized to other people and situations. Explanatory designs, therefore, are most able to provide valid and reliable research results that can serve as additions to our professions' knowledge base.

Unlike exploratory (Chapter 6) and descriptive (Chapter 7) designs, explanatory designs try to establish a causal connection between at least one independent and dependent variable. The value of the dependent variable could always result from chance rather than from the influence of the independent variable, but there are statistical techniques for calculating the probability that this will occur.

EXPLANATORY GROUP-LEVEL DESIGNS

There are three kinds of explanatory group-level research designs: (1) classical experimental design, (2) Solomon four-group design, and (3) randomized posttest-only control group design.

Classical Experimental Design

The first explanatory group-level design is the classical experimental design. It is the basis for all explanatory designs. It involves an experimental group and a control group, both created by a random assignment method (and if possible, random selection from a population). Both groups take a pretest (O_1) at the same time, after which the independent variable (X) is given only to the experimental group, and then both groups take the posttest (O_2). This design is written as follows:

Experimental Group: R O_1 X O_2
Control Group: R O_1 O_2

Where:

R = Random selection from a population and random assignment to group
O_1 = First measurement of the dependent variable
X = Independent variable, the intervention
O_2 = Second measurement of the dependent variable

Because the experimental and control groups have been randomly assigned, they are equivalent with respect to all important variables. This group equivalence in the design helps control for rival hypotheses, because both groups would be affected by them in the same way.

Solomon Four-Group Design

The second explanatory group-level design is the Solomon four-group research design. It involves four rather than two randomly assigned groups as in classical experimental design. There are two experimental groups and two control groups, but the pretest is taken by only one of each of these groups. Experimental Group 1 takes a pretest, receives the independent variable, and then takes a posttest. Experimental Group 2 also receives the independent variable but takes only the posttest. The same is true for the two control groups; Control Group 1 takes both the pretest and posttest, and Control Group 2 takes only the posttest. This design is written in symbols as follows:

Experimental Group 1:	R	O_1	X	O_2
Control Group 1:	R	O_1		O_2
Experimental Group 2:	R		X	O_2
Control Group 2:	R			O_2

Where:

R = Random assignment to group
O_1 = First measurement of the dependent variable
X = Independent variable, the intervention
O_2 = Second measurement of the dependent variable

The advantage of the Solomon four-group research design is that it allows for the control of testing effects, since one of the experimental groups and one of the control groups do not take the pretest. All of the threats to internal validity are addressed when this design is used. It has the disadvantage that twice as many research participants are required, and it is considerably more work to implement than the classical experimental design.

Randomized Posttest-Only Control Group Design

The third explanatory group-level design is the randomized posttest-only control group research design. It is identical to the descriptive comparison group posttest-only design, except that the research participants are randomly assigned to two groups. This design, therefore, has a control group rather than a comparison group.

The randomized posttest-only control group research design usually involves only two groups, one experimental and one control. There are no pretests. The experimental group receives the independent variable and takes the posttest; the control group only takes the posttest. This design can be written as follows:

Experimental Group:	R	X	O_1
Control Group:	R		O_1

Where:

R = Random selection from a population and random assignment to group

X = Independent variable, the intervention

O_1 = First and only measurement of the dependent variable

Suppose we want to test the effects of two different treatment interventions, X_1 and X_2. In this case, the randomized posttest-only control group research design could be elaborated upon to form three randomly assigned groups, two experimental groups (one for each intervention) and one control group. This design would be written as follows:

Experimental Group 1:	R	X_1	O_1
Experimental Group 2:	R	X_2	O_1
Control Group:	R		O_1

Where:

R = Random selection from a population and random assignment to group

X_1 = Different independent variable than X_2

X_2 = Different independent variable than X_1

O_1 = First and only measurement of the dependent variable

In addition to measuring change in a group or groups, a pretest also helps to ensure equivalence between the control and experimental groups. As you know, this design does not have a pretest. The groups have been randomly assigned, however, as indicated by R, and this, in itself, is theoretically enough to ensure equivalence without the need for a confirmatory pretest. This design is useful in situations where it is not possible to conduct a pretest or where a pretest would be expected to strongly influence the results of the posttest due to the effects of testing.

EXPLANATORY CASE-LEVEL DESIGNS

Our discussion of explanatory case-level designs (pages 170–180) has been adapted and modified from three sources: Grinnell and Williams (1990); Grinnell, Williams, and Tutty (1997); and Williams, Tutty, and Grinnell (1995). Explanatory case-level designs attempt to come to grips with the problem of cause and effect. If a worker wants to know whether a particular intervention is effective in a particular problem area, the following question needs to be answered: Did intervention *X* cause result *Y*? At an explanatory level, the worker needs to be sure that nothing other than the intervention caused the result.

As we will see in the following chapter, a research study in which changes in the dependent variable result only from changes in the independent variable is said to be internally valid. In order to conduct an internally valid study, three factors need to be taken into account:

- First, we must show that the independent variable occurred before the dependent variable.
- Second, the inevitable cohort of extraneous variables must be identified and dealt with.
- Third, a worker will need to consider other general factors that may pose a threat to internal validity.

An improvement in a client's level of self-esteem, for example, may occur not only from the interventive efforts. The improvement may be due to changes in another aspect of the client's life, such as getting a new job, or an intervention by another practitioner, such as being placed on medication. Alternatively, things may improve spontaneously.

Explanatory case-level designs attempt to control for such other occurrences by showing that there were two or more times in which improvement was noted in the client after a given intervention. If such is the case, then the likelihood of the improvement being related to other rival hypotheses is decreased. We will briefly discuss three types of explanatory case-level designs: (1) the *ABAB* design, (2) the *BAB* design, and (3) the *BCBC* design.

The *ABAB* Design

The first explanatory case-level design is the *ABAB* design. As the name might imply, an *ABAB* case-level design is simply two descriptive *AB* designs strung together. This design is most appropriate with interventions that produce temporary or easily removable effects, or when an intervention is withdrawn but measurements on the client's target problem continue to be made.

Referring back to Juan, whose target problem is social anxiety, Figure 7.5 illustrates a descriptive *AB* design as previously described. It shows a stable *A* or baseline phase, followed by a successful *B* phase, where his social anxiety level is gradually reduced to below 40 during the 10th week. It cannot be certain, however, that the intervention caused the reduction in anxiety until the same intervention has been tried again and has achieved the same result. The more times the same intervention is followed by the same result, the more certain it will become that the intervention caused the result.

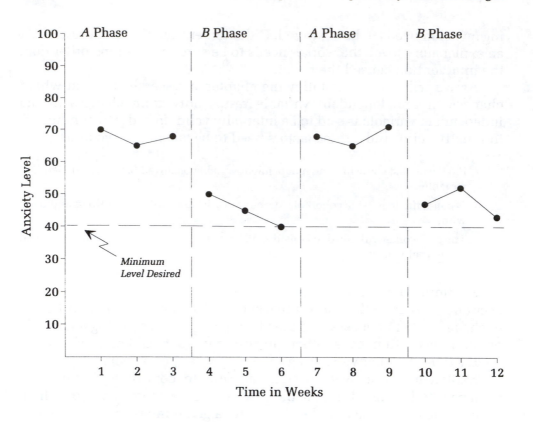

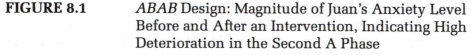

FIGURE 8.1   *ABAB* Design: Magnitude of Juan's Anxiety Level
                        Before and After an Intervention, Indicating High
                        Deterioration in the Second A Phase

Suppose, now, that Juan successfully reached his objective score of 40
during the first *B* phase (6th week) as illustrated in Figure 8.1. After
services are withdrawn, Juan then experiences some social reversals as his
anxiety mounts once more as indicated in the second *A* Phase in Figure
8.1. The worker provides services for the second time and has Juan
complete the same *IAAS* during the second *B* phase.

The worker goes through the same process as was done the first time,
establishing a baseline score, or *A* phase, in the first few weeks before the
introduction of an intervention. The same intervention is implemented,
and measurements of Juan's progress are obtained through the *B* phase,
producing almost the same result.

We can now be more certain that the intervention caused the result
since the same intervention was followed by the same result on two
separate occasions. In this example, Juan's social anxiety level returned to
the original baseline level—the level established in the first *A* phase. From
a research perspective, this is an ideal state of affairs, since the first *AB*
study can now be duplicated almost exactly. From a practice perspective,
however, it is worrisome as we would like to think that a client will
continue to benefit from an intervention after it has been withdrawn.

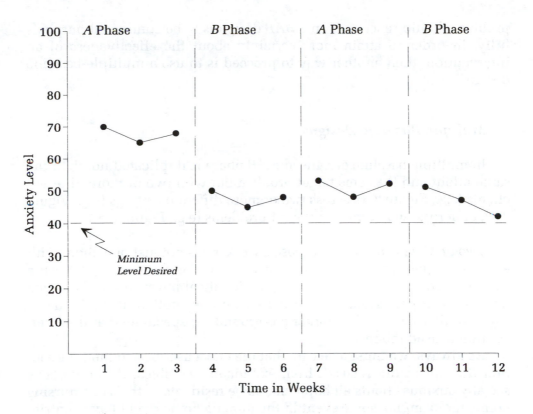

FIGURE 8.2   *ABAB* Design: Magnitude of Juan's Anxiety Level
Before and After an Intervention, Indicating Low
Deterioration in the Second *A* Phase

In fact, many clients do continue to benefit. Juan may have learned
and remembered techniques for reducing his anxiety, and it would be
unusual for his problem to return to its exact original level. Figure 8.2
illustrates a scenario in which Juan's anxiety problem did not return to its
original level.

In a case such as that shown in Figure 8.2, it is still quite possible to
conduct an *ABAB* study. The baseline scores in the second *A* phase are
relatively stable, even though they show an improvement over the first *A*
phase; and the second *B* phase shows once again that the intervention has
been followed by a reduction in Juan's social anxiety level.

Sometimes it is important to continue to measure the target problem
even after it appears to have been resolved and the intervention has been
withdrawn. Those workers who continue to measure a client's target
problem, perhaps while working on a different issue, are essentially constructing another baseline. This can be used as an additional *A* phase if
the client suffers a regression and needs the intervention to be repeated.

An *ABAB* design in which the target problem, once resolved, reverts
to its original level is known as a reversal design. Such a design may be
implemented accidentally. We never intend that the client's target

problem should reoccur. If an *ABAB* design is to be conducted purpose-fully, in order to attain more certainty about the effectiveness of an intervention, then another way to proceed is to use a multiple-baseline design.

Multiple-Baseline Designs

In multiple-baseline designs, the *AB* phase is duplicated not with the same client and the same target problem but with two or more different clients (e.g., Figure 8.3), across two or more different settings (e.g., Figure 8.4), or across two or more different problems (e.g., Figure 8.5).

Two or More Clients   Suppose a worker has not just one client with a social anxiety problem but two or more. He or she could establish a baseline with each client, implement an identical intervention with each one, and compare several *AB* designs with one another. If the *B* phases show similar results, the worker has grounds to speculate that the intervention caused the result.

As always, we must take care that the effect ascribed to the intervention did not result, instead, from extraneous variables. If the worker's socially anxious clients all happened to be residents of the same nursing home, for example, some event in the nursing home could have contrib-uted to the reduction in their anxiety: perhaps a newly instituted communal activity. This possibility can be controlled for—that is, we can ensure that extraneous variables have not occurred—by introducing the same intervention with each client at different times. Figure 8.3 illustrates an example of a multiple-baseline design across three clients who are being seen by a social worker for anxiety problems.

Had an extraneous variable been responsible for the reduced anxiety demonstrated by Breanne, the other two clients, Warren and Alison, would also have demonstrated reduced anxiety, even though the worker was not intervening on their behalf. The fact that the baseline scores of the second two clients remained stable until the introduction of the interven-tion is a good indication that no extraneous variables were present, and that the intervention is a probable cause of the result.

While a multiple-baseline design requires more effort than a simple *AB* design, it is often clinically feasible. A multiple-baseline study across clients can sometimes be carried out by several workers at the same time.

Two or More Settings   Another way to conduct a multiple-baseline study is to use not separate clients, but two or more separate settings. Suppose that an objective is to reduce the number of a child's temper tantrums. Three parallel single-case research studies could be conducted: one at home, one at school, and one at the day-care center where the child goes after school. At home, a parent might count the number of temper tantrums per day, both before and during the intervention. A teacher

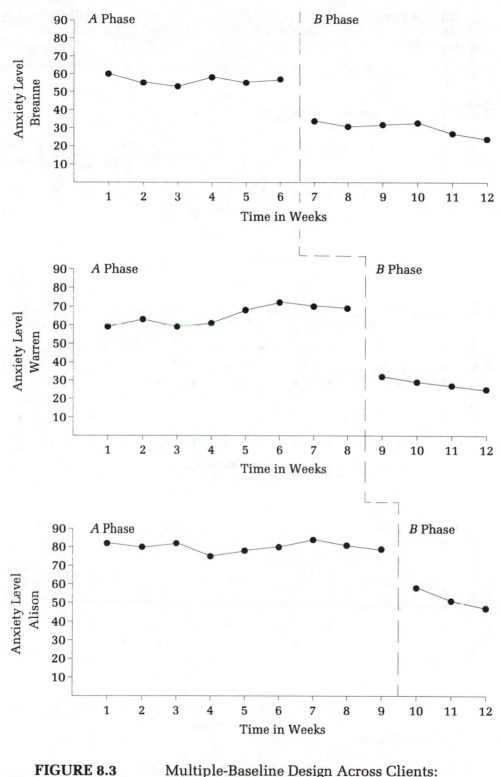

FIGURE 8.3   Multiple-Baseline Design Across Clients: Magnitude of Anxiety Levels for Three Clients, Indicating an Improvement

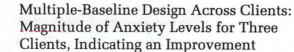

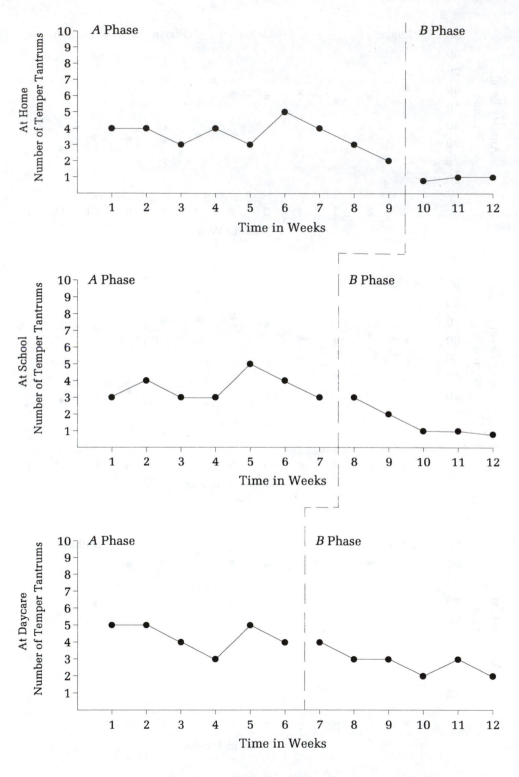

FIGURE 8.4   Multiple-Baseline Design Across Settings: Number of Temper Tantrums for One Client in Three Settings, Indicating an Improvement

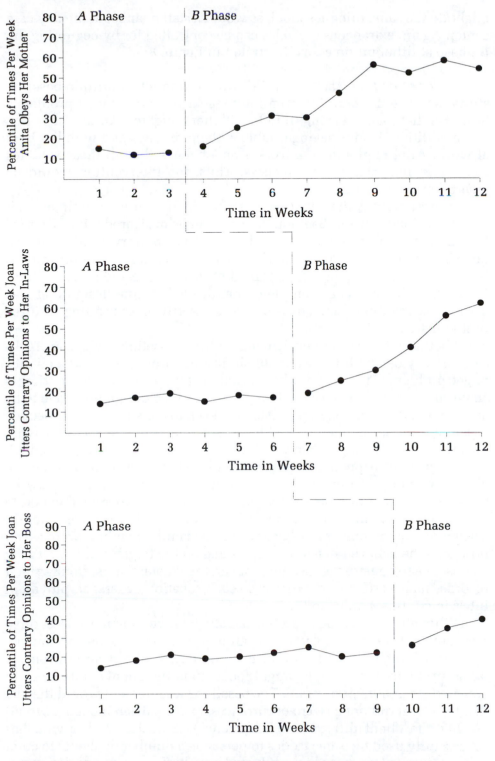

FIGURE 8.5   Multiple-Baseline Design Across Client
Target Problems: Magnitude of Three
Client Target Problem Areas for One Client,
Indicating an Improvement

might do the same thing at school, as would a staff member at the day-care center. Again, extraneous variables can be controlled for by beginning the *B* phase at different times, as illustrated in Figure 8.4.

Two or More Problems   A third way to conduct a multiple-baseline study is to use the same intervention to tackle different target problems. Suppose that Joan is having trouble with her daughter, Anita.

In addition, Joan is having trouble with her in-laws and with her boss at work. After exploration, a worker may believe that all these troubles stem from her lack of assertiveness. Thus, the intervention would be assertiveness training.

Progress with Anita might be measured by the number of times each day she is flagrantly disobedient. Progress can be measured with Joan's in-laws by the number of times she is able to utter a contrary opinion, and so on. Since the number of occasions on which Joan has an opportunity to be assertive will vary, these figures might best be expressed in percentiles. Figure 8.5 illustrates an example of a multiple-baseline design that was used to assess the effectiveness of Joan's assertiveness training in three problem areas.

Whether it is a reversal design or a multiple-baseline design, an *ABAB* explanatory design involves establishing a baseline level for the client's target problem. This will not be possible if the need for intervention is acute, and sometimes the very thought of an *A*-type design will have to be abandoned. It is sometimes possible, however, to construct a retrospective baseline—that is, to determine with a reasonable degree of accuracy what the level of the target problem was *before* an intervention is implemented.

The best retrospective baselines are those that do not depend on the client's memory. If the target problem occurs rarely, memories may be accurate. For example, Tai, a teenager, and his family may remember quite well how many times he ran away from home during the past month. They may not remember nearly so well if the family members were asked how often he behaved defiantly. Depending on the target problem, it may be possible to construct a baseline from archival data: that is, from written records, such as school attendance sheets, probation orders, employment interview forms, and so forth.

Although establishing a baseline usually involves making at least three measurements before implementing an intervention, it is also acceptable to establish a baseline of zero, or no occurrences of a desired event. A target problem, for example, might focus upon the client's reluctance to enter a drug treatment program. The baseline measurement would then be that the client did not go (zero occurrences) and the desired change would be that the client did go (one occurrence). A social worker who has successfully used the same tactics to persuade a number of clients to enter a drug treatment program has conducted a multiple-baseline design across clients.

As previously discussed in Chapter 7, a usable baseline should show either that the client's problem level is stable (e.g., Figure 7.1) or that it is growing worse (e.g., Figure 7.2). Sometimes an *A*-type design can be used even though the baseline indicates a slight improvement in the target problem (e.g., Figure 7.3). The justification must be that the intervention is expected to lead to an improvement that will exceed the anticipated improvement if the baseline trend continues.

Perhaps a child's temper tantrums are decreasing by one or two a week, for example, but the total number per week is still 18 to 20. If a worker thought the tantrums could be reduced to four or five a week, or they could be stopped altogether, the worker would be justified in implementing an intervention even though the client's target problem was improving slowly by itself.

In a similar way, a worker may be able to implement an *A*-type design if the client's baseline is unstable, provided that the intervention is expected to exceed the largest of the baseline fluctuations. Perhaps the child's temper tantrums are fluctuating between 12 and 20 per week in the baseline period and it is hoped to bring them down to less than 10 per week.

Nevertheless, there are some occasions when a baseline cannot be established or is not usable, such as when a client's behaviors involve self-injurious ones. Also, sometimes the establishment of a baseline is totally inappropriate.

The *BAB* Design

The second explanatory case-level design is the *BAB* design. As the name suggests, a *BAB* design is an *ABAB* design without the first *A* phase. Many times a social worker may decide that immediate intervention is needed and that there is not time to collect baseline data. The client's progress can be monitored, as is done in a *B* design, and the intervention can be withdrawn later when the problem appears to be resolved.

Previous experience has indicated that sometimes even the best-resolved client problems tend to reoccur, however, and the worker, therefore, continues to measure the target problem level, constructing an *A* phase almost incidentally. When the client's target problem does re-occur, the worker still has a good record of what happened to the problem level after the intervention was withdrawn. Figure 8.6 illustrates an example of a *BAB* design.

Since there is no initial baseline data, we cannot know whether the resolution of the client's target problem on the first occasion had anything to do with the intervention. The problem may have resolved itself, or some external event may have resolved it. Nor can we know the degree to which the problem level changed during the intervention, since there was no baseline data with which to compare the final result. An indication of the amount of change can be obtained by comparing the first and last measurements in the *B* phase, but the first measurement may have been an unreliable measure of the client's target problem level. The client may

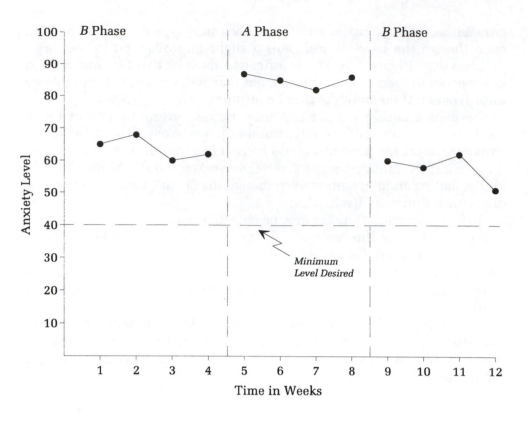

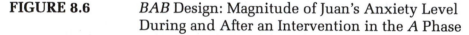

FIGURE 8.6   *BAB* Design: Magnitude of Juan's Anxiety Level
During and After an Intervention in the *A* Phase

have felt more or less anxious that day than usual; and a baseline is
necessary to compensate for such fluctuations.

Since the effectiveness of the intervention on the first occasion is
unknown, there can be no way of knowing whether the intervention was
just as effective the second time it was implemented, or less or more
effective. All we know is that the problem level improved twice, following
the same intervention; and this is probably enough to warrant using the
intervention again with another client.

The *BCBC* Design

The third explanatory case-level design is the *BCBC* design. In the same
way that an *ABAB* design comprises two *AB* designs, a *BCBC* design is
simply two *BC* designs strung together. In order to conduct a *BC* design,
we can implement an intervention without collecting baseline data, and
subsequently introduce a second intervention, both of which may be
potentially useful. Although the worker does not have baseline data, and
thus has no record of how serious the problem was initially, the worker
is able to compare the efficacy of the two or more different interventions.

SUMMING UP AND LOOKING AHEAD

When using either explanatory group- or case-level research designs, we are attempting to show causation; that is, we are trying to show that changes in one variable cause changes in another. As we will see in the following chapter, we try hard to control threats to internal validity because, if the study is not internally valid, we cannot demonstrate causation.

No explanatory research design is inherently inferior or superior to the others. Each has advantages and disadvantages in terms of time, cost, and the data that can be obtained. Those of us who are familiar with all of the explanatory designs will be equipped to select the one that is most appropriate to a particular research or practice situation. Now that we know the basic ingredients of exploratory (Chapter 6), descriptive (Chapter 7), and explanatory (Chapter 8) research designs, the next chapter will discuss the factors that we need to take into account when evaluating any one of them.

REVIEW QUESTIONS

1   Write an explanatory-level research hypothesis in which Variable A (some variable of your choice) is the independent variable and Variable B (some variable of your choice) is the dependent variable. Now rewrite the same hypothesis with the two variables reversed. Which hypothesis do you think is correct? Why? How would you go about testing the two hypotheses?

2   Design an explanatory group-level research study. What ethical issues do you see if your study were in fact implemented?

3   Out of all the explanatory group-level research designs presented in this chapter, which one do you think is used most often in social work research? Why? Justify your answer. Which one do you think is least utilized? Why? Justify your answer.

4   In groups of four, decide on a social work–related problem area. Design hypothetical studies using each one of the explanatory group- and case-level designs. For each study determine what data need to be gathered. Provide the graphic representation of the study detailing the *R*s, *O*s, and *X*s. Present the designs to the entire class with a detailed explanation of the population and the sampling procedures.

5   Discuss in your own words the purpose of explanatory case-level evaluation designs. Use a social work example throughout your discussion.

6   List and discuss in detail the three *explanatory* case-level evaluation designs. Provide a social work example of each.

7   What do descriptive case-level evaluation designs have that exploratory ones do not? Provide a social work example in your discussion.

8   What do explanatory case-level evaluation designs have that descriptive ones do not? Provide a social work example in your discussion.

9   What is the major purpose of multiple-baseline case-level evaluation designs? Discuss in detail. Provide a social work example of all three types.

10 List and discuss in detail the advantages and disadvantages of explanatory case-level evaluation designs. Provide a social work example throughout your discussion.

11 When is it inappropriate to implement an *A*-phase when trying to achieve an explanatory case-level research design? Provide a social work example throughout your discussion.

12 In your own words, discuss the similarities and differences between explanatory case-level designs and explanatory group-level designs. Use a social work example throughout your discussion.

13 In your own words, discuss the similarities and differences between *exploratory* case-level designs and *exploratory* group-level designs as presented in Chapter 6. Use a social work example throughout your discussion.

14 In your own words, discuss the similarities and differences between *descriptive* case-level designs and *descriptive* group-level designs as presented in Chapter 7. Use a social work example throughout your discussion.

15 In your own words, discuss the similarities and differences between *explanatory* case-level designs and *explanatory* group-level designs as presented in this chapter. Use a social work example throughout your discussion.

16 Out of all the explanatory case-level designs presented in this chapter, which one do you think is used most often in social work research? Why? Justify your answer. Which one do you think is least utilized? Why? Justify your answer. Use a social work example throughout your discussion.

17 Discuss why explanatory case-level designs are nothing more than interrupted time series group-level designs. Justify your answer. Use a social work example throughout your discussion.

This chapter has been adapted and modified from: Grinnell (1993a); Grinnell and Unrau (1997); Grinnell and Williams (1990); Grinnell, Williams, and Tutty (1997); and Williams, Tutty, and Grinnell (1995)

C h a p t e r   9

"Ideal" Research Designs

Aɴ "ɪᴅᴇᴀʟ" ʀᴇsᴇᴀʀᴄʜ ᴅᴇsɪɢɴ is one in which a research study most closely approaches certainty about the relationship between the independent and dependent variables. The purpose of creating an "ideal" research design is to ascertain whether it can be concluded from the study's findings that the independent variable is, or is not, the only cause of change in the dependent variable. As pointed out in previous chapters, some social work research studies have no independent variable—for example, those studies that just want to find out how many people in a certain community wish to establish a community-based halfway house for people who are addicted to drugs.

TOWARD THE CONCEPT OF AN "IDEAL" RESEARCH DESIGN

"Ideal" research designs are introduced with the word "ideal" in quotes because "ideal" designs are rarely achieved in social work research situations. In order to achieve this high degree of certainty and qualify as an "ideal" research design, it must meet six conditions:

1 The time order of the independent variable must be established.

2 The independent variable must be manipulated.

3 The relationship between the independent and dependent variables must be established.

4 The research design must control for rival hypotheses.

5 At least one control group should be used.

6 Random assignment procedures (and if possible, random sampling from a population) must be employed in assigning research participants (or objects) to groups.

Controlling the Time Order of Variables

In an "ideal" research design, the independent variable must precede the dependent variable in time. Time order is crucial if our research study is to show that one variable causes another, because something that occurs later cannot be the cause of something that occurred earlier. Suppose we want to study the relationship between adolescent substance abuse and gang-related behavior. The following hypothesis is formulated after some thought:

Adolescent substance abuse causes gang-related behavior.

In the hypothesis, the independent variable is adolescent drug use, and the dependent variable is gang-related behavior. The substance abuse must come *before* gang-related behavior because the hypothesis states that adolescent drug use causes gang-related behavior. We could also come up with the following hypothesis, however:

Adolescent gang-related behavior causes substance abuse.

In this hypothesis, adolescent gang-related behavior is the independent variable, and substance abuse is the dependent variable. According to this hypothesis, gang-related behavior must come *before* the substance abuse.

Manipulating the Independent Variable

Manipulation of the independent variable means that we must do something with the independent variable in terms of at least one of the research participants in the study. In the general form of the hypothesis, if X occurs then Y will result, the independent variable (X) must be manipulated in order to effect a variation in the dependent variable (Y). There are three ways in which independent variables can be manipulated:

1 **X present versus X absent**. If the effectiveness of a specific treatment intervention is being evaluated, an experimental group and a control group could be used. The experimental group would be given the intervention, the control group would not (see Box 3.3).

2 **A small amount of X versus a larger amount of X**. If the effect of treatment time on client's outcomes is being studied, two experimental groups could be used, one of which would be treated for a longer period of time.

3 **X versus something else**. If the effectiveness of two different treatment interventions is being studied, Intervention X_1 could be used with Experimental Group 1 and Intervention X_2 with Experimental Group 2.

There are certain variables, such as the gender or race of our research participants, that obviously cannot be manipulated because they are fixed. They do not vary, so they are called constants, not variables, as was pointed out in Chapter 3. Other constants, such as socioeconomic status or IQ, may vary for research participants over their life spans, but they are fixed quantities at the beginning of the study, probably will not change during the study, and are not subject to alteration by the one doing the study.

Any variable we can alter (e.g., treatment time) can be considered an independent variable. At least one independent variable must be manipulated in a research study if it is to be considered an "ideal" research design.

Establishing Relationships Between Variables

The relationship between the independent and dependent variables must be established in order to infer a cause-effect relationship at the explanatory knowledge level. If the independent variable is considered to be the cause of the dependent variable, there must be some pattern in the relationship between these two variables. An example is the hypothesis: The more time clients spend in treatment (independent variable), the better their progress (dependent variable).

Controlling Rival Hypotheses

Rival hypotheses, or alternative hypotheses as described in Chapter 3, must be identified and eliminated in an "ideal" research design. The logic of this requirement is extremely important, because this is what makes a cause-effect statement possible.

The prime question to ask when trying to identify a rival hypothesis is, "What other extraneous variables might affect the dependent variable?" (What else might affect the client's outcome besides treatment time?) At the risk of sounding redundant, "What else besides X might affect Y?" Perhaps the client's motivation for treatment, in addition to the time spent in treatment, might affect the client's outcome. If so, motivation for treatment is an extraneous variable that could be used as the independent variable in the rival hypothesis, "The higher the clients' motivation for treatment, the better their progress."

Perhaps the social worker's attitude toward the client might have an effect on the client's outcome, or the client might win the state lottery and ascend abruptly from depression to ecstasy. These extraneous variables could potentially be independent variables in other rival hypotheses. They must all be considered and eliminated before it can be said with reasonable certainty that a client's outcome resulted from the length of treatment time and not from any other extraneous variables.

Control over rival hypotheses refers to efforts on our part to identify and, if at all possible, to eliminate the extraneous variables in these alternative hypotheses. Of the many ways to deal with rival hypotheses, three of the most frequently used are to keep the extraneous variables constant, use correlated variation, or use analysis of covariance.

Keeping Extraneous Variables Constant

The most direct way to deal with rival hypotheses is to keep constant the critical extraneous variables that might affect the dependent variable. As we know, a constant cannot affect or be affected by any other variable. If an extraneous variable can be made into a constant, then it cannot affect either the study's real independent variable or the dependent variable.

Let us take an example to illustrate the above point. Suppose, for example, that a social worker who is providing counseling to anxious clients wants to relate client outcome to length of treatment time, but most of the clients are also being treated by a consulting psychiatrist with antidepressant medication. Because medication may also affect the clients' outcomes, it is a potential independent variable that could be used in a rival hypothesis. However, if the study included only clients who have been taking medication for some time before the treatment intervention began, and who continue to take the same medicine in the same way throughout treatment, then medication can be considered a constant (in this study, anyway).

Any change in the clients' anxiety levels after the intervention will, therefore, be due to the intervention with the help of the medication. The extraneous variable of medication, which might form a rival hypothesis, has been eliminated by holding it constant. In short, this study started out with one independent variable, the intervention, then added the variable of medication to it, so the final independent variable is the intervention plus the medication.

This is all very well in theory. In reality, however, a client's drug regime is usually controlled by the psychiatrist and may well be altered at any time. Even if the regime is not altered, the effects of the drugs might not become apparent until the study is under way. In addition, the client's level of anxiety might be affected by a host of other extraneous variables over which the social worker has no control at all: for example, living arrangements, relationships with other people, the condition of the stock market, or an unexpected visit from an IRS agent. These kinds of pragmatic difficulties tend to occur frequently in social work practice and research. It is often impossible to identify all rival hypotheses, let alone eliminate them by keeping them constant.

Using Correlated Variation

Rival hypotheses can also be controlled with correlated variation of the independent variables. Suppose, for example, that we are concerned that income has an effect on a client's compulsive behavior. The client's income, which in this case is subject to variation due to seasonal employment, is identified as an independent variable. The client's living conditions—in a hotel room rented by the week—are then identified as the second independent variable that might well affect the client's level of compulsive behavior. These two variables, however, are correlated since living conditions are highly dependent on income.

Correlated variation exists if one potential independent variable can be correlated with another. Then only one of them has to be dealt with in the research study.

Using Analysis of Covariance

In constructing an "ideal" research design, we must always aim to use two or more groups that are as equivalent as possible on all important variables. Sometimes this goal is not feasible, however. Perhaps we are obliged to use existing groups that are not as equivalent as we would like. Or, perhaps during the course of the study we discover inequivalencies between the groups that were not apparent at the beginning.

A statistical method called *analysis of covariance* can be used to compensate for these differences. The mathematics of the method is far beyond the scope of this discussion, but an explanation can be found in most advanced statistics texts.

Using a Control Group

An "ideal" research design should use at least one control group in addition to the experimental group. The experimental group may receive an intervention that is withheld from the control group, or equivalent groups may receive different interventions or no interventions at all.

A social worker who initiates a treatment intervention is often interested in knowing what would have happened if the intervention had not been used or had some different intervention been substituted. Would members of a support group for alcoholics have recovered anyway, without the social worker's efforts? Would they have recovered faster or more completely had family counseling been used instead of the support group approach?

The answer to these questions will never be known if only the support group is studied. But, what if another group of alcoholics is included in the research design? In a typical design with a control group, two equivalent groups, 1 and 2, would be formed, and both would be administered the same pretest to determine the initial level of the dependent variable (e.g., degree of alcoholism). Then an intervention would be initiated with Group 1 but not with Group 2. The group treated—Group 1 or the experimental group—would receive the independent variable (the intervention). The group not treated—Group 2 or the control group—would not receive it.

At the conclusion of the intervention, both groups would be given a posttest (the same measure as the pretest). The pretest and posttest consist of the use of some sort of data-gathering procedure, such as a survey or self-report measure, to measure the dependent variable before and after the introduction of the independent variable. As we know, group designs can be written in symbols as follows:

$$\text{Experimental Group:} \quad R \quad O_1 \quad X \quad O_2$$
$$\text{Control Group:} \quad R \quad O_1 \qquad\; O_2$$

Where:

R = Random assignment to group
O_1 = First measurement of the dependent variable
X = Independent variable
O_2 = Second measurement of the dependent variable

The two Rs in this design indicate that the research participants were randomly assigned to each group. The symbol X, which, as usual, stands for the independent variable, indicates that an intervention is to be given to the experimental group after the pretest (O_1) and before the posttest (O_2). The absence of X for the control group indicates that the intervention is not to be given to the control group. This design is called a classical experimental design because it comes closest to having all the characteristics necessary for an "ideal" research design.

Table 9.1 displays results from a research study of this type. If the experimental group is equivalent to the control group, the pretest results should be approximately the same for both groups. Within an acceptable margin of error, 24 is approximately the same as 26. Since the control

| **TABLE 9.1** | Clients' Outcomes by Group | | |

Group	Pretest	Posttest	Difference
Experimental	24	68	− 44
Control	26	27	− 1

group has not received the intervention, the posttest results for this group would not be expected to differ appreciably from the pretest results.

In fact, the posttest score, 27, differs little from the pretest score, 26, for the control group. Because the experimental and control groups may be considered equivalent, any rival hypotheses that affected the experimental group would have affected the control group in the same way. No rival hypothesis affected the control group, as indicated by the fact that without the intervention, the pretest and posttest scores did not differ. Therefore, it can be assumed that no rival hypothesis affected the experimental group, either, and the difference (–44) between pretest and posttest scores for the experimental group was probably due to the intervention and not to any other factor.

Randomly Assigning Research Participants to Groups

Once a sample has been selected (see Chapter 5), the individuals (or objects or events) in it are randomly assigned to either an experimental or a control group in such a way that the two groups are equivalent. This procedure is known as random assignment or randomization. In random assignment, the word *equivalent* means equal in terms of the variables that are important to the study, such as the clients' motivation for treatment, or problem severity.

If the effect of treatment time on clients' outcomes is being studied, for example, the research design might use one experimental group that is treated for a comparatively longer time, a second experimental group that is treated for a shorter time, and a control group that is not treated at all. If we are concerned that the clients' motivation for treatment might also affect their outcomes, the research participants can be assigned so that all the groups are equivalent (on the average) in terms of their motivation for treatment.

The process of random sampling from a population followed by random assignment of the sample to groups is illustrated in Figure 9.1. Let us say that the research design calls for a sample size of one-tenth of the population. From a population of 10,000, therefore, a random sampling procedure is used to select a sample of 1,000 individuals.

Then random assignment procedures are used to place the sample of 1,000 into two equivalent groups of 500 individuals each. In theory,

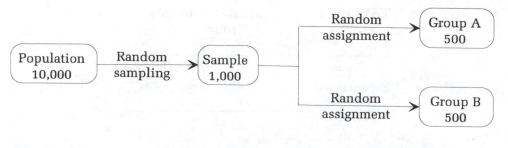

FIGURE 9.1   Random Sampling and Random Assignment
                     Procedures

Group A will be equivalent to Group B, which will be equivalent to the random sample, which will be equivalent to the population in respect to all important variables contained within the research study.

Matched Pairs

Besides randomization, another, more deliberate method of assigning people or other units to groups involves matching. The matched pairs method is suitable when the composition of each group consists of variables with a range of characteristics. One of the disadvantages of matching is that some individuals cannot be matched and so cannot participate in the study.

Suppose a new training program for teaching parenting skills to foster mothers is being evaluated, and it is important that the experimental and control groups have an equal number of highly skilled and less skilled foster parents before the training program is introduced. The women chosen for the sample would be matched in pairs according to their parenting skill level; the two most skilled foster mothers are matched, then the next two, and so on. One person in each pair of approximately equally skilled foster parents is then randomly assigned to the experimental group and the other is placed in the control group.

Let us suppose that in order to compare the foster mothers exposed to the new training program with women who were not, a standardized measuring instrument that measures parenting skill level (the dependent variable) is administered to a sample of ten women. The scores can range from 100 (excellent parenting skills) to zero (poor parenting skills).

Then their scores are rank-ordered from the highest to the lowest, and out of the foster mothers with the two highest scores, one is selected to be assigned to either the experimental group or the control group. It does not make any difference which group our first research participant is randomly assigned to, as long as there is an equal chance that she will go to either the control group or the experimental group. In this example the first person is randomly chosen to go to the experimental group, as illustrated as follows:

Rank Order of Parenting Skills Scores (in parentheses)
First Pair:
(99) Randomly assigned to the experimental group
(98) Assigned to the control group

Second Pair:
(97) Assigned to the control group
(96) Assigned to the experimental group

Third Pair:
(95) Assigned to the experimental group
(94) Assigned to the control group

Fourth Pair:
(93) Assigned to the control group
(92) Assigned to the experimental group

Fifth Pair:
(91) Assigned to the experimental group
(90) Assigned to the control group

The foster parent with the highest score (99) is randomly assigned to the experimental group, and this person's "match," with a score of 98, is assigned to the control group. This process is reversed with the next matched pair, where the first person is assigned to the control group and the match is assigned to the experimental group. If the assignment of research participants according to scores is not reversed for every other pair, one group will be higher than the other on the variable being matched.

To illustrate this point, suppose the first participant (highest score) in each match is always assigned to the experimental group. The experimental group's average score would be 95 (99 + 97 + 95 + 93 + 91 = 475/5 = 95), and the control group's average score would be 94 (98 + 96 + 94 + 92 + 90 = 470/5 = 94). If every other matched pair is reversed, however, as in the example, the average scores of the two groups are closer together; 94.6 for the experimental group (99 + 96 + 95 + 92 + 91 = 473/5 = 94.6) and 94.4 for the control group (98 + 97 + 94 + 93 + 90 = 472/5 = 94.4). In short, 94.6 and 94.4 (difference of 0.2) are closer together than 95 and 94 (difference of 1).

INTERNAL AND EXTERNAL VALIDITY

We must remember that the research design we finally select should always be evaluated on how close it comes to an "ideal" one in reference to the six characteristics presented in the beginning of this chapter. As stressed throughout this book, most research designs used in social work do not closely resemble an "ideal" research design. The research design finally selected needs to be evaluated on how well it meets its primary objective—to adequately answer a research question or to test a hypothesis. In short, a research design will be evaluated on how well it controls for internal and external validity factors.

Internal validity has to do with the ways in which the research design ensures that the introduction of the independent variable (if any) can be identified as the sole cause of change in the dependent variable. In contrast, external validity has to do with the extent to which the research design allows for generalization of the findings of the study to other groups and other situations.

Both internal and external validity are achieved in a research design by taking into account various threats that are inherent in all research efforts. A design for a study with both types of validity will recognize and attempt to control for potential factors that could affect our study's outcome or findings. An "ideal" research design, therefore, tries to control as many threats to internal and external validity as possible.

THREATS TO INTERNAL VALIDITY

In any explanatory research study, we should be able to conclude from our findings that the independent variable is, or is not, the only cause of change in the dependent variable. If our study does not have internal validity, such a conclusion is not possible, and the study's findings can be misleading.

Internal validity is concerned with one of the requirements for an "ideal" experiment—the control of rival hypotheses, or alternative explanations for what might bring about a change in the dependent variable. The higher the internal validity of any research study, the greater the extent to which rival hypotheses can be controlled; the lower the internal validity, the less they can be controlled. Thus, we must be prepared to rule out the effects of factors other than the independent variable that could influence the dependent variable.

There are ten threats to internal validity: (1) history, (2) maturation, (3) testing, (4) instrumentation error, (5) statistical regression, (6) differential selection of research participants, (7) mortality, (8) reactive effects of research participants, (9) interaction effects, and (10) relations between experimental and control groups.

History

The first threat to internal validity is history. It refers to any outside event, either public or private, that may affect the dependent variable and was not taken into account in our research design. Many times, it refers to events occurring between the first and second measurement of the dependent variable (the pretest and the posttest). If events occur that have the potential to alter the second measurement, there would be no way of knowing how much (if any) of the observed change in the dependent variable is a function of the independent variable and how much is attributable to these events.

Suppose, for example, we are investigating the effects of an educational program on racial tolerance. We may decide to measure the dependent variable, racial tolerance in the community, before introducing the independent variable, the educational program.

The educational program is then implemented. Since it is the independent variable, it is represented by X. Finally, racial tolerance is measured again, after the program has run its course. This final measurement yields a posttest score, represented by O_2. The one-group pretest-posttest study design can be written as:

$$O_1 \quad X \quad O_2$$

Where:

O_1 = First measurement, or pretest score, of racial tolerance
X = Educational program (independent variable) (see Box 6.2)
O_2 = Second measurement, or posttest score, of racial tolerance

The difference between the values O_2 and O_1 represent the difference in racial tolerance in the community before and after the educational program. If the study is internally valid, $O_2 - O_1$ will be a crude measure of the effect of the educational program on racial tolerance; and this is what we were trying to discover. Suppose, before the posttest could be administered, an outbreak of racial violence, such as the type that occurred in Los Angeles in the summer of 1992, occurred in the community. Violence can be expected to have a negative effect on racial tolerance, and the posttest scores may, therefore, show a lower level of tolerance than if the violence had not occurred. The effect, $O_2 - O_1$, will now be the combined effects of the educational program *and* the violence, not the effect of the program alone, as we intended.

Racial violence is an extraneous variable that we could not have anticipated and did not control for when designing the study. Other examples might include an earthquake, an election, illness, divorce, or marriage—any event, public or private that could affect the dependent variable.

Maturation

The second threat to internal validity is maturation. It refers to changes, both physical and psychological, that take place in our research participants over time and can affect the dependent variable. Suppose that we are evaluating an interventive strategy designed to improve the behavior of adolescents who engage in delinquent behavior. Since the behavior of adolescents changes naturally as they mature, the observed changed behavior may have been due as much to their natural development as it was to the intervention strategy.

Maturation refers not only to physical or mental growth, however. Over time, people grow older, more or less anxious, more or less bored, and more or less motivated to take part in a research study. All these factors and many more can affect the way in which people respond when the dependent variable is measured a second or third time.

Testing

The third threat to internal validity is testing. It is sometimes referred to as the initial measurement effect. Thus, the pretests that are the starting point for many research designs are another potential threat to internal validity. One of the most utilized research designs involves three steps: measuring some dependent variable, such as learning behavior in school or attitudes toward work; initiating a program to change that variable (the independent variable); then measuring the dependent variable again at the conclusion of the program. As we know, this simple one-group pretest-posttest design can be written as follows:

$$O_1 \quad X \quad O_2$$

Where:

O_1 = First measurement of the dependent variable, or pretest score
X = Independent variable (see Box 6.2)
O_2 = Second measurement of the dependent variable, or posttest score

The testing effect is the effect that taking a pretest might have on posttest scores. Suppose that Roberto, a research participant, takes a pretest to measure his initial level of racial tolerance before being exposed to a racial tolerance educational program. He might remember some of the questions on the pretest, think about them later, and change his views on racial issues before taking part in the educational program. After the program, his posttest score will reveal his changed opinions, and we may incorrectly assume that the program was responsible, whereas the true cause was his experience with the pretest.

Sometimes, a pretest induces anxiety in a research participant, so that Roberto receives a worse score on the posttest than he should have; or boredom with the same questions repeated again may be a factor. In order to avoid the testing effect, we may wish to use a design that does not require a pretest. If a pretest is essential, we then must consider the length of time that elapses between the pretest and posttest measurements. A pretest is far more likely to affect the posttest when the time between the two is short. The nature of the pretest is another factor. Questions dealing with factual matters, such as knowledge levels, may have a larger testing effect because they tend to be more easily recalled.

Instrumentation Error

The fourth threat to internal validity is instrumentation error. It refers to all the troubles that can afflict the measurement process. The instrument may be unreliable or invalid, as presented in Chapter 4. It may be a mechanical instrument, such as an electroencephalogram (EEG), that has malfunctioned. Occasionally, the term *instrumentation error* is used to refer to an observer whose observations are inconsistent; or to measuring instruments, such as the ones presented in Chapter 4, that are reliable in themselves, but not administered properly.

"Administration," with respect to a measuring instrument, means the circumstances under which the measurement is made: where, when, how, and by whom. A mother being asked about her attitudes toward her children, for example, may respond in one way in the social worker's office and in a different way at home when her children are screaming around her feet.

A mother's verbal response may differ from her written response; or she may respond differently in the morning than she would in the evening, or differently alone than she would in a group. These variations in situational responses do not indicate a true change in the feelings, attitudes, or behaviors being measured, but are only examples of instrumentation error.

Statistical Regression

The fifth threat to internal validity is statistical regression. It refers to the tendency of extremely low and extremely high scores to regress, or move toward the average score for everyone in the research study. Suppose that a student, named Maryanna, has to take a multiple-choice exam on a subject she knows nothing about. There are many questions, and each question has five possible answers. Since, for each question, Maryanna has a 20 percent (one in five) chance of guessing correctly, she might expect to score 20 percent on the exam just by guessing. If she guesses badly, she will score a lot lower; if well, a lot higher. The other members of the class take the same exam and, since they are all equally uninformed, the average score for the class is 20 percent.

Now suppose that the instructor separates the low scorers from the high scorers and tries to even out the level of the class by giving the low scorers special instruction. In order to determine if the special instruction has been effective, the entire class then takes another multiple-choice exam. The result of the exam is that the low scorers (as a group) do better than they did the first time, and the high scorers (as a group) worse. The instructor believes that this has occurred because the low scorers received special instruction and the high scorers did not.

According to the logic of statistical regression, however, both the average score of the low scorers (as a group) and the average score of the high scorers (as a group) would move toward the total average score for both groups (i.e., high and low). Even without any special instruction and still in their state of ignorance, the low scorers (as a group) would be expected to have a higher average score than they did before. Likewise, the high scorers (as a group) would be expected to have a lower average score than they did before.

It would be easy for the research instructor to assume that the low scores had increased because of the special instruction and the high scores had decreased because of the lack of it. Not necessarily so, however; the instruction may have had nothing to do with it. It may all be due to statistical regression.

Differential Selection of Research Participants

The sixth threat to internal validity is differential selection of research participants. To some extent, the participants selected for a research study are different from one another to begin with. "Ideal" experiments, however, require random sampling from a population (if at all possible) and random assignment to groups. This assures that the results of a study will be generalizable to a larger population, thus addressing threats to external validity. In respect to differential selection as a threat to internal validity, "ideal" experiments control for this since equivalency among the groups at pretest is assumed through the randomization process.

This threat is, however, present when we are working with preformed groups or groups that already exist, such as classes of students, self-help groups, or community groups. In terms of the external validity of such designs, because there is no way of knowing whether the preformed groups are representative of any larger population, it is not possible to generalize the study's results beyond the people (or objects or events) that were actually studied. The use of preformed groups also affects the internal validity of a study, though. It is probable that different preformed groups will not be equivalent with respect to relevant variables, and that these initial differences will invalidate the results of the posttest.

A child abuse prevention educational program for children in schools might be evaluated by comparing the prevention skills of one group of children who have experienced the educational program with the skills of a second group who have not. In order to make a valid comparison, the two groups must be as similar as possible, with respect to age, gender, intelligence, socioeconomic status, and anything else that might affect the acquisition of child abuse prevention skills. We would have to make every effort to form or select equivalent groups, but the groups are sometimes not as equivalent as might be hoped—especially if we are obliged to work with preformed groups, such as classes of students or community groups. If the two groups are different before the intervention was introduced, there is not much point in comparing them at the end.

Accordingly, preformed groups should be avoided whenever possible. If it is not feasible to do this, rigorous pretesting must be done to determine in what ways the groups are (or are not) equivalent, and differences must be compensated for with the use of statistical methods.

Mortality

The seventh threat to internal validity is mortality. This simply means that individual research participants may drop out before the end of the study. Their absence will probably have a significant effect on the study's findings because people who drop out are likely to be different in some ways from the other participants who stay in the study. People who drop out may be less motivated to participate in the intervention than people who stay in, for example.

Since dropouts often have such characteristics in common, it cannot be assumed that the attrition occurred in a random manner. If considerably more people drop out of one group than out of the other, the result will be two groups that are no longer equivalent and cannot be usefully compared. We cannot know at the beginning of the study how many people will drop out, but we can watch to see how many do. Mortality is never problematic if dropout rates are five percent or less *and* if the dropout rates are similar for the various groups.

Reactive Effects of Research Participants

The eighth threat to internal validity is reactive effects of research participants. Changes in the behaviors or feelings of research participants may be caused by their reaction to the novelty of the situation or the knowledge that they are participating in a research study. A mother practicing communication skills with her child, for example, may try especially hard when she knows the social worker is watching. We may wrongly believe that such reactive effects are due to the independent variable.

The classic example of reactive effects was found in a series of studies carried out at the Hawthorne plant of the Western Electric Company in Chicago many years ago. Researchers were investigating the relationship between working conditions and productivity. When they increased the level of lighting in one section of the plant, productivity increased; a further increase in the lighting was followed by an additional increase in productivity. When the lighting was then decreased, however, production levels did not fall accordingly but continued to rise. The conclusion was that the workers were increasing their productivity not because of the lighting level but because of the attention they were receiving as research participants in the study.

The term *Hawthorne effect* is still used to describe any situation in which the research participants' behaviors are influenced not by the independent variable but by the knowledge that they are taking part in a research project. Another example of such a reactive effect is the placebo or sugar pill given to patients, which produces beneficial results because they believe it is medication.

Reactive effects can be controlled by ensuring that all participants in a research study, in both the experimental and control groups, appear to be treated equally. If one group is to be shown an educational film, for example, the other group should also be shown a film—some film carefully chosen to bear no relationship to the variable being investigated. If the study involves a change in the participants' routine, this in itself may be enough to change behavior, and care must be taken to continue the study until novelty has ceased to be a factor.

Interaction Effects

The ninth threat to internal validity is interaction effects. Interaction among the various threats to internal validity can have an effect of its own. Any of the factors already described as threats may interact with one another, but the most common interactive effect involves differential selection and maturation.

Let us say we are studying two groups of clients who are being treated for depression. The intention was for these groups to be equivalent, in terms of both their motivation for treatment and their levels of depression. It turns out that Group A is more generally depressed than Group B, however. Whereas both groups may grow less motivated over time, it is likely that Group A, whose members were more depressed to begin with, will lose motivation more completely and more quickly than Group B. Inequivalent groups thus grow less equivalent over time as a result of the interaction between differential selection and maturation.

Relations Between Experimental and Control Groups

The tenth threat to internal validity is the relations between the experimental and control groups. This final group of threats to internal validity has to do with the effects of the use of experimental and control groups that receive different interventions. These effects include: (1) diffusion of treatments, (2) compensatory equalization, (3) compensatory rivalry, and (4) demoralization.

Diffusion of Treatments

Diffusion, or imitation, of treatments, may occur when the experimental and control groups talk to each other about the study. Suppose a study is designed that presents a new relaxation exercise to the experimental group and nothing at all to the control group. There is always the possibility that one of the participants in the experimental group will explain the exercise to a friend who happens to be in the control group. The friend explains it to another friend, and so on. This might be beneficial for the control group, but it invalidates the study's findings.

Compensatory Equalization

Compensatory equalization of treatment occurs when the person doing the study and/or the staff member administering the intervention to the experimental group feels sorry for people in the control group who are not receiving it and attempts to compensate them. A social worker might take a control group member aside and covertly demonstrate the relaxation exercise, for example. On the other hand, if our study has been ethically designed, there should be no need for guilt on the part of the social worker because some people are not being taught to relax. They can be taught to relax when our study is "officially" over.

Compensatory Rivalry

Compensatory rivalry is an effect that occurs when the control group becomes motivated to compete with the experimental group. For example, a control group in a program to encourage parental involvement in school activities might get wind that something is up and make a determined effort to participate too, on the basis that "anything they can do, we can do better." There is no direct communication between groups, as in the diffusion of treatment effect—only rumors and suggestions of rumors. However, rumors are often enough to threaten the internal validity of a study.

Demoralization

In direct contrast with compensatory rivalry, demoralization refers to feelings of deprivation among the control group that may cause them to give up and drop out of the study, in which case this effect would be referred to as mortality. The people in the control group may also get angry.

THREATS TO EXTERNAL VALIDITY

External validity is the degree to which the results of our research study are generalizable to a larger population or to settings outside the research situation or setting. There are six threats to external validity: (1) pretest-treatment interaction, (2) selection-treatment interaction, (3) specificity of variables, (4) reactive effects, (5) multiple-treatment interference, and (6) researcher bias. Box 9.1 presents an interesting discussion on how research studies that lack external validity can still be useful.

Pretest-Treatment Interaction

The first threat to external validity, pretest-treatment interaction, is similar to the testing threat to internal validity. The nature of a pretest can alter the way research participants respond to the experimental treatment, as well as to the posttest. Suppose, for example, that an educational program on racial tolerance is being evaluated. A pretest that measures the level of tolerance could well alert the participants to the fact that they are going to be educated into loving all their neighbors, but many people do not want to be "educated" into anything. They are satisfied with the way they feel and will resist the instruction. This will affect the level of racial tolerance registered on the posttest.

Selection-Treatment Interaction

The second threat to external validity is selection-treatment interaction. This threat commonly occurs when a research design cannot provide for random selection of participants from a population. Suppose we wanted to study the effectiveness of a family service agency staff, for example. If our research proposal was turned down by 50 agencies before it was accepted by the 51st, it is very likely that the accepting agency differs in certain important aspects from the other 50. It may accept the proposal because its social workers are more highly motivated, more secure, more satisfied with their jobs, or more interested in the practical application of the study than the average agency staff member.

Box 9.1

IS RESEARCH THAT LACKS EXTERNAL VALIDITY INVALID?

Mook (1983) argues that psychologists have overestimated the importance of external validity for experiments. Experiments most often are designed to test deductions made from theories, rather than to find results that generalize to the real world. Psychologists generalize from the theory, rather than from the experiment.

Mook argues that experiments apply only indirectly to the real world, through their contributions to theory development. Experimental psychologists "are not *making* generalizations, but *testing* them" (p. 380). They ask, "Under these specified conditions, are theoretical predictions accurate?"

Tightly controlled experiments offer "pure" investigations of a theory's limits. A valid theory should hold true for any population, so the exact population sampled is not necessarily important. If diffusion of responsibility leads to bystander apathy, this should be true for college sophomores in an introductory psychology course, nuns in a convent, and pedestrians on a street corner If the theory is not confirmed, it is amended to account for what has been found.

Carefully controlled conditions may have no analogue in the real world. The real world doesn't have cloth and wire monkey mothers, tachistoscopes that flash stimuli to the left visual field, or electrodes that measure brain waves; but psychologists have used these devices to develop important theoretical understandings of attachment, brain localization, and information processing. Psychologists conducting research in "artificial" laboratory settings are interested in uncovering what "can" happen.

Biofeedback technology and associated biofeedback therapies would never exist had psychologists restricted their research settings to what happens naturally in the real world. Moving into the laboratory, psychologists could ask previously unthought-of questions, such as "Can people control brain waves?"

Mook does not discount the importance of external validity for some studies. Research conducted to create generalizable results clearly requires external validity. For example, survey research conducted to predict the outcome of an upcoming election is designed to have direct, real-world application.

Representative samples are essential to avoid biased results, and the survey must contain questions that validly reveal citizens' actual behavior in the voting booth. Mook argues that the real test of a theory is its eventual usefulness, but experiments designed to examine a theory should not he judged on the direct external validity of their findings.

Source: Allen (1995)

As a result, we would be assessing the research participants on the very factors for which they were unwittingly (and by default) selected—motivation, job satisfaction, and so on. The study may be internally valid, but, since it will not be possible to generalize the results to other family service agencies, it would have little external validity.

Specificity of Variables

Specificity of variables has to do with the fact that a research project conducted with a specific group of people at a specific time and in a specific setting may not always be generalizable to other people at a different time and in a different setting. For example, a measuring instrument developed to measure the IQ levels of upper-socioeconomic level, Caucasian, suburban children does not provide an equally accurate measure of IQ when it is applied to lower-socioeconomic level children of racial minorities in the inner city.

Reactive Effects

The fourth threat to external validity is reactive effects which, as with internal validity, occur when the attitudes or behaviors of our research participants are affected to some degree by the very act of taking a pretest. Thus, they are no longer exactly equivalent to the population from which they were randomly selected, and it may not be possible to generalize our study's results to that population. Because pretests affect research participants to some degree, our results may be valid only for those who were pretested.

Multiple-Treatment Interference

The fifth threat to external validity, multiple-treatment interference, occurs if a research participant is given two or more interventions in succession, so that the results of the first intervention may affect the results of the second one. A client attending treatment sessions, for example, may not seem to benefit from one therapeutic technique, so another is tried. In fact, however, the client may have benefitted from the first technique but the benefit does not become apparent until the second technique has been tried. As a result, the effects of both techniques become commingled, or the results may be erroneously ascribed to the second technique alone.

Because of this threat, interventions should be given separately if possible. If our research design does not allow this, sufficient time should be allowed to elapse between the two interventions in an effort to minimize the possibility of multiple-treatment interference.

Researcher Bias

The final threat to external validity is researcher bias. Researchers, like people in general, tend to see what they want to see or expect to see. Unconsciously and without any thought of deceit, they may manipulate a study so that the actual results agree with the anticipated results. A practitioner may favor an intervention so strongly that the research study is structured to support it, or the results are interpreted favorably.

If we know which individuals are in the experimental group and which are in the control group, this knowledge alone might affect the study's results. Students who an instructor believes to be bright, for example, often are given higher grades than their performance warrants, while students believed to be dull are given lower grades. The way to control for such researcher bias is to perform a double-blind experiment in which neither the research participants nor the researcher knows who is in the experimental or control group or who is receiving a specific treatment intervention.

SUMMING UP AND LOOKING AHEAD

An explanatory group- or case-level research study is said to be internally valid if any changes in the dependent variable, *Y*, result *only* from the introduction of an independent variable(s), *X*. In order to demonstrate this we must control for the factors that threaten the design's internal and external (see Box 9.1) validities. Now that we know all about research designs, we will turn our attention to the various ways we can collect data to answer our research question or to test our hypothesis.

REVIEW QUESTIONS

1 Discuss why very few social work research studies ever come close to "ideal" research designs. What are some of the reasons why it would be unethical to do "ideal" design with clients?

2 Discuss in detail each one of the six characteristics that are necessary to approach an "ideal" research design in social work research. Provide a social work example in your discussion.

3 Construct an "ideal" research design with the general problem area of child sexual abuse.

4 Construct an "ideal" explanatory group-level research design with the research problem of suicide. What ethical problems did you run into?

5 Construct an "ideal" explanatory case-level research design with the research problem of abortion. What

ethical problems did you run into?

6 In your own words, discuss why it is important for you to know the six characteristics of an "ideal" research design when you design any given research study.

7 Why is it necessary to use at least one control group (or comparison group) when trying to construct an "ideal" research design?

8 Write an explanatory group-level research hypothesis in which Variable A (some variable of your choice) is the independent variable and Variable B (some variable of your choice) is the dependent variable. Now rewrite the same hypothesis with the two variables reversed. Which hypothesis do you think is correct? Why? How would you go about testing the two hypotheses? Include in your discussion how you would address all six of the char-

acteristics of an "ideal" research design.

9   Discuss in detail the similarities and differences between the concepts of internal and external validity. Provide a social work example throughout your discussion.

10 List and discuss the threats to internal validity by using a common social work example of your choice.

11 List and discuss the threats to external validity by using a common social work example of your choice.

12 Construct an "ideal" social work research design that controls for all the threats to internal and external validity. You may select any topic that you desire.

13 List other factors that you feel could be added as additional threats to *internal validity* besides the ones presented in this chapter. Provide a rationale for your response.

14 List other factors that you feel could be added as additional threats to *external validity* besides the ones presented in this chapter. Provide a rationale for your response.

15 List all the exploratory (Chapter 6), descriptive (chapter 7), and explanatory (Chapter 8) group research designs and indicate the threats to internal and external validity that each design controls for. Provide a rationale for each one of your responses. Provide a social work example to illustrate each one of your points.

16 Design a perfect group-level research study, at the explanatory level, that takes into account all the threats to internal and external validity. What ethical issues do you see if your study were in fact implemented?

17 Out of all the explanatory case-level designs presented in Chapter 8, which one do you think is used most often in social work research? Why? Justify your answer. Which one do you think is least utilized? Why? Justify your answer.

18 At your university library, find a published social work research article that controlled for as many threats to internal and external validity as possible. Go through the article and determine which internal and external validity factors the study controlled for, and which factors it did not control for. Hypothetically redesign the study in such a way that you could control for the factors that the original study did not. After doing this, would your hypothetical redesigned study have been feasible? Discuss in detail.

19 At your university library, find a social work article that reports on a research study that used an *exploratory* research design. How could have this study been done using a "higher level" group research design?

20 At your university library, find a social work article that reports on a research study that used a *descriptive* research design. How could have this study been done using a "higher level" group research design?

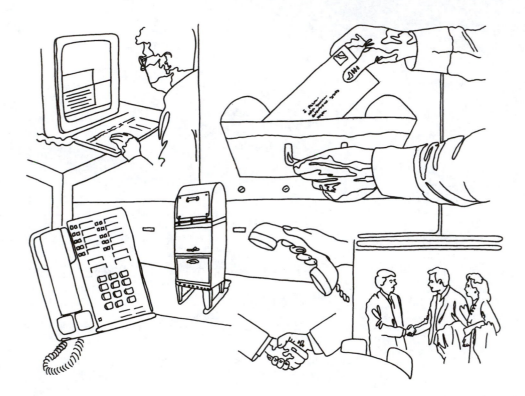

C h a p t e r   10

Collecting Data

DATA COLLECTION is the heartbeat of any research study—quantitative or qualitative. Our goal is to collect data—quantitative or qualitative—with a steady rhythm and in a systematic manner. When our data collection becomes erratic or stops prematurely, our study is in grave danger. With the above in mind, this chapter will discuss a variety of data collection methods that can produce data for our quantitative or qualitative research study.

DATA COLLECTION METHODS VERSUS DATA SOURCES

There is a critical distinction between a data collection method and a data source. This distinction must be clearly understood before we collect any data whatsoever. A *data collection method* consists of a detailed plan of procedures that aims to gather data for a specific purpose; that is, to answer a research question or to test a research hypothesis.

Any data collection method can tap into a variety of *data sources*. The primary source of data in most social work research studies is people.

Rarely do we use machines (e.g., biofeedback) to monitor change in people's attitudes, knowledge, or behaviors. Rather, we tend to collect data about people from the people themselves. Data collected directly from people can be first- or second-hand data. First-hand data are obtained from people who are closest to the problem we are studying. Single mothers participating in a parent support group, for example, can easily provide first-hand data to describe their own stresses as single mothers.

Second-hand data may come from other people who are indirectly connected to the primary problem (i.e., stress of single mothers) we are studying. A parent support group facilitator, for example, can record second-hand observations of "stress" behaviors displayed by parents in the parent support group. The facilitator can also collect data from family members. Grandparents, for example, can provide data that reflect their perceptions of how "stressed out" their daughters may be.

Regardless of the data collection method or the data source, *all* data are eventually collected, analyzed, and interpreted as part of the research process. We will discuss, shortly, the basic data collection methods that commonly produce quantitative data and those that commonly produce qualitative data.

TYPES OF DATA

What exactly are data? They are recorded units of information that are used as the basis for reasoning, calculation, and discussion (a single unit of information is called a *datum*). We can collect *original data* and/or *existing data*. The distinction between the two is a simple one. We collect original data (for the first time) during the course of our study to fulfill a specific purpose; that is, to answer our research question or test our research hypothesis. Unlike original data, we can use existing data that have been previously collected and stored, either manually or in a computer, before our study was even fully conceptualized.

We can also distinguish between types of data by the research approach used. In a quantitative study, for example, we analyze *numerical data* using mathematical computations and calculations. On the other hand, a qualitative study typically analyzes words or *text data*. We analyze text data by reading and rereading; our task is to look for common and differentiating characteristics and themes within the words. A single research study can easily incorporate both quantitative and qualitative types of data. In fact, quantitative and qualitative data collection methods can produce complimentary data.

QUANTITATIVE DATA

Quantitative data are used in research studies that utilize the quantitative research approach. Chapter 5 discussed how the approach aims to reduce research topics into concepts and clearly defined variables. One of the major steps in a quantitative study is "Focusing the Question," which requires that we develop operational definitions for all the variables in our study. Let us revisit our two-variable research question that was introduced in Chapter 3:

> *Research Question:*
> Do clients who come from an ethnic minority (independent variable) have difficulty in accessing social services (dependent variable)?

A quantitative research study requires that we operationally define "ethnicity"and "difficulty in accessing social services" in such a way that we can measure each variable. Recall that, in Chapter 3, we operationalized both of our study's variables using two categories each.

What is your ethnicity *(check one category below)*?
- Ethnic Minority
- Non–Ethnic Minority

Did you have difficulty in accessing any form of social services over the last 12-month period *(Check one category below)*?
- Yes
- No

In Chapter 5, however, we learned that our two variables (i.e., ethnicity and difficulty in accessing social services) can be operationally defined in a variety of ways. Let us consider the above two-variable research question for the various data collection methods that are most often associated with producing quantitative data: (1) survey questionnaires, (2) structured observation, (3) secondary data, and (4) existing statistics.

Survey Questionnaires

Survey research, or surveys, in itself is a method for researching social problems. Figure 10.1 illustrates the steps and tasks we would take in the survey research process. The aim of a survey is to collect data from a population, or a sample of research participants, in order to describe them as a group. One form that a survey can take is a questionnaire, which is a carefully selected set of questions that relate to our research question.

When data are collected using survey questionnaires, we get our research participants' perceptions about the variable being measured. Think about a survey questionnaire that you have filled out recently—a marketing survey, a consumer satisfaction questionnaire, or a teaching evaluation of your instructor. Your answers reflected your perceptions and were probably different from the perceptions of others who answered the same survey.

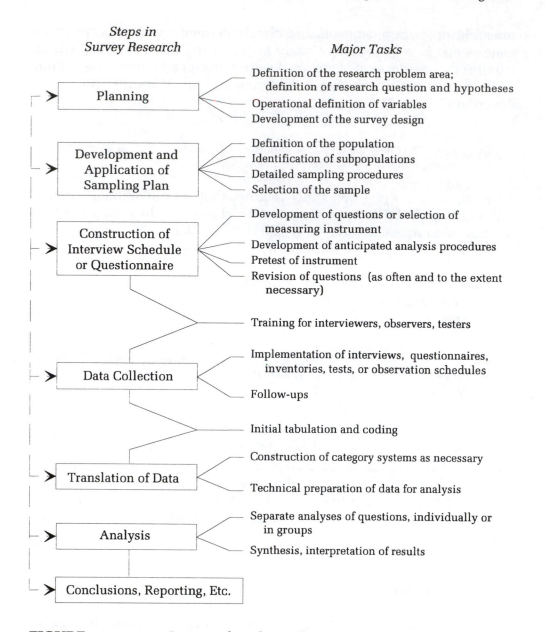

FIGURE 10.1 Steps and Tasks in the Survey Research Process

A survey questionnaire is one data collection method that we can use to collect data in order to answer our two-variable research question above. It would have to include items that measure our two variables—ethnicity and difficulty in accessing social services. We would ask clients within our study to "self-report" what they perceive their ethnicity to be and whether they have experienced difficulty in accessing social services over the last 12-month period.

There are two basic types of survey questionnaires. Nonstandardized survey questionnaires are one type. Our two questions posed above are a very basic example of a nonstandardized survey questionnaire. The two-question survey is nonstandardized because the items have not been tested for reliability or validity. We have no way of knowing whether our research participants will respond to our two questions in a uniform way. At best, we can comment on our survey questionnaire's face validity; that is, do its items "look" like they are measuring the variables we are interested in? Nonstandardized questionnaires are often developed when standardized questionnaires are not available or suited to our specific research question.

Standardized survey questionnaires are scientifically constructed to measure one specific variable. Let us say we have searched the library and computer data bases for a standardized survey questionnaire that measures our dependent variable, difficulty in accessing social services. Suppose the closest standardized questionnaire we find is *Reid-Gundlach Social Service Satisfaction Scale (R-GSSSS)*, which contains 34-items and measures clients' satisfaction with social services they have received (see Figure 4.2). Clients would read each item and rate how much they agree with each item. A five-point category partition scale is used: 1 strongly agree, 2 agree, 3 undecided, 4 disagree, and 5 strongly disagree.

The *R-GSSSS* specifically measures "satisfaction with social services," a concept that closely relates to our dependent variable but is not an exact measure of it. In other words, satisfaction with social services is not the same as difficulty in accessing social services but it could be used as a "proxy measure" to answer our research question. As a proxy measure, we would make the leap to say that clients who are most dissatisfied with the social services are the same clients that will have the most difficulty in accessing new social services.

How we proceed in collecting data survey questionnaire data varies depending upon whether we collect them via the mail, telephone interviews, or face-to-face interviews. When a questionnaire is sent through the mail, our research participants must also be provided with sufficient instructions to "self-administer" the questionnaire. This means that they must have all the necessary instructions to successfully complete the survey questionnaire alone. When telephone or face-to-face interviews are used, the interviewer is available to assist the research participant with any difficulties in completing the questionnaire. Regardless of how our questionnaires are administered, there are some basic procedures that we can use to increase the likelihood of their obtaining accurate and complete data.

Establishing Procedures for Data Collection

There are four basic procedures that must be considered before any survey questionnaire is administered to potential research participants. First, it is essential that straightforward and simple instructions accompany the questionnaire. Our objective is to have each research participant complete the questionnaire in exactly the same way, which means they must have the same understanding of each question. Suppose for a moment, that we ask one of our two questions posed earlier—Did you have difficulty in accessing any form of social services over the last 12-month period? It is clear that we want our research participants to answer our question with respect to the past 12 months and not any other time frame.

A second procedure that must be established is how informed consent will be obtained from the research participants. This is a task that can be accomplished by writing a cover letter explaining the purpose of the research study and questionnaire, who the researchers are, that participation is entirely voluntary, how data will be used, and the steps taken to guarantee confidentiality. A cover letter is usually sent out with mailed questionnaires, read aloud over the telephone, and presented in face-to-face interviews.

To decrease the likelihood of any misunderstanding, elementary language should be used in the cover letter (the same as in the questionnaire). It may even be possible to have the cover letter (and questionnaire) translated into our research participants' native language(s). In our study, we are asking about ethnicity, which suggests that English could be a second language for many of our research participants. Depending on the geographic area in which we are conducting our study, we may wish to translate our cover letter and questionnaire into the dominant language of the geographic area.

If our survey questionnaire is to be administered over the telephone or face-to-face by an interviewer, training of an interviewer will be a necessary third procedure. In the same way that we want research participants to have the same understanding of the questionnaire's items, we want interviewers to handle potential queries in a consistent manner. Interviewers must be trained to ask questions within our questionnaire in such a way that they do not influence research participants' answers. Basically, interviewers should refrain from discussing individual questions with research participants, from varying their tone of voice when asking questions, and from commenting on research participants' answers. The interviewer's task is to keep the research participant focused on answering the questions at hand, to answer questions for clarification, and to record the answers.

To save on time and resources, it may be possible to administer survey questionnaires in a group format. This usually means that we meet a group of research participants in their own environment. Suppose, for example, we were specifically interested in the accessibility of social services among Native people. We would need to travel to the reserve and administer our questionnaire at a central location on the reserve that would be convenient to our research participants.

Recording Data

The data we gather from questionnaires usually are in numerical form. Our question that asks whether clients had difficulty accessing any form of social services over the last 12 months will produce a number of "yes" responses and a number of "no" responses. We can add up the total sum of responses for each category and calculate the number of clients who had difficulty accessing social services broken down by ethnicity (i.e., ethnic minority and non–ethnic minority).

Neither of our questions directly translates into numerical terms. To get numerical data, we simply assign numerical codes to each category of a variable. We could code "no" responses as "1" and "yes" responses as "2," for our dependent variable (i.e., difficulty in accessing social services). For our independent variable (i.e., ethnicity), we could use similar codes—non–ethnic minority equals "1" and ethnic minority equals "2."

Reliability and Validity

Reliability and validity are critical to determining the credibility of any data collection instrument. Standardized questionnaires have associated with them values of both. Reliability values tell us how confident we can be in using our questionnaire over two or more time periods, across different people, and across different places. Validity values give us information about how good our questionnaire is at measuring what it purports to measure. The validity value for the *R-GSSSS*, for example, is reasonably high at .95 (the highest possible value is 1.0). Reports on the *R-GSSSS* also note that the standardized questionnaire is useful for measuring differences in race. Specifically, blacks and Mexican Americans are reported to predictably have lower scores. We can also assess the face validity of the *R-GSSSS* by simply looking at the 34 items contained within it (see Figure 4.2). A quick glance tells us that the items reflect the "idea" of client satisfaction with social services.

When using unstandardized questionnaires, we do not have the luxury of reporting reliability or validity. In this instance, we must ensure that our questionnaire, at the very least, has face validity.

Advantages and Disadvantages

Figure 10.2 displays the advantages and disadvantages of survey questionnaires when they are administered through the mail, telephone interviews, or face-to-face interviews.

Overall, the major advantage of survey questionnaires is that they offer a relatively inexpensive way to collect new data. In addition, they can: easily reach a large number of people; provide specific data; collect data

Technique	Advantages	Disadvantages
Face-to-face Interview	◦ Highest response rate ◦ Subjects tend to provide more thoughtful answers ◦ Allows for longer, more open-ended responses ◦ Allows recording of nonverbal information ◦ Can reach disabled or illiterate respondents ◦ Interviewer can clarify questions for respondent ◦ Subjects more willing to answer sensitive questions	◦ Highest cost ◦ Highest chance for introduction of experimenter bias ◦ Respondent may react to personality of interviewer rather than content of the interview ◦ Interviewer may mis-record response
Mail Survey	◦ Lowest cost ◦ Subjects can read and respond to questions at their own pace ◦ Visual arrangement of items on written instrument can facilitate comprehension ◦ Provides greatest sense of anonymity/ confidentiality ◦ Lowest chance of introduction of experimenter bias	◦ Lowest response rate ◦ Feasible only with subjects having relatively good reading skills ◦ No opportunity to clarify confusing items ◦ Difficult to get in-depth or open-ended responses ◦ Cannot ensure that intended respondents are the actual respondents
Telephone Survey	◦ Relatively low cost ◦ Can be completed quickly ◦ Interviewer can clarify questions for respondent ◦ Can reach respondents with poor reading/writing skills ◦ Allows direct computer data entry	◦ Not useful for low-income respondents who do not have a telephone ◦ High initial vocal interaction, misses nonverbal responses ◦ Requires simple questions, unless a copy of the survey instrument is mailed in advance

FIGURE 10.2   Advantages and Disadvantages to Three Principal Approaches to Data Collection in Survey Research

efficiently; and be input into a computer easily. An additional advantage of standardized questionnaires is that the data they generate can be compared with the data collected in other studies that used the same standardized questionnaire.

The overall disadvantages of survey questionnaires include: research participants must be literate, surveys usually get a low response rate, the research participants must have a mailing address or telephone to be reached, in-depth or open-end responses are missed, and simple questions are utilized to provide answers to complex research questions.

Structured Observation

The term "structured observation" describes itself as a data collection method. A trained observer records the interaction of others in a specific place over an agreed upon amount of time using specific procedures and measurements (Coleman, Collins, & Polster, 1997). Structured observation aims to observe the natural interactions between and among people that occur either in natural or in artificial settings. If we want to observe how people of different ethnic backgrounds interact with their social worker, for example, we could set up structured observations at the social worker's offices (natural environment), or we could artificially set up interviews behind one-way mirrors (artificial setting).

The data collected in structured observation reflect the trained observers' perceptions of the interactions. That is, the observers do not interact with the people they are observing. They simply watch the interactions and record the presence or absence of certain behaviors. Observers could, for example, count the number of times clients (comparing ethnic minority and non–ethnic minority groups) mention a barrier or obstacle to accessing a social service, or monitor whether or not social workers engage in behaviors that specifically assist clients in accessing new services. These observations, of course, would take place during "normal" meetings between social workers and their clients.

Structured observation requires that the variables being measured are specifically defined. We must "micro-define" our variables. In our two-variable research question, for example, we have already operationally defined "ethnicity" as having two categories: ethnic minority and non–ethnic minority. In measuring our dependent variable, "difficulty in accessing social services," we could operationalize it by the number of social services referred by a social worker in a 60-minute interview. We could then compare our measure on our dependent variable across our two ethnicity groups (the independent variable). Would we find that social workers are more or less likely to offer social service referrals to clients who are from an ethnic minority or a non–ethnic minority group?

There are three general types of recording that can be used with structured observation. Observations can be measured for frequency (e.g., count a behavior every time it occurs), for duration (e.g., how long does the behavior last each time it occurs), and for magnitude (e.g., the varying intensity of a behavior such as mild, moderate, or severe). Whether we use frequency, duration, or magnitude (or some combination), depends on the picture we want to develop to answer our research question. Do we want to describe difficulty in accessing social services by how many times services are offered to clients (frequency), by how much time social workers spend explaining how services can be accessed (duration), or by the degree of sincerity that the workers display when offering service referrals (magnitude)?

When we record the presence or absence of behaviors during an interaction between and among people, our observations can be structured in such a way as to help the observers record the behaviors accurately. Suppose for a moment, social worker interviews with clients take an average of one hour. We could set recording intervals every minute so that we have 60 recording intervals in one hour. The observers would sit with a stop-watch and record whether or not the social workers offered any social services to their clients, in the first minute, the second minute, and each minute thereafter until the interviews end. Interval recording assists the observers in making continuous observations throughout the interaction.

Spot-check recording is another way to schedule observation recordings. Unlike interval recording, which is continuous, spot-check recording is a way to record intermittent observations. It may be possible to observe and record the presence or absence of a behavior for one minute every five minutes, for example.

Establishing Procedures for Data Collection

The procedures established for structured observation are firmly decided upon before actual observations take place. That is, the observers are specifically trained to watch for the presence or absence of specific behaviors and the recording method is set. The types of data to be recorded are selected (i.e., frequency, duration, or magnitude) and the nature of the recording is decided (i.e., continuous, interval, or spot-check).

Data generally are recorded by observers and not the persons engaging in the behaviors. As such, it is essential that observers be trained to "see" behaviors in a reliable way. Imagine that you are one of the observers and your main task is to record magnitude ratings of the degree of sincerity that social workers display when they offer service referrals. You must decide if the social workers' gestures are mildly, moderately, or extremely sincere. How would you know to rate a behavior that you observed as "mildly sincere" versus "moderately sincere?"

Training of observers requires that all variables be unequivocally clear. Thus, observers are usually trained using "mock" trials. They are selected for their ability to collect data according to the "rules of the research study," not for their unique views or creative observations. In a nutshell, the observers are an instrument for data collection and an effort is made to calibrate all instruments of the research in the same way. To allow for several different observers to view the same situation, we may choose to videotape interactions.

A decision must also be made about who will be the best observers. Should only professionally trained outside observers be selected? This would include people who are completely unfamiliar with the context of the research but are skilled observers. How about indigenous observers—people who are familiar with the nature of the interaction to be observed? In our example, indigenous observers could include people such as other social workers, social work supervisors, other clients, or staff from other social service offices. Who we choose to observe may depend upon availability, expense, or how important we feel it is for the observers to be familiar or unfamiliar with the situation being observed. Measurement that reflects cultural variables, for example, may require indigenous observers.

Recording Data

The recording instrument for structured observation generally takes the form of a grid or checklist. The behaviors being observed and the method of recording are identified. The simplest recording form to construct is one that records frequency. The recording form would simply identify the period of observation and the number of times a specific behavior occurs:

Observation Period	Frequency
3:00 P.M. to 4:00 P.M.	✓✓✓✓✓

For duration recording it is necessary to add the duration in minutes at each occurrence of the behavior.

Observation Period	Frequency and Duration (in minutes)
3:00 P.M. to 4:00 P.M.	1(5); 2(11); 3(15)

For magnitude recording, we record the time of occurrence and give a corresponding rating for the behavior. To simplify recording, the magnitude ratings are generally coded by assigning a number to each category. For example, "1" is mildly sincere, "2" is moderately sincere, and "3" is extremely sincere.

Observation Time	Magnitude
3:17 P.M.	1
3:25 P.M.	1
3:29 P.M.	2

Reliability and Validity

As we know from Chapter 4, validity refers to whether we are measuring what we think we are measuring. In other words, are we really measuring or observing "difficulty in accessing social services?" Validity, in this instance, should make us think about whether our criteria for observation (i.e., how we operationalized our variable) are reasonable representations of the variable.

Reliability, on the other hand, can be assessed in more concrete ways. Once we have established an operational definition for each variable and the procedures for observation and recording, we can test their reliability. A simple method for determining reliability is to use two independent raters who observe the exact same situation. How well do their recordings match? Do the two observers produce the same frequencies? The same duration periods? The same magnitude ratings? Do they agree 100 percent or only 50 percent? One hundred percent agreement suggests that the measure is a reliable one, compared to 50 percent, which suggests we should go back to the drawing board to come up with more precise operational definitions for both variables or more exact recording procedures.

Advantages and Disadvantages

Structured observation helps us to collect precise, valid, and reliable data within complex interactions. We are able to tease out important behaviors that are direct (or indirect) measures of the variable we are interested in. The data produced are objective observations of behaviors and thus are not tainted by our individual self-perceptions. Think back to the survey questionnaire method of data collection that we discussed at the beginning of this chapter. The data collected using a survey questionnaire reflect research participants' own perceptions. Structured observation, on the other hand, gives a factual account of what actually took place. It can explain one component of a social interaction with objectivity, precision, and detail.

The major disadvantage of structured observation is the time and resources needed to train skilled observers. Think about the amount of time it would take, for example, to get you and, say, two other observers to agree on what constitutes "mild," "moderate," or "extremely" sincere behavior of social workers. Another disadvantage of structured observation is that it is a microscopic approach to dealing with complex social interactions. By focusing on one or two specific details (variables) of an interaction, we may miss out on many other important aspects of the interactions.

Secondary Data

When existing data are used to answer a newly developed research question (or to test a hypothesis), the data are considered secondary. In other words, the data are being used for some purpose other than the original one for which they were collected. Unlike survey questionnaires or structured observation mentioned previously, collecting secondary data is unobtrusive. Since data already exist, it is not necessary to ask people questions (as in survey questionnaires) or to be observed (as in structured observations). Furthermore, secondary data can exist in numerical form (quantitative) or text form (qualitative). Our discussion in this section focuses on existing quantitative data. We will discuss secondary text, or content, data later on in this chapter.

Let us go back to our two-variable research question that asks about the relationship between clients' ethnicity and whether they have difficulty in accessing social services. So far, we have discussed data collection methods within a social service context and have focused on the interaction between social workers and their clients. Within a social service agency there are many client records that could provide meaningful data to answer our simple research question. It is likely, for example, that client intake forms collect data about clients' ethnicity.

We can be assured that an "ethnicity" question on an existing client intake form was not "thought up" to answer our specific research question. Rather, the agency likely had other reasons for collecting the data such as needing to report the percentage of clients who come from an ethnic minority they see in a given fiscal period.

The social service agency may also have records that contain data that we could use for our dependent variable—difficulty in accessing social services. Social workers, for example, may be required to record each service referral made for each client. By reading each client file, we would be able to count the number of service referrals made for each client.

Secondary data can also be accessed from existing data bases around the world. Census data bases are a common example. With the advances of computer technology, data bases are becoming easier to access. The Inter-University Consortium for Political and Social Research (ICPSR) is the largest data archive in the world; it holds more than 17,000 files of data from more than 130 countries (Krysik, 1997). We could use the ICPSR data, for example, to compare the accessibility of social services for clients from different ethnic groups across various countries. Of course, we could only do this if meaningful data already exist within the data base to answer our research question.

Establishing Procedures for Data Collection

Given that secondary data already exist, there is no need to collect them. Rather, our focus shifts to evaluating the data set's worth with respect to answering our research question. The presence of data sets have important influences on how we formulate our research questions or test our hypotheses. When original data are collected, we design our research study and tailor our data collection procedures to gather the "best" data possible. When data exist, we can only develop a research question that is as good as the data that we have available.

Since secondary data influence how we formulate our research questions, we must firmly settle on a research question before analyzing them. Data sets can have a vertigo effect, leaving us to feel dizzy about the relationships between and among variables contained within them. It may be that we begin with a general research question, such as our two-variable question about ethnicity and difficulty in accessing social services and move to a more specific hypothesis. Suppose our existing data set had within it data about client ethnicity (e.g., Asians, African Americans, Caucasians, and Native Americans) and data about difficulty in accessing social services (e.g., yes or no). We could return to the literature for studies that might help us formulate a directional (one-tailed) research hypothesis.

A directional hypothesis would suggest that one or more of these four ethnic groups would have more (or less) difficulty accessing social services than the remaining groups. If no such literature exists, however, we would pose a nondirectional (two-tailed) hypothesis, which indicates that we have no basis to suggest that one of the four ethnic groups would have more or less difficulty accessing social services than any of the others.

Another influence of an existing data set is on how we operationally define the variables in our study. Simply put, our study's variables will have already been operationally defined for us. The definition used to collect the original data will be the definition we use in our study as well. It is possible to create a new variable by recasting one or more of the original variables in an existing data set. For instance, suppose we were interested to know whether or not our clients were parents. Existing agency records, however, only list the number of children in each family. We could recast this data by categorizing those clients that have one or more children versus those that have no children, thus creating a two-category variable. Clients with one or more children would be categorized as "parents" versus clients without any children who would be classified as "not parents."

One final consideration for using existing secondary data is that of informed consent. Just because data exist does not mean that we have free rein to use them in future studies. It may be that clients have provided information on intake forms because they believed it was necessary to do so in order to receive services. As we have seen in Chapter 2, when data are originally collected from clients, they must be informed of the present and future uses of the data and give their explicit consent.

Recording Data

Recording secondary data bases are a simple matter because data have already been collected, organized, and checked for accuracy. Our task is to work with them and determine the best possible procedures for data analyses. One feature of existing data bases is that they generally include a large number of cases and variables. Thus, some advanced knowledge of statistical software packages is required to extract the variables of interest and conduct the appropriate data analyses.

Reliability and Validity

Once our research question is formulated and our variables have been operationally defined, it is important to establish the data set's credibility. We must remember that "all data sets are not created equal," particularly with respect to their validity and reliability. Most importantly, we want to check out the data source. If ethnic status is recorded on a social service agency's client intake form, for example, we would want to know how the data were obtained. The data would be considered unreliable and, even invalid, if the workers simply looked at their clients and checked one of several ethnicity categories. A more reliable and valid procedure would be if they asked their clients what ethnic category they come from and, at the same time, showed them the categories to be selected. Data sets that are accompanied by clear data collection procedures are generally more valid and reliable than those data sets that are not.

Advantages and Disadvantages

The advancement of computer technology increases the likelihood that secondary data will be used more often in future social work research studies. It is a reasonably inexpensive way to gather and analyze data to answer a research question or to test a hypothesis. Given the data sets that are developing around the world, researchers can fairly easily compare data sets from different countries and across different time spans. Data sets are at "our fingertips," provided that we have a research question or hypothesis to match.

One major disadvantage of using an existing data set is that our research question is limited by the possibilities of the data set. We must make the best use of the data available to us, with the understanding that the "best" may not be good enough to answer our research question or test our hypothesis.

Existing Statistics

Existing statistics are a special form of secondary data. They *exist* in a variety of places. Box 10.1 provides an example of the many places that Fran, a clinical director of a private agency, accessed to gather existing statistics for her research question. One difference between existing statistics and secondary data is that statistics summarize data in aggregate form. Another unique feature of existing statistics is that they exist only in numerical form. We might have statistics, for example, that report: 20 percent of clients served by social services were Native, 30 percent were Hispanic, and 50 percent were Caucasian.

In the same way that secondary data are used for a purpose other than what was originally stated, so it is for existing statistics. With existing statistics, however, we are one step further removed from the original data. A statistic, for example, can be computed from 3,000 cases or from 30 cases—each produces only a single value.

There are two main types of statistics for us to be concerned with. The first is descriptive statistics, which simply describe the sample or population being studied. Statistics used for descriptive purposes include things like percentages, percentiles, means, standard deviations, medians, ranges, and so on. The second type of statistics, inferential statistics, include test statistics such as chi-square, *t*-test, ANOVA, regression, and correlation. Do not panic; we will give an introductory discussion on statistics in Chapter 12. For now, we need only to know that descriptive statistics tell us about the characteristics of a sample or a population. Inferential statistics tell us about the likelihood of a relationship between and among variables within a population.

When using existing statistics as our "data" we proceed in much the same way as when we use secondary data. Both are unobtrusive methods of data collection in that no persons will be asked to provide data about themselves—the data already exist and have been used to calculate a statistic. Therefore, we must establish their credibility.

Establishing Procedures for Data Collection

Using existing statistics in a research study influences our research question (and hypotheses) to a greater degree than when using secondary data. If existing statistics are to assist in developing a research question, then advanced knowledge of statistics is required. We would need to understand the purpose of each statistic, the assumptions behind it, and how it was calculated.

We would not want to gather existing statistics without also collecting information about how the original data (used to calculate our existing statistics) were collected and analyzed. This information is important to assessing the credibility of the statistics that we would use for our research study.

Box 10.1_____

USING GOVERNMENTAL AND PRIVATE-AGENCY STATISTICS

Fran is clinical director of a private, non-profit agency that provides foster care, group-home care, and residential treatment for children in a small city in Arizona. She has noticed that there is a higher number of ethnic minority children in her agency's caseload than would be expected based on the proportion of ethnic minority children in the general population. She decides to do a study of this issue using existing statistics already gathered by various sources as her data collection method.

Fran first talks with the information specialist at the local library, asking for help to conduct a computer search through the library's existing data bases. The search reveals a series of reports, titled *Characteristics of Children in Substitute and Adoptive Care,* that were sponsored by the American Public Welfare Association and that provide several years of data reported by states on their populations of children in various kinds of foster and adoptive care.

She also locates an annual publication produced by the Children's Defense Fund, and this provides a variety of background data on the well-being of children in the United States. Next, Fran checks in the library's government documents section. She locates recent census data on the distribution of persons under the age of 18 across different ethnic groups in her county.

Fran now quickly turns to state-level resources, where a quick check of government listings in the telephone book reveals two agencies that appear likely to have relevant data. One is the Foster Care Review Board, which is comprised of citizen volunteers who assist juvenile courts by reviewing the progress of children in foster care statewide.

A call to the Board reveals that they produce an annual report that lists a variety of statistics. These include the number of foster children in the state, where they are placed, and how long they have been in care, and descriptive data.

Fran also learns that the Board's annual reports from previous years contain similar data, thus a visit to the Board's office provides her with the historical data needed to identify trends in the statistics she is using. Finally, she discovers that two years earlier the Board produced a special issue of its annual report that was dedicated to the topic of ethnic minority children in foster care, and this issue offers additional statistics not normally recorded in most annual reports.

Another state agency is the Administration for Children, Youth, and Families, a division of the state's social services department. A call to the division connects her with a staff member who informs her that a special review of foster children was conducted by the agency only a few months before. Data from this review confirm her perception that minority children are overrepresented in foster care in the state, and it provides a range of other data that may be helpful in determining the causes of this problem.

From these sources Fran now has the data she needs to paint a detailed picture of minority foster children at the national and state levels. She also has the ability to examine the problem in terms of both point-in-time circumstances and longitudinal trends, and the latter suggest that the problem of overrepresentation has grown worse. There is also evidence to indicate that the problem is more severe in her state than nationally.

Finally, corollary data on related variables, together with the more intensive work done in the special studies by the Foster Care Review Board and the Administration for Children, Youth, and Families, gives Fran a basis for beginning to understand the causes of the problem and the type of research study that must be done to investigate solutions.

_____

Source: Sieppert, McMurtry, and McClelland (1997)

Recording Data

Recording existing statistics is different from recording secondary data. In the case of secondary data, the data are already in a recorded form. When working with existing statistics, it is usually necessary to extract the statistics from their original sources and reconfigure them in a way that permits us to conduct an appropriate data analysis. It may be, for example, that we need to extract percentage figures from a paragraph within a published article, or mean and standard deviation scores from an already existing table in a research report.

Reliability and Validity

Checking the reliability and validity of existing statistics requires advanced knowledge of statistics. There are, however, some basic things to look for. First, we want to be sure that the studies or reports from which we are extracting the statistics use comparable conceptual and operational definitions. If we were to compare statistical results about the accessibility of social services to clients who are from different ethnic groups across two different studies, we want to be certain that both studies had reasonably similar operational definitions for the two variables that we are interested in.

We can also examine previously conducted studies for their own assessment of their validity and reliability. Were sound procedures used to collect the original data? Were the original data analyzed in an appropriate way? What were the limitations of each study? By asking these types of questions about previous studies, we can get clues to the credibility of the statistics that we are about to use in our own study.

Advantages and Disadvantages

The advantages of using existing statistics are many. Given that existing data are used, via the form of statistics, it is a relatively inexpensive approach and is unobtrusive. By using existing statistics, we can push the knowledge envelope of what we already know and ask more complex research questions. The use of existing statistics also provides us with the opportunity to compare the results of several research studies in an empirical way.

One disadvantage of using existing statistics is that we are not provided with data for individual cases. We can only answer research questions and test hypotheses about groups of people. Because data are already presented in a summary (i.e., statistical) form, it is difficult to assess how the data were collected and analyzed. Since the data have been handled by different individuals, there is an increased chance that human error has occurred somewhere along the way.

QUALITATIVE DATA

Any research study requires data, regardless of whether a quantitative or qualitative research approach is used. We have already discussed that quantitative data are represented numerically, while qualitative data are expressed using text. A second key difference between these two types of data is that qualitative data are collected to "build" a story or understanding of a concept or variable, compared to quantitative data, which narrows in on a select few variables. A third difference worth noting is that qualitative data are generally "bulkier" than quantitative data. As we will see, qualitative data can be represented by a single word, a sentence, or even an entire page of text.

The exact point in time when data are collected in the research process is another difference between quantitative and qualitative data. We have stressed that quantitative data collection can only occur once variables have been completely operationally defined—in fact, the reliability and validity of our measurements depend on it. Qualitative data, on the other hand, can be collected during many different steps in the research process (Chapter 1). We may collect data near the beginning of our study to help us focus our research question (Step 2) and identify key variables to be explored later on in the research process. Qualitative data collected in later steps in our study can be used to check out any assumptions we may have and any new ideas that emerge (Chapter 6).

When collecting quantitative data, the rules for data collection are tried and tested *before* collecting any data—procedures can be outlined in a checklist format, where the data collector checks off each procedure as it is completed. For qualitative data, explicit procedures of data collection are not necessarily known before the data collection process starts. Rather, the procedures used are documented *as they happen*. It is only after data collection is complete that a detailed description of the procedure can be articulated.

This is not to say that in qualitative data collection we can "willy nilly" change our minds or that "anything goes." Research is still research, which means that a systematic approach to inquiry is used. The big difference for qualitative research is that the systematic nature of data collection applies to how we record and monitor the data collection process. Any changes in data collection (e.g., change in questions, research participants, or literature review) are based on data already collected. More will be explained about how qualitative data collection procedures are monitored in Chapter 13. For now, let us return to our research question introduced at the beginning of this chapter.

Research Question:
Do clients who come from an ethnic minority have difficulty in accessing social services?

We have already discussed four different methods of collecting quantitative data to answer the above research question. Now we will turn to four data collection methods that are more commonly associated with producing qualitative data: (1) narrative interviewing, (2) participant observation, (3) secondary content data, and (4) historical data.

Narrative Interviewing

Interviewing is a basic skill required for all obtrusive data collection methods. We have seen how interviewing is used to collect quantitative data via survey questionnaires, in which interviewers are trained to ask questions of research participants in a uniform way and interaction between interviewers and their research participants is minimized. Interviewing for qualitative data, on the other hand, has a completely different tone. The aim of narrative interviewing is to have research participants tell stories in their own words. Their stories usually begin when we ask our identified research question. For example, we could begin an interview by saying, "Could you tell me about your experiences as a Native client in terms of accessing social services?" If we wanted to begin with a more general research question, we could simply ask Native clients to tell us about their experiences with accessing social services.

Qualitative interviewers are not bound by strict rules and procedures. Rather, they make every effort to engage research participants in meaningful discussions. In fact, the purpose is to have research participants tell their own stories in their own ways. The direction the interviews take may deviate from the original research problem being investigated depending on what research participants choose to tell interviewers. Data collected in one research interview can be used to develop or revise further research questions in subsequent research interviews.

The narrative interview is commonly used in case study research where numerous interviews are usually conducted to learn more about a "case," which could be defined as a person, a group of people, an event, or an organization. The narrative interview is also a component of other research pursuits, such as feminist research.

Establishing Procedures for Data Collection

Data collection and data analysis are intertwined in a qualitative research study. Thus, the steps we take in collecting data from a narrative interview will evolve with our study. Nevertheless, we must be clear about our starting point and the procedures that we will use to "check and balance" the decisions we make along the way.

One of the aims of a qualitative research approach is to tell a story about a problem without the cobwebs of existing theories, labels, and interpretations. As such, we may choose to limit the amount of literature we review before proceeding with data collection. The amount of literature we review is guided by the qualitative research approach we use. A grounded theory approach, for example, suggests that we review some literature at the beginning of our study in order to help frame our research question. We would then review more literature later on, taking direction from the new data that we collect.

It is necessary for us to decide when and how to approach potential research participants before data collection occurs. Think about our simple research question for a moment—Do clients who come from an ethnic minority have difficulty in accessing social services? Who would we interview first? Would we interview someone receiving multiple social services or someone not receiving any? Is there a particular ethnic group that we would want represented in our early interviews?

Remember that the data we collect in our beginning interviews will directly influence how we proceed in later interviews. It is possible for the professional literature, or our expert knowledge, to point us to a particular starting place. Regardless of where we begin, it is critical for us to document our early steps in the data collection process. The notes we take will be used later on to recall the steps we took, and more importantly, why we took them.

Let us say, for example, that our interest in our research question stems from the fact that many ethnic minority people we know in our personal lives (not our professional lives) have complained about access to social services. We may choose to begin interviewing an individual whom we already know. On the other hand, we may decide after a cursory review of the literature that most of the existing research on our research problem is based on interviews with people who, in fact, are receiving services. We may then choose to begin interviewing clients who are from an ethnic minority and who are not currently receiving any social services but who are named on social service client lists.

We must also establish how the interview will be structured. Interviewing for qualitative data can range from informal casual conversations to more formal guided discussions. An informal interview is unplanned. The interviewer begins, for example, by asking Native clients a general question, such as the one presented earlier—Could you tell me about your experiences in accessing social services? The discussion that would follow would be based on the natural and spontaneous interaction between the interviewer and the research participant. The interviewer has no way of knowing at the outset what direction the interview will take or where it will end.

A guided interview, on the other hand, has more structure. The exact amount of structure varies from one guided interview to another. In any case, the interviewer has an interview schedule, which essentially amounts to an outline of questions and/or concepts, to guide the interview with the research participant. A loosely structured interview schedule may simply identify key concepts or ideas to include in the interview at the appropriate time. In our study, for example, we might want the interviewer to specifically ask each research participant about language barriers and social isolation, if these concepts do not naturally emerge in the interviews. A highly structured interview schedule would list each question to be asked during the interviews. The interviewer would read the question out to the research participants and record their answers.

Recording Data

The most reliable way to record interview data is through the use of audiotape. Videotape is also a possibility but many people are uncomfortable with being filmed. The audiotape is an excellent record of an interview because it gives us research participants' verbatim answers. The tone, pace, and "atmosphere" of the interview can be recalled by simply replaying the tape.

To prepare data for analysis, however, it is necessary to transcribe every word of the interview. As we will see in Chapter 13, the transcription provides text data, which will be read (and reread) and analyzed. Because audio data are transformed into text data, verbatim statements are used. In addition, any pauses, sighs, and gestures are noted in the text. The following is an example of an excerpt of text data based on our question asked earlier.

> **Research Participant Number 6:** Being a Native in social services, huh . . .well, it's not good, eh people don't know . . .they don't see the reserve or the kids playing...even when they see they don't see. The kids you know, they could have some help, especially the older ones (sighs and pauses for a few seconds). My oldest you know, he's 12 and he goes to school in the city. He comes home and doesn't know what to do. He gets into trouble. Then the social services people come with their briefcases and tell you what to do (voice gets softer). They put in stupid programs and the kids don't want to go you know, they just want to play, get into trouble (laughs). . . .

> **Interviewer:** Hmmm. And how would you describe your own experiences with social services?

Because the interviewing approach to data collection is based on the interaction of the interviewer and the research participant, both parts of the discussion are included in the transcript. But data collection and recording do not stop here. The interviewer must also keep notes on the interview to record impressions, thoughts, perspectives, and any data that will shed light on the transcript during analysis. An example of the interviewer's notes from the above excerpt is:

> **September 12 (Research Participant Number 6):** I was feeling somewhat frustrated because the research participant kept talking about his children. I felt compelled to get him to talk about his own experiences but that seemed sooooo much less important to him.

As we will see in Chapter 13, the verbatim transcript and the interviewer's notes are key pieces of data that will be jointly considered when text data are analyzed.

Trustworthiness and Truth Value

Regardless of the type of interview or the data recording strategy that we select, we must have some way to assess the credibility of the data we collect. With quantitative data, we do this by determining the reliability and validity of the data—usually by calculating a numerical value. In contrast, with qualitative data we are less likely to generate numerical values and more likely to document our own personal observations and procedures.

An important question to assess the trustworthiness and truth value of the text data (and our interpretation of it) is whether we understand what our research participants were telling us from their points of view. Two common ways to check the credibility of interview data are triangulation and member checking. These procedures will be discussed in more detail in Chapter 13. Briefly, triangulation involves comparing data from multiple perspectives. It may be that we interview several people (i.e., data sources) on one topic, or even that we compare quantitative and qualitative data for the same variable. Member checking simply involves getting feedback from our research participants about our interpretation of what they said.

Advantages and Disadvantages

The major advantage of narrative interviewing is the richness of data that are generated. Narrative interviewing allows us to remain open to learning new information or new perspectives about old ideas. Because the interviewer is usually the same person who is the researcher, there is a genuine interest expressed in the interviews.

The major disadvantage associated with narrative interviewing is that it is time consuming. Not only does it take time to conduct the interviews, but considerable time also must be allotted for transcribing the text data. Narrative interviews produce reams and reams of text, which make it difficult to conduct an analysis. Researchers can tire easily and are subject to imposing their own biases and perspectives on what the research participants say.

Participant Observation

Participant observation is a way for us to be a part of something and study it at the same time. This method of data collection requires us to establish and maintain ongoing relationships with research participants in the field setting. We not only listen, observe, and record data, but also participate in events and activities as they happen.

Our role in participant observation can be described on a continuum (see Figure 10.3), with one end emphasizing the *participant role* and the other end emphasizing the *observer role*. An "observer-participant" has the dominant role of observation, while the "participant-observer" is predominantly a participant.

Suppose we were to use participant observation as a data collection method for our study. An example of an observer-participant is a researcher who joins a group of people, say Natives living on their reserve, for events related to our research study. We may travel with a community social worker, for example, and participate in community meetings on the reserve to discuss access to social services. An example of a participant-observer could be when a social worker has the dual responsibility of conducting the meeting and observing the interactions of community members. A participant-observer could also be identified within his or her unique community. A Native resident of the reserve, for example, could participate in the meeting as a resident and as an observer.

In any case, participant observation always requires that one person assumes a dual role. For ethical reasons, the role must be made explicit to all persons participating in the research study. Whether the researcher is a social worker or a Native resident of the reserve, he or she must declare his or her dual role before the community meeting gets underway.

Establishing Procedures for Data Collection

Given the dual role of researchers in participant observation, formulating steps for data collection can be tricky. It is essential for the researcher to keep a balance between "participation" and "observation." Suppose our Native resident who is a participant-observer gets so immersed in the issues of the community meeting that she forgets to look around or ask others questions related to the research study. Someone who completely participates will not be very effective in noting important detail with respect to how other people participated in the meeting. On the other hand, if our Native researcher leans too far into her observation role, others might see her as an outsider and express their views differently than if they believed she had a vested interest within the community.

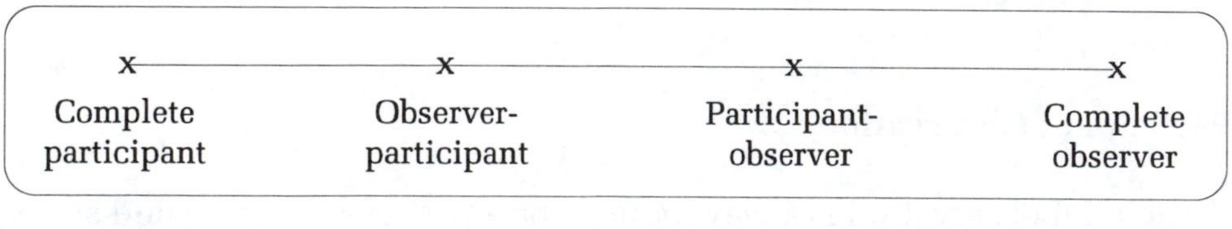

Complete participant	Observer-participant	Participant-observer	Complete observer
x	x	x	x

FIGURE 10.3   Continuum of Participant Observation

An important consideration for a participant observation study is how to gain access to the group of people being studied. Imagine who might be welcomed into a community meeting on a Native reserve and who might be rejected. Chances are that the Native people on a reserve would be more accepting of a Native person, a person known to them, or a person whom they trust, as compared to a non-Native person, a stranger, or a person whom they know but do not trust.

In participant observation we would need to understand the culture of the reserve in order to know who to seek permission from. In participant observation, entry and access is a process "more analogous to peeling away the layers of an onion than it is to opening a door" (Rogers & Bouey, 1997). Forming relationships with people is a critical part of data collection. The more meaningful relationships we can establish, the more meaningful data we will collect. This is not to say, however, that we somehow trade relationship "tokens" for pieces of information. Rather, research participants should feel a partnership with the researcher that is characterized by mutual interest, reciprocity, trust, and cooperation.

One way to better understand participant observation as a data collection method is to compare it with a more common data collection method that we have already discussed—surveys. Figure 10.4 outlines critical differences between survey interviews and participant observation interviews.

Recording Data

The data generated from participant observation come from observing, interviewing, using existing documents and artifacts, and reflecting on personal experiences. The following are a few examples:

Observation (September 12, 9:30 A.M. Meeting Start Time): When the social worker announced the purpose of the meeting was to discuss access to social services for people living on the reserve, there was a lot of agreement from a crowd of 42 people. Some cheered, some nodded their heads, and others made comments like, "it's about time."

Research participant's verbatim comment (September 12, 10:15 A.M.): "Native people don't use social services because they are not offered on the reserve."

Existing document: A report entitled, "The Social Service Needs of a Reserve Community" reports that there have been three failed attempts by state social workers to keep a program up and running on the reserve. Worker turnover is identified as the main contributing factor of program failures.

Researcher's personal note (September 12, 10:44 A.M. Meeting End Time): I feel amazed at the amount of positive energy in the room. I can sense peoples' frustrations (including my own), yet I am in awe of the hopeful and positive outlook everyone has to want to develop something that works for our community. I am proud to be a part of this initiative to improve services in the community.

Survey Interview		*Participant Observation Interview*	
1	It has a clear beginning and conclusion.	1	The beginning and end are not clearly defined. The interview can be picked up later.
2	The same standard questions are asked of all research participants in the same order.	2	The questions and the order in which they are asked are tailored to certain people and situations.
3	The interviewer remains neutral at all times.	3	The interviewer shows interest in responses, encourages elaboration.
4	The interviewer asks questions, and the interviewee answers.	4	It is like a friendly conversational exchange, but with more interview-like questions.
5	It is almost always with a single research participant.	5	It can occur in group setting or with others in area, but varies.
6	Professional tone and businesslike focus. Diversions are ignored.	6	It is interspersed with jokes, asides, stories, diversions, and anecdotes, which are recorded.
7	Closed-ended questions are common, with rare probes.	7	Open-ended questions are common, and probes are frequent.
8	The interviewer alone controls the speed and direction of the interview.	8	The interviewer and insider jointly influence the pace and direction of the interview.
9	The social context in which the interview takes place is not considered and is assumed to make little difference.	9	The social context of the interview is noted and seen as essential for interpreting the meaning of responses.
10	The interviewer attempts to shape the communication pattern into a standard framework.	10	The interviewer adjusts to the insider's norms and language usage, following his or her lead.

FIGURE 10.4   Survey Research Interviews versus
                         Participant Observation Interviews

Overall, participant observers produce "participant observational" data through the use of detailed and rich notes. Several strategies can be used for documenting notes. We can take notes on an ongoing basis, for example, by being careful to observe the time and context for all written entries. A more efficient method, however, would be to carry a dicta-phone, which gives us the flexibility to state a thought, to record a conversation, and to make summary comments about what we observe. Collecting data on an ongoing basis is preferable because it increases the likelihood of producing accurate notes in addition to remembering key events. In some instances, however, participation in a process prevents us from recording any data, which leaves us to record our notes after the event we are participating in has ended.

Trustworthiness and Truth Value

Given that multiple data sources are possible in participant observation, it is possible to check the credibility of the data through triangulation. By reviewing the four data recording examples above, we can be reasonably confident that there is agreement about the state of social services on the reserve. The four separate data entries seem to agree that social services on the reserve are inadequate in terms of the community's needs.

The flexibility of participant observation allows us to seek out opportunities to check out our personal assumptions and ideas. After hearing the general response of Native community members at the beginning of the meeting, for example, we may choose to ask related questions to specific individuals. We can also check our perceptions along the way by sharing our own thoughts, asking people to comment on data summaries, or asking people how well they think two data sources fit together.

Advantages and Disadvantages

A major advantage of participant observation is that we can collect multiple sources of data and check the credibility of the data as we go. Because of the participant role, any observations made are grounded within the context in which they were generated. A complete participant is more likely to pick up subtle messages, for example, than would be a complete observer (as in structured observation).

The disadvantages of participant observation are related to time considerations. As with narrative interviewing, a considerable amount of time must be allotted to data recording and transcription. The researcher also runs the risk of becoming too immersed as a participant or too distant as an observer—two situations that will compromise the data collected.

Secondary Content Data

Secondary content data are existing text data. In the same way that existing quantitative data can be used to answer newly developed research questions, so can existing qualitative (or content) data. In this case, the text data were recorded at some other time and for some other purpose than the research question that we have posed. Let us return to our research question—Do clients who come from an ethnic minority have difficulty in accessing social services?

With the use of content data, we could answer our question using context data that already exist. It may be, for example, that social workers are mandated to record any discussion they had about barriers to accessing social services for their clients on their client files. Case notes, for example, may read "client does not have reliable transportation" or "client has expressed a strong wish for a worker who has the same ethnic background." These types of comments can be counted and categorized according to meaningful themes. In this instance, we are zeroing in on text data for specific examples of recorded behaviors; much like the microscopic approach of structured observation.

We must be aware that content data can be first- or second-hand. In our example, first-hand data would be generated when the social workers document their own behaviors in relation to offering services to their clients. When social workers record their own impressions about how their clients respond to offers of services, second-hand data are produced.

Establishing Procedures for Data Collection

Content data are restricted to what is available. That is, if 68 client files exist, then we have exactly 68 client files to work from. We do not have the luxury of collecting more data. Like secondary quantitative data, we are in a position only to compile the existing data, not to collect new data. It is possible, however, that content data are available from several sources. Client journals may be on file, or perhaps the agency recently conducted an open-ended client satisfaction survey, which has hand-written responses to satisfaction-type questions from clients.

A major consideration of content data is whether or not a sufficient amount exists to adequately answer our research question. If there are not enough data, we do not want to spend precious time reading and analyzing them. We must also remember that we are reading and reviewing text data for a purpose that they were not originally intended for. Suppose, for example, you kept a daily journal of your personal experience in your research course. Would you write down the same thoughts if you knew your journal would be private, compared to if you were to share your writings with your research instructor? The original intent of writing is essential to remember because it provides the context in which the writing occurred.

Because we are examining confidential client case files, we must establish a coding procedure to ensure that our clients' confidentiality and anonymity are maintained. In fact, it is not at all necessary for us, as researchers, to know the names of the client files we are reading. Given our research question, we need only to have access to those portions of clients' files that contain information about client ethnicity and the difficulty clients have in accessing social services.

Recording Data

As we know, content data exist in text form. If they exist in hand-written form, it is necessary to type them out into transcript form. It is useful to make several copies of the transcripts to facilitate data analysis. More will be said about preparing transcripts in Chapter 13.

Trustworthiness and Truth Value

Clearly, first-hand data are more credible than second-hand data when dealing with existing text data. Because the data are secondary, questions of credibility center more around data analysis than data collection. In our example, it may be possible to triangulate data by comparing files of different workers or by comparing different client files with the same worker. It also may be possible to member check (Chapter 13) if workers are available and consent to it.

Advantages and Disadvantages

A major advantage of content data is that they already exist. Thus, time and money are saved in the data collection process. The task of the researcher is simply to compile data that are readily available and accessible.

The disadvantages of content data are that they are limited in scope. The data were recorded for some other purpose and may omit important detail that would be needed to answer our research question.

Historical Data

Historical data are collected in an effort to study the past (Stuart, 1997). Like the participant observation method to data collection, historical data can come from different data sources. Data collection can be obtrusive, as in the case of interviewing people about past or historical events, or unobtrusive, as in the case when existing documents (primarily content data) are compiled. When our purpose is to study history, however, special cases of content data and interviewing are required.

Suppose we recast our research question to ask—Did clients who come from an ethnic minority have difficulty accessing social services from 1947 to 1965? Phrased this way, our question directs us to understand *what has been* rather than *what is*. In order for us to answer our new research question, we would need to dig up remains from the past that could help us to describe the relationship, if any, between ethnicity and difficulty in accessing social services for our specified time period. We would search for documents such as, related reports, memos, letters, transcription, client records, and documentaries, all dating back to the time period. Many libraries store this information in their archives.

We could also interview people (e.g., social workers and clients) who were part of social services between 1947 and 1965. People from the past might include clients, workers, supervisors, volunteers, funders, or ministers. The purpose of our interviews would be to have people remember the past—that is, to describe factual events from their memories. We are less interested in people's opinions about the past than we are about what "really" happened.

When collecting historical data, it is important to sort out first-hand data from second-hand data. First-hand data, of course, are more highly valued because the data are less likely to be distorted or altered. Diaries, autobiographies, letters, home videos, photographs, and organizational minutes are all examples of first-hand data. Second-hand data, on the other hand, include documents like biographies, history books, and published articles.

Establishing Procedures for Data Collection

It is probably more accurate to say that we retrieve historical data than it is to say that we collect it. The data already exist, whether in long-forgotten written documents, dusty videotapes, or in peoples' memories. Our task is to resurface a sufficient amount of data so that we can describe, and sometimes explain, what happened (Stuart, 1997).

One of the first considerations for conducting a historical research study is to be sure that the variable being investigated is one that existed in the past. Suppose, for example, we had a specific interest in the relationship among three variables: client ethnicity, difficulty in accessing social services, and computer technology. More specifically, let us say that we were interested in knowing about the relationship among these three variables, if any, for our specified time period, 1947 to 1965. It would be impossible to determine the relationship among these three variables from a historical perspective since computers were not (or were rarely) used in the social services from 1947 to 1965. Thus, there would be no past to describe or explain—at least not where computers are concerned.

Once we have established that our research question is relevant, we can delineate a list of possible data sources and the types of data that each can produce. The total list of data sources and types must be assessed to determine if, in fact, sufficient data exist to answer our research question. It is possible, however, that data do exist but they are not accessible. Client records, for example, may be secured. Documents may be out of circulation; thus, requiring a researcher to travel to where the data are stored.

Recording Data

Despite the fact that historical data, in many cases, already exist, it is usually necessary to reproduce the data. When interviews are used, interview notes are recorded and the interviews are transcribed as we have discussed in other qualitative data collection methods. When past documents are used, they ought to be duplicated to create "working" copies. Original documents should be protected and preserved so that they can be made available to other interested researchers.

Trustworthiness and Truth Value

Assessing the trustworthiness and truth value of historical data, in many ways, is the process of data analysis. Do different people recall similar facts? Do independent events from the past tell the same story? Much effort goes into triangulating pieces of data. The more corroboration we have among our data, the stronger our resulting conclusions will be.

When reconstructing the past, our conclusions can only be as good as the data we base them on. Are the data authentic? How much of our data are first-hand, compared to second-hand? Do we have sufficient data to describe the entire time period of interest? Perhaps, we might have to cut back a few years. Or, if other data emerge, perhaps we can expand our time period.

Advantages and Disadvantages

Historical data are unique and used for a specific purpose—to describe and explain the past. It is the only way for us to research history. When secondary data are readily available and accessible, the cost is minimized. When interviews are used, they provide us with an opportunity to probe further into the past and our area of interest.

The disadvantages of historical data are that they are not always easily available or accessible. There is also a risk of researcher bias such as when a letter or document is analyzed out of context. The past cannot be reconstructed, for example, if we impose present-day views, standards, and ideas.

SUMMING UP AND LOOKING AHEAD

In this chapter we have described eight different methods for data collection. We have demonstrated that one research question can be answered using any data collection method. Different data collection methods produce different types of data. Data collection methods that are more commonly associated with quantitative or numerical data are: survey questionnaires, structured observation, secondary data, and existing statistics. Data collection methods that are more commonly associated with qualitative or text data are: narrative interviewing, participant observation, historical data, and content data.

In the next chapter, we will look more closely at how data collection fits into the entire research process. We will also discuss several factors that directly influence which data collection method we choose in a research study.

REVIEW QUESTIONS

1 Describe, in your own words, the differences between a data collection method and a data source. Provide an example of each.

2 Describe data. Provide a social work example of data.

3 Describe quantitative data. What exactly are they? Provide an example of quantitative data that would be derived from survey questionnaires, structured observations, secondary data, and existing statistics.

4 Describe qualitative data. What exactly are they? Provide an example of qualitative data that would be derived from narrative interviews, participant observations, secondary content data, and historical data.

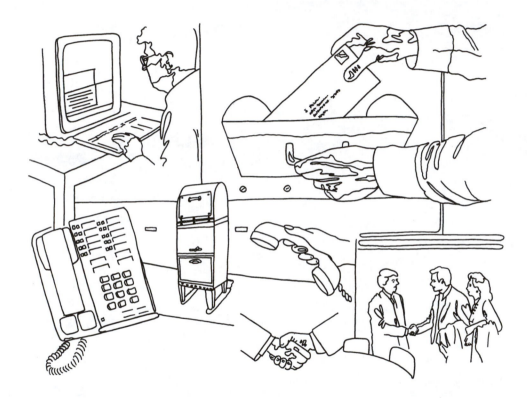

This chapter has been adapted and modified from: Unrau (1997b)

Chapter 11

Selecting a Data Collection Method

IN THE LAST CHAPTER, we discussed eight methods of data collection, which were divided by the type of data that each is most likely to produce—quantitative or qualitative. This chapter examines the data collection process from the vantage point of choosing the most appropriate data collection method and data source for a given research question.

DATA COLLECTION AND THE RESEARCH PROCESS

Data collection is a critical step in the research process because it is the link between theory and practice. Our research study always begins with an idea that is molded by a conceptual framework, which uses preexisting knowledge about our study's problem area. Once our research problem and question have been refined to a researchable level, data are sought from a selected source and gathered using a data collection method. The data collected are then used to support or supplant our original study's conceptions about our research problem under investigation.

The role of data collection in connecting theory and practice is understood when looking at the entire research process. As we have seen in Chapter 1, choosing a data collection method and data source follows the steps of selecting a research topic area, focusing the topic into a research question, and designing the research study. It comes before the steps of analyzing the data and writing the research report. Although data collection is presented in this text as a distinct phase of the research process, it cannot be tackled separately or in isolation.

All steps of the research process must be considered if we hope to come up with the best strategy to gather the most relevant, reliable, and valid data to answer a research question or to test a hypothesis. This section discusses the role of data collection (Step 4) in relation to the other five steps of the research process as outlined in Chapter 1:

- **Steps 1 and 2**—selecting a general research topic and focusing the topic into a research question
- **Steps 3 and 4**—designing the research study and collecting the data
- **Step 5**—analyzing and interpreting the data
- **Step 6**—writing the research report

Steps 1 and 2: Selecting a General Research Topic and Focusing the Topic into a Research Question

Our specific research question identifies the general problem area and the population to be studied. It tells us what we want to collect data about and alerts us to potential data sources. It does not necessarily specify the exact manner in which our data will be gathered, however. Let's return to our research question from Chapter 10:

> Do clients who come from an ethnic minority have difficulty in accessing social services?

Our research question identifies a problem area (difficulty in accessing social services for people who are ethnic minorities) and a population (social service clients). It does not state how the question will be answered.

We have seen in Chapter 10 that our research question, in fact, could be answered using various data collection methods. One factor that affects how our question is answered depends upon how we conceptualize and operationalize the variables within it. As we know, "accessing social services" could be measured in a variety of ways.

Another factor that affects how a research question is answered (or a hypothesis is tested) is the source of data; that is, who or what is providing them. If we want to get first-hand data about the accessibility of social services, for example, we could target the clients as a potential data source. If such first-hand data sources were not a viable option, second-hand data sources could be sought. Social workers, for example, can be asked for their perceptions of how accessible social services are to clients who come from ethnic minorities. In other instances, second-hand data can be gleaned from existing reports (secondary data or content data) written about clients (or client records) that monitor client progress and social worker–client interactions.

By listing all possible data collection methods and data sources that could provide sound data to answer a research question, we develop a fuller understanding of our initial research problem. It also encourages us to think about our research problem from different perspectives, via the data sources. Because social work problems are complex, data collection is strengthened when two or more data sources are used. For example, if social workers and clients were to each report their perceptions of service accessibility in a similar way, then we could be more confident that the data (from both these sources) accurately reflect the research problem.

Steps 3 and 4: Designing the Research Study and Collecting the Data

As we know, the research design flows from the research question, which flows from the problem area. A research design organizes our research question into a framework that sets the parameters and conditions of the study. As mentioned, the research question directs *what* data are collected and *who* data could be collected from. In a quantitative study, the research design refines the *what* question by operationalizing variables and the *who* question by developing a sampling strategy. In a qualitative study, the research design identifies the starting point for data collection and how such procedures will be monitored and recorded along the way. In both research approaches, the research design also dictates (more or less) *when, where,* and *how* data will be collected.

The research design outlines how many data collection points our study will have and specifies the data sources. Each discrete data gathering activity constitutes a data collection point and defines *when* data are to be collected. Thus, using an exploratory one-group, posttest-only design, we will collect data only once from a single group of research participants. On the other hand, if a classical experimental design is used, data will be collected at two separate times with two different groups of research participants—for a total of four discrete data collection points.

Where the data are collected is also important to consider. If our research question is too narrow and begs for a broader issue that encompasses individuals living in various geographic locations, then mailed survey questionnaires would be more feasible than face-to-face interviews. If our research question focuses on a specific population where all research participants live in the same geographic location, however, it may be possible to use direct observations or individual or group interviews.

Because most social work studies are applied, the setting of our study usually involves clients in their natural environments where there is little control over extraneous variables. If we want to measure the clients' perceptions about their difficulty in accessing social services, for example, do we observe clients in agency waiting rooms, observe how they interact with their social workers, or have them complete a survey questionnaire of some kind? In short, we must always consider which method of data collection will lead to the most valid and reliable data to answer a specific research question or to test a specific hypothesis.

The combination of potential data collection methods and potential data sources is another important consideration. A research study can have one data collection source and still use multiple data collection methods. Agency clients (data source 1) in our study, for example, can fill out a standardized questionnaire that measures their perceptions of how accessible social services are (data collection method 1) in addition to participating in face-to-face interviews (data collection method 2).

In the same vein, another study can have multiple data sources and one data collection method. In this case, we can collect data about difficulty in accessing social services through observation recordings by social workers (data source 1), administrators (data source 2), or other citizens (data source 3). The combination of data collection methods should not be too taxing on any research participant or any system, such as the social service agency itself. That is, data collection should not interfere greatly with the day-to-day activities of the persons providing (or responsible for collecting) the data.

In some studies, there is no research design *per se*. Instead we can use existing data to answer our research question. Such is the case when secondary or content data are used. When the data already exist, we put more effort into ensuring that the research question is a good fit with the data at hand. Regardless, of what data collection method is used, once the data are collected, they are subject to data analysis.

Step 5: Analyzing and Interpreting the Data

Collecting data is a resource intensive endeavor that can be expensive and time consuming—both for quantitative and qualitative research studies. The truth of this statement is realized in the data analysis step of our research study. Without a great deal of forethought about what data to collect, data can be thrown out because they cannot be organized or analyzed in any meaningful way. In short, data analyses should always be considered when choosing a data collection method and data source because the analysis phase must summarize, synthesize, and ultimately organize the data in an effort to have as clear-cut an answer as possible to our research question. When too much (or too little) data are collected, we can easily become bogged down (or stalled) by difficult decisions that could have been avoided with a little forethought.

After thinking through our research problem and research question and selecting a viable data collection and data source, it is worthwhile to list out the details of the type of data that will be produced. Specifically, we must think about how the data will be used in our data analysis. This exercise provides a clearer idea of the type of results we can expect.

The dependent variable in our example research question is difficulty in accessing social services. Suppose the agency social worker decides to collect data about this variable by giving clients (data source) a brief standardized questionnaire (data collection method) to measure their perceptions. Many standardized questionnaires contain several subscales that, when combined, give a quantitative measure of a larger concept.

The *R-GSSSS* contained in Figure 4.2, for example, is made up of three subscales: (1) relevance, (2) impact, and (3) gratification. Thus, it has four scores associated with it: a relevance score, an impact score, a gratification score, and a total score (which is a measure of satisfaction). With three separate subscales, we can choose to use any one subscale (one variable), all three subscales (three variables), or a total score (one variable).

Alternatively, if data about difficulty in accessing social services were to be collected using two different data sources such as social worker (data source 1) and a client (data source 2) observations, we must think about how the two data sources "fit" together. That is, will data from the two sources be treated as two separate variables? If so, will one variable be weighted differently in our analysis than the other? Thinking about how the data will be summarized helps us to expose any frivolous data—that is, data that are not suitable to answer our research question.

Besides collecting data about our study's variables, we must also develop a strategy to collect demographic data about the people who participate in our study. Typical demographic variables include: age, gender, education level, and family income. These data are not necessarily used in the analysis of the research question. Rather, they provide a descriptive context for our study. Some data collection methods, such as standardized questionnaires, include these types of data. Often, however, we are responsible for obtaining them as part of the data collection process.

Step 6: Writing the Research Report

It is useful to think about our final research report when choosing a data collection method and data source as it forces us to visualize how our study's findings will ultimately be presented. It identifies both who the audience of the study will be and the people interested in our findings. Knowing who will read our research report and how it will be disseminated helps us to take more of an objective stance toward our study.

In short, we can take a third-person look at what our study will finally look like. Such objectivity helps us to think about our data collection method and data source with a critical eye. Will consumers of our research study agree that the clients in fact were the best data collection source? Were the data collection method and analysis sound? These are some of the practical questions that bring scrutiny to the data collection process.

CRITERIA FOR SELECTING A DATA COLLECTION METHOD

Thinking through the steps in the research process, from the vantage point of collecting data, permits us to refine the conceptualization of our study and the place of data collection within it. It also sets the context within which our data will be gathered. Clearly, there are many viable data collection methods and data sources that can be used to answer any research question.

Nevertheless, there are many practical criteria that ultimately refine the final data collection method (and sources) to fit the conditions of any given research study. These criteria are: (1) size, (2) scope, (3) program participation, (4) worker cooperation, (5) intrusion into the lives of research participants, (6) resources, (7) time, and (8) previous research findings. They all interact with one another, but for the sake of clarity each one is presented separately.

Size

The size of our study reflects just how many people, places, or systems are represented in it. As with any planning activity, the more people involved, the more complicated the process and the more difficult it is to arrive at a mutual agreement. Decisions about which data collection method and which data source to use can be stalled when several people, levels, or systems are involved. This is simply because individuals have different interests and opinions.

Imagine if our research question about whether ethnicity is related to difficulty in accessing social services were examined on a larger scale such that all social service agencies in the country were included. Our study's complexity is dramatically increased because of such factors as the increased number of agencies, clients, funders, administrators, politicians, government representatives, and social workers involved. The biases within each of these stakeholder groups make it much more difficult to agree upon the best data collection method and data source for our study.

Our study's sample size is also a consideration. This is particularly true for quantitative studies, which aim to have a sample that is representative of the population of interest. With respect to sample size, this means that we should strive for a reasonable representation of the sampling frame. When small-scale studies are conducted, such as a program evaluation in one social work agency, the total number of people in the sampling frame may be in the hundreds or fewer. Thus, randomly selecting clients poses no real problem.

On the other hand, when large-scale studies are conducted, such as when the federal government chooses to examine a social service program that involves hundreds of thousands of people, sampling can become more problematic. If our sample is in the hundreds, it is unlikely that we would be able to successfully observe or interview all participants to collect data for our study. Rather, a much more efficient manner of data collection—say a survey—may be more appropriate.

Scope

The scope of our research study is another matter to consider. Scope refers to how much of our *problem area* will be covered. If in our research question, for example, we are interested in gathering data on other client-related variables such as language ability, degree of social isolation, and level of assertiveness, then three different aspects of our problem area will be covered. In short, we need to consider whether one method of data collection and one data source can be used to collect all the data. It could be that client records, for example, are used to collect data about clients' language abilities, interviews with clients are conducted to collect data about social isolation, and observation methods are used to gather data about clients' assertiveness levels.

Program Participation

Many social work research efforts are conducted in actual real-life program settings. Thus, it is essential that we gain the support of program personnel to conduct our study. Program factors that can impact the choice of our data collection methods and data sources include variables such as the program's clarity in its mandate to serve clients, its philosophical stance toward clients, and its flexibility in client record keeping.

First, if a program is not able to clearly articulate a client service delivery plan, it will be difficult to distinguish between clinical activity and research activity, and to determine when the two overlap.

Second, agencies tend to base themselves on strong beliefs about a client population, which affect who can have access to clients and in what manner. A child sexual abuse investigation program, for example, may be designed specifically to avoid the problem of using multiple interviewers and multiple interviews of children in the investigation of an allegation of sexual abuse. As a result, the program would be hesitant for us to conduct interviews with the children to gather data for "research purposes."

Third, to save time and energy there is often considerable overlap between program client records and research data collection. The degree of willingness of a program to change or adapt to new record-keeping techniques will affect how we might go about collecting certain types of data.

Worker Cooperation

On a general level, programs have fewer resources than they need and more clients than they can handle. Such conditions naturally lead their administrators and social workers to place intervention activity as a top priority (versus research activity). When our research study has social workers collecting data as a part of their day-to-day activities, it is highly likely that they will view data collection as additional paperwork and not as a means to expedite decision making in their work.

Getting cooperation of social workers within a program is a priority in any research study that relies directly or indirectly on their meaningful participation. Program workers will be affected by our study whether they are involved in the data collection process or not. They may be asked to schedule additional interviews with families or adjust their intervention plans to ensure that data collection occurs at the optimal time. Given the fiscal constraints faced by programs, the workers themselves often participate as data collectors. They may end up using new client recording forms or administer questionnaires. Whatever the level of their participation, it is important for us to strive to achieve a maximum level of their cooperation.

There are three factors to consider when trying to achieve maximum cooperation from workers. First, we should make every effort to work effectively and efficiently with the program's staff. Cooperation is more likely to be achieved when workers participate in the development of our study plan from the beginning. Thus, it is worthwhile to take time to explain the purpose of our study and its intended outcomes at an early stage in the study. Furthermore, administrators and frontline workers can provide valuable information about which data collection method(s) may work best.

Second, we must be sensitive to the workloads of the program's staff. Data collection methods and sources should be designed to enhance the work of professionals. Client recording forms, for example, can be designed to provide focus for supervision meetings, as well as summarize facts and worker impressions about a case.

Third, a mechanism ought to be set up by which workers receive feedback based on the data they have collected. When a mechanism for feedback is put in place, workers are more likely to show interest in the data collection activity. When data are reported back to the program's staff before the completion of our study, however, we must ensure that the data will not bias later measurements (if any).

Intrusion into the Lives of Research Participants

When clients are used as a data source, client self-determination takes precedence over research activity. As we know, clients have every right to refuse participation in a research study and cannot be denied services because they are unwilling to participate. It is unethical, for example, when a member of a group-based treatment intervention has not consented to participate in the study, but participant observation is used as the data collection method. This is unethical because the group member ends up being observed as part of the group dynamic in the data collection process after refusing to give his or her consent. The data collection method(s) we finally select must be flexible enough to allow our study to continue, even with the possibility that some clients will not participate.

Ethnic and cultural consideration must also be given to the type of data collection method used. One-to-one interviewing with Cambodian refugees, for example, may be extremely terrifying for them, given the interrogation they may have experienced in their own country. Moreover, if we, as data collectors, have different ethnic backgrounds than our research participants, it is important to ensure that interpretation of the data (e.g., their behaviors, events, or expressions) is accurate from the clients' perspectives and not our own.

We must also recognize the cultural biases of standardized measuring instruments, since most are based on testing with Caucasian groups. The problems here are twofold. First, we cannot be sure if the concept that the instrument is measuring is expressed the same way in different cultures. For instance, a standardized self-report instrument that measures family functioning may include an item such as, "We have flexible rules in our household that promote individual differences," which would likely be viewed positively by North American cultures, but negatively by many Asian cultures. Second, because standardized measuring instruments are written in English, research participants must have a good grasp of English to ensure that the data collected from them are valid and reliable.

Another consideration comes into play when particular populations have been the subject of a considerable amount of research study already. Many aboriginal people living on reserves, for example, have been subjected to government surveys, task force inquiries, independent research projects, and perhaps even to the curiosities of social work students learning in a practicum setting. When a population has been extensively researched, it is even more important that we consider how the data collection method will affect those people participating in the study. Has the data collection method been used previously? If so, what was the nature of the data collected?

Resources

There are various costs associated with collecting data in any given research study. Materials and supplies, equipment rental, transportation costs, and training for data collectors are just a few things to consider when choosing a data collection method. In addition, once the data are collected, additional expenses can arise when the data are entered into a computer or transcribed.

An efficient data collection method is one that collects credible data to answer a research question or test a hypothesis while requiring the least amount of time and money. In our example, to ask clients about their perceptions about the difficulty in accessing social services via an open-ended interview may offer rich data, but we take the risk that clients will not fully answer our questions in the time allotted for the interview. On the other hand, having them complete a self-report questionnaire about access to social services is a quicker and less costly way to collect data, but it gives little sense about how well the clients understood the questions being asked of them or whether the data obtained reflect their true perceptions.

Time

Time is a consideration when our study has a fixed completion date. Time constraints may be self- or externally imposed. Self-imposed time constraints are personal matters we need to consider. Is our research project a part of a thesis or dissertation? What are our personal time commitments?

Externally imposed time restrictions are set by someone other than the person who is doing the study. For instance, our research study may be limited by the fiscal year of a social service agency. Other external pressures may be political, such as an administrator who wants research results for a funding proposal or to present at a conference.

Previous Research

Having reviewed the professional literature on our problem, we need to be well aware of other data collection methods that have been used in similar studies. We can evaluate earlier studies for the strengths and weaknesses of their data collection methods and thereby make a more informed decision as to the best data collection strategy to use in our specific situation. Further, we need to look for diversity when evaluating other data collection approaches. That is, we can triangulate results from separate studies that used different data collection methods and data sources to answer a research question or test a hypothesis.

TRYING OUT THE SELECTED DATA COLLECTION METHOD

Data collection is a particularly vulnerable time for a research study because it is the point where "talk" turns to "action." So far, all the considerations that have been weighed in the selection of a data collection method have been in theory. All people involved in our research endeavor have cast their suggestions and doubts on the entire process. Once general agreement has been reached about which data collection method and data source to use, it is time to test the waters.

Trying out a data collection method can occur informally by simply testing it out with available and willing research participants or, at the very least, with anyone who has not been involved with the planning of the study. The purpose of this trial run is to ensure that those who are going to provide data understand the questions and procedures in the way that they were intended. Data collection methods might also be tested more formally, such as when a pilot study is conducted.

A pilot study involves carrying out all aspects of the data collection plan on a mini-scale. That is, a small portion of our study's actual sample is selected and run through all steps of the data collection process. In a pilot study, we are interested in the process of the data collection as well as the content. In short, we want to know whether our chosen data collection method produces the expected data. Are there any unanticipated barriers to gathering the desired data? How do research participants (data source) respond to our data collection procedures?

IMPLEMENTATION AND EVALUATION

The data collection step of a research study can go smoothly if we act proactively. That is, we should guide and monitor the entire data collection process according to the procedures and steps that were set out in the planning stage of our study and were tested in the pilot study.

Implementation

The main guiding principle to implementing the selected data collection method is that a systematic approach to data collection must be used. This means that the steps to gathering data should be methodically detailed so that there is no question about the tasks of the person(s) collecting the data—the data collector(s). This is true whether using a quantitative or qualitative research approach. As we know from Chapter 3, the difference between these two research approaches is that the structure of the data collection process within a qualitative research study is documented as the study progresses. On the other hand, in a quantitative research study, the data collection process is decided at the study's outset and provides much less flexibility after the study is underway.

It must be very clear who is responsible for collecting the data. When we take on the task, there is reasonable assurance that the data collection will remain objective and be guided by our research interests. Data collection left to only one person may be a formidable task. We must determine the amount of resources available to decide what data collection method is most realistic. We must attempt to establish clear roles and boundaries with those involved in the data collection process.

The clearer our research study is articulated, the less difficulty there will be in moving through all the steps of the study. In particular, it is critical to identify who will and will not be involved in the data collection process. To further avoid mix-up and complications, specific tasks must be spelled out for all persons involved in our study. Where will the data be stored? Who will collect them? How will the data collection process be monitored?

In many social work research studies, frontline social workers are involved in data collection activities as part of their day-to-day activities. They typically gather intake and referral data, write assessment notes, and even use standardized questionnaires as part of their assessments. Data collection in programs can easily be designed to serve the dual purposes of research *and* intervention inquiry. Thus, it is important to establish data collection protocols to avoid problems of biased data. As mentioned, everyone in a research study must agree *when* data will be collected, *where*, and in *what* manner. Agreement is more likely to occur when we have fully informed and involved everyone participating in our study.

Evaluation

The process of selecting a chosen data collection method is not complete without evaluating it. Evaluation occurs at two levels. First, the strengths and weaknesses of a data collection method and data source are evaluated, given the research context in which our study takes place. If, for example, data are gathered about clients presenting problems by a referring social worker, it must be acknowledged that the obtained data offer a limited (or restricted) point of view about the clients' problems. The strength of this approach may be that it was the only means for collecting the data.

A second level of evaluation is monitoring the implementation of the data collection process itself. When data are gathered using several methods (or several sources), it is beneficial to develop a checklist of what data have been collected for each research participant. Developing a strategy for monitoring the data collection process is especially important when the data must be collected in a timely fashion. If pretest data are needed before a client enters a treatment program, for example, the data collection must be complete before admission occurs. Once a client has entered the program, opportunity to collect pretest data is lost forever.

Another strategy for monitoring evaluation is to keep a journal of the data collection process. The journal records any questions or queries that arise in the data collection step. We may find, for example, that several research participants completing a questionnaire have difficulty understanding one particular question. In addition, sometimes research participants have poor reading skills and require assistance with completion of some self-report standardized questionnaires. Documenting these idiosyncratic incidents accumulates important information by which to comment on our data's credibility.

SUMMING UP AND LOOKING AHEAD

There are many possible data collection methods and data sources that can be used in any given research situation. We must weigh the pros and cons of both within the context of a particular research study to arrive at the best data collection method and data source. This process involves both conceptual and practical considerations.

On a conceptual level, we review the steps of the research process through a "data collection and data source lens." We think about how various data collection methods and data sources fit with each step of the research process. At the same time, considering the different data collection methods and data sources helps us to gain a fuller understanding of our problem area and research question.

On a practical level, there are many considerations that need to be addressed when deciding upon the best data collection method(s) and data source(s) for a particular study. Factors such as worker cooperation, available resources, and consequences for the clients all influence our final choices.

Now that we know how to collect quantitative and qualitative data for any given research study (i.e., Chapters 10 & 11), we will turn our attention to analyzing them. Thus, Chapter 12 presents how to analyze quantitative data and Chapter 13 discusses how to analyze qualitative data.

REVIEW QUESTIONS

1   Discuss in detail what is meant by a data collection method. Provide a social work example in your discussion.

2   Discuss in detail what is meant by a data source. Provide a social work example in your discussion.

3   Discuss in detail how available data collection methods influence the selection of data sources, and vice versa. Provide a social work example in your discussion.

4   Discuss in detail how available data collection methods and data sources influence the selection of research problems and research questions, and vice versa. Provide a social work example in your discussion.

5   Discuss in detail how available data collection methods and data sources influence the selection of research designs, and vice versa. Provide a social work example in your discussion.

6   List and discuss in detail the criteria that can be used to select a data collection method. Provide a social work example in your discussion.

7   List and discuss in detail the criteria that can be used to select a data source. Provide a social work example in your discussion.

8   Describe in detail how you could use two or more different data sources in a single research study that focused on one specific research question (or hypothesis). Provide a social work example in your discussion.

This chapter has been adapted and modified from: Grinnell, Williams, and Tutty (1997); and Williams, Tutty, and Grinnell (1995)

C h a p t e r   12

Quantitative Data Analysis

After quantitative data are collected they need to be analyzed—the topic of this chapter. To be honest, a thorough understanding of quantitative statistical methods is far beyond the scope of this book. Such comprehension necessitates more in-depth study, through taking one or more statistics courses. Instead, we briefly describe a select group of basic statistical analytical methods that are used frequently in many quantitative *and* qualitative social work research studies. Our emphasis is not on providing and calculating formulas, but rather on helping the reader to understand the underlying rationale for their use.

We present two basic groups of statistical procedures. The first group is called *descriptive statistics*, which simply describe and summarize one or more variables for a sample or population. They provide information about only the group included in the study. The second group of statistical procedures is called *inferential statistics*, which determine if we can generalize findings derived from a sample to the population from which the sample was drawn. In other words, knowing what we know about a particular sample, can we infer that the rest of the population is similar to the sample that we have studied? Before we can answer this question, however, we need to know the level of measurement for each variable being analyzed. Let us now turn to a brief discussion of the four different levels of measurement that a variable can take.

LEVELS OF MEASUREMENT

The specific statistic(s) used to analyze the data collected is dependent on the type of data that are gathered. The characteristics or qualities that describe a variable are known as its *attributes*. The variable *gender*, for example, has only two characteristics or attributes—*male* and *female*—since gender in humans is limited to male and female, and there are no other possible categories or ways of describing gender. The variable *ethnicity* has a number of possible categories: *African American, Native American, Asian, Hispanic American,* and *Caucasian* are just five examples of the many attributes of the variable ethnicity. A point to note here is that the attributes of gender differ in kind from one another—male is different from female—and, in the same way, the attributes of ethnicity are also different from one another.

Now consider the variable *income*. Income can only be described in terms of amounts of money: $15,000 per year, $288.46 per week, and so forth. In whatever terms a person's income is actually described, it still comes down to a number. Since every number has its own category, as we mentioned before, the variable income can generate as many categories as there are numbers, up to the number covering the research participant who earns the most. These numbers are all attributes of income and they are all different, but they are not different in *kind*, as male and female are, or Native American and Hispanic; they are only different in *quantity*.

In other words, the attributes of income differ in that they represent more or less of the same thing, whereas the attributes of gender differ in that they represent different kinds of things. Income will, therefore, be measured in a different way from gender. When we come to measure income, we will be looking for categories that are lower or higher than each other; when we come to measure gender, we will be looking for categories that are different in kind from each other.

Mathematically, there is not much we can do with categories that are different in kind. We cannot subtract Hispanics from Caucasians, for example, whereas we can quite easily subtract one person's annual income from another and come up with a meaningful difference. As far as mathematical computations are concerned, we are obliged to work at a lower level of complexity when we measure variables like ethnicity than when we measure variables like income. Depending on the nature of their attributes, all variables can be measured at one (or more) of four measurement levels: (1) nominal, (2) ordinal, (3) interval, or (4) ratio.

Nominal Measurement

Nominal measurement is the lowest level of measurement and is used to measure variables whose attributes are different in kind. As we have seen, gender is one variable measured at a nominal level, and ethnicity is another. *Place of birth* is a third, since "born in California," for example, is different from "born in Chicago," and we cannot add "born in California" to "born in Chicago," or subtract them or divide them, or do anything statistically interesting with them at all.

Ordinal Measurement

Ordinal measurement is a higher level of measurement than nominal and is used to measure those variables whose attributes can be rank-ordered: for example, socioeconomic status, sexism, racism, client satisfaction, and the like. If we intend to measure *client satisfaction*, we must first develop a list of all the possible attributes of client satisfaction: That is, we must think of all the possible categories into which answers about client satisfaction might be placed. Some clients will be *very satisfied*—one category, at the high end of the satisfaction continuum; some will be *not at all satisfied*—a separate category, at the low end of the continuum; and others will be *generally satisfied*, *moderately satisfied*, or *somewhat satisfied*—three more categories, at differing points on the continuum, as illustrated in Figure 12.1.

Figure 12.1 is a five-point scale, anchored at all five points with a brief description of the degree of satisfaction represented by the point. Of course, we may choose to express the anchors in different words, substituting *extremely satisfied* for *very satisfied*, or *fairly satisfied* for *generally satisfied*. We may select a three-point scale instead, limiting the choices to *very satisfied*, *moderately satisfied,* and *not at all satisfied*; or we may even use a ten-point scale if we believe that our respondents will be able to rate their satisfaction with that degree of accuracy.

Whichever particular method is selected, some sort of scale is the only measurement option available because there is no other way to categorize client satisfaction except in terms of more satisfaction or less satisfaction. As we did with nominal measurement, we might assign numbers to each of the points on the scale. If we used the scale in Figure 12.1, we might assign a 5 to *very satisfied*, a 4 to *generally satisfied*, a 3 to *moderately satisfied*, a 2 to *somewhat satisfied*, and a 1 to *not at all satisfied*.

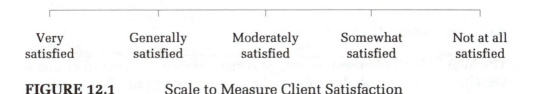

| Very
satisfied | Generally
satisfied | Moderately
satisfied | Somewhat
satisfied | Not at all
satisfied |

FIGURE 12.1   Scale to Measure Client Satisfaction

Here, the numbers do have some mathematical meaning. Five (*very satisfied*) is in fact better than 4 (*generally satisfied*), 4 is better than 3, 3 is better than 2, and 2 is better than 1. The numbers, however, say nothing about *how much better* any category is than any other. We cannot assume that the difference in satisfaction between *very* and *generally* is the same as the difference between *generally* and *moderately*. In short, we cannot assume that the intervals between the anchored points on the scale are all the same length. Most definitely, we cannot assume that a client who rates a service at 4 (*generally satisfied*) is twice as satisfied as a client who rates the service at 2 (*somewhat satisfied*).

In fact, we cannot attempt any mathematical manipulation at all. We cannot add the numbers 1, 2, 3, 4, and 5, nor can we subtract, multiply, or divide them. As its name might suggest, all we can know from ordinal measurement is the order of the categories.

Interval Measurement

Some variables, such as client satisfaction, have attributes that can be rank-ordered—from *very satisfied* to *not at all satisfied*, as we have just discussed. As we saw, however, these attributes cannot be assumed to be the same distance apart if they are placed on a scale; and, in any case, the distance they are apart has no real meaning. No one can measure the distance between *very satisfied* and *moderately satisfied*; we only know that the one is better than the other.

Conversely, for some variables, the distance, or interval, separating their attributes *does* have meaning, and these variables can be measured at the interval level. An example in physical science would is the Fahrenheit or Celsius temperature scales. The difference between 80 degrees and 90 degrees is the same as the difference between 40 and 50 degrees. Eighty degrees is not twice as hot as 40 degrees; nor does zero degrees mean no heat at all.

In social work, interval measures are most commonly used in connection with standardized measuring instruments, as presented in Chapter 4. When we look at a standardized intelligence test, for example, we can say that the difference between IQ scores of 100 and 110 is the same as the difference between IQ scores of 95 and 105, based on the scores obtained by the many thousands of people who have taken the test over the years. As with the temperature scales mentioned above, a person with an IQ score of 120 is not twice as intelligent as a person with a score of 60: nor does a score of 0 mean no intelligence at all.

Ratio Measurement

The highest level of measurement, ratio measurement, is used to measure variables whose attributes are based on a true zero point. It may not be possible to have zero intelligence, but it is certainly possible to have zero children or zero money. Whenever a question about a particular variable might elicit the answer "none" or "never," that variable can be measured at the ratio level. The question, "How many times have you seen your social worker?" might be answered, "Never." Other variables commonly measured at the ratio level include length of residence in a given place, age, number of times married, number of organizations belonged to, number of antisocial behaviors, number of case reviews, number of training sessions, number of supervisory meetings, and so forth.

With a ratio level of measurement we can meaningfully interpret the comparison between two scores. A person who is 40 years of age, for example, is twice as old as a person who is 20 and half as old as a person who is 80. Children aged 2 and 5, respectively, are the same distance apart as children aged 6 and 9. Data resulting from ratio measurement can be added, subtracted, multiplied, and divided. Averages can be calculated and other statistical analyses can be performed.

It is useful to note that, while some variables *can* be measured at a higher level, they may not need to be. The variable *income*, for example, can be measured at a ratio level because it is possible to have a zero income but, for the purposes of a particular study, we may not need to know the actual incomes of our research participants, only the range within which their incomes fall. A person who is asked how much he or she earns may be reluctant to give a figure ("mind your own business" is a perfectly legitimate response) but may not object to checking one of a number of income categories, choosing, for example, between:

1 less than $5,000 per year

2 $5,001 to $15,000 per year

3 $15,001 to $25,000 per year

4 $25,001 to $35,000 per year

5 more than $35,000 per year

Categorizing income in this way reduces the measurement from the ratio level to the ordinal level. It will now be possible to know only that a person checking Category 1 earns less than a person checking Category 2, and so on. While we will not know *how much* less or more one person earns than another and we will not be able to perform statistical tasks such as calculating average incomes, we will be able to say, for example, that 50 percent of our sample falls into Category 1, 30 percent into Category 2, 15 percent into Category 3, and 5 percent into Category 4. If we are conducting a study to see how many people fall in each income range, this may be all we need to know.

In the same way, we might not want to know the actual ages of our sample, only the range in which they fall. For some studies, it might be enough to measure age at a nominal level—to inquire, for example, whether people were born during the Depression, or whether they were born before or after 1990. In short, when studying variables that can be measured at any level, the measurement level chosen depends on what kind of data are needed, and this in turn is determined by why the data are needed, which in turn is determined by our research question.

COMPUTER APPLICATIONS

The use of computers has revolutionized the analysis of quantitative and qualitative data. Where previous generations of researchers had to rely on hand-cranked adding machines to calculate every small step in a data analysis, today we can enter raw scores into a personal computer, and, with few complications, direct the computer program to execute just about any statistical test imaginable. Seconds later, the results are available. While the process is truly miraculous, the risk is that, even though we have conducted the correct statistical analysis, we may not understand what the results mean, a factor that will almost certainly affect how we interpret the data.

We can code data from all four levels of measurement into a computer for any given data analysis. The coding of nominal data is perhaps the most complex, because we have to create categories that correspond with certain possible responses for a variable. One type of nominal level data that is often gathered from research participants is *place of birth*. If, for the purposes of our study, we are interested in whether our research participants were born in either the United States or Canada, we would assign only three categories to *place of birth*:

1 United States
2 Canada
9 Other

The *other* category appears routinely at the end of lists of categories and acts as a catch-all, to cover any category that may have been omitted.

When entering nominal level data into a computer, because we do not want to enter *Canada* every time the response on the questionnaire is Canada, we may assign it the code number 2, so that all we have to enter is 2. Similarly, the United States may be assigned the number 1, and "other" may be assigned the number 9. These numbers have no mathematical meaning: We are not saying that the United States is better than Canada because it comes first, or that Canada is twice as good as the United States because the number assigned to it is twice as high. We are merely using numbers as a shorthand device to record *qualitative* differences: differences in *kind*, not in amount.

Most coding for ordinal, interval, and ratio level data is simply a matter of entering the final score, or number, from the measuring instrument that was used to measure the variable directly into the computer. If a person scored a 45 on a standardized measuring instrument, for example, the number 45 would be entered into the computer. Although almost all data entered into computers are in the form of numbers, we need to know at what level of measurement the data exist, so that we can choose the appropriate statistic(s) to describe and compare the variables. Now that we know how to measure variables at four different measurement levels, let us turn to the first group of statistics that can be helpful for the analysis of data—descriptive statistics.

DESCRIPTIVE STATISTICS

Descriptive statistics are commonly used in most quantitative and qualitative research studies. They describe and summarize a variable(s) of interest and portray how that particular variable is distributed in the sample, or population. Before looking at descriptive statistics, however, let us examine a social work research example that will be used throughout this chapter.

Thea Black is a social worker who works in a treatment foster care program. Her program focuses on children who have behavioral problems who are placed with "treatment" foster care parents. These parents are supposed to have parenting skills that will help them provide the children with the special needs they present. Thus, Thea's program also teaches parenting skills to these treatment foster care parents. She assumes that newly recruited foster parents are not likely to know much about parenting children who have behavioral problems. Therefore, she believes that they would benefit from a training program that teaches these skills in order to help them to deal effectively with the special needs of these children who will soon be living with them.

Thea hopes that her parenting skills training program will increase the knowledge about parental management skills for the parents who attend. She assumes that, with such training, the foster parents would be in a better position to support and provide clear limits for their foster children.

After offering the training program for several months, Thea became curious about whether the foster care providers who attended the program were, indeed, lacking in knowledge of parental management skills as she first believed (her tentative hypothesis). She was fortunate to find a valid and reliable standardized instrument that measures the knowledge of such parenting skills, the Parenting Skills Scale (*PSS*). Thea decided to find out for herself how much the newly recruited parents knew about parenting skills—clearly a descriptive research question.

At the beginning of one of her training sessions (before they were exposed to her skills training program), she handed out the *PSS*, asking the 20 individuals in attendance to complete it and also to include data about their gender, years of education, and whether they had ever participated in a parenting skills training program before. All of these three variables could be potentially extraneous ones that might influence the level of knowledge of parenting skills of the 20 participants.

TABLE 12.1 Data Collected for Four Variables from Foster Care Providers

Number	PSS Score	Gender	Previous Training	Years of Education
01	95	male	no	12
02	93	female	yes	15
03	93	male	no	08
04	93	female	no	12
05	90	male	yes	12
06	90	female	no	12
07	84	male	no	14
08	84	female	no	18
09	82	male	no	10
10	82	female	no	12
11	80	male	no	12
12	80	female	no	11
13	79	male	no	12
14	79	female	yes	12
15	79	female	no	16
16	79	male	no	12
17	79	female	no	11
18	72	female	no	14
19	71	male	no	15
20	55	female	yes	12

For each foster care parent, Thea calculated the *PSS* score, called a *raw score* because it has not been sorted or analyzed in any way. The total score possible on the *PSS* is 100, with higher scores indicating greater knowledge of parenting skills. The scores for the *PSS* scale, as well as the other data collected from the 20 parents, are listed in Table 12.1.

At this point, Thea stopped to consider how she could best utilize the data that she had collected. She had data at three different levels of measurement. At the nominal level, Thea had collected data on gender (3rd column), and whether the parents had any previous parenting skills training (4th column). Each of these variables can be categorized into two responses.

The scores on the *PSS* (2nd column) are ordinal because, although the data are sequenced from highest to lowest, the differences between units cannot be placed on an equally spaced continuum. Nevertheless, many measures in the social sciences are treated as if they are at an interval level, even though equal distances between scale points cannot be proved. This assumption is important because it allows for the use of inferential statistics on such data.

Finally, the data on years of formal education (5th column) that were collected by Thea are clearly at the ratio level of measurement, because there are equally distributed points and the scale has an absolute zero.

TABLE 12.2   Frequency
                       Distribution

PSS Score	Absolute Frequency
95	1
93	3
90	2
84	2
82	2
80	2
79	5
72	1
71	1
55	1

In sum, it seemed to Thea that the data could be used in at least two ways. First, the data collected about each variable could be described to provide a picture of the characteristics of the group of foster care parents. This would call for descriptive statistics. Secondly, she might look for relationships between some of the variables about which she had collected data, procedures that would utilize inferential statistics. For now let us begin by looking at how the first type of descriptive statistic can be utilized with Thea's data set.

Frequency Distributions

One of the simplest procedures that Thea can employ is to develop a frequency distribution of her data. Constructing a frequency distribution involves counting the occurrences of each value, or category, of the variable and ordering them in some fashion. This *absolute* or *simple frequency distribution* allows us to see quickly how certain values of a variable are distributed in our sample or population.

The *mode*, or the most commonly occurring score, can be easily spotted in a simple frequency distribution (see Table 12.2). In this example, the mode is 79, a score obtained by five parents on the *PSS* scale. The highest and the lowest score are also quickly identifiable. The top score was 95, while the foster care parent who performed the least well on the *PSS* scored 55.

There are several other ways to present frequency data. A commonly used method that can be easily integrated into a simple frequency distribution table is the *cumulative frequency distribution*, shown in Table 12.3.

In Thea's data set, the highest *PSS* score, 95, was obtained by only one individual. The group of individuals who scored 93 or above on the *PSS* measure includes four foster care parents. If we want to know how many scored 80 or above, if we look at the number across from 80 in the

TABLE 12.3   Cumulative Frequency and
                      Percentage Distributions of
                      Parental Skill Scores

PSS Score	Absolute Frequency	Cumulative Frequency	Percentage Distribution
95	1	1	5
93	3	4	15
90	2	6	10
84	2	8	10
82	2	10	10
80	2	12	10
79	5	17	25
72	1	18	5
71	1	19	5
55	1	20	5
Totals	20		100

cumulative frequency column, we can quickly see that 12 of the parents scored 80 or better.

Other tables utilize percentages rather than frequencies, sometimes referred to as a *percentage distribution*, shown in the right-hand column in Table 12.3. Each of these numbers represents the percentage of participants who obtained each *PSS* value. Five individuals, for example, scored 79 on the *PSS*. Since there was a total of 20 foster care parents, 5 out of the 20, or one-quarter of the total, obtained a score of 79. This corresponds to 25 percent of the participants.

Finally, *grouped frequency distributions* are used to simplify a table by grouping the variable into equal-sized ranges, as is shown in Table 12.4. Both absolute and cumulative frequencies and percentages can also be displayed using this format. Each is calculated in the same way that was previously described for nongrouped data, and the interpretation is identical.

Looking at the absolute frequency column, for example, we can quickly identify the fact that seven of the foster care parents scored in the 70–79 range on the *PSS*. By looking at the cumulative frequency column, we can see that 12 of 20 parents scored 80 or better on the *PSS*. Further, from the absolute percentage column, it is clear that 30 percent of the foster parents scored in the 80–89 range on the knowledge of parenting skills scale. Only one parent, or 5 percent of the group, had significant problems with the *PSS*, scoring in the 50–59 range.

Note that each of the other variables in Thea's data set could also be displayed in frequency distributions. Displaying years of education in a frequency distribution, for example, would provide a snapshot of how this variable is distributed in Thea's sample of foster care parents. With two category nominal variables, such as gender (male, female) and previous parent skills training (yes, no), however, cumulative frequencies become

TABLE 12.4   Grouped Frequency Distribution of Parental Skill Scores

PSS Scores	Absolute Frequency	Cumulative Frequency	Absolute Percentage
90 – 100	6	6	30
80 – 89	6	12	30
70 – 79	7	19	35
60 – 69	0	19	0
50 – 59	1	20	5

less meaningful and the data are better described as percentages. Thea noted that 55 percent of the foster care parents who attended the training workshop were women (obviously the other 45 percent were men) and that 20 percent of the parents had already received some form of parenting skills training (while a further 80 percent had not been trained).

Measures of Central Tendency

We can also display the values obtained on the *PSS* in the form of a graph. A *frequency polygon* is one of the simplest ways of charting frequencies. The graph in Figure 12.2 displays the data that we had previously put in Table 12.2. The *PSS* score is plotted in terms of how many of the foster care parents obtained each score.

As can be seen from Figure 12.2, most of the scores fall between 79 and 93. The one extremely low score of 55 is also quickly noticeable in such a graph, because it is so far removed from the rest of the values.

A frequency polygon allows us to make a quick analysis of how closely the distribution fits the shape of a normal curve. A *normal curve*, also known as a *bell-shaped distribution* or a *normal distribution*, is a frequency polygon in which the greatest number of responses fall in the middle of the distribution and fewer scores appear at the extremes of either very high or very low scores (see Figure 12.3).

Many variables in the social sciences are assumed to be distributed in the shape of a normal curve. Low intelligence, for example, is thought to be relatively rare as compared to the number of individuals with average intelligence. On the other end of the continuum, extremely gifted individuals are also relatively uncommon.

Of course, not all variables are distributed in the shape of a normal curve. Some are such that a large number of people do very well (as Thea found in her sample of foster care parents and their parenting skill levels). Other variables, such as juggling ability, for example, would be charted showing a fairly substantial number of people performing poorly. Frequency distributions of still other variables would show that some

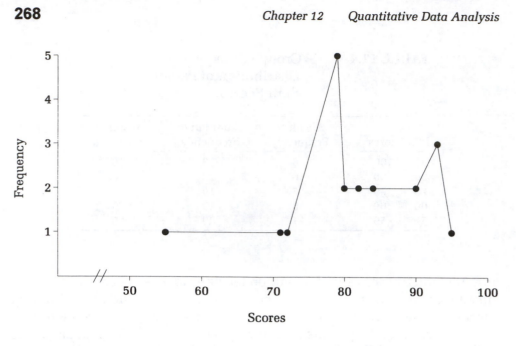

FIGURE 12.2   Frequency Polygon of Parental Skill Scores (from
                        Table 12.2)

people do well, and some people do poorly, but not many fall in between.
What is important to remember about distributions is that, although all
different sorts are possible, most statistical procedures assume that there
is a normal distribution of the variable in question in the population.

When looking at how variables are distributed in samples and
populations it is common to use measures of *central tendency*, such as the
mode, median, and mean, which help us to identify where the typical or
the average score can be found. These measures are utilized so often
because, not only do they provide a useful summary of the data, they also
provide a common denominator for comparing groups to each other.

Mode

As mentioned earlier, the mode is the score, or value, that occurs the
most often—the value with the highest frequency. In Thea's data set of
parental skills scores the mode is 79, with five foster care parents
obtaining this value. The mode is particularly useful for nominal level
data. Knowing what score occurred the most often, however, provides
little information about the other scores and how they are distributed in
the sample or population. Because the mode is the least precise of all the
measures of central tendency, the median and the mean are better
descriptors of ordinal level data and above. We now turn our attention to
the second measure of central tendency, the median.

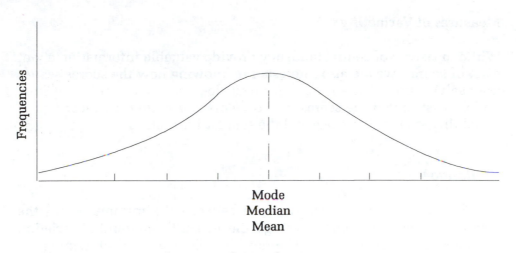

Mode
Median
Mean

FIGURE 12.3   The Normal Distribution

Median

The median is the score that divides a distribution into two equal parts or portions. In order to do this, we must rank-order the scores, so at least an ordinal level of measurement is required. In Thea's sample of 20 *PSS* scores, the median would be the score above which the top ten scores lie and below which the bottom ten fall. As can be seen in Table 12.2, the top ten scores finish at 82, and the bottom ten scores start at 80. In this example, the median is 81, since it falls between 82 and 80.

Mean

The mean is the most sophisticated measure of central tendency and is useful for interval or ratio levels of measurement. It is also one of the most commonly utilized statistics. A mean is calculated by summing the individual values and dividing by the total number of values. The mean of Thea's sample is $95 + 93 + 93 + 93 + 90 + 90 + \ldots 72 + 71 + 55/20 = 81.95$. In this example, the obtained mean of 82 (we rounded off for the sake of clarity) is larger than the mode of 79 or the median of 81.

The mean is one of the previously mentioned statistical procedures that assumes that a variable will be distributed normally throughout a population. If this is not an accurate assumption, then the median might be a better descriptor. The mean is also best used with relatively large sample sizes where extreme scores (such as the lowest score of 55 in Thea's sample) have less influence.

Measures of Variability

While measures of central tendency provide valuable information about a set of scores, we are also interested in knowing how the scores scatter themselves around the center. A mean does not give a sense of how widely distributed the scores may be: This is provided by measures of variability such as the range and the standard deviation.

Range

The range is simply the distance between the minimum and the maximum score. The larger the range, the greater the amount of variation of scores in the distribution. The range is calculated by subtracting the lowest score from the highest. In Thea's sample, the range is 40 (95 – 55).

The range assumes equal intervals and so should be used only with interval or ratio level data. It is, like the mean, sensitive to deviant values, because it depends on only the two extreme scores. We could have a group of four scores ranging from 10 to 20: 10, 14, 19, and 20, for example. The range of this sample would be 10 (20 – 10). If one additional score that was substantially different from the first set of four scores was included, this would change the range dramatically. In this example, if a fifth score of 45 was added, the range would become 35 (45 – 10), a number that would suggest quite a different picture of the variability of the scores.

Standard Deviation

The standard deviation is the most well-used indicator of dispersion. It provides a picture of how the scores distribute themselves around the mean. Used in combination with the mean, the standard deviation provides a great deal of information about the sample or population, without our ever needing to see the raw scores. In a normal distribution of scores, described previously, there are six standard deviations: three below the mean and three above, as is shown in Figure 12.4.

In this perfect model we always know that 34.13 percent of the scores of the sample fall within one standard deviation above the mean, and another 34.13 percent fall within one standard deviation below the mean. Thus, a total of 68.26 percent, or about two-thirds of the scores, is between +1 standard deviation and –1 standard deviation from the mean. This leaves almost one-third of the scores to fall farther away from the mean, with 15.87 percent (50% – 34.13%) above +1 standard deviation, and 15.87 percent (50% – 34.13%) below –1 standard deviation. In total, when looking at the proportion of scores that fall between +2 and –2 standard deviations, 95.44 percent of scores can be expected to be found within these parameters. Furthermore, 99.74 percent of the scores fall between +3

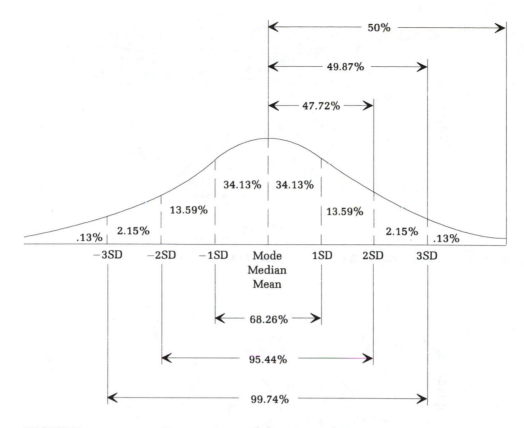

FIGURE 12.4   Proportions of the Normal Curve

standard deviations and –3 standard deviations about the mean. Thus, finding scores that fall beyond 3 standard deviations above and below the mean should be a rare occurrence.

The standard deviation has the advantage, like the mean, of taking all values into consideration in its computation. Also similar to the mean, it is utilized with interval or ratio levels of measurement and assumes a normal distribution of scores.

Several different samples of scores could have the same mean, but the variation around the mean, as provided by the standard deviation, could be quite different, as is shown in Figure 12.5a. Two different distributions could have unequal means and equal standard deviations, as in Figure 12.5b, or unequal means and unequal standard deviations, as in Figure 12.5c.

The standard deviation of the scores of Thea's foster care parents was calculated to be 10. Again, assuming that the variable of knowledge about parenting skills is normally distributed in the population of foster care parents, the results of the *PSS* scores from the sample of parents about whom we are making inferences can be shown in a distribution like Figure 12.6.

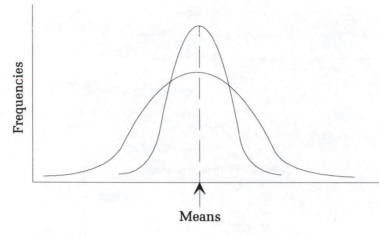

(*a*)   Equal means, unequal standard deviations

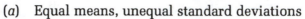

(*b*)   Unequal means, equal standard deviations

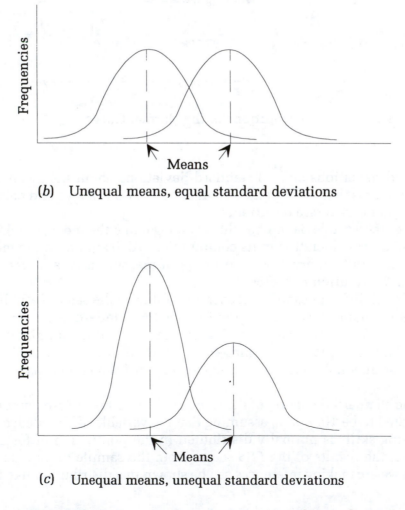

(*c*)   Unequal means, unequal standard deviations

FIGURE 12.5   Variations in Normal Distributions

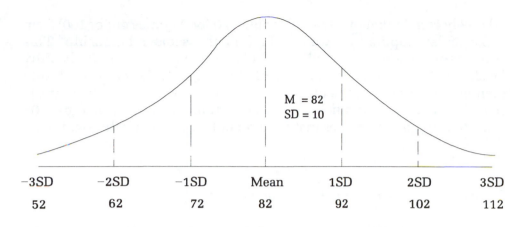

M = 82
SD = 10

−3SD	−2SD	−1SD	Mean	1SD	2SD	3SD
52	62	72	82	92	102	112

FIGURE 12.6   Distribution of Parental Skill Scores

As can also be seen in Figure 12.6, the score that would include two standard deviations, 102, is beyond the total possible score of 100 on the test. This is because the distribution of the scores in Thea's sample of parents does not entirely fit a normal distribution. The one extremely low score of 55 (see Table 12.1) obtained by one foster care parent would have affected the mean, as well as the standard deviation.

INFERENTIAL STATISTICS

The goal of inferential statistical tests is to rule out chance as the explanation for finding either associations between variables or differences between variables in our samples. Since we are rarely able to study an entire population, we are almost always dealing with samples drawn from that population. The danger is that we might make conclusions about a particular population based on a sample that is uncharacteristic of the population it is supposed to represent.

For example, perhaps the group of foster parents in Thea's training session happened to have an unusually high level of knowledge of parenting skills. If she assumed that all the rest of the foster parents that she might train in the future were as knowledgeable, she would be overestimating their knowledge, a factor that could have a negative impact on the way she conducts her training program.

To counteract the possibility that the sample is uncharacteristic of the general population, statistical tests take a conservative position as to whether or not we can conclude that there are relationships between the variables within our sample. The guidelines to indicate the likelihood that we have, indeed, found a relationship or difference that fits the population of interest are called *probability levels.*

The convention in most social science research is that variables are significantly associated or groups are significantly different if we are relatively certain that in 19 samples out of 20 (or 95 times out of 100) from a particular population, we would find the same relationship. This corresponds to a probability level of .05, written as ($p < .05$). Probability levels are usually provided along with the results of the statistical test to demonstrate how confident we are that the results actually indicate statistically significant differences. If a probability level is greater than .05 (e.g., .06, .10), this indicates that we did not find a statistically significant difference.

Statistics That Determine Associations

There are many statistics that can determine if there is an association between two variables. We will briefly discuss two: chi-square and correlation.

Chi-Square

The *chi-square test* requires measurements of variables at only the nominal or ordinal level. Thus, it is very useful since most data in social work are gathered at these two levels of measurement. In general, the chi-square test looks at whether specific values of one variable tend to be associated with specific values of another. In short, we use it to determine if two variables are related. It cannot be used to determine if one variable *caused* another, however.

In thinking about the foster care parents who were in her training program, Thea was aware that women are more typically responsible for caring for their own children than men. Even if they are not mothers themselves, they are often in professions such as teaching and social work where they are caretakers. Thus, she wondered whether there might be a relationship between having had previous training in parenting skills and gender, such that women were less likely to have taken such training since they already felt confident in their knowledge of parenting skills. As a result, her one-tailed hypothesis was that fewer women than men would have previously taken parenting skills training courses. Thea could examine this possibility with her 20 foster care parents using a chi-square test.

In terms of gender, Thea had data from the nine (45%) men and 11 (55%) women. Of the total group, four (20%) had previous training in foster care training, while 16 (80%) had not. As shown in Table 12.5, the first task was for Thea to count the number of men and women who had previous training and the number of men and women who did not have previous training. She put these data in one of the four categories in Table 12.5. The actual numbers are called *observed frequencies*. It is helpful to transform these raw data into percentages, making comparisons between categories much easier.

TABLE 12.5   Frequencies (and Percentages) of Gender by Previous Training (from Table 12.1)

	Previous Training		
Gender	Yes	No	Totals
Male	1 (11)	8 (89)	9
Female	3 (27)	8 (73)	11
Totals	4 (20)	16 (80)	20

We can, however, still not tell simply by looking at the observed frequencies whether there is a statistically significant relationship between gender (male or female) and previous training (yes or no). To do this, the next step is to look at how much the observed frequencies differ from what we would expect to see if, in fact, if there was no relationship. These are called *expected frequencies*. Without going through all the calculations, the chi-square table would now look like Table 12.6 for Thea's data set.

Since the probability level of the obtained chi-square value in Table 12.6 is greater than .05, Thea did not find any statistical relationship between gender and previous training in parenting skills. Thus, statistically speaking, men were no more likely than women to have received previous training in parenting skills; her research hypothesis was not supported by the data.

Correlation

Tests of correlation investigate the strength of the relationship between two variables. As with the chi-square test, correlation cannot be used to

TABLE 12.6   Chi-Square Table for Gender by Previous Training (from Table 12.5)

Gender	Previous Training	No Previous Training
Male	$O = 1$ $E = 1.8$	$O = 8$ $E = 7.2$
Female	$O = 3$ $E = 2.2$	$O = 8$ $E = 8.8$

$\chi^2 = .8$, $df = 1$, $p > .05$
O = observed frequencies (from Table 12.5)
E = expected frequencies

imply causation, only association. Correlation is applicable to data at the interval and ratio levels of measurement. Correlational values are always decimalized numbers, never exceeding ±1.00.

The size of the obtained correlation value indicates the strength of the association, or relationship, between the two variables. The closer a correlation is to zero, the less likely it is that a relationship exists between the two variables. The plus and minus signs indicate the direction of the relationship. Both high positive (close to +1.00) or high negative numbers (close to −1.00) signify strong relationships.

In positive correlations, though, the scores vary similarly, either increasing or decreasing. Thus, as parenting skills increase, so does self-esteem, for example. A negative correlation, in contrast, simply means that as one variable increases the other decreases. An example would be that, as parenting skills increase, the stresses experienced by foster parents decrease.

Thea may wonder whether there is a relationship between the foster parents' years of education and score on the *PSS* knowledge test. She might reason that the more years of education completed, the more likely the parents would have greater knowledge about parenting skills. To investigate the one-tailed hypothesis that years of education is positively related to knowledge of parenting skills, Thea can correlate the *PSS* scores with each person's number of years of formal education using one of the most common correlational tests, Pearson's *r*.

The obtained correlation between *PSS* score and years of education in this example is $r = -.10$ ($p > .05$). It was in the opposite direction of what she predicted. This negative correlation is close to zero, and its probability level is greater than .05. Thus, in Thea's sample, the parents' *PSS* scores are not related to their educational levels. If the resulting correlation coefficient (*r*) had been positive and statistically significant ($p < .05$), it would have indicated that as the knowledge levels of the parents increased so would their years of formal education. If the correlation coefficient had been statistically significant but negative, this would be interpreted as showing that as years of formal education increased, knowledge scores decreased.

If a correlational analysis is misinterpreted, it is likely to be the case that the researcher implied causation rather than simply identifying an association between the two variables. If Thea were to have found a statistically significant positive correlation between knowledge and education levels and had explained this to mean than the high knowledge scores were a result of higher education levels, she would have interpreted the statistic incorrectly.

Statistics That Determine Differences

Two commonly used statistical procedures, *t*-tests and analysis of variance (ANOVA), examine the means and variances of two or more separate groups of scores to determine if they are statistically different from one another. *T*-tests are used with only two groups of scores, whereas ANOVA is used when there are more than two groups. Both are characterized by having a dependent variable at the interval or ratio level of measurement, and an independent, or grouping, variable at either the nominal or ordinal level of measurement. Several assumptions underlie the use of both *t*-tests and ANOVA.

First, it is assumed that the dependent variable is normally distributed in the population from which the samples were drawn. Second, it is assumed that the variance of the scores of the dependent variable in the different groups is roughly the same. This assumption is called *homogeneity of variance*. Third, it is assumed that the samples are randomly drawn from the population.

Nevertheless, as mentioned in Chapters 6–9 on group research designs, it is a common occurrence in social work that we can neither randomly select nor randomly assign individuals to either the experimental or the control group. In many cases this is because we are dealing with already preformed groups, such as Thea's foster care parents.

Breaking the assumption of randomization, however, presents a serious drawback to the interpretation of the research findings that must be noted in the limitations and the interpretations section of the final research report. One possible difficulty that might result from nonrandomization is that the sample may be uncharacteristic of the larger population in some manner. It is important, therefore, that the results not be used inferentially; that is, the findings must not be generalized to the general population. The design of the research study is, thus, reduced to an exploratory or descriptive level, being relevant to only those individuals included in the sample.

Dependent t-Tests

Dependent *t*-tests are used to compare two groups of scores from the same individuals. The most frequent example in social work research is looking at how a group of individuals change from before they receive a social work intervention (pre) to afterwards (post). Thea may have decided that, while knowing the knowledge levels of the foster care parents before receiving training was interesting, it did not give her any idea whether her program helped the parents to improve their skill levels. In other words her research question became: "After being involved in the program, did parents know more about parenting skills than before they started?" Her hypothesis was that knowledge of parenting skills would improve after participation in her training program.

Thea managed to contact all of the foster care parents in the original group (Group A) one week after they had graduated from the program and asked them to fill out the *PSS* knowledge questionnaire once again. Since it was the same group of people who were responding twice to the same questionnaire, the dependent *t*-test was appropriate. The research design is as follows:

$$O_1 \quad X \quad O_2$$

Where:

O_1 = First administration of the *PSS*, the dependent variable
X = The skills training program, the independent variable
O_2 = Second administration of the *PSS*, the dependent variable

Using the same set of scores collected by Thea previously as the pre-test, the mean *PSS* was 82, with a standard deviation of 10. The mean score of the foster care parents after they completed the program was calculated as 86, with a standard deviation of 8.

A *t*-value of 3.9 was obtained, significant at the .05 level, indicating that the levels of parenting skills significantly increased after the foster care parents participated in the skill training program.

The results suggest that the average parenting skills of this particular group of foster care parents significantly improved (from 82 to 86) after they had participated in Thea's program.

Independent t-Tests

Independent *t*-tests are used for two groups of scores that have no relationship to each other. If Thea had *PSS* scores from one group of foster care parents and then collected more *PSS* scores from a second group of foster care parents, for example, these two groups would be considered independent, and the independent *t*-test would be the appropriate statistical analysis to determine if there was a statistically significant difference between the means of the two groups' *PSS* scores. This design could be written as:

$$
\begin{array}{ll}
\text{Mean of Group A:} & O_1 \\
\text{Mean of Group B:} & O_1
\end{array}
$$

Where:

O_1 = Mean score on the *PSS* before they went through the skills training program

Thea decided to compare the average *PSS* score for the first group of foster care parents (Group A) to the average *PSS* score of parents in her next training program (Group B). This would allow her to see if the first group (Group A) had been unusually talented, or conversely, were less well-versed in parenting skills than the second group (Group B). Her hypothesis was that there would be no differences in the levels of knowledge of parenting skills between the two groups.

Since Thea had *PSS* scores from two different groups of participants (Groups A & B), the correct statistical test to identify if there are any statistical differences between the means of the two groups is the independent *t*-test. Let us use the same set of numbers that we previously used in the example of the dependent *t*-test in this analysis, this time considering the posttest *PSS* scores as the scores of the second group of foster care parents. As can be seen from Figure 12.7, the mean *PSS* of Group A was 82 and the standard deviation was 10. Group B scored an average of 86 on the *PSS*, with a standard deviation of 8. Although the means of the two groups are four points apart, the standard deviations in the distribution of each are fairly large, so that there is considerable overlap between the two groups. This would suggest that statistically significant differences will not be found.

The obtained *t*-value to establish whether this four-point difference (86 – 82) between the means for two groups was statistically significant was calculated to be $t = 1.6$ with a $p > .05$. The two groups were, thus, not statistically different from one another and Thea's hypothesis was supported. Note, however, that Thea's foster care parents were not randomly assigned to each group, thus breaking one of the assumptions of the *t*-test. As discussed earlier, this is a serious limitation to the interpretation of the study's results. We must be especially careful not to generalize the findings beyond the groups included in the study.

Note that in the previous example, when using the same set of numbers but a dependent *t*-test, we found a statistically significant difference. This is because the dependent *t*-test analysis is more robust than the independent *t*-test, since having the same participant fill out the questionnaire twice, under two different conditions, controls for many extraneous variables, such as individual differences, that could negatively influence an analysis of independent samples.

One-Way Analysis of Variance

A one-way ANOVA is the extension of an independent *t*-test that uses three or more groups. Each set of scores is from a different group of

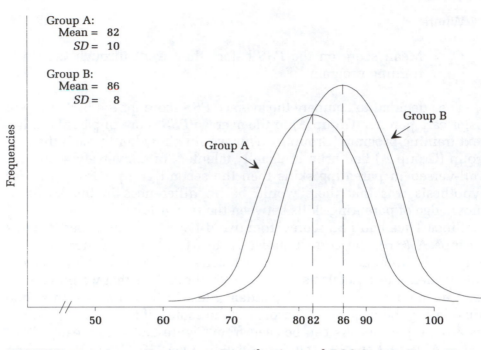

FIGURE 12.7   Frequency Distributions of *PSS* Scores From Two Groups of Foster Care Providers

participants. For example, Thea might use the scores on the *PSS* test from the first group of foster care parents from whom she collected data before they participated in her program, but she might also collect data from a second and a third group of parents before they received the training. The test for significance of an ANOVA is called an *F*-test. We could actually use an ANOVA procedure on only two groups and the result would be identical to the *t*-test.

Unlike the *t*-test, however, obtaining a significant *F*-value in a one-way ANOVA does not complete the analysis. Because ANOVA looks at differences between three or more groups, a significant *F*-value only tells us that there is a statistically significant difference among the groups: It does not tell us between which ones.

To identify this, we need to do a *post-hoc* test. A variety are available, such as Duncan's multiple range, Tukey's Honestly Significant Difference test, and Newman-Keuls, and are provided automatically by most computer statistical programs. But one caution applies: A post-hoc test should be used *only after finding a significant F*-value, because some of the post-hoc tests are more sensitive than the *F* test and so might find significance when the *F*-test does not. Generally, we should use the most conservative test first, in this case the *F*-test.

In the example of Thea's program, let us say that she collected data on a total of three different groups of foster care parents. The research design could be written as follows:

$$
\begin{array}{ll}
\text{Group A:} & O_1 \\
\text{Group B:} & O_1 \\
\text{Group C:} & O_1 \\
\end{array}
$$

There is no X in the design, since the measures were taken before the training (the X) was provided. The first group of foster care parents scored an average of 82 on the *PSS* (standard deviation 10). The second group scored an average of 86 (standard deviation 8), while the mean score of the third group was 88 with a standard deviation of 7.

The obtained F-value for the one-way ANOVA is 2.63, with a $p > .05$. Thus, we must conclude that there are no statistically significant differences between the means of the groups (i.e., 82, 86, 88). Since the F-value was not significant, we would not conduct any post-hoc tests. This finding would be interesting to Thea, since it suggests that all three groups of foster care parents started out with approximately the same knowledge levels, on the average, before receiving training.

SUMMING UP AND LOOKING AHEAD

This chapter provided a beginning look at the rationale behind some of the most commonly used statistical procedures, both those that describe samples and those that analyze data from a sample in order to make inferences about the larger population.

The level of measurement of the data is key to the kind of statistical procedures that can be utilized. Descriptive statistics are utilized with data from all levels of measurement. The mode is the most appropriate measure of central tendency for measurements of this level. It is only when we have data from interval and ratio levels that we can utilize inferential statistics—those that extend the statistical conclusions made about a sample by applying them to the larger population.

Descriptive measures of central tendency, such as the mode, median, and mean of a sample or population, all provide different kinds of information, each of which is applicable only to some levels of measurement. In addition to knowing the middle or average of a distribution of scores as provided by measures of central tendency, it is useful to know the value of the standard deviation that shows us how far away from the mean the scores are distributed. It is assumed that many variables studied in social work can be found in a normal distribution in the total population. Consequently many descriptive and inferential statistics assume such a distribution for their tests to be valid.

Chi-square and correlation are both statistical tests that determine whether variables are associated, although they do not show causation. In contrast, *t*-tests and analysis of variance (ANOVA) are statistical procedures for determining whether the mean and variance in one group (often a treatment group) are significantly different from those in another (often a comparison or control group).

REVIEW QUESTIONS

1   Describe in detail each level of measurement. Use a social work example in your discussion. Discuss how the variable, educational level, could be classified at all four levels.

2   Describe the purpose of descriptive statistics. How can they be used in social work research situations? Provide a social work example in your discussion.

3   Describe the purpose of inferential statistics. How can they be used in social work research situations? Provide a social work example in your discussion.

4   Discuss how computers can help aid in the data analysis phase of the research process.

5   What are the benefits to the reader when statistics are reported in a journal article? Be specific and concrete in your response.

6   List and fully describe the three measures of central tendency and the two measures of variability. Provide a social work example throughout your discussion.

7   List and fully describe the two statistics that can help us to determine if there is an association between two variables. When is one used over the other? Why?

8   List and fully describe the three statistics that can help us to determine if there are any statistically significant differences between the means of two or more groups. Use a social work example throughout your discussion.

9   Describe the main differences between *t*-tests and ANOVA. When is one used over the other?

10   In groups of four, decide on a social work–related problem area. Derive a research question (or hypothesis) out of the problem area. Describe how you could carry out a quantitative research study that would use statistics that could answer your research question (or test your hypothesis). In your description, define all relevant variables (e.g., independent, dependent, extraneous, intervening), the research question (or hypothesis), potential rival hypotheses, the specific research design, the sample, the data collection method(s), the data source(s) for each data collection method(s), and the specific statistics that you would use. Discuss the limitations of your hypothetical study. Present your discussion to the entire class.

11   With the same research question (or hypothesis) used in Exercise 1, design a qualitative study and answer the same questions contained at the end of Exercise 1.

12   At your university library, locate as many articles as needed to demonstrate the four levels of measurement. If the measuring instruments are not included in the article(s), find copies of the instruments. Discuss how the authors used measurement by answering the following four questions: (a) Which variable(s) was (were) measured at the *nominal* level? (b) Which variable(s) was (were) measured at the *ordinal* level? (c) Which variable(s) was (were) measured at the *interval* level? (d) Which variable(s) was (were) measured at the *ratio* level?

C h a p t e r　13

Qualitative Data Analysis

IN THE LAST CHAPTER, we looked at methods of analyzing quantitative data. In this chapter, we turn to the analysis of qualitative data: that is, data collected in the form of words (i.e., text data), most often through interviews, open-ended items on questionnaires, or personal logs. Unlike *numbers*, which are used in quantitative analyses, *words* give us descriptions or opinions from the unique point of view of the person who spoke or wrote the words (see Box 13.1).

Text data have both disadvantages and advantages. The disadvantages are that words tend to be open to different interpretations and cannot be collected from large numbers of people at a time because the process of collection and analysis is much more time-consuming than is the case for numerical data. The major advantage is that the material is very rich, containing multiple facets, and may provide us with a deeper understanding of the underlying meaning than would be possible if we just collected numbers. Usually, we need the deeper understanding provided by qualitative data when we know very little about the problem we are investigating and are not yet in a position to formulate theories about it for testing. We are seeking to form patterns out of individual experiences so that we can develop more general theories.

Box 13.1

WRITING THE QUALITATIVE RESEARCH REPORT

Writing up and disseminating our research findings is a critical phase of the qualitative research process. Without an adequate plan and strategy for the dissemination of our findings, they will not reach practitioners who may find them useful. As far as we are concerned, too many research reports gather dust on shelves because the researchers have overlooked the significance of disseminating their findings.

A commitment to adding to our knowledge base requires a carefully conceived and implemented publishing method for informing our practice community. It is extremely important to know that qualitative research findings can result either in improved social scientific understanding or in meaningless gibberish, as is so aptly pointed out by Berg (1994):

> My children, Alex and Kate, were eating alphabet soup for lunch one Sunday afternoon. Kate, then about four years old, was stirring her soup with great care and deliberation. She managed to capture several of the letters on her spoon, carefully spill off the liquid, and spell out her name.
>
> "Look daddy, I wrote my name with my noodles!" She held her spoon up for my inspection. She had arranged the letters to spell "KATIE." Alex, seeing the attention his sister had received, pulled his dripping spoon from his soup, and spilling much of it onto the floor exclaimed, "Me too!" Unfortunately, his letters spelled out "XCYU," a unique spelling of "Alex," or simply failure to "sort the noodles from the soup" in a fashion that made his noodles mean something to others.

With the above quote in mind, it must be noted, however, that our research findings may not merit dissemination. This is true regardless of the type of research approach undertaken—quantitative or qualitative. All researchers must assess the utility and practical significance of their findings before they decide whether a report should be written for possible publication. Several assessment criteria can be applied to qualitative research studies:

- Do our research findings extend current theory?
- Has our research study added anything to the theoretical base of social work practice?
- How well does our research study meet the test of trustworthiness? How credible is our research study?
- To what extent could our study's findings inform day-to-day social work practice activities?

Each of the above criteria must be evaluated keeping in mind the audience we want to reach. Effective distribution requires a clear idea of who should know about our study. Such clarity will greatly assist in selecting and implementing a strategy for its dissemination. There can be little doubt that the written word has dominated publication activities over time. In addition to journals and books, improved access to the literature is now available through on-line bibliographic searches.

Nevertheless, publication methods have diversified and the presentation of qualitative research findings through nonprint outlets is growing. Social work practitioners who are developing agency-specific models of intervention may find the nonprint approach useful as a supplement to staff training.

Video- and audiotapes are particularly effective ways to disperse information that involves practice skills. Unfortunately, most of us do not have access to the means of creating nonprint media products, so these approaches may prove difficult to develop.

Source: Adapted and modified from: Berg 1994); McClelland and Austin (1996)

The primary purpose of a qualitative data analysis is to sift and sort the masses of words we have collected from our research participants in such a way that we can derive patterns related to our research question: to identify the similarities and differences presented by individuals and the possible links between them. Suppose for a moment, that we are investigating postnatal depression among women. We may be interested in what the symptoms are, how new mothers experience them, and how they feel their depression affects their relationships with their newborns. We may also be interested in whether the women who experience postnatal depression are similar in any way with respect to various characteristics, such as age, ethnic background, desire for the baby, partner or family support, socioeconomic status, medical history, and so on.

Indeed, we may have structured our interviews to collect specific data related to these kinds of variables. If we did, then we have already theorized that these characteristics or variables are related to postnatal depression, and we may, even subconsciously, look for patterns in the data that will confirm our theories. There is nothing evil about this. Researchers are human beings with a normal human tendency to make connections between events on the frailest of evidence, and it is a rare researcher who starts on a study with no preconceived notions at all.

The important thing is to be aware of our human frailties with respect to drawing unwarranted conclusions, and to organize our data collection and analysis so that these frailties are minimized as far as possible. A look at some of the assumptions underlying qualitative research might help us to accomplish this:

- We are assuming that the goal of qualitative research is to reach an in-depth understanding of each of our research participants, with respect to the research question, including experiences that are unique to them. We will not achieve this goal if we do not allow participants to express their uniqueness during data collection. Neither will we achieve it if we ignore the uniqueness during data analysis because we were hoping to uncover patterns and this is an anomaly that does not quite fit. It is also easy to ignore uniqueness if it does not fit with the findings of other researchers. An exploratory topic tends to reveal little in the way of previous research, but there is usually some, and it is tempting to disregard a unique experience if it seems to contravene what others have found.

- Information is always provided in some context. In the case of a research study, the context is the way in which the information was elicited: for example, the phrasing of a question. In an interview, the context is the relationship between the interviewer and the interviewee. Preconceptions on the part of the interviewer tend to elicit responses that fit with the preconceptions. Thus, it is important in analysis not to look at just the response but at the emotional atmosphere surrounding the response and the question that was responded to.

There are three major phases involved in a qualitative analysis:

- First, we must plan how we will do the analysis: how we will transcribe spoken or written data into a usable form and what rules we will use to fit the pieces of data together in a meaningful way.

- Second, we must do the analysis, following the general rules we set out at the beginning and perhaps revising these rules along the way if we come across some data to which our rules cannot be sensibly applied. It is important to note though that whatever rules we finally decide on must be applied to all our data. Changing our minds about rules will mean going back over the material we have worked on already; and, indeed, qualitative analysis is usually a back-and-forth sort of process, involving many rereadings and reworkings as new insights appear and we begin to question our initial theories or assumptions.

- Third, we need to draw meaning from our analysis: that is, to identify relationships between the major themes that have emerged and to build theories around these for testing in the future.

PLANNING THE ANALYSIS

There are two steps involved in planning a qualitative analysis: (1) transcribing the data, and (2) establishing general rules for the analysis.

Transcribing the Data

Transcribing our data itself involves two tasks: (1) deciding what computer program to use, if any; and (2) deciding who will transcribe the data.

Deciding What Computer Program to Use, If Any

If responses are written, as in open-ended items on a questionnaire or personal logs, transcription may be a matter of typing the responses, either just for easier reading or with the aim of using a computer program to assist with the analysis. A few researchers, distrustful of computers, prefer to use a traditional "cut-and-paste" method, physically cutting the manuscript and grouping the cut sections together with other related sections. A computer need not be used for transcription in this case. A typewriter would do, or even legible handwriting. Some researchers trust the computer just sufficiently to allow it to move selected passages together with other selected passages to electronically form a group of related data: the majority of word-processing programs can accomplish this.

An increasing number of researchers, however, use computer programs that have been developed specifically to assist with the analysis of qualitative data. Two familiar names are *The Ethnograph* and *Nudist* but new programs are always coming on to the market and it is wise to consult colleagues or computer companies about which programs might be most helpful for a particular project. It is important to note that no computer program can do the analysis for us. The most it can do is free up time for us to spend on considering the meaning of our data.

Deciding Who Will Transcribe the Data

Some researchers are fortunate enough to have a research or administrative assistant to help them in the transcription process. If this is the case, it is necessary to lay down guidelines right at the beginning about how the material should be transcribed. If an interview has been audio- or videotaped, for example, the questions should be included in the transcript as well as the answers. Nonverbal communications such as pauses, laughing or crying, and voice tone should be included in brackets so that the emotional context of the interview is captured as far as possible in the transcript. Those fortunate researchers with assistants are nevertheless well advised to transcribe at least the first few interviews themselves so that assistants can see what ought to be included.

Another concern is how to format the transcript so that it is easy to read and analyze. It is a good idea to leave a margin of at least two inches along the right-hand side so that we can write notes and codes alongside the corresponding text. It is also a good idea to number each line of the transcript so that we can readily identify each segment of data. Computer programs designed to assist in qualitative analysis will automatically do this. For example, suppose we worked in a foster care agency and we were asking foster parents who had resigned from the agency in the past year why they had resigned. A few lines from one of our interviews might be transcribed like this:

1 **Sue** (angrily): His behavior was just too much and nobody from the agency told

2 us that he'd set fires before and was probably going to burn our house down. I

3 suppose they thought that if they'd told us that we wouldn't have taken him but

4 I do feel that we were set up from the beginning (sounding very upset). And when

5 we called the agency, there was only an answering machine and it was a whole

6 day before the social worker called us back.

7 **Interviewer**: That's dreadful.

Reading these lines after the transcript is completed might immediately set us thinking about how foster parents' reasons for resigning could be separated into categories. One category might be the foster child's behavior (much worse than the foster parents had been led to expect). Or this might be two categories: (1) the child's behavior and (2) the discrepancy between the actual behavior and the expected behavior.

Another category might be negative feelings toward the agency, with two subcategories: the feeling of having been set up, and the perceived lack of support in a time of crisis. It might not take long at all for these tentative categories to harden into certainties. Having read six lines from one interview, we now feel we know why foster parents resign and it only remains to confirm the reasons we have found by picking out similar sentiments from our interviews with other foster parents. Job completed!

Actually, we have barely begun. Since we cannot—and do not wish to—stop our minds from jumping ahead in this fashion, we must find some way to organize our thoughts such that our intuitive leaps do not blind us to different and perhaps contradictory insights yielded by other interviews. There are two techniques that might help us to do this: previewing the data, and keeping a journal. Both these techniques will also help us to establish general rules for our analysis.

Establishing General Rules for the Analysis

Establishing general rules for the analysis ensures that our efforts are systematic and the same rules are applied to all our data. We use rules to decide how we could fit together pieces of data in a meaningful way and how these groups of data could be categorized and coded (to be discussed shortly). For example, what criteria or rule do we use to decide whether a child's worsened behavior after a visit with the biological parents should be categorized under "child's behaviors" or under "relationships with biological parents"? Although we clarify and refine the rules throughout the study, by the time we have finished we should have a set of rules that have been consistently applied to every piece of data. We start to think about what rules might apply during the previewing task.

Previewing the Data

The process of transcription might be ongoing throughout the study, with each interview transcribed as soon as it is completed, or transcription might not begin until all the data have been assembled. Whichever method is used, it is important to read all of the transcripts before beginning to formally identify categories. It is also important to give all of the transcripts and all parts of the transcripts the same amount of attention. We may be in peak form at the beginning of the day while reading the first few pages of the first transcript, for example, but by the end of the day and the end of the third transcript, this initial peak has waned to weary impatience.

We would be better advised to read only for as long as we remain interested in the material. This will obviously mean that the process of previewing the data extends over a longer period, but qualitative data analysis takes time. It is a lengthy process of discovery, whose pace cannot be forced. If we are rereading material, it sometimes helps to read the last third of an interview at moments of high energy instead of the first third. That way, we will not lose valuable insights from later sections of the interview transcript.

Keeping a Journal

Some people love journals and others hate them, but the qualitative researcher cannot afford to be without one. The journal should have been started at the same time as the study was started. It should include notes on the planned method and any changes in the plan, with dates and reasons. For example, perhaps the plan was to interview all of the foster parents who had resigned from the agency during the last year, but some of them would not agree to be interviewed.

We may believe that those who agreed differed in some important respects from those who refused: They were more satisfied with the agency perhaps. If this were the case, the data from our more satisfied sample might lead us to faulty conclusions, possibly causing us to place more emphasis on personal reasons for resignation, such as failing health or family circumstances, and less on agency-related reasons, such as poor information-sharing or support. Whatever the difficulties we encounter and the assumptions we make, our journal should keep an accurate record of them as we move along in the data analysis. Since the work we do must be open to scrutiny by others, it is essential to keep a record of all our activities and the feelings and reasonings behind them.

When the data-collection stage begins, the journal can be used to record personal reactions to the interview situation. For example, we might feel more personal empathy with one foster parent than with another and be tempted to give more weight to the remarks of the parent with whom we sympathized. An unconscious overreliance on one research participant or one subset of research participants will hopefully reveal itself as we read through our journal entries later during the course of the analysis.

When we begin to categorize and code the data, we can use the journal to keep notes about the process, writing down the general rules, revisions to the rules, and questions or comments with respect to how particular pieces of data might be categorized.

DOING THE ANALYSIS

Once all the data have been previewed, we can start on coding. There are two levels of coding: (1) first-level coding, which deals with the concrete ideas evident in the transcript and (2) second-level coding, which looks for and interprets the more abstract meanings underlying these ideas.

First-Level Coding

There are four tasks in first-level coding: (1) identifying meaning units, (2) creating categories, (3) assigning codes to categories, and (4) refining and reorganizing categories.

Identifying Meaning Units

A meaning unit is a piece of data, which we consider to be meaningful by itself. It might be a word, a partial or complete sentence, or a paragraph or more. Let us look once again at the interview segment presented earlier:

1 **Sue** (angrily): <u>His behavior was just too much</u> and *nobody from the agency told*

2 *us that he'd set fires before and was probably going to burn our house down.* **I**

3 **suppose they thought that if they'd told us that we wouldn't have taken him but**

4 **I do feel that we were set up from the beginning (sounding very upset).** *And when*

5 *we called the agency, there was only an answering machine and it was a whole*

6 *day before the social worker called us back.*

7 **Interviewer**: That's dreadful.

In this segment, we might identify four meaning units. The first (<u>under-lined</u>, line 1) relates to the child's behavior. The second (*italics*, lines 1 and 2) relates to lack of information provided by the agency. The third (**bold**, lines 2, 3 and 4) relates to feeling set up by the agency. The fourth (***bold italics***, lines 4, 5 and 6) relates to poor support on the part of the agency. Of course, different researchers might identify different meaning units or label the same units differently. For example, lines 4, 5 and 6 might be identified as relating to agency response style rather than poor support and might involve two distinct meaning units, "response method" and "response time." Similarly, the partial sentence in line 2 "he'd set fires before" might be viewed as a separate meaning unit relating to the child's past rather than present behavior.

The first run-through to identify meaning units will always be somewhat tentative and subject to change. If we are not sure whether to break a large meaning unit into smaller ones, it may be preferable to leave it as a whole. We can always break it down later in the analysis; and breaking down large units tends to be easier than combining smaller ones, especially once second-level coding begins.

Creating Categories

Once we have identified meaning units in the transcript, our next task is to consider which of them fit together into categories. Perhaps we should have a category labeled "child's behavior" into which we put all meaning units related to the child's behavior, including the second meaning unit identified above "nobody from the agency told us that he'd set fires before and was probably going to burn our house down."

Or perhaps we should have two categories, "child's present behavior" and "child's past behavior," in which case the second meaning unit might belong in the latter category. Or perhaps we feel that the vital words are "nobody told us" and this second meaning unit really belongs in a different category labeled "provision of information by agency." All other meaning units to do with foster parents being given information by the agency would then belong in this same category even though they had nothing to do with the child's behavior.

Since these kinds of decisions are often difficult to make, it is a good idea to note in our journal how we made the decisions we did and what alternatives we considered at the time. What rules did we use to decide whether a particular meaning unit was similar to or different from another meaning unit? How did we define our categories in order to decide whether a group of similar meaning units should be placed in one category or in another?

As we continue to examine new meaning units, we will use these rules to decide whether each new unit is similar to existing units and belongs in an existing category or whether it is different from existing units and needs a new separate category. The number of categories will therefore expand every time we identify meaning units that are different in important ways from those we have already categorized.

Since too many categories will make the final analysis very difficult, we should try to keep the number within manageable limits. This may mean revising our initial rules about how categories are defined and what criteria are used to decide whether meaning units are similar enough to be grouped together. Of course, any change in rules should be noted in our journal, together with the rationale for the change.

The complexity of our categorization scheme also needs to be considered. One meaning unit may, in fact, fall into more than one category, or a group of meaning units may overlap with another group. Large, inclusive categories may consist of a number of smaller, more exclusive subcategories. For example, as we saw, the meaning unit *"nobody from the agency told us that he'd set fires before and was probably going to burn our house down"* has to do both with lack of information provided by the agency and with the child's past behavior.

Sometimes, meaning units cannot be clearly placed into any category and fall into the category of "miscellaneous." When we are tired, most everything may seem to be "miscellaneous," but miscellaneous units should make up no more than ten percent of the total data set. More than that suggests that there is a problem with the original categorization scheme. The real purpose of a "miscellaneous" category is to prevent our throwing out meaning units which, at first glance, appear to be irrelevant. Such throwing out is risky because at some point we may decide that our whole categorization scheme needs massive revision and we must start the whole process again from scratch.

Assigning Codes to Categories

Codes are simply a shorthand form of the category name. They typically take the form of strings of letters and/or symbols. Codes used in

The Ethnograph, for example, may be up to ten letters long and can also include symbols. Codes are usually displayed in the margins (often the right margin) of the transcribed text.

If we had a category labeled "child's behavior" we might simply code this CB where the C stands for the foster child and the B stands for behavior. If we want to distinguish between past and present behavior, we might use the codes CPASTB and CPRESB respectively. If there is a category relating to the behavior of the foster parents' own children (perhaps this has worsened since the foster child moved in), we might use the codes FPCPASTB and FPCPRESB respectively, where the FPC stands for the foster parents' child.

In fact, we might make it a rule that codes starting with C, FP, FPC, and A stand for things to do with the foster child, the foster parents, the foster parents' children, and the agency respectively. Then AINF>FP might mean information provided by the agency to the foster parents and AINF<FP might mean information provided by the foster parents to the agency. It is a good idea to keep the codes as short as possible in the beginning since they tend to become longer as the analysis grows more complex. However, there are many different ways to assign codes and, so long as the code is clearly related to the category, it does not really matter which system is utilized (see Box 13.2).

Refining and Reorganizing Categories

Before moving on from first-level coding, we need to make a final sweep through the data to ensure that our analysis reflects what our research participants have said. We should consider the logic underlying the rules we made for grouping meaning units and defining categories. We may, for example, be confused about why we created some categories, or feel uncertain about why a particular meaning unit was put into a particular category. We might find that some categories are too complex and need to be split into smaller categories; or some categories are poorly defined; or some of the categories that we expected to emerge from the data are missing altogether.

We might, for example, have expected that some foster parents would resign because of poor health, but there is no category coded FPHEA. Investigation reveals that foster parents did indeed mention their poor health but they always ascribed it to the strain of dealing with the foster child or the foster child's biological parents or the agency. Hence, the meaning units including poor health have been categorized under "foster child's present behavior (CPRESB)" or "relationships with agency (AREL)" or "relationships with biological parents (BPREL)" and have not been broken down finely enough to isolate poor health as a separate category. We may wish to create such a category or we may prefer to note its absence in our journal, together with other categories that are incomplete or in some way unsatisfactory.

Box 13.2_____

BUILDING A CONCEPTUAL FRAMEWORK
FOR THE FOUNTAIN HOUSE STUDY

In the Fountain House study, Ellen Finch wanted to find out why staff members there had not experienced the burnout that had been reported for other such helping professionals. She began by spending a week at Independence Center, Missouri, a setting closer to home but modeled on Fountain House, a New York facility for former mental patients.

After this preliminary study, she had a much better idea of what to look for, what to expect, and how to approach people at Fountain House, which was four times as large and nine times as old. Once at Fountain House, she reviewed agency documents, attended unit meetings, spoke with members and staff, went to the social programs, and instituted formal staff interviews.

Finch's study was guided by a linked set of concepts that formed a conceptual framework. The concepts were drawn primarily from role theory and provided the terms, ideas, cues, categories, and assumptions that determined how the study was to be conducted. She therefore structured the interviews to cover at least the following conceptual categories:

- Individual background
- Recruitment/selection into the Fountain House staff
- Fountain House model and ideology
- Initial and ongoing socialization
- Role expectations
- Organizational processes, such as leadership, supervision, evaluation, communication, decision making, recognition, rewards
- Occupational stress
- Role adaptations and negotiation
- Organizational changes
- Growth in recent years

By thinking through in advance what the interviews should cover, Finch was well on her way to a preliminary list of categories and codes. Her field notes from the first site visit filled a large notebook.

They were organized into five types of notes: interview, observational, theoretical, methodological, and personal. She explains her procedures as follows:

> Every few days I would carefully review these notes and write descriptive code words developed prior to the fieldwork in the left margin . . . . These code words were derived from the interview questions and common categories of response . . . . The brief analytic reviews during the data collection period were used to increase awareness of patterns and recurrent themes, speculate on apparent processes, redirect interview questions and strategies, point out gaps, and develop explanatory paradigms.

After her first two-week visit she went through her notes again, seeking to clarify and refine concepts and to think through issues to be covered on a second site visit. She used the cut-and-paste method to organize field notes into coded categories, which helped make evident the patterns in the responses and observed processes. Codes were checked and revised if necessary; the original categories were modified to incorporate emergent themes. The answers to questionnaires administered to measure burnout were scored.

From this immersion in the data, new ideas and insights become evident. In this conceptualization, Finch observes, "Some patterns which emerged were consistent with initial thinking; some did not support earlier assumptions; and some were altogether new pieces of the organizational puzzle." To explain the new concepts and patterns, she had to review a large, diverse body of literature.

Finch then made plans for the second site visit. She determined that she needed to follow certain conceptual threads and drop others. More verbatim information derived from audiotaped interviews was needed to tap the information available from members. More material was needed on unit activities.

Box 13.2 Continued

This evaluation led to a much revised set of categories and codes. The number of categories was reduced from 37 to 24, and the descriptors were more finely focused. The final version included such codes and categories as:

Code	Category
Stress/soc	Stressor related to socialization
Stress/wrk	Stressor related to work overload
Stress/mem	Stressor related to member
R exp	Role expectations
Refram	Reframing stressors (adaptation)
Sur skil	Survival skills (adaptation)
Recruit	Recruitment and selection of staff
Soc sup	Social support
Ideo	Ideology
C lead	Charismatic leadership

Interviews during the second visit covered less material but were more in-depth, lasted longer, and seemed more relaxed. Finch was feeling more at home with the staff, and the staff was more at ease with her. After this visit came a second round of conceptualization and analysis, which included ongoing revision of concepts and evaluation of patterns. The initial data analysis was supplemented with theoretical notes and summaries made in the field. The field notes and transcribed interviews were reviewed and coded, and additional demographic information was combined with the earlier data.

Without the processes of categorizing, coding, and conceptualization, Finch's strenuous work in building relationships, framing the sample, and collecting and logging the data would have yielded only so many pages of text.

Source: Taylor (1993)

This is a good time to ask a colleague to analyze one or two of our interviews using the rules we have devised. In this way, we can check that the categories themselves and the rules that define them make sense. If our colleague organizes meaning units in a significantly different way, our categorization scheme may need to be substantially revised.

It is probably time to stop first-level coding when all our meaning units fit easily into our current categorization scheme and there are no more units that require the creation of new categories. If interviews are continuing during first-level coding, we will probably find the data becoming repetitive, yielding no new piece of information that cannot be fitted into the present scheme.

Second-Level Coding

The next major step in the data analysis process is second-level coding. As noted earlier, this is more abstract and involves interpreting what the first-level categories mean. During first-level coding, we derived meaning units from interviews with individuals, and we derived categories by comparing the meaning units to see which were similar enough to be grouped together. During second-level coding we will compare the categories themselves in order to uncover possible relationships between them. The point of doing this is to identify themes based on patterns that repeatedly occur among our categories.

Comparing Categories

A comparison of categories in any qualitative study will probably yield many different types of relationships. The following three types are among those most commonly found:

- **A temporal relationship**   One category may be found to often precede another. For example, foster children whose own parents are abusive might initially behave well because they are happy to be living away from the abuse. Later, however, they may push for a return to their families of origin, and their response to the foster parents may become less positive.

- **A causal relationship**   One category may be perceived to be the cause of another. For example, foster parents may believe that the child's bad behavior after every visit with the biological parent was the cause of their own negative attitudes toward the biological parent. However, it is always risky to assume that one category caused another when, in fact, the opposite may be true. Perhaps the foster parents started off with a negative attitude toward the child's biological parents, the child was more than usually angry about this after visits home, and the child demonstrated rage by behaving badly.

- **One category may be contained within another category**   At this stage of the analysis, we may decide that two categories that we had thought to be separate are in fact linked. For example, foster parents may have said that they were never introduced to the child's biological parents by the agency, and we have categorized this separately from their statement that the agency was not entirely truthful with them about the child's past behavior. Now, we realize that these are both examples of lack of information provided to the foster parent by the agency. Furthermore, foster parents complained that they were not invited to agency meetings in which the child's progress was reviewed. Lack of information and nonattendance at meetings might combine to form a theme related to the agency's attitude toward the foster parents: The theme might be that the agency does not appear to accept the foster parents as equal partners in the task of helping the child.

When we have identified themes based on patterns among our categories, we code these themes in the same way as we coded our categories. If one of our themes is that the agency does not view foster parents as equal partners, for example, we might code this as A<FP-PART. Once themes have been identified and coded, the process of second-level coding is complete.

LOOKING FOR MEANING

Drawing meaning from our data is perhaps the most rewarding step of a qualitative data analysis. It involves two important steps: (1) interpreting data and building theory, and (2) assessing the trustworthiness of the results.

Interpreting Data and Building Theory

This step involves two tasks: (1) developing conceptual classifications systems, and (2) presenting themes or theory.

Developing Conceptual Classifications Systems

The ultimate goal of a qualitative research study is to identify any relationships between the major themes that emerge from the data set. During first-level coding, we used meaning units to form categories. During second-level coding, we used categories to form themes. Now we will use themes to build theories. In order to do this, we must understand the interconnections between themes and categories. There are several strategies that might be useful in helping us to identify these connections:

- **Draw a cluster diagram**   This form of diagram helps us to think about how themes and categories may or may not be related to one another. Draw and label circles for each theme and arrange them in relation to each other. Some of the circles will overlap, others will stand alone. The circles of the themes of more importance will be larger, in comparison to themes and categories that are not as relevant to our conclusions. The process of thinking about what weight to give the themes, how they interact, and how important they will be in the final scheme will be valuable in helping us to think about the meaning of our research study.

- **Make a matrix**   Matrix displays may be helpful for noting relations between categories or themes. Designing a two-dimensional matrix involves writing a list of categories along the left side of a piece of paper and then another list of categories across the top. For example, along the side, we might write categories related to the theme of the degree of partnership between the agency and the foster parents: One such category might be whether the foster parents were invited to agency meetings held to discuss the child's progress. Then, along the top we might write categories related to the theme of foster parents' attitudes toward the agency: One category here might be whether foster parents felt their opinions about the child were listened to by the agency. Where two categories intersect on the matrix, we could note with a plus sign (+), those indicators of partnership or lack of partnership that positively affect parents' attitudes. Conversely, we would mark with a minus sign (–) those that seem to have a negative affect. Such a matrix gives us a sense of to what degree and in what ways foster parents' attitudes toward the agency are molded by the agency's view of foster parents as partners.

- **Count the number of times a meaning unit or category appears**   Although numbers are typically associated with quantitative studies, it is acceptable to use numbers in qualitative work in order to document how many of the participants expressed a particular theme. We might be interested, for example, in finding out how many participants experienced specific problems related to lack of agency support. We would write the code names for the foster parents interviewed down the left side of a piece of paper and the list of problems across the top. To fill in the chart, we would simply place a check mark beside each foster parent's code name if she or he experienced that particular problem. Numbers will help protect our analysis against bias that occurs when intense but rare examples of problems are presented. For example, many foster parents may have felt that they were not given sufficient information about the child's past behavior, but only one may have felt that the agency deliberately set her up. Although, we will certainly not discount this foster parent's experience, we might prefer to view it as an extreme example of the results of poor information sharing.

- **Create a metaphor**   Developing metaphors that convey the essence of our findings is another mechanism for extracting meaning. One example of a metaphor concerning battered women is "the cycle of violence," which effectively describes the tension building between a couple until the husband beats his wife, followed by a calm, loving phase until the tension builds again.

- **Look for missing links**   If two categories or themes seem to be related but not directly so, it may be that a third variable connects the two.

- **Note contradictory evidence**   It is only natural to want to focus on evidence that supports our ideas. Because of this human tendency, it is particularly important to also identify themes and categories that raise questions about our conclusions. All contradictory evidence must be accounted for when we come to derive theories pertaining to our study area: for example, theories about why foster parents resign.

Presenting Themes or Theory

Sometimes it is sufficient to conclude a qualitative study merely by describing the major themes that emerged from the data. For example, we may have used the experiences of individual foster parents to derive reasons for resignation common to the majority of foster parents we studied. When categorized, such reasons might relate to: inadequate training; poor support from the agency; failure on the agency's part to treat the foster parents as partners; negative attitudes on the part of the foster parents' friends and extended family; unrealistic expectations on the part of the foster parents with respect to the foster child's progress and behavior; poor relations between the biological and foster parents; the perceived negative influence of the foster child on the foster parents' own children; marital discord attributed to stress; failing health attributed to stress; and so on. We might think it sufficient in our conclusions to present and describe these categories, together with recommendations for improvement.

On the other hand, we might wish to formulate questions to be answered in future studies. What would change if agencies were to view foster parents as partners rather than clients? If we think, we know what would change, we might want to formulate more specific questions: for example:

> Are agencies that view foster parents as partners more likely to provide foster parents with full information regarding the child's background than agencies that do not view foster parents as partners?

Or, we might want to reword this question to form a hypothesis for testing:

> Agencies that view foster parents as partners are more likely to provide foster parents with full information regarding the child's background than agencies that do not view parents as partners.

In order to arrive at this hypothesis, we have essentially formulated a theory about how two of our concepts are related. We could carry this further by adding other concepts to the chain of relationships and formulating additional hypotheses:

> Foster parents who have full information about the child's background are less likely to have unrealistic expectations about the child's behavior and progress than foster parents who do not have full information about the child's background.

And,

> Foster parents who have unrealistic expectations about the child's behavior and progress are more likely to experience marital discord (due to the fostering process) than foster parents who do not have unrealistic expectations.

Indeed, we might weave all the various woes our study has uncovered into an elaborate pattern of threads, beginning with the agency's reluctance to view foster parents as partners and ending with the foster parents' resignations.

In our excitement, we might come to believe that we have solved the entire problem of resigning foster parents. If agencies would only change their attitudes with respect to foster parents' status and behave in accordance with this change in attitude, then all foster parents would continue to be foster parents until removed by death. It is at this point that we need to focus on the second stage of our search for meaning: assessing the trustworthiness of our results.

Assessing the Trustworthiness of the Results

There are three major reasons why disgruntled agencies, as well as other actors, may not agree that our results are as trustworthy as we believe: (1) they may doubt our personal credibility as researchers, (2) they may doubt the dependability of our data, and (3) they may think that we have been led astray by our own biases and preconceptions.

Establishing Our Own Credibility

Since a qualitative study depends so much on human judgment, it is necessary to demonstrate that our own personal judgment is to be trusted. Part of this relates to our training and experience. Another important part is the record we made in our journal detailing the procedures we followed, the decisions we made and why we made them, and the thought processes that led to our conclusions. If we can demonstrate that we were qualified to undertake this study and we carried it out meticulously, others are far more likely to take account of our conclusions.

Establishing the Dependability of the Data

If we have been consistent in such things as interview procedures and developing rules for coding, and if we have obtained dependable data through a rigorous, recorded process, then another researcher should be able to follow the same process, make the same decisions, and arrive at essentially the same conclusions. Also, if we ourselves redo part of the analysis at a later date, the outcome should be very similar to that produced in the original analysis. In order to ensure that we or others could duplicate our work, we need to pay attention to the following issues:

- **The context of the interviews**   Some data-collection situations yield more credible data than others, and we may choose to weight our interviews accordingly. Some authors claim, for example, that data collected later in the study are more dependable than data collected at the beginning because our interviewing style is likely to be more relaxed and less intrusive. In addition, data obtained first-hand are considered to be more dependable than second-hand data, which are obtained through a third party. Similarly, data offered voluntarily are thought to be stronger than data obtained through intensive questioning; and data obtained from research participants while in their natural enviornments (e.g., home or neighborhood coffee shop) are more to be trusted than data provided by research participants in a foreign and sterile environment (e.g., researcher's office or interviewing room).

- **Triangulation**   Triangulation is commonly used to establish the trustworthiness of qualitative data. There are several different kinds of triangulation, but the essence of the method lies in a comparison of several perspectives. For example, we might collect data from the agency about what information was provided to foster parents in order to compare the agency's perspective with what foster parents said. With respect to data analysis, we might ask a colleague to use our rules to see if he or she makes the same decisions about meaning units, categories, and themes. The hope is that different perspectives will confirm each other, adding weight to the credibility of our analysis.

- **Member checking**   Obtaining feedback from research participants is a credibility technique that is unique to qualitative studies. While such feedback should be an ongoing part of the study (interview transcripts may be presented to research participants for comment, for example), it is particularly useful when our analysis has been completed, our interpretations made, and our conclusions drawn. Research participants may not agree with our interpretation or conclusions, and may differ among each other. If this is the case, we need to decide whether to exclude the interpretations to which they object, or whether to leave them in, merely recording the dissenting opinions and our position in relation to them.

Establishing Our Control of Biases and Preconceptions

Since all human beings inevitably have biases and preconceptions about most everything, one way to demonstrate that we are in control of ours is to list them. Such a list is useful to both ourselves and others when we want to check that our conclusions have emerged from the data rather than from our established beliefs. Also useful is our journal where we documented our attempts to keep ourselves open to what our research participants had to say. We may want to consider the following points in relation to bias:

- Our personal belief systems may affect our interpretation of the data. Member checking has already been mentioned as a way to safeguard against this.
- We might draw conclusions before the data are analyzed or before we have decided about the trustworthiness of the data collected. Such conclusions tend to set to a cement-like hardness and are likely to persist despite all future indications that they were wrong.
- We might censor, ignore, or dismiss certain parts of the data. This may occur as a result of data overload or because the data contradict an established way of thinking.
- We might make unwarranted or unsupported causal statements based on impressions rather than on solid analysis. Even when our statements are based on solid analysis, it is a good idea to actively hunt for any evidence that might contradict them. If we can demonstrate that we have genuinely searched for (but failed to find) negative evidence, looking for outliers and using extreme cases, our conclusions will be more credible.
- We might be too opinionated and reduce our conclusions to a limited number of choices or alternatives.
- We might unthinkingly give certain people or events more credibility than others. Perhaps we have relied too much on information that was easily accessible or we have given too much weight to research participants we personally liked. If we detect such a bias, we can interview more people, deliberately searching for atypical events and research participants who differ markedly from those we have already interviewed. Hopefully, these new data will provide a balance with the data originally collected.

Once we have assessed the trustworthiness of our results, it only remains to write the report describing our methods and findings. Writing qualitative reports will be discussed in detail in Chapter 15.

SUMMING UP AND LOOKING AHEAD

This chapter has presented a systematic and purposeful approach to data analysis in a qualitative research study. The major steps of a data analysis include transcript preparation, planning the analysis, first-level coding, second-level coding, interpretation and theory building, and assessing the trustworthiness of the results. Although these steps have been presented in a linear fashion, any real qualitative analysis will involve moving back and forth between them in order to produce rich and meaningful findings.

REVIEW QUESTIONS

1   In your own words, describe the major differences between a qualitative data analysis and a quantitative data analysis.

2   Discuss how you could answer a single research question through qualitative and quantitative data. Provide an example.

3   What is the major purpose of a qualitative data analysis? What is the major purpose of a quantitative data analysis? Compare and contrast the two purposes in relation to the role that research plays in generating social work knowledge. Provide one common social work example in your discussion.

4   List and discuss all the assumptions that underlie the qualitative research approach that are directly relevant to the data analysis phase of a qualitative research study. Provide one common social work example in your discussion.

5   Discuss how you would go about preparing qualitative data in transcript form, using the steps as outlined in the chapter. Provide one common social work example in your discussion.

6   Discuss how you would go about establishing a plan for qualitative data analysis using the steps as outlined in the chapter. Provide one common social work example in your discussion.

7   Describe in detail the purpose of first-level coding. Discuss how you would do first-level coding using the steps as outlined in the chapter. Provide one common social work example in your discussion.

8   Describe in detail the purpose of second-level coding. Discuss how you would do first-level coding using the steps as outlined in the chapter. Provide one common social work example in your discussion.

9   Discuss in detail the purpose of interpreting qualitative data and building theory from the data. Discuss how you would interpret data using the steps as outlined in the chapter. Provide one common social work example in your discussion.

10   Discuss in detail the purpose of assessing the trustworthiness of a qualitative study's findings. Discuss

how you would establish the study's trustworthiness using the steps as outlined in the chapter. Provide one common social work example in your discussion.

11   In groups of four, decide on a social work–related problem area. Derive a research question (or hypothesis) out of the problem area that you wish to answer. Describe how you could carry out a qualitative research study that would answer your research question (or test your hypothesis). In your description, define all relevant variables (e.g., independent, dependent, extraneous, intervening), the research question (or hypothesis), potential rival hypotheses, the specific research design, the sample (research participants), the data collection method(s), and the data source(s) for each data collection method(s). Discuss in detail how you would go about analyzing data generated from your study using all the steps as outlined in the chapter. Discuss the limitations of your hypothetical study. Present your discussion to the entire class.

12   With the same research question (or hypothesis) used in the above exercise, design a quantitative study and answer the same questions contained at the end of the exercise using statistics as outlined in the previous chapter.

13   In groups of four, design a quantitative research study that used interviewing as a data collection method for answering a social work–related research question (or testing a hypothesis) of your choice. With the same research question (or hypothesis), design a qualitative research study. Compare the advantages and disadvantages of using both research approaches in answering the research question (or testing the hypothesis).

This chapter has been adapted and modified from: Grinnell and Williams (1990); and Williams, Tutty, and Grinnell (1995)

C h a p t e r   14

Quantitative Proposals and Reports

Iₙ THIS CHAPTER, we discuss both how to write a quantitative research proposal, which is done *before* the study begins, and how to write a quantitative research report, which is done *after* the study is completed. They will be presented together because a quantitative research proposal describes what is *proposed* to be done, while a quantitative research report describes what *has been* done. As will be emphasized throughout the chapter, there is so much overlap between the two that a majority of the material written for a quantitative research proposal can be used in writing the final quantitative research report.

This chapter will incorporate most of the contents of the preceding ones, so it is really a summary of the entire quantitative research process (and this book) up to report writing. We will use an example of Lula Wilson, a social work practitioner and researcher who wants to do a quantitative research study on children who come to her women's emergency shelter with their mothers. She has been working at the shelter for the past two years. The shelter is located in a large urban city.

WRITING PROPOSALS

When writing a quantitative research proposal, we must always keep in mind the purposes for its development and be aware of politically sensitive research topics (see Box 14.1). These are, primarily, to get permission to do the study and, second, perhaps to obtain some funds with which to do it.

There is a third purpose—to persuade the people who will review the proposal that its author, Lula, is competent to carry out the intended study. Finally, the fourth purpose of a proposal is to force Lula to write down exactly what is going to be studied, why it is going to studied, and how it is going to studied. In doing this, she may think of aspects of the study that had not occurred before. For example, she may look at the first draft of her proposal and realize that some essential detail was forgotten—for instance, that the research participants (in her case, children) who are going to fill out self-report standardized measuring instruments must be able to read.

The intended readers of the proposal determine how it will be written. It is important to remember that the reviewers will probably have many proposals to evaluate at once. Some proposals will need to be turned down because there will not be sufficient funds, space, or staff time, to accept all of them. Thus, proposal reviewers are faced with some difficult decisions on which to accept and which ones to reject. People who review quantitative research proposals often do so on a voluntary basis.

With the above in mind, the proposal should be written so that it is easy to read, easy to follow, easy to understand, clearly organized, and brief. It must not ramble or go off into anecdotes about how Lula became interested in the subject in the first place. Rather, Lula's proposal must describe her proposed research study simply, clearly, and concisely.

Now that we know the underlying rationale for the proposal, the next step is to consider what content it should include. This depends to some extent on who will be reviewing it. If the proposal is submitted to an academic committee, for example, it will often include more of a literature review and more details of the study's research design than if it were submitted to a funding organization. Some funding bodies specify exactly what they want included and in what order; others leave it to the author's discretion.

The simplest and most logical way to write the proposal is in the same order that a quantitative research study is conducted. For example, when a quantitative research study is done, a general topic area is decided upon as presented in Chapter 1. This is followed by a literature review in an attempt to narrow the broad research area into more specific research questions or hypotheses as presented in Chapter 3. We will now go back and look at how each step of a quantitative research study leads to the writing of a parallel section in a quantitative research proposal. Let us turn to the first task of proposal writing, specifying the research topic.

Box 14.1 _____

RESEARCH ON POLITICALLY SENSITIVE TOPICS

Sensitivity to cultural pluralism some-times creates conflicts for researchers. It is no longer "politically correct" to refer to African-American citizens as Negroes, women as girls, or gay people as homosex-uals. Researchers who wish to examine cultural differences may be accused of having an "ism" (racism, sexism, ageism, heterosexism), especially if they uncover results unflattering to minority groups.

Sandra Scarr, who has conducted research on race and genetics, reports that researchers who examine racial and ethnic issues are "in danger of ostracism and worse from one's socially well-intentioned colleagues. The messenger with the bad news seems to be blamed for having in-vented the message" (1988, p.56).

Although empirically verified weak-nesses may be incorrectly used to justify exploitation or oppression, remediation programs will not be established and funded until we understand what needs must be met and their etiology. Under-standing differences also should reduce misunderstandings between groups. For example, personal space requirements (the distance around the body that is main-tained between people) vary across cul-tures; people unaware of these differences may misinterpret the behaviors of those from another culture.

In addition, if we don't look for differ-ences, we don't uncover similarities; thus, we allow inaccurate stereotypes to persist. Rather than ignore possible differences, perhaps researchers should routinely look for them and report both significant and nonsignificant results (Eagly, 1987).

Fearing criticism, researchers may abandon lines of research that could have politically unpopular results. For exam-ple, Baumeister (1988) suggests that we should stop studying sex differences be-cause "politically, the study of sex differ-ences may do more harm than good. By seeking, reporting, and discussing sex differences, psychologists lend scientific prestige to the distinction between men and women" and this "endorses a way of looking at the world in which men and women are fundamentally different" (p. 1094). This line of reasoning could be applied to other group differences. IRBs may be so sensitive to this perspective that they refuse to approve research stud-ies that follow stated ethical guidelines, but that examine politically sensitive issues, such as affirmative action and reverse discrimination (Ceci, Peters, & Plotkin, 1985). Concerns about politically sensitive research may lead to censorship.

Scarr (1988) enumerates a number of research programs with results that were misused by others, such as the application of aversive conditioning to political pris-oners and the application of sleep research to brainwashing. She concludes that researchers have the obligation to consider possible misuses of their results and to take a proactive stand explaining their conclusions in a public forum. Their explanations need not be consistent with politically correct ideology, but science "must operate with free inquiry, free dis-cussion, and the competition of ideas" (p. 58).

A number of publications in the *American Psychologist* (the major publica-tion of the American Psychological Asso-ciation) have suggested ways to reduce biased research (e.g., Denmark, Russo, Frieze, & Sechzer, 1988; Herek, Kimmel, Amaro, & Melton, 1991; Zuckerman, 1990). Bias may affect every stage of a research study, from its first formulation to the final explanation of results. Here are some examples of bias in research:

1 Researchers who compare other groups to their own group and assume their group is "normal" are bound to find other groups "abnormal." IQ tests may have cultural biases that work against some minority cultures, and definitions of healthy behaviors and ways to handle stress and conflict may vary across cultures. Groups may be different, but this does not imply that one group is deficient compared to the other.

Box 14.1 Continued

2 Literature reviews may lead to biased conclusions, especially if results are based on samples restricted to one group. For example, research on male subjects shows that aggressive stimuli are sexually stimulating, but other studies have shown that this is not true for female subjects (Denmark et al., 1988).

Much research leaves minority groups "invisible." For example, lesbian, gay male, and bisexual research participants may not be identified or separately analyzed in studies in which they may respond differently from subjects with a heterosexual orientation, such as studies concerning marital relationships.

Members of other minority groups may not be identified or separately analyzed. Studies may involve biased samples for comparison purposes. For example, gender and ethnic comparisons among employees of a major corporation might compare people who also vary in income, educational level, and social class. Differences may reflect these other factors, rather than gender or ethnicity.

3 Biological explanations that do not take possible cultural differences into account may not be justified, and researchers should not assume genetic or cultural uniformity within groups. For example, Latino or Asian-American subjects may include recent immigrants, fifth-generation American citizens with few ties to their ethnic roots, and people with backgrounds from a variety of cultural traditions.

4 Definitions of group membership may be inaccurate. For example, ethnic backgrounds may be mixed in American samples of minority groups. The whole concept of race is questionable among American samples because its definition assumes isolated inbreeding groups, a situation probably never true in our society (Zuckerman, 1990).

The researcher's assumptions about group membership may be in error People who attend Alcoholics Anonymous meetings may not be alcoholic; people at gay bars may not be gay; people who claim to be in a group may not belong to it.

5 Small differences may be exaggerated, leading to discussions of trivial, but statistically significant differences. This is especially common in studies with large sample sizes. In addition, group differences cannot be applied to individuals. For example, the average man scores higher than the average woman on tests of mathematical reasoning, but some women score higher than most men and some men score lower than most women. Group differences cannot be used to justify discrimination against individuals, such as barring women from engineering programs.

6 Alternative interpretations may be ignored. For example, women use more tag questions than men. (Tag questions are short questions at the end of declarative sentences, as in *It's hot today, isn't it?*) This could be interpreted as an indicator of the lack of self-confidence in women or as an indicator that women make more attempts to involve others in mutual conversation (Hyde, 1991).

Openly discussing research issues with members of other groups is an excellent way to highlight biased assumptions. A willingness to discuss group differences in an open forum should lead to increased mutual understanding and awareness. Researchers who examine socially important issues without bias are following APA ethical guidelines that promote research for the benefit of human welfare.

Source: Allen (1995)

Part 1: Research Topic

The first step in beginning a quantitative research study is to decide what the study will be about. The first procedure in writing a proposal, therefore, is to describe, in general terms, what it is that is going to be studied. Lula may describe, for example, her proposed study's general problem area as:

> *General Problem Area:*
> Problems experienced by children who witness the husband physically abusing the wife (wife abuse).

The first task is to convince the proposal reviewers that the general problem area is a good one to study. This task is accomplished by outlining the significance of Lula's proposed study in three specific social work areas: its practical significance, its theoretical significance, and its social policy significance.

Depending on to whom the proposal is submitted, Lula may go into detail about these three areas or describe them briefly. It may be known, for example, that the funding organization that will review the proposal is mostly interested in improving the effectiveness of individual social workers in their day-to-day practice activities. If this is the case, the reviewers will more likely be interested in the practical significance of Lula's proposed study than its theoretical and/or policy significance.

Therefore, Lula's proposal would neither go into detail about how her study might generate new social work theory, nor elaborate on the changes in social policy that might follow directly from the study's results. Since Lula is going to submit the proposal to the women's emergency shelter where she works, she would be smart in obtaining informal input from the agency's executive director at this stage in writing the proposal. Informal advice at an early stage is astronomically important to proposal writers.

In sum, Part 1 of the proposal describes *what* is going to be studied and *why* it should be studied. One should thoroughly reread Chapters 1–3 in this book before writing Part 1 of a quantitative research proposal.

Part 2: Literature Review

The second part of a proposal contains the literature review. This is not simply a list of all the books and journal articles that vaguely touch on the general problem area mentioned in Part 1. When a quantitative research study is done, it is basically trying to add another piece to a jigsaw puzzle already begun by other researchers. The purpose of a literature review, then, is to show how *Lula's* study fits into the whole.

The trouble is that it might be a very big whole. There may be literally hundreds of articles and books filled with previous research studies on the study's general topic area. If Lula tries to list every one of these, the reviewers of the proposal, probably her colleagues who work with her at the shelter, will lose both interest and patience somewhere in the middle of Part 2. The literature review has to be selective—listing enough material to show that Lula is thoroughly familiar with her topic area, but not enough to induce stupor in the reviewer. This is a delicate and sensitive balance. She should include findings from recent research studies along with any classical ones.

On the other side of the coin, another possibility is that previous research studies on Lula's general topic area may be limited. In this case, all available material is included. However, her proposal can also branch out into material that is partially related or describes a parallel topic area. Lula might find a research article, for example, that claims that children whose parents are contemplating divorce have low social interaction skills. This does not bear directly on the matter of problems children have who witnessed wife abuse (the general problem area mentioned above). However, since marital separation can be a result of wife abuse, it might be indirectly relevant.

A literature review serves a number of purposes. First, it shows the reviewers that Lula understands the most current and central issues related to the general topic area that she proposes to study. Second, it points out in what ways her proposed study is the same as, or different from, other similar studies. Third, it describes how the results of her proposed study will contribute to solving the puzzle. Fourth, it introduces and conceptually defines all the variables that will be examined throughout the study.

At this stage, Lula does not operationally define her study's variables—that is, in such a way that allows their measurement. They are only abstractly defined. For example, if Lula is going to study the social interaction skills of children who witness wife abuse, her proposal so far introduces only the concepts of children, wife abuse, children witnessing wife abuse, and children's social interaction skills. They will be operationally defined in Part 5. Elaine Bouey and Gayla Rogers (1993) and Gayla Rogers and Elaine Bouey (1993) have written two book chapters on how to do literature reviews that are recommended reading before writing Part 2 of a quantitative research proposal.

Part 3: Conceptual Framework

A conceptual framework takes the variables that have been mentioned in Part 2, illustrates their possible relationship to one another, and discusses why the relationship exists the way it is proposed and not in some other, equally possible way. The author's suppositions might be based on past professional experience. For example, Lula has observed numerous children who accompanied their mothers to women's emergency shelters. She has made subjective observations of these children over the past two years and finally wishes to test out two hunches objectively. First, Lula believes that children who have witnessed wife abuse *seem to* have lower social interaction skills than children who have not witnessed wife abuse. Second, Lula believes that of the children who have been a witness to wife abuse, boys *seem to* have lower social interaction skills than girls. However, these two hunches are based on only two-year subjective observations, which need to be objectively tested—the purpose of her quantitative research study.

As we know from Chapter 3, ideally, Lula's hunches should be integrated with existing theory or findings derived from previous research studies. In any case, Lula should discuss these assumptions and the reasons for believing them as the basis for the variables that are included in her proposed study.

In sum, Lula wants to see if children who have witnessed wife abuse have lower social interaction skills than do children who have not witnessed it. And of the children who have witnessed wife abuse, she wants to determine whether boys have lower social interaction skills than girls. It must be remembered that the two areas her study proposes to explore have been delineated out of her past experiences and have not been formulated on existing theory or previous research findings.

Part 4: Questions and Hypotheses

As discussed in Chapters 6–9, when an exploratory or descriptive study is done on a topic that little is known about, only general research questions are asked. Many general research questions relating to Lula's general problem area can be asked. One of the many could be:

> *General Research Question*:
> Is there a relationship between children witnessing wife abuse and their social interaction skills?

On the other hand, when a descriptive or explanatory study is done on a topic where a lot of previous research studies have been previously done, a specific hypothesis can be formulated. A specific hypothesis derived from the above general research question might be:

> *Specific Research Hypothesis*:
> Children who have witnessed wife abuse will have lower social interaction skills than children who have not witnessed such abuse.

Part 5: Operational Definitions

As mentioned, variables are abstractly and conceptually defined in the conceptual framework part of the proposal (Part 3). Part 5 provides operational definitions of them; that is, they must be defined in ways in which they can become measurable.

Let us take Lula's simple research hypothesis previously mentioned. In this hypothesis there are four main variables that must be operationalized before Lula's study can begin: children, wife abuse, children witnessing wife abuse, and children's social interaction skills. Each must be described in such a way that there is no ambiguity as to what they mean.

Variable 1: Childen

For example, what constitutes a child? How old must the child be? Does the child have to be in a certain age range, for example between the ages of 5–10? Does the child have to be a biological product of either the mother or the father? Can the child be a stepchild? Can the child be adopted? Does the child have to live full-time at home?

Since Lula's study is at the descriptive level, she may wish to define a child operationally in such a way that permits the largest number of children to be included in the study. She would, however, go to the literature and find out how other researchers have operationally defined "children," and she would use this operational definition if it made sense to her.

However, in a simple study such as this one, a child could be operationally defined as "any person who is considered to be a child as determined by the mother." This is a very vague operational definition, at best, but it is more practical than constructing one such as, "a person between the ages of 5–17 who has resided full-time with the biological mother for the last 12-month period."

If such a complex operational definition was utilized, Lula would have to provide answers to questions as: Why the ages of 5–17, why not 4–18? What is the specific reason for this age range? Why must the child live at home full-time, why not part-time? Why must the mother be the biological mother, why not a nonbiological mother? What about biological fathers? Why must the child have had to live at home for the past 12 months, why not two years, four years? In short, Lula's operational definition of a child must make sense and be based on a rational or theoretical basis. For now, Lula is going to make matters simple: A child in her study will be operationally defined as any child whose mother validates their relationship. This simple operational definition makes the most practical sense to Lula.

Variable 2: Wife Abuse

Let us now turn to Lula's second variable—wife abuse. What is it? Does one partner have to shove, push, or threaten the other? How would a child, as operationally defined above, know when it occurs? Does a husband yelling at his wife imply wife abuse? If so, does it have to last a long time? If it does, what is a long time? Is Lula interested in the frequency, duration, or magnitude of yelling—or all three? A specific operational definition of wife abuse has to be established in order for the study to be of any value.

Like most variables, there are as many operational definitions of wife abuse as there are people willing to define it. For now, Lula is going to continue to make her descriptive study simple by operationally defining wife abuse as, "women who say they have been physically abused by their partners." Lula can simply ask each woman who enters the shelter if she believes she has been physically abused by her partner. The data provided by the women will be "yes" or "no." Lula could have looked at the frequency, duration, or magnitude of such abuse, but for this study, the variable is a dichotomous one: Either wife abuse occurred, or it did not occur—as reported by the women. Questions regarding its frequency (how many times it occurred), its duration (how long each episode lasted), and its magnitude (the intensity of each episode) are not asked.

Variable 3: Children Witnessing Wife Abuse

The third variable in Lula's hypothesis is the child (or children) who witness wife abuse. Now that operational definitions of a "child" and "wife abuse" have been formulated, how will she know that a child has witnessed such an abuse? Each child could be asked directly, or a standardized checklist of possible verbal and physical abuses that a child might have witnessed can be given to the child, who is then asked how many times such abuse has been observed.

Obviously, the child would have to know what constitutes wife abuse to recognize it. In addition, the child would have to be old enough to respond to such requests, and the operational definition that is used for wife abuse must be consistent with the age of the child. For example, the child must be able to communicate to someone that wife abuse has in fact occurred—not to mention the question of whether the child could recognize it in the first place.

In Lula's continuing struggle to keep her study as simple as possible, she operationally defines "a child witnessing wife abuse" by asking the mothers who come to the women's emergency shelter if their child(ren) witnessed the physical abuse. She is interested only in the women who come to the shelter as a result of being physically abused by their partners. Women who come to the shelter for other reasons are not included in her study. It must be kept in mind that Lula's study is focusing only upon physical abuse and not emotional or mental abuse.

So far, Lula's study is rather simple in terms of operational definitions. Up to this point she is studying mothers who bring their child(ren) with them to one women's emergency shelter. She simply asks the mother if the person(s) with her is her child(ren), which operationally defines "child." The mother is asked if she believes her partner physically abused her, which defines "wife abuse." The mother is also asked if the child(ren) who is accompanying her to the shelter saw the physical abuse occur, which operationally defines "children witnessing wife abuse."

Variable 4: Children's Social Interaction Skills

Let us now turn to Lula's fourth and final variable in her hypothesis—the children's social interaction skills. How will they be measured? What constitutes the social skills of a child? They could be measured in a variety of ways through direct observations of parents, social work practitioners, social work researchers, social work practicum students, teachers, neighbors, and even members from the children's peer group. They could also be measured by a standardized measuring instrument such as the ones discussed in Chapter 4. Lula decides to use one of the many standardized measuring instruments that measure social interaction skills of children, named the Social Interaction Skills of Children Assessment Instrument (*SISOCAI*).

All in all, Part 5 of a proposal provides operational definitions of all important variables that were abstractly defined in Part 3. It should be noted that the four variables that have been operationally defined should be defined from the available literature, if appropriate. (This procedure makes a study's results generalizable from one research situation to another.) However, there may be times when this is not possible. The proposal must specify what data gathering instruments are going to be used, including their validity and reliability, as presented in Chapter 4.

In summary, let us review how Lula intends to operationally define her four key variables: child, wife abuse, child witnessing wife abuse, and children's social interaction skills:

1 **Child**   Any person who the mother claims is her child.

2 **Wife Abuse**   Asking the mother if her partner physically abused her.

3 **Child Witnessing Wife Abuse**   Asking the mother if the child(ren) who accompanied her to the shelter witnessed the abuse.

4 **Children's Social Interaction Skills**   The *SISOCAI* score for each child in the study.

The above four operational definitions are rather rudimentary, at best. There are many more sophisticated ways of operationally defining them. However, alternative definitions will not be explored, because Lula wants to keep her quantitative research proposal as uncomplicated as possible as she knows that the shelter does not want a study that would intrude too heavily into its day-to-day operations. On a very general level, the more complex the operational definitions of variables used in a quantitative research study, the more the study will intrude on the research participants' lives—in addition to the agency's day-to-day operations.

There are a few criteria that need to be examined when evaluating Parts 1–5 of a quantitative research proposal (Fischer, 1993):

1   Adequacy of the proposal's literature review

2   Clarity of the problem area and research question under investigation

3   Clarity of the statement of the research hypothesis (if applicable)

4   Clarity of the specification of the independent variable, at an abstract and conceptual level (if applicable)

5   Clarity of the specification of the dependent variable, at an abstract and conceptual level

6   Reasonableness of the described relationship between the independent and dependent variables (if applicable)

7   Specification of other rival hypotheses

8   Clarity of the researcher's orientation

9   Clarity of the study's purpose

10   Clarity of the study's auspices

11   Reasonableness of the author's assumptions

The eleven criteria above should be gone over very carefully, and authors of proposals should try to respond to them all before going on to Part 6, the study's research design.

Part 6: Research Design

This part of a quantitative research proposal presents the study's research design. Suppose Lula formulated two related research hypotheses from her general problem area mentioned above:

Research Hypothesis 1:
Children who have witnessed wife abuse will have lower social interaction skills than children who have not witnessed such abuse.

Research Hypothesis 2:
Of those children who have witnessed wife abuse, boys will have lower social interaction skills than girls.

In relation to Research Hypothesis 1, Lula's study would use the children who accompanied their mothers to the women's emergency shelter. These children would then be broken down into two groups, (1) those children who witnessed wife abuse, and (2) those children who did not witness it (as determined by the mother).

A very simple two-group research design could be used to test Research Hypothesis 1, such as:

Children Who Have Witnessed Wife Abuse: O_1
Children Who Have Not Witnessed Wife Abuse: O_1

Where:

O_1 = Measurement of the child's social interaction skills (*SISOCAI*)

The average social interaction skill score, via the *SISOCAI*, between the two groups can then be compared.

In relation to Research Hypothesis 2, within the group of children who have witnessed wife abuse, the children's social interaction skills, via the *SISOCAI*, between the boys and girls can be compared. This simple procedure would test Research Hypothesis 2. A simple two-group research design could be used to test Research Hypothesis 2, such as:

$$\text{Boys: } O_1$$
$$\text{Girls: } O_1$$

Where:

O_1 = Measurement of the child's social interaction skills (*SISOCAI*)

In Lula's study, there are two separate miniresearch studies running at the same time—Research Hypotheses 1 and 2. All Lula wants to do is to see if there is an association between the social interaction skills of children who have and have not witnessed wife abuse (Research Hypothesis 1). In addition, for those children who have witnessed wife abuse, she wants to see if boys have lower social interaction skills than girls (Research Hypothesis 2).

In Part 6 of a quantitative research proposal, information should be included about what data will be collected, how these data will be collected, and who will be the research participants.

Next, Lula must now describe the data to be collected. She will have her research assistant complete the *SISOCAI* for each child during a half-hour interview. Finally, the conditions under which the data will be gathered are discussed; that is, the research assistant will complete the *SISOCAI* for each child one day after the mother entered the shelter.

Of necessity, recording all of this will involve some repetition. For example, Part 5, when discussing operational definitions, discussed what data would be collected, and how. Part 7, the next part, will discuss the study's sample and population (i.e., who will be studied) in much more detail. It is repeated in Part 6, both to give an overview of the whole quantitative research process, and to form links between Parts 5 and 7 so that the entire proposal flows smoothly.

Part 7: Population and Sample

This part of the proposal presents a detailed description of who will be studied. Lula's quantitative research study will use the children who accompanied their mothers to one women's emergency shelter who wish to voluntarily participate, and whose mothers agree that they can be included in the study. The children will then each go into one of two distinct groups: those who have witnessed wife abuse, and those who have not (according to the mothers, that is). Lula's study could have used a comparison group of children from the same local community who have never witnessed wife abuse and have never been to a women's emergency shelter. However, Lula chose to use only those children who accompanied their mothers to the shelter where she works.

There is no question of random selection from some population, and it is not possible to generalize the study's findings to any general population of children who have and have not witnessed wife abuse. The results of Lula's study will apply only to the children who participated in it. Chapter 5 in this book should be reread before writing Part 8 of a quantitative research proposal.

Part 8: Data Collection

This part of a quantitative research proposal presents a detailed account of how the data are going to be collected—that is, the specific data collection method(s) that will be used. As we know, data can be collected using interviews (individual or group), surveys (mail or telephone), direct observations, participant observations, secondary analyses, and content analyses. Lula is going to collect data on the dependent variable by having her research assistant complete the *SISOCAI* for each identified child during a one-half hour interview one day after the mother enters the shelter with her child(ren). Those mothers who do not bring their children with them will not be included in Lula's study.

In addition to the children, their mothers are also going to be interviewed to some small degree. Each mother will be asked by Lula if she believes her partner physically assaulted her. These responses will then be used to operationally define "wife abuse." Each mother will also provide data on whether or not her child(ren) who accompanied her to the shelter saw the abuse occur. The mothers' responses will then operationally define whether or not the child(ren) witnessed wife abuse.

Finally, this section should discuss ethical issues involved in data collection, such as the ones presented in Chapter 2. Chapter 10 in this book present various data collection methods that can be used in research studies. This chapter should be reread thoroughly before writing Part 8 of a quantitative research proposal.

Part 9: Data Analysis

This part of a quantitative research proposal describes the way the data will be analyzed, including the statistical procedures to be used, if any.

Having clearly specified the research design in Part 6, this part specifies exactly what statistical test(s) will be used to answer the research questions or hypotheses. Most of the more common statistical procedures were presented in the previous chapter.

The *SISOCAI* produces interval-level data, and a child's social interaction skill score on this particular instrument can range from 0–100, where higher scores mean higher (better) social skills than lower scores. Since there are two groups of children that are being used to test both research hypotheses, and the dependent variable (*SISOCAI*) is at the interval-level of measurement, an independent *t*-test would be used to test both research hypotheses. In addition to Chapter 12 in this book, Robert W. Weinbach and Richard M. Grinnell's book (1998) should be read before completing Part 9 of a quantitative research proposal.

Part 10: Limitations

There are limitations in every quantitative research study, often due to problems that cannot be eliminated entirely—even though steps can be taken to reduce them. Lula's study is certainly no exception. Limitations inherent in a study might relate to the validity and reliability of the measuring instruments, or to the generalizability of the study's results. Sometimes the data that were needed could not be collected, for some reason. In addition, this part should mention all extraneous variables that have not been controlled for.

For example, Lula may not have been able to control for all the factors that affect the children's social interaction skills. Although she believes that having witnessed wife abuse leads to lower social skills for boys as compared to girls, it may not be possible to collect reliable and valid data about whether the children saw or did not see an abuse occur. In Lula's study, she is going to simply ask the mothers, so in this case, she has to take the mothers' word for it.

She could ask the children, however. This would produce another set of limitations in and of itself. For example, it would be difficult for Lula to ascertain whether a child did or did not see a form of wife abuse as perceived by the child. It may be hard for a child to tell what type of abuse occurred. Also the frequency, duration, and magnitude of a particular form of wife abuse may be hard for the child to recall. All of these limitations, and a host of others, must be delineated in this part of the proposal. In addition, asking a child if he or she saw the abuse occur might prove to be a traumatic experience for the child.

Some limitations will not be discovered until the study is well underway. However, many problems can be anticipated and these should be included in the proposal, together with the specific steps that are intended to minimize them.

Part 11: Administration

The final part of a quantitative research proposal contains the organization and resources necessary to carry out the study. First, Lula has to find a base of operations (e.g., a desk and telephone). She has to think about who is going to take on the overall administrative responsibility for the study. What staff will be involved? How many individuals will be needed? What should their qualifications be? What will be their responsibilities? To whom are they responsible? What is the chain of command? Finally, Lula has to think about things such as a computer, stationery, telephone, travel, and parking expenses.

When all of the details have been put together, an organizational chart can be produced that shows what will be done, by whom, where, and in what order. The next step is to develop a time frame. By what date should each anticipated step be completed? Optimism about completion dates should be avoided, particularly when it comes to allowing time to analyze the data and writing the final report (to be discussed shortly). Both of these activities always take far longer than anticipated, and it is important that they be properly done—which takes more time than originally planned.

When the organizational chart and time frame have been established, the final step is to prepare a budget. Lula has to figure out how much each aspect of the study—such as office space, the research assistant's time, staff time, and participants' time, if any—will cost.

We have now examined eleven parts that should be included when writing a quantitative research proposal. Not all proposals are organized in precisely this way; sometimes different headings are used or information is put in a different part of the proposal. For example, in some proposals, previous studies are discussed in the conceptual framework section rather than in the literature review. Much depends on for whom the proposal is being written and on the author's personal writing style.

Much of the content that has been used to write the eleven parts of a quantitative research proposal can be used to write the final quantitative research report. Let us now turn to that discussion.

WRITING REPORTS

A quantitative research report is a way of describing the completed study to other people. The findings can be reported by way of an oral presentation, a book, or a published paper. The report may be addressed solely to colleagues at work or to a worldwide audience. It may be written simply, so that everyone can understand it, or it may be so highly technical that it can only be understood by a few.

The most common way of sharing a study's findings is to publish a report in a journal. Most journal reports run about twenty-five double-spaced, typewritten pages, including figures, tables, and references.

As we know, quantitative research proposals are written with the proposal reviewers in mind. Similarly, a quantitative research report is written with its readers in mind. However, some of the readers who read research reports will want to know the technical details of how the study's results were achieved, others will only want to know how the study's results are relevant to social work practice, without the inclusion of the technical details.

There are a number of ways to deal with this situation. First, a technical report can be written for those who can understand it, without worrying too much about those who cannot. In addition, a second report can be written that skims over the technical aspects of the study and concentrates mostly on the practical application of the study's findings. Thus, two versions of the same study can be written; a technical one, and a nontechnical one.

The thought of writing two reports where one would suffice will not appeal to very many of us, however. Usually, we try to compensate for this by including those technical aspects of the study that are necessary to an understanding of the study's findings. This is essential, because readers will not be able to evaluate the study's findings without knowing how they were arrived at.

However, life can be made easier for nontechnical audiences by including some explanation of the technical aspects and, in addition, paying close attention to the practical application of the study's results. In this way, we will probably succeed in addressing the needs of both audiences—those who want all the technical details and those who want none.

A quantitative research report can be organized in many different ways depending on the intended audience and the author's personal style. Often, however, the same common-sense sequence is followed that was laid out in Chapter 1, when the basic problem-solving method was discussed. In order to solve a problem, the problem must be specified, ways of solving it must be explored, a solution to solve the problem must be tried, and an evaluation must take place to see if the solution worked.

In general, this is the way to solve practice and research problems. It is also the order in which a quantitative research report is written. First, a research problem is defined. Then, the method used to solve it is discussed. Next, the findings are presented. Finally, the significance of the findings to the social work profession are discussed.

Part 1: Problem

Probably the best way to begin a quantitative research report is to explain simply what the research problem is. Lula might say, for example, that the study's purpose was to ascertain if children who have witnessed wife abuse have lower social interaction skills than children who have not witnessed such abuse. In addition, the study wanted to find out, of those children who have witnessed wife abuse, if boys have lower social interaction skills than girls.

But why would anyone want to know about that? How would the knowledge derived from Lula's study help social workers? Thinking back to Part 1 of her proposal, this question was asked and answered once before. In the first part of her proposal, when the research topic was set out, the significance of the study was discussed in the areas of practice, theory, social policy. This material can be used, suitably paraphrased, in Part 1 of the final report.

One thing that should be remembered, though, is that a quantitative research report written for a journal is not, relatively speaking, very long. A lot of information must be included in less than twenty-five pages, and the author cannot afford to use too much space explaining to readers why this particular study was chosen. Sometimes, the significance of the study will be apparent and there is no room to belabor what is already obvious.

In Part 2 of the proposal, a literature review, was done in which Lula's proposed study was compared to other similar studies, highlighting similarities and differences. Also, key variables were conceptually defined. In her final report, she can use both the literature review and her conceptually defined variables that she presented in her proposal. The literature review might have to be cut back if space is at a premium, but the abstract and conceptual definitions of all key variables must be included.

In Part 3 of her proposal, she presented a conceptual framework. This can be used in Part 1 of the final report, where Lula must state the relationships between the variables she is studying.

In Part 4 of the quantitative research proposal, a research question or hypothesis to be answered or tested was stated. In the final report, we started out with that, so now we have come full circle. By using the first four parts of the proposal for the first part of the quantitative research report, we have managed to considerably cut down writing time. In fact, Part 1 of a quantitative research report is nothing more than a cut-and-paste job of the first four parts of the quantitative research proposal. Actually, if the first four parts of the quantitative research proposal were done correctly, there should be very little original writing within Part 1 of a quantitative research report.

One of the most important things to remember when writing Part 1 of a quantitative research report is that the study's findings have to have some form of utilization potential for social workers, or the report would not be worth writing in the first place. More specifically, the report must have some practical, theoretical, or policy significance. Part 1 of a quantitative research report tells why the study's findings would be useful to the social work profession. This is mentioned briefly but is picked up later in Part 4.

Part 2: Method

Part 2 of a quantitative research report contains the method(s) used to answer the research problem. This section usually includes descriptions of the study's research design, a description of the research participants who were a part of the study (study's sample), and a detailed description of the data gathering procedures (who, what, when, how), and presents the operational definition of all variables.

Once again, sections of the original quantitative research proposal can be used. For example, in Part 5 of the proposal, key variables were operationally defined; that is, they were defined in a way that would allow them to be measured. When and how the measurements would occur were also presented. This material can be used again in the final report.

Part 6 of the proposal described the study's research design. This section of the proposal was used—about half way through—to link the parts of the study together into a whole. Since a research design encompasses the entire quantitative research process from conceptualizing the problem to disseminating the findings, Lula could take this opportunity to give a brief picture of the entire process. This part presents who would be studied (the research participants, or sample), what data would be gathered, how the data would be gathered, when the data would be gathered, and what would be done with the data once obtained (analysis).

In the final report, there is not a lot of space to provide this information in detail. Instead, a clear description of how the data were obtained from the measuring instruments must be presented. For example, Lula could state in this part of the report, that "a research assistant rated each child on the *SISOCAI* during a one-half hour interview one day after the mother entered the shelter."

There are a few criteria that need to be examined when evaluating the method section of a quantitative research report (Fischer, 1993):

1   Clarity of the specification of the kinds of changes desired (if applicable)

2   Appropriateness of the outcome measures in relation to the purpose of the study (if applicable)

3   Degree of validity of the outcome measures (if applicable)

4   Degree of reliability of the outcome measures (if applicable)

5   Degree of use of a variety of outcome measures such as subjective and objective measures (if applicable)

6   Clarity about how the data were collected

7   Clarity about who collected the data

8   Degree of error in the collection of data

9   Clarity of the description of the research design

10 Adequacy of the research design (in terms of purpose)

11 Clarity and adequacy of time between pretest and posttest (if applicable)

12 Appropriateness in the use of a control group(s) (if applicable)

13 Appropriateness in the use of random assignment procedures (if applicable)

14 Appropriateness in the use of matching procedures (if applicable)

15 Degree of experimental and control group equivalency at pretest (if applicable)

16 Degree of control for effects of history (if applicable)

17 Degree of control for effects of maturation (if applicable)

18 Degree of control for effects of testing (if applicable)

19 Degree of control for effects of instrumentation (if applicable)

20 Degree of control for statistical regression (if applicable)

21 Degree of control for differential selection of clients (if applicable)

22 Degree of control for differential mortality (if applicable)

23 Degree of control for temporal bias (if applicable)

24 Degree of control for integrity of the intervention (if applicable)

25 Ability to distinguish causal variable(s) (if applicable)

26 Degree of control for interaction effects (if applicable)

27 Overall degree of success in maximizing internal validity (16–26)

28 Adequacy of sample size

29 Degree of accuracy in defining the population

30 Degree of adequacy in the representativeness of the sample drawn from the population (if applicable)

31 Degree of control for reactive effects of testing—interaction with independent variable (if applicable)

32 Degree of control for interaction between selection and experimental variable (if applicable)

33 Degree of control for special effects of experimental arrangements (if applicable)

34 Degree of control for multiple-treatment interference (if applicable)

35 Overall degree of success in maximizing external validity

Many of the above criteria are not applicable to Lula's study. However, they can be used in evaluating other, more complex, studies.

Part 3: Findings

Part 3 of a report presents the study's findings. Unfortunately, Lula's original proposal will not be of much help here because she did not know what she would find when it was written—only what she hoped to find.

One way to begin Part 3 of a report is to prepare whatever figures, tables, or other data displays that are going to used. For now, let us take Lula's Research Hypothesis 1 as an example of how to write up a study's findings. Suppose that there were 80 children who accompanied their mothers to the shelter. All of the mothers claimed they were physically abused by their partners. Lula's research assistant rated the 80 children's social skills, via the *SISOCAI*, one day after they accompanied their mothers to the shelter. Thus, there are 80 *SISOCAI* scores. What is she going to do with all that data? The goal of tables and figures is to organize the data in such a way that the reader takes them in at a glance and says, "Ah! Well, it's obvious that the children who witnessed wife abuse had lower *SISOCAI* scores than the children who did not see such abuse."

As can be seen from Table 14.1, the average *SISOCAI* score for all of the 80 children is 60. These 80 children would then be broken down into two subgroups: those who witnessed wife abuse, and those who did not—according to their mothers, that is. For the sake of simplicity let us say there were 40 children in each subgroup. In the first subgroup, the average *SISOCAI* score for the 40 children is 45; in the second subgroup, the average *SISOCAI* score for the 40 children is 75.

Table 14.1 allows the reader to quickly compare the average *SISOCAI* score for each subgroup. The reader can see, at a glance, that there is a 30-point difference between the two average *SISOCAI* scores (75 − 45 = 30). The children who witnessed wife abuse scored 30 points lower, on the average, on the *SISOCAI* than those children who did not witnesses wife abuse. Thus, by glancing at Table 14.1, Lula's Research Hypothesis 1 is supported in that children who witness wife abuse had lower social interaction skills than children who did not witness it.

However, it is still not known from Table 14.1 whether the 30-point difference between the two average *SISOCAI* scores is large enough to be statistically significant. The appropriate statistical procedure for this design is the independent *t*-test, as described in Chapter 12. The results of the *t*-test could also be included under Table 14.1, or they could be described in the findings section as follows:

> The result of an independent *t*-test between the *SISOCAI* scores of children who witnessed wife abuse as compared to those children who did not witness it was statistically significant ($t = 3.56$, $df = 78$, $p < .05$). Thus, children who witnessed wife abuse had statistically significantly lower social interaction skills, on the average, than children who did not witness such abuse.

Table 14.2 presents the study's findings for Lula's second research hypothesis. This table uses the data from the 40 children who witnessed wife abuse (from Table 14.1). As can be seen from Tables 14.1 and 14.2, the average social skill score for the 40 children who witnessed wife abuse

TABLE 14.1   Means and Standard Deviations of Social Interaction Skills of Children Who Did and Did Not Witness Wife Abuse

Witness Wife Abuse?	Mean	Standard Deviation	N
Yes	45	11	40
No	75	9	40
Averages	60	10	

TABLE 14.2   Means and Standard Deviations of Social Interaction Skills of Boys and Girls Who Witnessed Wife Abuse (from Table 14.1)

Gender	Mean	Standard Deviation	N
Boys	35	12	20
Girls	<u>55</u>	<u>10</u>	20
Averages	45	11	

is 45. Table 14.2 further breaks down these 40 children into two sub groups: boys and girls. Out of the 40 children who witnessed wife abuse, 20 were boys and 20 were girls. As can be seen from Table 14.2, boys had an average social skill score of 35 as compared with the average score for girls of 55. Thus, the boys scored, on the average, 20 points lower than the girls. So far, Lula's second research hypothesis is supported.

However, it is still not known from Table 14.2 whether the 20-point difference between the two average *SISOCAI* scores is large enough to be statistically significant. The appropriate statistical procedure for this design is the independent *t*-test, as described in the previous chapter. The results of the *t*-test could also be included under Table 14.2, or they could be described in the findings section as follows:

> The result of an independent *t*-test between the *SISOCAI* scores for boys and girls who witnessed wife abuse was statistically significant ($t = 2.56$, $df = 38$, $p < .05$). Thus, boys had statistically significant lower social interaction skills, on the average, than girls.

Once a table (or figure) is constructed, the next thing that has to be done is to describe in words what it means. Data displays should be self-explanatory if done correctly. It is a waste of precious space to repeat in the text something that is perfectly apparent from a table or figure.

At this point, Lula has to decide whether she is going to go into a lengthy discussion of her findings in this part of the report or whether she is going to reserve the discussion for the next part. Which option is chosen often depends on what there is to discuss. Sometimes it is more sensible to combine the findings with the discussion, pointing out the significance of what has been found as she goes along.

There are a few criteria that need to be examined when evaluating the findings section of a quantitative research report (Fischer, 1993):

1   Adequacy of the manipulation of the independent variable (if applicable)
2   Appropriateness in the use of follow-up measures (if applicable)
3   Adequacy of data to provide evidence for testing of the hypotheses (if applicable)
4   Clarity in reporting the statistics (if applicable)
5   Appropriateness in the use of statistical controls (if applicable)

    6 Appropriateness of statistics utilized (if applicable)
       a Statistics appropriate to level of measurement
       b Use of between-groups procedures
       c Multivariate statistics used appropriately
       d Post hoc tests used appropriately
       e Overall appropriateness of statistics

Many of the above criteria are not applicable to Lula's study. However, they can be used in evaluating other, more complex, studies.

Part 4: Discussion

The final part of a quantitative research report presents a discussion of the study's findings. Care should be taken not to merely repeat the study's findings that were already presented in Part 3. It can be tempting to repeat one finding in order to remind the reader about it preliminary to a discussion, and then another finding, and then a third . . . and, before we know it, we have written the whole of the findings section all over again and called it a discussion. What is needed here is control and judgment—a delicate balance between not reminding the reader at all and saying everything twice.

On the other hand, Lula might be tempted to ignore her findings altogether, particularly if she did not find what she expected. If the findings did not support her hypothesis, she may have a strong urge to express her viewpoint anyway, using persuasive prose to make up for the lack of quantitative objective evidence. This temptation must be resisted at all costs. The term "discussion" relates to what she found, not to what she thinks she ought to have found, or to what she might have found under slightly different circumstances.

Perhaps she did manage to find a relationship between the variables in both of her hypotheses. However, to her dismay, the relationship was the opposite of what she predicted. For example, suppose her data indicated that children who did not witness wife abuse had lower social interaction skills than children who witnessed it (this is the opposite of what she predicted). This unexpected result must be discussed, shedding whatever light on the surprising finding. Any relationship between two variables is worthy of discussion, particularly if they seem atypical or if they are not quite what was anticipated.

A common limitation in social work research has to do with not being able to randomly sample research participants from a population. Whenever we cannot randomly select or assign research participants to two or more groups, the sample cannot be considered to be truly representative of the population in question, and we cannot generalize the study's results back to the population of children who witnessed or did not witness wife abuse in the community.

Another major limitation in this study is that we will never know the social skills of children who did not accompany their mothers to the shelter. The social skills of children who stay home may somehow be quite different from those children who accompanied their mothers. In fact, there are a host of other limitations in this simple study, including the simple fact that, in reference to Research Hypothesis 2, boys who did not see wife abuse may also have lower social interaction skills than girls—this was never tested in Lula's study. Nevertheless, we should also bear in mind the fact that few social work studies are based on truly representative random samples. In Lula's study, however, she still managed to collect some interesting data.

There are a few criteria that need to be examined when evaluating the utilization potential of a study's findings (Fischer, 1993):

1   Degree of relevance to social work practice

2   Overall soundness of the study (internal validity)

3   Degree of generalizability of the study's findings to other populations and settings (external validity)

4   Degree to which the independent variables are accessible to control by the social workers (if applicable)

5   Extent to which a meaningful difference would occur if the independent variable were utilized in actual social work practice situations (if applicable)

6   Degree of economic feasibility of the independent variable if utilized in actual social work practice settings (if applicable)

7   Degree of ethical suitability of the manipulation of the independent variable

8   Extent to which the research question or hypothesis has been addressed (if applicable)

Many of the above criteria are not applicable to Lula's study. However, they can be used in evaluating other, more complex, studies. All social work researchers would like to be able to generalize their findings beyond the specific research setting and sample. From a quantitative research perspective (not a practice perspective), Lula is not really interested in the specific children in this particular study. She is more interested in children who witness wife abuse in general. Technically, the results of her study cannot be generalized to other populations of children who witness wife abuse, but she can suggest that she might find similar results with other children who accompany their mothers to similar women's shelters. She can imply and can recommend further research studies into the topic area.

Sometimes we can find support for our suggestions in the results of previous studies that were not conclusive either, but that also managed to produce recommendations. It might even be a good idea to extract these studies from the literature review section in Part 1 of the report and resurrect them in the discussion section.

On occasion, the results of a study will not agree with the results of previous studies. In this case, we should give whatever explanations seem reasonable for the disagreement and make some suggestions whereby the discrepancy can be resolved. Perhaps another research study should be undertaken that would examine the same or different variables. Perhaps, next time, a different research design should be used or the research hypothesis should be reformulated. Perhaps other operational definitions could be used. Suggestions for future studies should always be specific, not just a vague statement to the effect that more research studies need to be done in this area.

In some cases, recommendations can be made for changes in social work programs, interventions, or policies based on the results of a study. These recommendations are usually contained in reports addressed to people who have the power to make the suggested changes. When changes are suggested, the author has to display some knowledge about the policy or program and the possible consequences of implementing the changes.

Finally, a report is concluded with a summary of the study's findings. This is particularly important in longer reports or when a study's findings and discussion sections are lengthy or complex. Sometimes, indeed, people reading a long report read only the summary and a few sections of the study that interests them.

There are a few criteria that need to be examined when evaluating the discussion section of a quantitative research report (Fischer, 1993):

1   Degree to which the data support the research hypothesis (if applicable)
2   Extent to which the researcher's conclusions are consistent with the data gathered
3   Degree of uniformity between tables and text
4   Degree of researcher bias
5   Clarity as to cause of changes in the dependent variable (if applicable)
6   Degree to which potential rival hypotheses were dealt with in the discussion
7   Reasonableness of opinions about the study's implications
8   Adequacy in relating the study's findings to previous studies through the literature
9   Adequacy of conclusions for generalizing beyond the study's data
10   Appropriateness in the handling of unexpected consequences

SUMMING UP AND LOOKING AHEAD

The purpose of writing a quantitative research proposal is fourfold. A quantitative research proposal is necessary, first, to obtain permission to carry out the study and, second, to secure the funds with which to do it. Third, the researcher needs to convince the proposal reviewers that he or she is competent enough to do the study. Fourth, we need to think over precisely what we want to study, why we want to study it, what methods we should use, and what difficulties we are likely to encounter.

A quantitative research proposal should be well organized and easy to read so that reviewers have a clear picture of each step of the study. The information included in most proposals can be set out under eleven general headings, or parts: research topic, literature review, conceptual framework, questions and hypotheses, operational definitions, research design, population and sample, data collection, data analysis, limitations, and administration.

Using a majority of the material from the quantitative research proposal, a quantitative research report is written that can be broken down into four general headings, or parts: problem, method, findings, and discussion. The four parts of a quantitative research report parallel the eleven parts of the quantitative research proposal. This is not surprising, since both the report and the proposal are describing the same study.

Now that we know how to write quantitative research proposals and reports, the next chapter presents how to write qualitative research proposals and reports.

REVIEW QUESTIONS

1. Discuss the purpose of a quantitative research proposal. Present the benefits of writing one before a quantitative research study is actually conducted. Present a social work example throughout your discussion.

2. Thoroughly describe in your own words the eleven parts of a quantitative research proposal. Present a social work example throughout your discussion.

3. Discuss the purpose of quantitative research reports. Why are they necessary for the social work profession?

4. Thoroughly describe in your own words the four parts of a quantitative research report. Present a social work example throughout your discussion.

5. Go to the library and select a social work article. Did the article follow the same sequence of parts as presented in this chapter? How could the contents of the article have been reformulated to fit the four parts as described in this chapter? Discuss in detail.

6. What other limitations, besides the ones mentioned in this chapter, should Lula include in her final quantitative research report? Discuss each one in detail. For example, what about the social interaction skills of children who not only witnessed wife abuse but were also physically abused by their fathers?

7. Go to the library and select a social work quantitative research article. Write a hypothetical quantitative research proposal for the study using the contents of this chapter as a guide.

8. Write an explanatory-level quantitative research proposal that Lula could have written with her same general problem area: problems experienced by children who witness one parent physically abusing the other.

9. Write a hypothetical quantitative research report based on the quantitative research proposal that you wrote for Question 8.

10. Write a final quantitative research report that Lula could submit to a professional social work journal using the findings of her study.

Chapter 15

Qualitative Proposals and Reports

I N THEORY, qualitative research proposals and their corresponding reports are similar to one another. If we explain clearly what we intend to do when we write our proposal, for example, and we actually carry out our study as we originally planned, then writing our research report is largely a matter of changing "we will do" (as in the proposal) to "we did" (as in the report). This is true for everything but describing our study's findings in the research report.

As we will see, there is a good deal of similarity between quantitative and qualitative research proposals and reports. After all, the research process follows a logical progression whether it is quantitative or qualitative. We need to know from the beginning of our research study what we want to study, why we want to study it, what methods we will use to study it, how long our research study will take, and how much it will cost. In addition, we need to know what data will be collected, from whom, in what way, and how they will be analyzed.

For the sake of continuity, this chapter—on qualitative proposals and reports—will use the same headings and subheadings that were used in the last chapter that described quantitative proposals and reports. We will also uses the same example: Lula Wilson, a social work practitioner who wants to do a qualitative research study on children and their mothers in the women's emergency shelter where she works.

WRITING PROPOSALS

Before we begin to write the very first word of a research proposal—whether quantitative or qualitative—we need to know why we want to write it and who will read it. Knowing the purpose and our intended audience helps us to make important decisions about what we should include, in what order, and what writing style should be used.

Purpose of Writing a Proposal

There are three general purposes for writing a research proposal, no matter whether the study being proposed is quantitative or qualitative:

1 We need to obtain permission to do the study
2 We need to obtain funding for the study
3 We need to write down exactly what we intend to study, why, and how

As we know from Chapter 2, obtaining permission to do our study is often a matter of resolving ethical and informed consent issues to the satisfaction of various ethics committees. Most universities and colleges have ethics committees, which decide whether our proposed study is designed in such a way that the interests of its research participants are ethically addressed. Many social services agencies have their own ethics committees, which vet all proposed research endeavors that involve the their clients and staff.

If Lula were associated in any way with a university, for example, and if her women's emergency shelter had its own ethics committee, she would have to obtain permission from both ethics committees before she could begin her study. Even if no ethics committees are involved, Lula would have to discuss her proposed study with her supervisor, who would probably have to obtain official permission from the shelter's board of directors.

All research studies require some level of funding. Even if Lula is prepared to do all the work on her own time using her own clients, there will still be direct and indirect costs such as photocopying, travel, phone, fax, and postage. If Lula wants her shelter to cover these costs, she must include a budget in her proposal and get the budget approved before she begins her study. If it is a larger study, necessitating money from a funding body, then Lula must tailor her research proposal to meet the requirements of the particular funding body to which she is applying.

Most funding bodies have application forms that ask the applicant to supply the study's details under specific headings. Usually, funding bodies also want to know how qualified the particular applicant is to undertake the proposed study. In other words, Lula will have to convince the funding body that she, personally, has the experience and educational qualifications necessary to obtain meaningful and trustworthy results from her proposed study.

After permission and funding, the third purpose of writing a proposal is to force Lula to clarify her thoughts a bit more. In the process of describing her proposed study in sufficient detail in an attempt to convince others of its importance, Lula may think of aspects of her study that she has not thought of before. She may realize, for example, that she has little experience with interviewing children, and someone who has more experience with interviewing children may be in a better position to interview them.

Intended Audience

Most research proposals are reviewed by busy people who have a great deal of other work and probably a number of proposals to review. Lula's proposal, therefore should be as short as she can possibly make it. It should concisely describe her proposed study, its budget, and time frame, in a way that is easy to read, to follow, and to understand. Many proposals have to be rejected because there is insufficient funding or facilities to support them all, and those that are rejected are not necessarily the least worthy in terms of their importance. They are, however, often the least worthy in terms of how well they were organized and written. Lula will therefore be well advised to keep her proposal simple, clear, and brief.

Content and Writing Style

A proposal's content and writing style will largely depend on who is going to review it. As already noted, some funding bodies stipulate on their application forms what, and how much, they want included, and in what format and order. If there is no such stipulation, it is simplest and most logical to write the research proposal in the order that the study will be conducted: that is, the order followed in this chapter. How much to include under what heading depends on the intended audience: A research proposal submitted to an academic committee, for example, often requires more of a literature review than a proposal submitted to a funding organization.

Style similarly depends on the recipient. In most cases, it is safest to write formally, using the third person. As we know, however, qualitative research studies are often more subjective than quantitative ones, their terminology is different, their underlying assumptions are different, and the researcher's own thoughts and feelings are an important component. It may therefore be appropriate to acknowledge the qualitative nature of the study by using a more personal writing style. As will be the case in writing the final research report, the style used depends on the proposal's intended audience and the author's personal judgment.

Organizing the Proposal

As previously noted, if the proposal's recipients have provided no guidance as to how its contents should be organized, it is simplest to present the proposed study in the order in which it would be conducted. That is, the order that follows.

Part 1: Research Topic

This first section of a research proposal does nothing more than introduce the study to its readers. It examines the nature of the research question being explored and its significance, both to social work in general and to the recipient of the proposal in particular. As with quantitative studies, a qualitative study should have practical significance, theoretical significance, or significance with respect to social policy; or it may touch on all three areas. The author's task is to explain what research question is being asked and why the answer to this question will be of benefit, paying particular attention to the interests of the proposal's reviewers.

Lula may write, for example, about the general topic area in her study as follows:

> *General Topic Area:*
> The problems experienced by children who witness their mothers being physically abused by their fathers.

The results of such a study—knowing what these problems are—might generate new social work theory or it might lead to changes in social policy. If Lula is going to submit her proposal to the women's emergency shelter where she works, however, her fellow social workers are more likely to be interested in how an understanding of the children's problems might help them to address the children's needs on a very practical level. Lula will therefore emphasize the practical significance of her study in the first part of her proposal.

Part 2: Literature Review

As with quantitative research studies, there are four purposes in carrying out a literature review for qualitative studies:

1 **To assure the reviewers that Lula understands the current issues related to her research topic.**

2 **To point out ways in which her study is similar to, or different from, other studies that have been previously conducted**   Since many qualitative studies deal with topics about which little is known, Lula may find very few studies that have explored children's experiences with respect to their witnessing wife abuse. Such a paucity of information will support Lula's contention that her study needs to be conducted.

3 **To fit Lula's study into the jigsaw puzzle of present knowledge**   Even if there is little knowledge in the area, there will still be some, and Lula's task is to explain how her study will fit with what is known already and will help to fill the knowledge gaps.

4 **To introduce and conceptualize the variables that will be used throughout the study**   Lulu's proposal, for example, will include such concepts as children, wife abuse (or partner or marital abuse, whichever term is preferred) and children witnessing wife abuse.

Part 3: Conceptual Framework

As we know from Box 3.2, in quantitative research studies, the conceptual framework identifies the possible relationships between and among concepts to one another. Identifying the ways that concepts might be connected lays the groundwork for developing a research question or research hypothesis. In the last chapter, for example, Lula formulated the research hypothesis as follows:

Research Hypothesis:
Children who have witnessed wife abuse will have lower social interaction skills than children who have not witnessed such abuse.

That is, her conceptual framework included the idea that a particular concept—children's social interaction skills—was directly related to another concept—whether the children witnessed the abuse or not.

In qualitative studies, the level of knowledge in the topic area will probably be too low to allow such possible connections between and among concepts to be envisaged. Children's poor social interaction skills may indeed be one of the problems experienced by children who witness their mothers being physically abused by their fathers, but Lula does not know that yet. Her simple research question at this stage is simply, "What problems do these children experience?"

Relationships between and among concepts can still be hypothesized, however, even at an exploratory level, and even if the hypothesized relationships will not be tested during the course of the study. People reading a qualitative study, for example, are usually more interested in where the study took place and whether the influence of the clinical setting (i.e., the shelter) was appropriately acknowledged in the data analysis.

Lula must therefore take into account the possibility that the problems experienced by the children in her study may have been due to the study's setting (i.e., the shelter) and not so much from their witnessing the abuse. If she conceptualizes this possibility early, she may decide to interview the children's mothers, asking them not only to identify their children's problems, but to describe each problem before and after coming into the shelter. Similarly, she may want to explore the possibility that the children's problems may have been related to the children being abused themselves and not just to their witnessing their mothers being physically abused by their fathers.

Part 4: Questions and Hypotheses

A qualitative research study rarely tests a research hypothesis. It is very important, however, that the questions to be answered during the course of a qualitative study be clearly formulated before it begins. Lula could formulate quite specific research questions, such as:

Specific Research Questions:
- What types of problems are experienced by children who have witnessed wife abuse?
- Does the type of abuse witnessed (e.g., hitting, yelling) affect the type of problems experienced by the children?
- Does the intensity of the abuse—witnessed by the children—affect the problems they experience?
- Does the frequency (e.g., daily, weekly) of the abuse—witnessed by the children—affect the problems they experience?
- Does the duration (e.g., over months, years) of the abuse—witnessed by the children—affect the problems they experience?
- Does the child's gender affect the types of problems they experience?
- Does the child's age affect the types of problems they experience?
- Do the child's problems, as perceived by the mother, affect the mother's decision to leave the abusive relationship?
- Do the child's problems, as perceived by the mother, affect the mother's decision about whether or not to return to the abusive relationship?

If Lula is going to formulate specific research questions, she will probably need to use a fairly structured interview schedule when she collects interview data from the mothers and their children. On the other hand, she may prefer to formulate just a few, more general research questions, such as:

General Research Questions:
- What types of problems are experienced by children who have witnessed wife abuse?
- What effects do these problems have on the children and their mothers?

In this case, she would use an unstructured interview schedule, which would allow the mothers and children to guide the interviews themselves, relating what is important to them in their own way.

Lula's decision about whether to formulate specific or general research questions depends on the level of knowledge about the study's topic area. If enough knowledge is available to enable her to formulate specific research questions, she will probably do that. If not, one of the purposes of her study would be to gain enough knowledge to allow specific research questions to be formulated in the future.

Part 5: Operational Definitions

As we know, operationally defining a variable in a quantitative research study means defining the variable in such a way that it can be measured. In the last chapter, for example, Lula operationally defined the level of a child's social interaction skills in terms of the child's score derived from a standardized measuring instrument (*SISOCIA*). The idea behind operationally defining a variable in this way is that both its definition and its measurement are consistent and objective. Lula did not define "children's social interaction skills" herself (except insofar as she selected the measuring instrument) and she did not ask the children or their mothers what they perceived "children's social interaction skills" to be. Similarly, the measured result for each child (a numerical score) did not depend on anyone's personal perception on how well, or how badly, the child interacted socially with others.

Conversely, in qualitative studies, we are not as interested in objectively defining or measuring our concepts as we are when doing quantitative studies. Indeed, we actively encourage our research participants to provide us with their own, subjective definitions, since we are trying to understand their problems as they perceive them to be (see Boxes 3.4 & 3.5). Similarly, we measure the extent, or effect, of a problem in terms of the research participants' subjective viewpoints.

Hence, Lula will not have to worry about how to operationally define "a child" or "a child's problem," and she will not have to decide whether "a child witnessing wife abuse" means seeing it, or hearing it, or merely being aware that it is occurring. Lula might want to collect data about the ages of the children in her study, whether they are the biological children of their mothers, and whether they live full time at home, but none of these data will be used to exclude any child from the study on the grounds that the child is too old or too young, or otherwise does not fit Lula's operational definition of "a child."

Lula does not have an operational definition of a child. In her study, "a child" is operationally defined as "any person whom the mother considers to be her child." Similarly, "a problem" is whatever the mother and/or child considers to be problematic. "Wife abuse" is defined as whatever the research participants think it is; and children who have "witnessed wife abuse" if they and/or their mothers believe that they have.

It might be as well here to put in a word about measurement. The word "measurement" is often associated with numbers, and hence with quantitative studies. To "measure" something, however, only means to describe it as accurately and completely as possible. If we cannot describe it with numbers, we may still be able to describe it with words, and this qualitative type of measurement is just as valid as a quantitative numerical measurement. Hence, Lula is "measuring" the problems experienced by children when she encourages the mothers and their children to describe those problems as accurately and completely as they can.

The first five parts of a research proposal deal with *what* is to be studied and *why* it is to be studied. Before moving on to *how* it is to be studied, it is as well to review the *what* and *why* sections to ensure that nothing has been omitted. As presented in the last chapter, Fischer (1993) has provided a few criteria that need to be examined when reviewing Parts 1–5 of a research proposal. These criteria were designed for quantitative studies but some of them are also useful in qualitative ones. The following six criteria should be considered:

1 Adequacy of the proposal's literature review
2 Clarity of the problem area and research questions under investigation
3 Clarity of the researcher's orientation
4 Clarity of the study's purpose
5 Clarity of the study's auspices
6 Reasonableness of the author's assumptions

The last four criteria are particularly important for qualitative studies since the trustworthiness of the subjective nature of the data provided by research participants might easily be compromised by bias on the part of the researcher. Researchers engaged in both quantitative and qualitative studies often have strong feelings about their research topics.

In quantitative studies, efforts are made to mitigate the effects of researcher bias through objective measurement (see Chapter 9). In qualitative studies, however, the use of measurement is to capture the subjective experiences of the research participants. Thus, it is vital for Lula to be aware of the effects of her own feelings upon the research participants she will be interviewing. Any prior assumptions she has made, and any position she might hold, must be clearly outlined at the beginning of her study, so that the reader of her proposal can evaluate the degree to which her study's potential findings would reflect the research participants' opinions rather than Lula's opinions.

Similarly, it is important to record the interests and possible biases of the organization who is funding the study in addition to the agency where the study actually takes place. Would certain findings be more welcome to the funding body or the agency than other findings? Is the researcher under any pressure to emphasize certain aspects of the study's results to the detriment of other aspects? Again, the reader of a research proposal must be able to evaluate the degree to which the proposed study's auspices would potentially affect the study's findings.

A clear statement of the study's purpose might deflect critics who argue that the proposed study did not fulfill other purposes which the critics, themselves, may perceive as more important. Lula's research study might have a practical purpose, for example, where it would be in tune with staff interests who work within the women's emergency shelter that would provide both funding for the study and access to its clients.

Lula simply wants to know what the children's problems are so that the shelter can better meet the needs of the children and their mothers. She is not overly interested in adding to social work theory or changing social policy, although her study's results may indeed have implications in both of these areas. She is less likely to be criticized for not placing sufficient emphasis on theory and policy in her discussion if she has clearly stated from the beginning that her proposed study's purpose is to inform day-to-day practice activities within her specific shelter.

Part 6: Research Design

We come now to the *how* of the study. This section includes information about what data will be collected, in what way and from whom, and how they will be analyzed.

While writing about these matters, there will be many opportunities to address issues related to the study's *trustworthiness*. Evidence of a study's trustworthiness is provided by paying attention to four major concerns:

- Credibility, or truth value
- Transferability, or applicability
- Dependability, or consistency
- Confirmability, or neutrality

The above are roughly equivalent to the quantitative concepts of internal validity, external validity or generalizability, reliability, and objectivity (see Chapter 9). The first issue related to trustworthiness, credibility (akin to internal validity), is particularly important and is built on the following aspects of a qualitative research study:

- **Triangulation of data sources**—collecting data about the same thing from a number of different data sources (see Chapters 10 and 11); also engagement with research participants over a long period of time.
- **Consulting with colleagues**—consulting with them about ethical and legal matters, and about the methods chosen to select the sample of research participants and to collect and analyze the data.

- **Negative case analysis**—ensuring that information from all data sources is included in the data analysis, even when information from one data source seems to contradict themes or conclusions common to other data sources.
- **Referential adequacy**—keeping a complete and accurate record of all personal interviews and observations, such as videotapes, audiotapes, case notes, and transcriptions.
- **Member checks**—research participants are asked to provide feedback on the information collected from the researcher and the conclusions drawn by the researcher.

The second issue related to trustworthiness, transferability (akin to external validity, or generalizability) is addressed through a rich description of the study's clinical setting and research participants. Findings from a qualitative research study are usually not generalized beyond the setting in which the study took place. The findings may be applicable, however, to other similar client populations: women and children in similar women's emergency shelters elsewhere, for example. Readers can only judge to what degree a study's findings may be applicable to their own clientele if the researcher provides a detailed description of the study's research participants in addition to their special needs and circumstances.

The third issue, dependability (akin to reliability) relates to efforts to maintain consistency throughout the study. Were all interviews conducted in the same setting, according to the same format, and recorded in the same way? Were all research participants asked to provide feedback on the data collected, or only some? During data analysis, were rules concerning categorization and coding consistently applied? Aspects of the study related to credibility and described above may be used to demonstrate dependability as well: for example, referential adequacy, providing evidence of consistent interviewing procedures, and providing evidence that all research participants were asked for their feedback.

The last issue, confirmability (akin to objectivity) has to do with Lula's awareness of her own role in influencing the data provided by the research participants and the conclusions she drew from the data. As discussed in Chapters 3 and 13, all qualitative researchers should keep journals in which they record their own thoughts and feelings about the study's research participants and about their interviews and observations. Lula should note in her journal, for example, why she made the decisions she did about methodological matters, such as sampling procedures, and data collection and analysis techniques. While conducting the data analysis, she will record decisions and concerns about organizing and interpreting the data she collected.

These journal entries disclose the degree of impartiality she brought to the entire research process; and, where she was not impartial, it discloses her awareness, or lack thereof, about her own assumptions and biases. With respect to dependability (discussed above), it provides a record of how consistent her decision making was and how consistently she conducted her interviews and analyzed her data.

Part 7: Population and Sample

In this part of the proposal, Lula provides only a general description of who her research participants will be, together with a rationale for selecting these and not others. In qualitative studies, there is no attempt to select a random sample. Indeed, the sample often consists of all those persons available to be studied who fit broad criteria. Lula could draw her sample of research participants, for example, from all those women who are residents in her women's emergency shelter at a specific time.

Since Lula's study involves the effects on children who witnessed wife abuse, she will need to exclude from her sample all women who do not have children *and* all women who say that their children did not witness the abuse. Lula may personally believe that no child whose mother is being abused can remain unaware of that abuse, and the definition of "witnessing" for her may include a child's awareness, as well as seeing or hearing.

In addition, it would be interesting to explore conflicting perceptions between the mothers and their children, when the children believe that they have witnessed wife abuse and their mothers believe that they have not. Lula is unlikely, however, to elicit information about the effects of witnessing wife abuse from women who do not believe that their children witnessed it; nor are these women likely to give Lula permission to interview their children on the subject.

Lula may decide to include women who do not have their children with them at the shelter. Whether she does so or not will depend on a number of factors. First, how many women can she interview, given her own and the women's time constraints? This will depend on how long she expects each interview to take, which, in turn, depends on such factors as the structure and depth of the interview. In addition, she must consider the time involved in transcribing and analyzing each interview in its entirety. If the number of women who have their children at the shelter is equal to, or larger than, the number of women Lula can reasonably interview, then she will exclude women whose children are not present.

If the number is smaller, she may consider including these women, but that decision, as well, will depend on a number of factors. Uppermost in the mind of any qualitative researcher is the notion of the study's trustworthiness. As discussed earlier, one way of establishing the trustworthiness of data is to collect data about the same thing from a number of different data sources.

As presented in Chapters 10 and 11, data on the problems experienced by children, for example, may be collected from three data sources: (1) the children themselves, (2) their mothers, and (3) shelter staff who have observed the children. Such a triangulation of data sources allows assessment of the trustworthiness of the data obtained from any one given source. If children are not present at the shelter, then data on their problems can be obtained only from their mothers and there will be no way to check on the accuracy of the data they provide.

Another way to establish trustworthiness is to ask each research participant to comment on the data gathered and the conclusions that the researcher drew from the data. Lula might want to submit the transcript of each interview to the research participant concerned to make sure that she has adequately captured what the participant was trying to say. Then, she might want to discuss her findings with the other research participants to see if they believe that she has interpreted what they said correctly and has drawn conclusions that seem reasonable to them as well.

None of this will be possible if the research participants have left the emergency shelter and disappeared before Lula has transcribed and analyzed her data. She might, therefore, want to restrict her sample of women to those who are likely to remain in her shelter for a number of weeks or who will go on to a halfway house or some other traceable address. Of course, if she does this, she will lose data from women whose very transience might affect their children's problems and the way those problems are perceived.

Lula must also consider whether to interview the children and, if so, children in what age groups. She may not be skilled in interviewing young children and may feel that children under school age cannot be meaningfully interviewed at all. If there are enough women in the shelter who have older children present, she may consider restricting her sample of research participants to women whose children are, say, 10 years old or older. She will have to justify selecting age 10 instead of 8 or 12, for example, and she will lose data pertaining to the problems experienced by these younger children.

With this in mind, she may consider enlisting the assistance of a colleague who is more skilled at eliciting information from younger children—through data collection methods such as drama, art, or play—than she is. But, now, she has to think about how such interview data would be analyzed and how she would integrate them with the data collected through her own personal interviews with the mothers.

The child's gender may be another consideration. Perhaps Lula has an idea that girls tend to display more internalizing problem behaviors—such as withdrawal and depression—than boys. And, she may believe that boys tend to display more externalizing behaviors—such as hostility and aggression—than girls. She might therefore want to ensure that her study contains approximately equal numbers of girls and boys.

If she purposefully drew her sample of research participants in this way, she would have to explain that she expected to find more internalizing behaviors in girls and more externalizing behaviors in boys. This would constitute a research hypothesis, which would need to be included in the Questions and Hypotheses section and justified through the literature review. Or perhaps, Lula would phrase it as a research question, simply asking whether the gender of the child was related to the type of problem behavior he or she exhibited.

Similarly, Lula might have an idea that the types of problem behaviors exhibited by children depend on their ethnic background. If she were able to conduct only a small number of interviews, for example, she might purposefully select women and children from different ethnic backgrounds to make up her sample of research participants (called *purposive sampling*, see Chapter 5). Here again, she would have to justify her choice, including a relevant research question or research hypothesis and addressing the matter in the literature review.

Lula thus has a number of factors to consider in deciding whom to include as research participants in her study. The main consideration, however, is always the willingness of the research participant to take part in the study. Like most social work populations, women in emergency shelters are an extremely vulnerable group, and it is vital to ensure that they feel freely able to refuse to participate in the study, knowing that their refusal will in no way affect the quality of the services they receive (see Chapter 2).

Similarly, the social workers within Lula's women's emergency shelter must also feel able to refuse, knowing that their refusal will not affect the terms of their employment. It is quite likely that Lula will not have the luxury of selecting her research participants in terms of the age, gender, or ethnic background of the children. More probably, Lula will just interview those women who agree to be interviewed and who also give permission for her, or a colleague, to interview their children as well. The children will not be in a position to sign an informed consent form, as their mothers and the social workers will do, but it is still extremely important to ensure that they understand their rights with respect to refusing to take part in the study or withdrawing from it at any time.

Part 8: Data Collection

This part of the qualitative research proposal provides a detailed account of how the data are going to be collected, together with a justification for using the data collection method selected rather than some other method. Lula could use focus groups, for example, rather than unstructured interviews to collect data from the women. She could decide not to interview children, but instead to observe the children's behaviors herself, without involving a colleague or other social workers. If she does involve the shelter's social workers, she might decide just to interview them and ask how they define the children's problem behaviors and what problem behaviors they have observed in the children under study. On the other hand, she might ask them first to define children's problem behaviors, then to purposefully observe certain children with respect to these behaviors, and finally to report their observations back to her. She might even ask them to use structured methods of observation, such as frequency, magnitude, or duration recording instruments (see Chapter 10).

Whatever she decides, she must first justify her decisions and then clearly describe the methods to be used. She should state, for example, that the abused women, the shelter's social workers, and the children aged

10 or over will be interviewed by herself, if that is what she has decided to do.

She should also specify where these interviews will take place, how long approximately each is expected to last, and to what degree the content will be guided by an interview schedule. She should also specify the time frame within which all the interviews will be completed and how the interviews will be recorded. Videotaping, audiotaping, and taking notes during the interview all have their advantages and disadvantages, which need to be discussed.

If a colleague is to work with the younger children, for example, details of the methods used to elicit interview data from these children must be given. In addition, the colleague's credentials must be included at the beginning of the proposal, since this colleague is now a coresearcher and her experience and qualifications will affect the trustworthiness of the study's findings.

Ethical considerations that were not covered in the discussion about selecting research participants should also be addressed in this section. Should Lula obtain informed consent from the mothers and their children, for example, before she asks the shelter's social workers to observe the children, or to discuss their behaviors with her? Should she share the social worker's comments with the mothers and their children concerned and tell the social workers beforehand that this is to be done? Should she share data obtained from the children with their mothers, or make it clear that such data will not be shared? Social workers might not be so honest in their comments if they know that the data will be shared: and neither might the children.

In addition, children who know they are being observed might not behave as they otherwise would. These are old dilemmas that always affect data collection methods, and Lula must specify what dilemmas she may encounter and how she plans to resolve them. It is as well to state how the mothers, children, and social workers are to be approached, and precisely what they are going to be told about her study and their own part in it. Samples of informed consent forms should be included as an appendix at the end of the proposal.

Lula's journal is also a form of data. While it will include little in the way of data collected from her study's research participants, it will include Lula's reactions to these data and a chronology of her study's process. Lula might therefore want to state in her proposal that she will keep a journal, recording notes on the decisions she is going to make during every stage of her study, with particular reference to the study's trustworthiness.

Part 9: Data Analysis

This part of the research proposal describes the way the data will be analyzed. There are usually no statistical procedures to be discussed, as there may be in a quantitative study, but there are a number of other matters. As presented in Chapter 13, a decision must be made about whether to use a software computer program to aid in the data analysis and, if so, which one. Then, Lula must decide who will transcribe the interviews and how the transcripts should be formatted. She must establish a plan for her data analysis, including some plan for making journal entries. She might want to add in her proposal that, after she has analyzed the data, using first- and second-level coding methods, and after she has drawn conclusions, she will assess the trustworthiness of her study's findings. She will do this by documenting what she is going to do to establish credibility, transferability, dependability (consistency), and confirmability (control of biases and preconceptions).

Part 10: Limitations

All research studies have limitations. It might even be suggested that one of the main limitations of a qualitative study is that it is not a quantitative one. This is simply not true. Every study is judged on how well it fulfills its own purpose; and one of the purposes of a qualitative study is usually to understand the experiences of the research participants in depth, including experiences that are unique to them. The purpose of Lula's study is to gain a better understanding of the problems experienced by children who have witnessed wife abuse, from the different perspectives of the mothers, their children, and the shelter's social workers, so that the needs of these children can be better identified and met.

A discussion of a study's limitations should include only factors that impede the fulfillment of this purpose. Lula's study, for example, is not limited because she did not operationally define the concepts "wife abuse" and "children witnessing wife abuse." Part of her study's purpose is to find out how the mothers and their children, themselves, define "wife abuse;" that is, to find out what it was that the children in her study actually witnessed, and what they and their mothers think that "witnessing" includes.

From an ideal standpoint, Lula's study is limited with respect to its transferability (generalizability, in quantitative terms). It would have been ideal if she could have constructed a sampling frame of all the children in the world who had witnessed wife abuse, taken a random sample, and interviewed all these children and their mothers in depth.

A quantitative researcher restricts the study to a manageable population of research participants and then generalizes from the sample to the population from which it was drawn. It is a limitation if the sample did not adequately represent its population, thus restricting the ability to generalize; but it is not considered a limitation that the study did not use a larger population in the first place. Similarly, Lula does not need to apologize for having chosen to work only with those women and their children who were residents in her particular women's emergency shelter at the time she wanted to conduct her study. On the other hand, some of these women whose children had witnessed wife abuse may have refused to participate, and that would be a limitation to Lula's study, since those women may have felt particularly traumatized by their children's involvement, to the point where they felt unable to discuss it. By losing them, Lula would lose a different and valuable perspective.

Another limitation to Lula's study is that many of the children who have witnessed wife abuse may have been abused themselves. It may be impossible for the mothers and/or children to distinguish between the effects of being abused themselves and the effects of witnessing the abuse. The only way Lula could deal with this is to divide her population of children who have witnessed abuse into two groups: those who have been abused, according to their mothers; and those who have not. Of course, it might be argued that witnessing wife abuse constitutes emotional abuse. If Lula subscribes to this view, she might wish to ask the mothers specifically if their children have been physically or sexually abused, since all the children in her sample will have been emotionally abused according to her own definition.

Nevertheless, in practical terms, Lula can form her two groups of children merely by including a question about physical or sexual abuse during her interviews with them and with their mothers. If Lula identifies this limitation early on while she is conceptualizing her study, she can include the two groups in her study's research design, mentioning the question about wife abuse in the data collection section, and noting, in the data analysis section, that she will accord each group a separate category. Thus, her study's limitation will have ceased to be a limitation and will have become an integral part of her study. This is one of the purposes of a research design, of course: to identify and address a study's potential limitations so that they can be eliminated, or at least alleviated, to the greatest possible extent.

Essentially, what Lula has done in thinking about children who have been abused themselves is to identify a confounding or intervening variable that might interfere with the relationship between their witnessing wife abuse and their experiencing problems, if any, due to witnessing it. Inevitably, there will be a host of other confounding variables since no one can tell for certain whether children's particular problematic behaviors are due to witnessing wife abuse or to some other factor(s). Without random assignment to a control group, which is not possible in this study, Lula will be able to conclude only that children who witnessed wife abuse experienced certain problems, not that the problems were caused by witnessing the wife abuse in the first place.

Failure to establish causality, however, is only a limitation if the establishment of causality was one of the purposes of the study. In this case, it was not; and indeed the kind of rigorous research design needed to establish causality is usually inappropriate in a qualitative study.

Lula may find that her sample of children is not diverse enough in terms of age, gender, or ethnic background to allow her to draw conclusions about the effects of these variables on their problem behaviors. Again, this is a study limitation only if she has stated her intention to draw such a conclusion. The major limitation that Lula is likely to encounter in her study is related to the issue of credibility or truth value (internal validity, in quantitative terms). How will she know whether the mothers and their children were truthful in relating their experiences or whether their remarks were geared more toward pleasing her or making themselves appear more socially desirable? And, if their remarks were based on memories of previous abusive behaviors, how far were those memories reliable?

These are common dilemmas in both research and clinical interviews. One way to handle them is through triangulation: obtaining data on the same issue from more than one data source. Another way is to constantly reflect on the quality of the data being obtained throughout the interview process, and to record the results of these reflections in the study's journal. The following are examples of the kinds of questions Lula might ask herself while she is pursuing her reflections:

- Is the interviewee withholding something—and what should I do about it?
- What impact might my race, age, social status, gender, or beliefs have on my interviewee?
- What difference might it make that I work at the women's emergency shelter?
- Did what the interviewee said ring true—or did she want to please me, or look good, or protect someone else, or save herself embarrassment?
- Why am I feeling so stressed after this interview?
- Am I getting the kinds of data that are relevant for my study?

These questions might improve the quality of the data obtained by making Lula more aware of possible sources of error. Even if they do not, Lula will have shown that she has recognized her study's limitations and will take the necessary steps to deal with each limitation.

Part 11: Administration

The final part of a research proposal deals with the organization and resources necessary to carry out the proposed study. Lula might want to separate her role as a researcher from her role as one of the shelter's social workers, for example, by equipping herself with a desk and computer in a room other than that which she usually uses. If "researcher space" is not a problem, Lula will still need to think about where she should base her operations: where she will write up her notes, analyze her data, and keep the records of her interviews. Then, she has to think about administrative responsibilities. Will she take on the overall responsibility for her study herself or will that fall to her supervisor? What will be the responsibilities of her colleague and the shelter's social workers? To whom will they report? What is the chain of command?

When Lula has put together the details of who does what, in what order, and who is responsible to whom, she will be in a position to consider a time frame. How long will each task take and by what date ought it to be completed? It is very easy to underestimate the amount of time needed to analyze qualitative data and to feed the information back to the research participants for their comments. It is also easy to underestimate the time needed to write the final report. Neither of these tasks should be skimped and it is very important to allow adequate time to complete them thoroughly: more time, that is, than the researcher believes will be necessary at the beginning of the qualitative study.

Finally, Lula must consider a budget. If she has to purchase a software computer program to help her analyze her interview data, who will pay for it? Who will cover the costs related to transcribing the data and preparing and disseminating the final report? How much money should she allocate to each of these areas? How much should she ask for overall?

When she has decided on all this, Lula will have completed her research proposal. As discussed, not all proposals are organized in this way, but all essentially contain the information that has been discussed in the preceding sections.

This same information can be used to write the final research report, and it is to this that we now turn our attention.

WRITING REPORTS

As with a quantitative research report, a qualitative research report is a way of describing the research study to other people. How it is written, and to some degree what it will contain, depends on the audience it is written for. Lula may want to present her study's findings, for example, only to the board of directors and staff of the women's emergency shelter where she works. In this case, it will be unnecessary to describe the clinical setting (i.e., the shelter) in detail since the audience is already familiar with it. This very familiarity will also mean that Lula must take extra care to protect the identities of her research participants since personal knowledge of the women and children concerned will make it easier for her audience to identify them. Lula will probably want to submit a written report—particularly if her shelter funded her study—but she may also want to give an oral presentation.

As she imagines herself speaking the words she has written, she may find that she wants to organize the material differently or use a different style than she would if she were preparing a written report. Perhaps she will use less formal language, or include more detail about her own thoughts and feelings, or shorten the direct quotes made by the research participants.

Other possible outlets for her work include books, book chapters, journal articles, and presentations at conferences. Again, depending on the audience, she might write quite simply or she might include a wealth of technical detail, perhaps describing at length the methods she used to categorize and code her interview data. In order to avoid writing a number of reports on the same study aimed at different audiences, she might choose to include in the main body of the report just sufficient technical detail to establish the study's trustworthiness, while putting additional technical material in an appendix for those readers who are interested. Whatever approach she chooses, it is important to remember that qualitative research studies are based on a different set of assumptions than quantitative ones.

As we know from Chapters 3 and 13, the goal of a qualitative study is to understand the experiences of the study's research participants in depth, and the personal feelings of the researcher cannot be divorced from this understanding. It is therefore often appropriate to report a qualitative study using a more personal style, including both quotes from interviews with the research participants and the researcher's own reflections on the material. The aim is to produce a credible and compelling account that will be taken seriously by the reader.

The material itself can be organized in a number of ways, depending on whether it is to be presented in book form or more concisely, in the form of a journal article. An article usually contains six parts: (1) an abstract; (2) an introduction; (3) a discussion of methodology; (4) a presentation of the analysis and findings; (5) a conclusion, or discussion of the significance of the study's findings; and (6) a list of references.

Abstract

An abstract is a short statement—often about 200 words—that summarizes the purpose of the study, its methodology, its findings, and its conclusions. Journal readers often decide on the basis of the abstract whether they are sufficiently interested in the topic to want to read further. Thus, the abstract must provide just enough information to enable readers to assess the relevance of the study to their own work. A statement of the study's research question, with enough context to make it meaningful, is usually followed by a brief description of the study's methodology that was used to answer the research question.

Lula might say, for example, that she interviewed eight women and eleven children who were residents in a women's emergency shelter in a small town in Alberta, Canada, plus three of the shelter's social workers. She might go on to identify the problems experienced by the children who had witnessed wife abuse, stating that these problems were derived from analyses of interview data. Finally, she would outline the practical implications from the study for social work practice resulting from a greater understanding of the children's problems.

Introduction

The main body of the report begins with the introduction. It describes the *what* and *why* components of the study, which Lula has already written about in the first five parts of her research proposal. If she goes back to what she wrote before, she will see that she has already identified her research question and put it into the context of previous work through a literature review.

She has discussed why she thinks this question needs to be answered, clarified her own orientation and assumptions, and commented on the interests of the women's emergency shelter or other funding organizations. In addition, she has identified the variables relevant to her study and placed them within an appropriate framework. In short, she has already gathered the material needed for her introduction, and all that remains is to ensure that it is written in an appropriate style.

Method

After the *what* and *why* components of the study comes the *how*. In the methods section, Lula describes how she selected her sample of research participants and how she collected her data. She would provide a justification for why she chose to use the particular sampling and data collection methods. Again, if she looks back at her research proposal, she will see that she has already written about this in Parts 6, 7, and 8: research design, population and sample, and data collection, respectively. As before, she can use this same material, merely ensuring that it is written in a coherent and appropriate style.

However, before leaving the methods section of the report, Lula might want to check that nothing of importance has been omitted. Fischer (1993) has provided criteria by which to evaluate the methods section of a quantitative report, and a few of these criteria, with some modifications, are also applicable to qualitative reports:

1 Clarity about how the data were collected
2 Clarity about who collected the data
3 Degree of error in the collection of data
4 Degree of credibility associated with data collection instruments
5 Degree of use of a variety of data sources
6 Adequacy of the research design in terms of the study's purpose
7 Degree of accuracy in defining the population and sample
8 Degree of transferability (applicability to other similar populations)

We might add to these:

9 Degree of evidence of the study's trustworthiness

Casting her eye over these criteria, Lula will try to ensure that her methods section explains clearly what data were collected, by whom, from whom, where, in what time frame, and by what methods. She will not forget that her personal journal also constitutes data and will pay attention to it when it comes to trustworthiness.

Analysis and Findings

Materials on data analysis and findings are often presented together. Descriptive profiles of research participants and their direct quotes from interviews are used to answer the research question being explored. In her proposal, Lula has already written the part on data analysis in her research proposal, which stated which computer program she was going to use (if any), and the utilization of first- and second-level coding methods. In her research report, however, she would want to identify and provide examples of the meaning units she derived from the first-level coding process. One segment from one of her interviews might have gone as follows:

1 **Pam** (sounding upset): The poor kid was never the same after that. **The**

2 **first time, you know, it was just a slap on the butt that she might even**

3 **have mistaken for affection, but that second time he slammed me right**

4 **against the wall and he was still hitting my face after I landed.** (pause) No

5 mistaking that one, is there, even for a four-year old? (longer pause) No, well,

6 I guess I'm kidding myself about that first time. She knew all right. *She was*

7 *an outgoing sort of kid before, always out in the yard with friends,* but then

8 she stopped going out, and she'd follow me around, kind of, as if she was

9 afraid to let me out of her sight.

Lula may have identified three meaning units in this data segment. The first (in **bold**, lines 1 to 4) relates to what might and might not constitute wife abuse in the mind of a 4-year-old child. The second (in *italics*, lines 6 and 7) relates to the child's behavior prior to witnessing the abuse; and the third (underlined, lines 7 to 9) relates to the child's behavior after witnessing the abuse. In her report, Lula might want to identify and briefly describe the meaning units she derived from all her interviews, occasionally illustrating a unit with a direct quote to provide context and meaning.

As discussed in Chapter 13, Lula's next task in the analysis is to identify categories, assign each meaning unit to a category, and assign codes to the categories. A description of these categories will also come next in her report. She may have found, for example, that a number of mothers interpreted their child's behavior after witnessing wife abuse as indicative of fear for the mother's safety. Instead of one large category "child's behavior after witnessing wife abuse."

Lula may have chosen instead to create a number of smaller categories reflecting distinct types of behavior. One of these was "after witnessing wife abuse, child demonstrates fear for mother's safety," and Lula coded it as *CAWFMSAF*, where *C* stands for "the child," *AW* stands for "after witnessing wife abuse," and *FMSAF* stands for "fear for mother's safety." See Box 13.2 for more information on how to build a conceptual framework for a qualitative research study.

Depending on the number and depth of the interviews conducted, Lula may have a very large number of meaning units, and may have gone through an intricate process of refining and reorganizing in order to come up with appropriate categories. In a book, there will be room to describe all this, together with Lula's own reflections on the process; but in a journal article, running to perhaps 25 pages overall, Lula will have to be selective about what parts of the process she describes and how much detail she provides.

Although meaning units and categories are certainly a major part of Lula's findings, the majority of readers will be more interested in the next part of the analysis: comparing and contrasting the categories to discover the relationships between and among them in order to develop tentative themes or theories. By doing this, Lula may have been able to finally identify the problems most commonly experienced by children who have witnessed wife abuse.

She may even have been able to put the children's problems in an order of importance as perceived by the mothers and their children. In addition, she may have been able to add depth by describing the emotions related to the children's problems: perhaps guilt, on the mother's part, or anger toward the father, or a growing determination not to return to the abusive relationship. These themes will constitute the larger part of Lula's analysis and findings section, and it is to these themes that she will return in her discussion.

Discussion

This part of the research report presents a discussion of the study's findings. Here, Lula will point out the significance of her study's findings as they relate to the original purpose. If the purpose of her study was to inform practice by enabling the shelter's social workers to better understand the needs of children who have witnessed wife abuse, then Lula must provide a link between the children's problems and their needs resulting from those problems. She must also point out exactly how the shelter's social workers' practice might be informed. If she has found from her study, for example, that children who witnessed wife abuse tend to experience more fear for their mothers' safety than children who had not witnessed the abuse, then a related need might be to keep the mother always within sight.

Social workers within the shelter who understand this need might be more willing to tolerate children underfoot in the shelter's kitchen, for example, and might be less likely to tell Mary to "give Mom a moment's peace and go and play with Sue." These kinds of connections should be made for each theme that Lula identified in her study.

The final part of a research report often has to do with suggestions for future research studies. During the process of filling knowledge gaps by summarizing the study's findings, Lula will doubtless find other knowledge gaps that she believes ought to be filled. She might frame new research questions relating to these gaps; or she might even feel that she has sufficient knowledge to enable her to formulate research hypotheses for testing in future research studies (see Chapter 3).

Before concluding her discussion and moving on to the report's references, Lula might want to check that nothing has been left out. Fischer (1993) has provided a few criteria to be used in evaluating the discussion section of a report. These criteria, modified for use with a qualitative study, are presented below:

1 Degree to which researcher bias has been made overt

2 Extent to which the researcher's conclusions are consistent with the data gathered

3 Reasonableness of opinions about the study's implications

4 Adequacy in relating the study's findings to previous studies through the literature review

5 Adequacy of the conclusions for application to other similar populations

References

Finally, both quantitative and qualitative researchers are expected to provide a list of references that will enable the reader to locate the materials used for documentation within the report. If the manuscript is accepted for publication, the journal will certainly ask for any revisions it considers appropriate with regard to its style. It is important to note that quotes from a study's research participants do not have to be referenced, and adequate steps should always be taken to conceal their identities.

SUMMING UP

The purposes of writing a research proposal are threefold: to obtain permission to do the study; to obtain funding for the study; and to encourage the author to think carefully through what he or she wants to study and what difficulties are likely to be encountered.

The proposal itself should be clear, brief, and easy to read. Although proposals may be differently organized depending on who is to receive them, the information included in most proposals may be logically set out under general headings identified in this chapter.

The information contained under all these headings—except for limitations and administration—can also be used to write the research report. Since the proposal outlines *what will be done* and the research report describes *what was done*, the proposal and the report should parallel each other closely, unless the implementation of the study differed widely from what was planned.

A research report is often written under four general headings: introduction, method, analysis and findings, and discussion.

REVIEW QUESTIONS

1   Discuss the purpose of a qualitative research proposal. Present the benefits of writing one before a qualitative research study is actually conducted. Present a social work example throughout your discussion.

2   Thoroughly describe in your own words the eleven parts of a qualitative research proposal. Present a social work example throughout your discussion.

3   Discuss the purpose of qualitative research reports. Why are they necessary for the social work profession?

4   Thoroughly describe in your own words the four parts of a qualitative research report. Present a social work example throughout your discussion.

5   Go to the library and select a social work article. Did the article follow the same sequence of parts as presented in this chapter? How could the contents of the article have been reformulated to fit the four parts as described in this chapter? Discuss in detail.

6   What other limitations, besides the ones mentioned in this chapter, should Lula include in her final qualitative research report? Discuss each one in detail. For example, what about the social interaction skills of children who not only witnessed wife abuse but were also physically abused by their fathers?

7   Go to the library and select a social work qualitative research article. Write a hypothetical qualitative research proposal for the study using the contents of this chapter as a guide.

8   Write an explanatory-level qualitative research proposal that Lula could have written with her same general problem area: problems experienced by children who witness one parent physically abusing the other.

9   Write a hypothetical qualitative research report based on the qualitative research proposal that you wrote for Question 8.

10   Write a final qualitative research report that Lula could submit to a professional social work journal using the findings of her study.

Glossary

Abstracting indexing services
Providers of specialized reference tools that make it possible to find information quickly and easily, usually through subject headings and/or author approaches.

Abstracts   Reference materials consisting of citations and brief descriptive summaries from quantitative and qualitative research studies.

Accountability   A system of responsibility in which program administrators account for all program activities by answering to the demands of a program's stakeholders and by justifying the program's expenditures to the satisfaction of its stakeholders.

Aggregated case-level evaluation designs   The collection of a number of case-level evaluations to determine the degree to which a program objective has been met.

Aggregate-level data   Derived from micro-level data, aggregate-level data are grouped so that the characteristics of individual units of analysis are no longer identifiable; for example, the variable, "gross national income," is an aggregation of data about individual incomes.

Alternate-forms method   A method for establishing reliability of a measuring instrument by administering, in succession, equivalent forms of the same instrument to the same group of research participants.

Alternative hypothesis   See Rival hypothesis.

Analytical memos   Notes made by the researcher in reference to qualitative data that raise questions or make comments about meaning units and categories identified in a transcript.

Analytic generalization   The type of generalizability associated with case studies; the research findings of case studies are not assumed to fit another case no matter how apparently similar; rather, research findings are tested to see if they do in fact fit; used as working hypotheses to test practice principles.

Annual report   A detailed account or statement describing a program's processes and results over a given year; usually produced at the end of a fiscal year.

Antecedent variable   A variable that precedes the introduction of one or more dependent variables.

Antiquarianism   An interest in past events without reference to their importance or significance for the present; the reverse of presentism.

A phase   In case-level evaluation designs, a phase (*A* Phase) in which the baseline measurement of the target problem is established before the intervention (*B* Phase) is implemented.

Applied research approach   A search for practical and applied research results that can be applied in actual social work practice situations; complementry to the pure research approach.

Area probability sampling   A form of cluster sampling which uses a three-stage process to provide the means to carry out a research study when no comprehensive list of the population can be compiled.

Assessment-related case study   A type of case study that generates knowledge about specific clients and their situations; focuses on the perspectives of the study's participants.

Audit trail   The documentation of critical steps in a qualitative research study that allows for an independent reviewer to examine and verify the steps in the research process and the conclusions of the research study.

Authority   The reliance on authority figures to tell us what is true; one of the six ways of knowing.

Availability sampling   See Convenience sampling.

Axes   Straight horizontal and vertical lines in a graph upon which values of a measurement, or the corresponding frequencies, are plotted.

Back-translation   The process of translating an original document into a second language, then having an independent translator conduct a subsequent translation of the first translation back into the language of origin; the second translation is then compared with the original document for equivalency.

Baseline   A period of time, usually three or four data collection periods, in which the level of the client's target problem is measured while no intervention is carried out; designated as the *A* phase in case-level evaluation designs.

Between research methods approach   Triangulation by using different research methods available in *both* the qualitative and the quantitative research approaches in a single research study.

Bias   Not neutral; an inclination to some form of prejudice or preconceived position.

Biased sample   A sample unintentionally selected in such a way that some members of the population are more likely than others to be picked for sample membership.

Binomial effect size display (BESD)   A technique for interpreting the *r* value in a meta-analysis by converting it into a 2 by 2 table displaying magnitude of effect.

Biography   Tells the story of one individual's life, often suggesting what the person's influence was on social, political, or intellectual developments of the times.

B phase   In case-level evaluation designs, the intervention phase, which may, or may not, include simultaneous measurements.

Case   The basic unit of social work practice, whether it be an individual, a couple, a family, an agency, a community, a county, a state, or a country.

Case-level evaluation designs   Designs in which data are collected about a single client system—an individual, group, or community—in order to evaluate the outcome of an intervention for the client system; a form of appraisal that monitors change for individual clients; designs in which data are collected about a single client system—an individual, group, or community—in order to evaluate the outcome of an intervention for the client system; also called single-system research designs.

Case study   Using research approaches to investigate a research question or hypothesis relating to a specific case; used to develop theory and test hypotheses; an in-depth form of research in which data are gathered and analyzed about an individual unit of analysis, person, city, event, society, etc.; it allows more intensive analysis of specific details; the disadvantage is that it is hard to use the results to generalize to other cases.

Categories   Groupings of related meaning units that are given one name; used to organize, summarize, and interpret qualitative data; categories in a qualitative study can change throughout the data analysis process, and the number of categories in a given study depends upon the breadth and depth the researcher aims for in the analysis.

Category   In a qualitative data analysis, an aggregate of meaning units that share a common feature.

Category saturation   The point in qualitative data analysis when all identified meaning units fit easily into the existing categorization scheme and no new categories emerge; the point at which first-level coding ends.

Causality   A relationship of cause and effect; the effect will invariably occur when the cause is present.

Causal relationship   A relationship between two variables for which we can state that the presence of, or absence of, one variable determines the presence of, or absence of, the other variable.

CD-ROM sources   Computerized retrieval systems that allow searching for indexes and abstracts stored on compact computer discs (CDs).

Census data   Data from the survey of an entire population in contrast to a survey of a sample.

Citation   A brief identification of a reference that includes name of author(s), title, source, page numbers, and year of publication.

Classical experimental design   An explanatory research design with randomly assigned experimental and control groups in which the dependent variable is measured before and after the treatment (the independent variable) for both groups, but only the experimental group receives the treatment (the dependent variable).

Client system   *An* individual client, *a* couple, *a* family, *a* group, *an* organization, or *a* community that can be studied with case- and program-level evaluation designs and with quantitative and qualitative research approaches.

Closed-ended questions   Items in a measuring instrument that require respondents to select one of several response categories provided; also known as fixed-alternative questions.

Cluster diagram   An illustration of a conceptual classification scheme where the researcher draws and labels circles for each theme that emerges from the data; the circles are organized in a way to depict the relationships between themes.

Cluster sampling   A multistage probability sampling procedure in which the population is divided into groups (or clusters) and the groups, rather than the individuals, are selected for inclusion in the sample.

Code   The label assigned to a category or theme in a qualitative data analysis; shortened versions of the actual category or theme label; used as markers in a qualitative data analysis; usually no longer than eight characters in length and can use a combination of letters, symbols, and numbers.

Codebook   A device used to organize qualitative data by applying labels and descriptions that draw distinctions between different parts of the data that have been collected.

Coding   (1) In data analysis, translating data from respondents onto a form that can be read by a computer; (2) In qualitative research, marking the text with codes for content categories.

Coding frame   A specific framework that delineates what data are to be coded and how they are to be coded in order to prepare them for analyses.

Coding sheets   In a literature review, a sheet used to record for each research study the complete reference, research design, measuring instrument(s), population and sample, outcomes, and other significant features of the study.

Cohort study   A longitudinal survey design that uses successive random samples to monitor how the characteristics of a specific group of people, who share certain characteristics or experiences (cohorts), change over time.

Collaterals   Professionals or staff members who serve as indigenous observers in the data collection process.

Collective biographies   Studies of the characteristics of groups of people who lived during a past period and had some major factor in common.

Collectivist culture   Societies that stress interdependence and seek the welfare and survival of the group above that of the individual; collectivist cultures are characterized by a readiness to be influenced by others, preference for conformity, and cooperation in relationships.

Comparative rating scale   A rating scale in which respondents are asked to compare an individual person, concept, or situation, to others.

Comparative research design   The study of more than one event, group, or society to isolate explanatory factors; there are two basic strategies in comparative research: (1) the study of elements that differ in many ways but that have some major factor in common, and (2) the study of elements that are highly similar but different in some important aspect, such as modern industrialized nations that have different health insurance systems.

Comparison group   A nonexperimental group to which research participants have not been randomly assigned for purposes of comparison with the experimental group. Not to be confused with control group.

Comparison group posttest-only design   A descriptive research design with two groups, experimental and comparison, in which the dependent variable is measured once for both groups, and only the experimental group receives the treatment (the independent variable).

Comparison group pretest-posttest design   A descriptive research design with two groups, experimental and comparison, in which the dependent variable is measured before and after the treatment for both groups, but only the experimental group receives the treatment.

Compensation Attempts by researchers to compensate for the lack of treatment for control group members by administering it to them; a threat to internal validity.

Compensatory rivalry Motivation of control group members to compete with experimental group members; a threat to internal validity.

Completeness One of the four criteria for evaluating research hypotheses.

Complete observer A term describing one of four possible research roles on a continuum of participant observation research; the complete observer acts simply as an observer and does not participate in the events at hand.

Complete participant The complete participant is at the far end of the continuum from the complete observer in participant observation research; this research role is characterized by total involvement.

Comprehensive qualitative review A nonstatistical synthesis of representative research studies relevant to a research problem, question, or hypothesis.

Computerized retrieval systems

Systems in which abstracts, indexes, and subject bibliographies are incorporated in computerized data bases to facilitate information retrieval.

Concept An understanding, an idea, or a mental image; a way of viewing and categorizing objects, processes, relations, and events.

Conceptual classification system The strategy for conceiving how units of qualitative data relate to each other; the method used to depict patterns that emerge from the various coding levels in qualitative data.

Conceptual framework A frame of reference that serves to guide a research study and is developed from theories, findings from a variety of other research studies, and the author's personal experiences and values.

Conceptualization The process of selecting the specific concepts to include in quantitative and qualitative research studies.

Conceptual validity See Construct validity.

Concurrent validity A form of criterion validity that is concerned with the ability of a measuring instrument to predict accurately an individual's status by comparing concurrent ratings (or scores) on one or more measuring instruments.

Confidentiality An ethical consideration in research whereby anonymity of research participants is safeguarded by ensuring that raw data are not seen by anyone other than the research team and that data presented have no identifying marks.

Confounding variable A variable operating in a specific situation in such a way that its effects cannot be separated; the effects of an extraneous variable thus confound the interpretation of a research study's findings.

Consistency Holding steadfast to the same principles and procedures in the qualitative data analysis process.

Constant A concept that does not vary and does not change; a characteristic that has the same value for all research participants or events in a research study.

Constant comparison A technique used to categorize qualitative data; it begins after the complete set of data has been examined and meaning units identified; each unit is classified as similar or different from the others; similar meaning units are lumped into the same category and classified by the same code.

Constant error Systematic error in measurement; error due to factors that consistently or systematically affect the variable being measured and that are concerned with the relatively stable qualities of respondents to a measuring instrument.

Construct See Concept.

Construct validity The degree to which a measuring instrument successfully measures a theoretical construct; the degree to which explanatory concepts account for variance in the scores of an instrument; also referred to as conceptual validity in meta-analyses.

Content analysis A data collection method in which communications are analyzed in a systematic, objective, and quantitative manner to produce new data.

Content validity The extent to which the content of a measuring instrument reflects the concept that is being measured and in fact measures that concept and not another.

Contextual detail The particulars of the environment in which the case (or unit of analysis) is embedded; provides a basis for understanding and interpreting case study data and results.

Contradictory evidence Identifying themes and categories that raise questions about the conclusions reached at the end of qualitative data analysis; outliers or extreme cases that are inconsistent or contradict the conclusions drawn from qualitative data; also called negative evidence.

Contributing partner A social work role in which the social worker joins forces with others who perform different roles in quantitative and qualitative research studies.

Control group A group of randomly assigned research participants in a research study who do not receive the experimental treatment and are used for comparison purposes. Not to be confused with comparison group.

Control variable A variable, other than the independent variable(s) of primary interest, whose effects we can determine; an intervening variable that has been controlled for in the study's research design.

Convenience sampling A nonprobability sampling procedure that relies on the closest and most available research participants to constitute a sample.

Convergent validity The degree to which different measures of a construct yield similar results, or converge.

Correlated variables Variables whose values are associated; values of one variable tend to be associated in a systematic way with values in the others.

Cost-benefit analysis An analytical procedure that not only determines the costs of the program itself but also considers the monetary benefits of the program's effects.

Cost-effectiveness analysis An analytical procedure that assesses the costs of the program itself; the monetary benefits of the program's effects are not assessed.

Cover letter A letter to respondents or research participants that is written under the official letterhead of the sponsoring organization and describes the research study and its purpose.

Credibility The trustworthiness of both the steps taken in qualitative data analysis and the conclusions reached.

Criterion validity The degree to which the scores obtained on a measuring instrument are comparable to scores from an external criterion believed to measure the same concept.

Criterion variable The variable whose values are predicted from measurements of the predictor variable.

Cross-cultural comparisons Research studies that include culture as a major variable; studies that compare two or more diverse cultural groups.

Cross-sectional research design A survey research design in which data are collected to indicate characteristics of a sample or population at a particular moment in time.

Cross-tabulation table A simple table showing the joint frequency distribution of two or more nominal level variables.

Cultural encapsulation The assumption that differences between groups represent some deficit or pathology.

Culturally equivalent Similarity in the meaning of a construct between two cultures.

Cultural relativity The belief that human thought and action can be judged only from the perspective of the culture out of which they have grown.

Cut-and-paste method A method of analyzing qualitative data whereby the researcher cuts segments of the typed transcript and sorts these cuttings into relevant groupings; it can be done manually or with computer assistance.

Data The numbers, words, or scores, generated by quantitative and qualitative research studies; the word "data" is plural.

Data analyses The process of turning data into information; the process of reviewing, summarizing, and organizing isolated facts (data) such that they formulate a meaningful response to a research question.

Data archive A place where many data sets are stored and from which data can be accessed.

Data coding Translating data from one language or format into another, usually to make it readable for a computer.

Data collection method Procedures specifying techniques to be employed, measuring instruments to be utilized, and activities to be conducted in implementing a quantitative or qualitative research study.

Data set A collection of related data items, such as the answers given by respondents to all the questions in a survey.

Data source The provider of the data, whether it be primary—the original source—or secondary—an intermediary between the research participant and the researcher analyzing the data.

Datum Singular of data.

Decision-making rule A statement that we use (in testing a hypothesis) to choose between the null hypothesis; indicates the range(s) of values of the observed statistic that leads to the rejection of the null hypothesis.

Deduction A conclusion about a specific case(s) based on the assumption that it shares a characteristic with an entire class of similar cases.

Deductive reasoning Forming a theory, making a deduction from the theory, and testing this deduction, or hypothesis, against reality; in research, applied to theory in order to arrive at a hypothesis that can be tested; A method of reasoning whereby a conclusion about specific cases is reached based on the assumption that they share characteristics with an entire class of similar cases.

Demand needs When needs are defined by only those individuals who indicate that they feel or perceive the need themselves.

Demographic data Vital and social facts that describe a sample or a population.

Demoralization Feelings of deprivation among control group members that may cause them to drop out of a research study; a threat to internal validity.

Dependability The soundness of both the steps taken in a qualitative data analysis and the conclusions reached.

Dependent events Events that influence the probability of occurrence of each other.

Dependent variable A variable that is dependent on, or caused by, another variable; an outcome variable, which is not manipulated directly but is measured to determine if the independent variable has had an effect.

Derived scores   Raw scores of research participants, or groups, converted in such a way that meaningful comparisons with other individuals, or groups, are possible.

Descriptive research   Research studies undertaken to increase precision in the definition of knowledge in a problem area where less is known than at the explanatory level; situated in the middle of the knowledge continuum.

Descriptive statistics   Methods used for summarizing and describing data in a clear and precise manner.

Design bias   Any effect that systematically distorts the outcome of a research study so that the study's results are not representative of the phenomenon under investigation.

Determinism   A contention in quantitative research studies that only an event that is true over time and place and that will occur independent of beliefs about it (a predetermined event) permits the generalization of a study's findings; one of the four main limitations of the quantitative research approach.

Deterministic causation   When a particular effect appears, the associated cause is always present; no other variables influence the relationship between cause and effect; the link between an independent variable that brings about the occurrence of the dependent variable exists every time.

Dichotomous variable   A variable that can take on only one of two values.

Differential scale   A questionnaire-type scale in which respondents are asked to consider questions representing different positions along a continuum and select those with which they agree.

Differential selection   A potential lack of equivalency among preformed groups of research participants; a threat to internal validity.

Diffusion of treatments   Problems that may occur when experimental and control group members talk to each other about a research study; a threat to internal validity.

***d* index**   A measure of effect size in a meta-analysis.

Directional hypothesis   See One-tailed hypotheses.

Directional test   See One-tailed hypotheses.

Direct observation   An obtrusive data collection method in which the focus is entirely on the behaviors of a group, or persons, being observed.

Direct observation notes   These are the first level of field notes, usually chronologically organized, and they contain a detailed description of what was seen and heard; they may also include summary notes made after an interview.

Direct relationship   A relationship between two variables such that high values of one variable are found with high values of the second variable, and vice versa.

Discriminant validity   The degree to which a construct can be empirically differentiated, or discriminated from, other constructs.

Divergent validity   The extent to which a measuring instrument differs from other instruments that measure unrelated constructs.

Dominant–less dominant research model   A model combining qualitative and quantitative research approaches in a single study where one approach stands out as having the major role in the research design; the other approach has a minor or complementary role.

Double-barreled question   A question in a measuring instrument that contains two questions in one, usually joined by an *and* or an *or*.

Duration recording   A method of data collection that includes direct observation of the target problem and recording of the length of time each occurrence lasts within a specified observation period.

Ecological fallacy   An error of reasoning committed by coming to conclusions about individuals based only on data about groups.

Edge coding   Adding a series of blank lines on the right side of the response category in a measuring instrument to aid in processing the data.

Effect size   In meta-analysis, the most widely used measure of the dependent variable; the effect size statistic provides a measure of the magnitude of the relationship found between the variables of interest and allows for the computation of summary statistics that apply to the analysis of all the studies considered as a whole.

Empirical   Knowledge derived from the six ways of knowing.

Error of central tendency   A measurement error due to the tendency of observers to rate respondents in the middle of a variable's value range, rather than consistently too high or too low.

Error of measurement   See Measurement error.

Ethical research project   The systematic inquiry into a problem area in an effort to discover new knowledge or test existing ideas; the research study is conducted in accordance with professional standards.

Ethics in research   Quantitative and qualitative data that are collected and analyzed with careful attention to their accuracy, fidelity to logic, and respect for the feelings and rights of research participants; one of the four criteria for evaluating research problem areas *and* formulating research questions out of the problem areas.

Ethnicity   A term that implies a common ancestry and cultural heritage and encompasses customs, values, beliefs, and behaviors.

Ethnocentricity   Assumptions about normal behavior that are based on one's own cultural framework without taking cultural relativity into account; the failure to acknowledge alternative world views.

Ethnograph   A computer software program that is designed for qualitative data analysis.

Ethnographic   A form of content analysis used to document and explain the communication of meaning, as well as to verify theoretical relationships; any of several methods of describing social or cultural life based on direct, systematic observation, such as becoming a participant in a social system.

Ethnography   The systematic study of human cultures and the similarities and dissimilarities between them.

Ethnomethodology   Pioneered by Harold Garfinkel, this method of research focuses on the common-sense understanding of social life held by ordinary people (the ethos), usually as discovered through participant observation; often the observer's own methods of making sense of the situation become the object of investigation.

Evaluation   A form of appraisal using valid and reliable research methods; there are numerous types of evaluations geared to produce data that in turn produce information that helps in the decision-making process; data from evaluations are used to develop quality programs and services.

Evaluative research designs   Case- and program-level research designs that apply various research designs and data collection methods to find out if an intervention (or treatment) worked at the case-level and if the social work program worked at the program level.

Existing documents   Physical records left over from the past.

Existing statistics   Previously calculated numerical summaries of data that exist in the public domain.

Experience and intuition   Learning what is true through personal past experiences and intuition; two of the six ways of knowing.

Experiment   A research study in which we have control over the levels of the independent variable and over the assignment of research participants, or objects, to different experimental conditions.

Experimental designs   (1) Explanatory research designs or "ideal experiments;" (2) Case-level research designs that examine the question, "Did the client system improve because of social work intervention?"

Experimental group   In an experimental research design, the group of research participants exposed to the manipulation of the independent variable; also referred to as a treatment group.

Explanatory research   "Ideal" research studies undertaken to infer cause-effect and directional relationships in areas where a number of substantial research findings are already in place; situated at the top end of the knowledge continuum.

Exploratory research   Research studies undertaken to gather data in areas of inquiry where very little is already known; situated at the lowest end of the knowledge continuum. See Non-experimental design.

External evaluation   An evaluation that is conducted by someone who does not have any connection with the program; usually an evaluation that is requested by the agency's funding sources; this type of evaluation complements an in-house evaluation.

External validity   The extent to which the findings of a research study can be generalized outside the specific research situation.

Extraneous variables   See Rival hypothesis.

Face validity   The degree to which a measurement has self-evident meaning and measures what it appears to measure.

Feasibility   One of the four criteria for evaluating research problem areas *and* formulating research questions out of the problem areas.

Feedback   When data and information are returned to the persons who originally provided or collected them; used for informed decision making at the case- and program-levels; a basic principle underlying the design of evaluations.

Field notes   A record, usually written, of events observed by a researcher; the notes are taken as the study proceeds, and later they are used for analyses.

Field research   Research conducted in a real-life setting, not in a laboratory; the researcher neither creates nor manipulates anything within the study, but observes it.

Field-tested   The pilot of an instrument or research method in conditions equivalent to those that will be encountered in the research study.

File drawer problem   (1) In literature searches or reviews, the difficulty in locating studies that have not been published or are not easily retrievable; (2) In meta-analyses, errors in effect size due to reliance on published articles showing statistical significance.

Firsthand data   Data obtained from people who directly experience the problem being studied.

First-level coding   A process of identifying meaning units in a transcript, organizing the meaning units into categories, and assigning names to the categories.

Flexibility   The degree to which the design and procedures of a research study can be changed to adapt to contextual demands of the research setting.

Focus group interview   A group of people brought together to talk about their lives and experiences in free-flowing, open-ended discussions that usually focus on a single topic.

Formative evaluation   A type of evaluation that focuses on obtaining data that are helpful in planning the program and in improving its implementation and performance.

Frequency recording A method of data collection by direct observations in which each occurrence of the target problem is recorded during a specified observation period.

Fugitive data Informal information found outside regular publishing channels.

Gaining access A term used in qualitative research to describe the process of engagement and relationship development between the researcher and the research participants.

Generalizable explanation evaluation model An evaluation model whose proponents believe that many solutions are possible for any one social problem and that the effects of programs will differ under different conditions.

Generalizing results Extending or applying the findings of a research study to individuals or situations not directly involved in the original research study; the ability to extend or apply the findings of a research study to subjects or situations that were not directly investigated.

Goal Attainment Scale (*GAS*) A modified measurement scale used to evaluate case or program outcomes.

Government documents Printed documents issued by local, state, and federal governments; such documents include reports of legislative committee hearings and investigations, studies commissioned by legislative commissions and executive agencies, statistical compilations such as the census, the regular and special reports of executive agencies, and much more.

Grand tour questions Queries in which research participants are asked to provide wide-ranging background information; mainly used in qualitative research studies.

Graphic rating scale A rating scale that describes an attribute on a continuum from one extreme to the other, with points of the continuum ordered in equal intervals and then assigned values.

Grounded theory A final outcome of the qualitative research process that is reached when the insights are grounded on observations and the conclusions seem to be firm.

Group evaluation designs Evaluation designs that are conducted with groups of cases for the purpose of assessing to what degree program objectives have been achieved.

Group research designs Research designs conducted with two or more groups of cases, or research participants, for the purpose of answering research questions or testing hypotheses.

Halo effect A measurement error due to the tendency of an observer to be influenced by a favorable trait(s) of a research participant(s).

Hawthorne effect Effects on research participants' behaviors or attitudes attributable to their knowledge that they are taking part in a research study; a reactive effect; a threat to external validity.

Heterogeneity of respondents The extent to which a research participant differs from other research participants.

Heuristic A theory used to stimulate creative thought and scientific activity.

Historical research The process by which we study the past; a method of inquiry that attempts to explain past events based on surviving artifacts.

History in research design The possibility that events not accounted for in a research design may alter the second and subsequent measurements of the dependent variable; a threat to internal validity.

Homogeneity of respondents The extent to which a research participant is similar to other research participants.

Hypothesis A theory-based prediction of the expected results of a research study; a tentative explanation that a relationship between or among variables exists.

Hypothetico-deductive method A hypothesis-testing approach that a hypothesis is derived on the deductions based from a theory.

Ideographic research Research studies that focus on unique individuals or situations.

Implementation of a program The action of carrying out a program in the way that it was designed.

Independent variable A variable that is not dependent on another variable but is believed to cause or determine changes in the dependent variable; an antecedent variable that is directly manipulated in order to assess its effect on the dependent variable.

Index A group of individual measures that, when combined, are meant to indicate some more general characteristic.

Indigenous observers People who are naturally a part of the research participants' environment and who perform the data collection function; includes relevant others (e.g., family members, peers) and collaterals (e.g., social workers, staff members).

Indirect measures A substitute variable, or a collection of representative variables, used when there is no direct measurement of the variable of interest; also called a proxy variable.

Individualism A way of living that stresses independence, personal rather than group objectives, competition, and power in relationships; achievement measured through success of the individual as opposed to the group.

Individual synthesis Analysis of published studies related to the subject under study.

Inductive reasoning Building on specific observations of events, things, or processes to make inferences or more general statements; in research studies, applied to data collection and research results to make generalizations to see if they fit a theory; a method of reasoning whereby a conclusion is reached by building on specific observations of events, things, or processes to make inferences or more general statements.

Inferential statistics Statistical methods that make it possible to draw tentative conclusions about the population based on observations of a sample selected from that population and, furthermore, to make a probability statement about those conclusions to aid in their evaluation.

Information anxiety A feeling attributable to a lack of understanding of information, being overwhelmed by the amount of information to be accessed and understood, or not knowing if certain information exists.

Informed consent Signed statements obtained from research participants prior to the initiation of the research study to inform them what their participation entails and that they are free to decline participation.

In-house evaluation An evaluation that is conducted by someone who works within a program; usually an evaluation for the purpose of promoting better client services; also known as an internal evaluation; this type of evaluation complements an external evaluation.

Institutional review boards (IRBs) Boards set up by institutions in order to protect research participants and to ensure that ethical issues are recognized and responded to in the a study's research design.

Instrumentation   Weaknesses of a measuring instrument, such as invalidity, unreliability, improper administrations, or mechanical breakdowns; a threat to internal validity.

Integration   Combining evaluation and day-to-day practice activities to develop a complete approach to client service delivery; a basic principle underlying the design of evaluations.

Interaction effects   Effects produced by the combination of two or more threats to internal validity.

Internal consistency   The extent to which the scores on two comparable halves of the same measuring instrument are similar; inter-item consistency.

Internal validity   The extent to which it can be demonstrated that the independent variable within a research study is the only cause of change in the dependent variable; overall soundness of the experimental procedures and measuring instruments.

Interobserver reliability   The stability or consistency of observations made by two or more observers at one point in time.

Interpretive notes   Notes on the researcher's interpretations of events that are kept separate from the record of the facts noted as direct observations.

Interquartile range   A number that measures the variability of a data set; the distance between the 75th and 25th percentiles.

Interrater reliability   The degree to which two or more independent observers, coders, or judges produce consistent results.

Interrupted time-series design   An explanatory research design in which there is only one group of research participants and the dependent variable is measured repeatedly before and after treatment; used in case- and program evaluation designs.

Interval level of measurement   The level of measurement with an arbitrarily chosen zero point that classifies its values on an equally spaced continuum.

Interval recording   A method of data collection that involves a continuous direct observation of an individual during specified observation periods divided into equal time intervals.

Intervening variable   See Rival hypothesis.

Interview data   Isolated facts that are gathered when research participants respond to carefully constructed research questions; data, which are in the form of words, are recorded by transcription.

Interviewing   A conversation with a purpose.

Interview schedule   A measuring instrument used to collect data in face-to-face and telephone interviews.

Intraobserver reliability   The stability of observations made by a single observer at several points in time.

Intrusion into lives of research participants   The understanding that specific data collection methods can have negative consequences for research participants; a criterion for selecting a data collection method.

Itemized rating scales   A measuring instrument that presents a series of statements that respondents or observers rank in different positions on a specific attribute.

Journal   A written record of the process of a qualitative research study. Journal entries are made on an ongoing basis throughout the study and include study procedures as well as the researcher's reactions to emerging issues and concerns during the data analysis process.

Key informants   A subpopulation of research participants who seem to know much more about "the situation" than other research participants.

Knowledge base   A body of knowledge and skills specific to a certain discipline.

Knowledge creator and disseminator   A social work role in which the social worker actually carries out and disseminates the results of a quantitative and/or qualitative research study to generate knowledge for our profession.

Knowledge level continuum   The range of knowledge levels, from exploratory to descriptive to explanatory, at which research studies can be conducted.

Latent content   In a content analysis, the true meaning, depth, or intensity of a variable, or concept, under study.

Levels of measurement   The degree to which characteristics of a data set can be modeled mathematically; the higher the level of measurement, the more statistical methods that are applicable.

Limited review   An existing literature synthesis that summarizes in narrative form the findings and implications of a few research studies.

Literature review   See Literature search and Review of the literature.

Literature search   In a meta-analysis, scanning books and journals for basic, up-to-date research articles on studies relevant to a research question or hypothesis; sufficiently thorough to maximize the chance of including all relevant sources. See Review of the literature.

Logical consistency   The requirement that all the steps within a quantitative research study must be logically related to one another.

Logical positivism   A philosophy of science holding that the scientific method of inquiry is the only source of certain knowledge; in research, focuses on testing hypotheses deduced from theory.

Logistics   In evaluation, refers to getting research participants to do what they are supposed to do, getting research instruments distributed and returned; in general, the activities that ensure that procedural tasks of a research or evaluation study are carried out.

Longitudinal case study   An exploratory research design in which there is only one group of research participants and the dependent variable is measured more than once.

Longitudinal design   A survey research design in which a measuring instrument(s) is administered to a sample of research participants repeatedly over time; used to detect dynamic processes such as opinion change.

Magnitude recording   A direct-observation method of soliciting and recording data on amount, level, or degree of the target problem during each occurrence.

Management information system (MIS)   System in which computer technology is used to process, store, retrieve, and analyze data collected routinely in such processes as social service delivery.

Manifest content   Content of a communication that is obvious and clearly evident.

Manipulable solution evaluation model   An evaluation model whose proponents believe that the greatest priority is to serve the public interest, not the interests of its stakeholders who have vested interests in the program being evaluated; closely resembles an outcome evaluation.

Matching   A random assignment technique that assigns research participants to two or more groups so that the experimental and control groups are approximately equivalent in pretest scores or other characteristics, or so that all differences except the experimental condition are eliminated.

Maturation Unplanned change in research participants due to mental, physical, or other processes operating over time; a threat to internal validity.

Meaning units In a qualitative data analysis, a discrete segment of a transcript that can stand alone as a single idea; can consist of a single word, a partial or complete sentence, a paragraph, or more; used as the basic building blocks for developing categories.

Measurement The assignment of labels or numerals to the properties or attributes of observations, events, or objects according to specific rules.

Measurement error Any variation in measurement that cannot be attributed to the variable being measured; variability in responses produced by individual differences and other extraneous variables.

Measuring instrument Any instrument used to measure a variable(s).

Media myths The content of television shows, movies, and newspaper and magazine articles; one of the six ways of knowing.

Member checking A process of obtaining feedback and comments from research participants on interpretations and conclusions made from the qualitative data they provided; asking research participants to confirm or refute the conclusions made.

Meta-analysis A research method in which mathematical procedures are applied to the quantitative findings of studies located in a literature search to produce new summary statistics and to describe the findings for a meta-analysis.

Methodology The procedures and rules that detail how a single research study is conducted.

Micro-level data Data derived from individual units of analysis, whether these data sources are individuals, families, corporations, etc.; for example, age and years of formal schooling are two variables requiring micro-level data.

Missing data Data not available for a research participant about whom other data are available, such as when a respondent fails to answer one of the questions in a survey.

Missing links When two categories or themes seem to be related, but not directly so, it may be that a third variable connects the two.

Mixed research model A model combining aspects of qualitative and quantitative research approaches within all (or many) of the methodological steps contained within a single research study.

Monitoring approach to evaluation Evaluation that aims to provide ongoing feedback so that a program can be improved while it is still underway; it contributes to the continuous development and improvement of a human service program; this approach complements the project approach to evaluation.

Mortality Loss of research participants through normal attrition over time in an experimental design that requires retesting; a threat to internal validity.

Multicultural research Representation of diverse cultural factors in the subjects of study; such diversity variables may include religion, race, ethnicity, language preference, gender, etc.

Multigroup posttest-only design An exploratory research design in which there is more than one group of research participants and the dependent variable is measured only once for each group.

Multiple-baseline design A case-level evaluation design with more than one baseline period and intervention phase which allows the causal inferences regarding the relationship between a treatment intervention and its effect on clients' target problems and which helps control for extraneous variables. See Interrupted time-series design.

Multiple-group design An experimental research design with one control group and several experimental groups.

Multiple-treatment interference Effects of the results of a first treatment on the results of second and subsequent treatments; a threat to external validity.

Multistage probability sampling Probability sampling procedures used when a comprehensive list of the population does not exist and it is not possible to construct one.

Multivariate (1) A relationship involving two or more variables; (2) A hypothesis stating an assertion about two or more variables and how they relate to one another.

Multivariate analysis A statistical analysis of the relationship among three or more variables.

Narrowband measuring instrument Measuring instruments that focus on a single, or a few, variables.

Nationality A term that refers to country of origin.

Naturalist A person who studies the facts of nature as they occur under natural conditions.

Needs assessment Program-level evaluation activities that aim to assess the feasibility for establishing or continuing a particular social service program; an evaluation that aims to assess the need for a human service by verifying that a social problem exists within a specific client population to an extent that warrants services.

Negative case sampling Purposefully selecting research participants based on the fact that they have different characteristics than previous cases.

Nominal level of measurement The level of measurement that classifies variables by assigning names or categories that are mutually exclusive and exhaustive.

Nondirectional test See Two-tailed hypotheses.

Nonexperimental design A research design at the exploratory, or lowest level, of the knowledge continuum; also called preexperimental.

Nonoccurrence data In the structured-observation method of data collection, a recording of only those time intervals in which the target problem did not occur.

Nonparametric tests Refers to statistical tests of hypotheses about population probability distributions, but not about specific parameters of the distributions.

Nonprobability sampling Sampling procedures in which all of the persons, events, or objects in the sampling frame have an unknown, and usually different, probability of being included in a sample.

Nonreactive Methods of research that do not allow the research participants to know that they are being studied; thus, they do not alter their responses for the benefit of the researcher.

Nonresponse The rate of nonresponse in survey research is calculated by dividing the total number of respondents by the total number in the sample, minus any units verified as ineligible.

Nonsampling errors Errors in a research study's results that are not due to the sampling procedures.

Norm In measurement, an average or set group standard of achievement that can be used to interpret individual scores; normative data describing statistical properties of a measuring instrument such as means and standard deviations.

Normalization group The population sample to which a measuring instrument under development is administered in order to establish norms; also called the norm group.

Normative needs When needs are defined by comparing the objective living conditions of a target population with what society—or, at least, that segment of society concerned with helping the target population—deems acceptable or desirable from a humanitarian standpoint.

Null hypothesis A statement concerning one or more parameters that is subjected to a statistical test; a statement that there is no relationship between the two variables of interest.

Numbers The basic data unit of analysis used in quantitative research studies.

Objectivity A research stance in which a study is carried out and its data are examined and interpreted without distortion by personal feelings or biases.

Observer One of four roles on a continuum of participation in participant observation research; the level of involvement of the observer participant is lower than the complete participant and higher than the participant observer.

Obtrusive data collection methods Direct data collection methods that can influence the variables under study or the responses of research participants; data collection methods that produce reactive effects.

Occurrence data In the structured-observation method of data collection, a recording of the first occurrence of the target problem during each time interval.

One-group posttest-only design An exploratory research design in which the dependent variable is measured only once.

One-group pretest-posttest design A descriptive research design in which the dependent variable is measured twice—before and after treatment.

One-stage probability sampling Probability sampling procedures in which the selection of a sample that is drawn from a specific population is completed in a single process.

One-tailed hypotheses Statements that predict specific relationships between independent and dependent variables.

On-line sources Computerized literary retrieval systems that provide printouts of indexes and abstracts.

Open-ended questions Unstructured questions in which the response categories are not specified or detailed.

Operational definition Explicit specification of a variable in such a way that its measurement is possible.

Operationalization The process of developing operational definitions of the variables that are contained within the concepts of a quantitative and/or qualitative research study.

Ordinal level of measurement The level of measurement that classifies variables by rank-ordering them from high to low or from most to least.

Outcome The effect of the manipulation of the independent variable on the dependent variable; the end product of a treatment intervention.

Outcome measure The criterion or basis for measuring effects of the independent variable or change in the dependent variable.

Outcome-oriented case study A type of case study that investigates whether client outcomes were in fact achieved.

Outside observers Trained observers who are not a part of the research participants' environment and who are brought in to record data.

Paired observations An observation on two variables, where the intent is to examine the relationship between them.

Panel research study A longitudinal survey design in which the same group of research participants (the panel) is followed over time by surveying them on successive occasions.

Parametric tests Statistical methods for estimating parameters or testing hypotheses about population parameters.

Participant observation An obtrusive data collection method that the researcher, or the observer, participates in the life of those being observed; both an obtrusive data collection method and a research approach, this method is characterized by the one doing the study undertaking roles that involve establishing and maintaining ongoing relationships with research participants who are often in the field settings, and observing and participating with the research participants over time.

Participant observer The participant observer is one of four roles on a continuum of participation in participant observation research; the level of involvement of the participant observer is higher than of the complete observer and lower than of the observer participant.

Permanent product recording A method of data collection in which the occurrence of the target problem is determined by observing the permanent product or record of the target problem.

Pilot study See Pretest (2).

Population An entire set, or universe, of people, objects, or events of concern to a research study, from which a sample is drawn.

Positivism See Logical positivism.

Posttest Measurement of the dependent variable after the introduction of the independent variable.

Potential for testing One of the four criteria for evaluating research hypotheses.

Practitioner/researcher A social worker who guides practice through the use of research findings; collects data throughout an intervention using research methods, skills, and tools; disseminates practice findings.

Pragmatists Researchers who believe that both qualitative and quantitative research approaches can be integrated in a single research study.

Predictive validity A form of criterion validity that is concerned with the ability of a measuring instrument to predict future performance or status on the basis of present performance or status.

Predictor variable The variable that, it is believed, allows us to improve our ability to predict values of the criterion variable.

Preexposure Tasks to be carried out in advance of a research study to sensitize the researcher to the culture of interest; these tasks may include participation in cultural experiences, intercultural sharing, case studies, ethnic literature reviews, value statement exercises, etc.

Preliminary plan for data analysis A strategy for analyzing qualitative data that is outlined in the beginning stages of a qualitative research study; the plan has two general steps: (1) previewing the data, and (2) outlining what to record in the researcher's journal.

Presentism Applying current thinking and concepts to interpretations of past events or intentions.

Pretest (1) Measurement of the dependent variable prior to the introduction of the independent variable; (2) Administration of a measuring instrument to a group of people who will not be included in the study to determine difficulties the research participants may have in answering questions and the general impression given by the instrument; also called a pilot study.

Pretest-treatment interaction Effects that a pretest has on the responses of research participants to the introduction of the independent variable or the experimental treatment; a threat to external validity.

Previous research Research studies that have already been completed and published; they provide information about data collection methods used to investigate research questions that are similar to our own; a criterion for selecting a data collection method.

Primary data Data in its original form, as collected from the research participants; a primary data source is one that puts as few intermediaries as possible between the production and the study of the data.

Primary language The preferred language of the research participants.

Primary reference source A report of a research study by the person who conducted the study; usually an article in a professional journal.

Probability sampling Sampling procedures in which every member of the designated population has a known probability of being selected for the sample.

Problem area In social work research, a general expressed difficulty about which something researchable is unknown; not to be confused with research question.

Problem-solving process A generic method with specified phases for solving problems; also described as the scientific method.

Process-oriented case study A type of case study that illuminates the micro-steps of intervention that lead to client outcomes; describes how programs and interventions work and gives insight to the "black box" of intervention.

Professional standards Rules for making judgments about evaluation activity that are established by a group of persons who have advanced education and usually have the same occupation.

Program An organized set of political, administrative, and clinical activities that function to fulfill some social purpose.

Program development The constant effort to improve program services to better achieve outcomes; a basic principle underlying the design of evaluations.

Program efficiency Assessment of a program's outcome in relation to the costs of obtaining the outcome.

Program evaluation A form of appraisal, using valid and reliable research methods, that examines the processes or outcomes of an organization that exists to fulfill some social purpose.

Program goal A statement defining the intent of a program that cannot be directly evaluated; it can, however, be evaluated indirectly by the program's objectives, which are derived from the program goal; not to be confused with program objectives.

Program-level evaluation A form of appraisal that monitors change for groups of clients and organizational performance.

Program objectives A statement that clearly and exactly specifies the expected change, or intended result, for individuals receiving program services; qualities of well-chosen objectives are meaningfulness, specificity, measurability, and directionality; not to be confused with program goal.

Program participation The philosophy and structure of a program that will support or supplant the successful implementation of a research study within an existing social service program; a criterion for selecting a data collection method.

Program process The coordination of administrative and clinical activities that are designed to achieve a program's goal.

Program results A report on how effective a program is at meeting its stated objectives.

Project approach to evaluation Evaluation that aims to assess a completed or finished program; this approach complements the monitoring approach.

Proxy   An indirect measure of a variable that a researcher wants to study; it is often used when the variable of inquiry is difficult to measure or observe directly.

Pure research approach   A search for theoretical results that can be utilized to develop theory and expand our profession's knowledge bases; complementary to the applied research approach.

Purists   Researchers who believe that qualitative and quantitative research approaches should never be mixed.

Purpose statement   A declaration of words that clearly describes a research study's intent.

Purposive sampling   A nonprobability sampling procedure in which research participants with particular characteristics are purposely selected for inclusion in a research sample; also known as judgmental or theoretical sampling.

Qualitative data   Data that measure a quality or kind; when referring to variables, qualitative is another term for categorical or nominal variable values; when speaking of kinds of research, qualitative refers to studies of subjects that are hard to quantify; qualitative research produces descriptive data based on spoken or written words and observable behaviors.

Qualitative research approach   Research studies that focus on the facts of nature as they occur under natural conditions and emphasize qualitative description and generalization; a process of discovery sensitive to holistic and ecological issues; a research approach that is complementry to the quantitative research approach.

Quantification   In measurement, the reduction of data to numerical form

in order to analyze them by way of mathematical or statistical techniques.

Quantitative data   Data that measure a quantity or amount.

Quantitative research approach   A research approach to discover relationships and facts that are generalizable; research that is "independent" of subjective beliefs, feelings, wishes, and values; a research approach that is complementry to the qualitative research approach.

Quasi-experiment   A research design at the descriptive level of the knowledge continuum that resembles an "ideal" experiment but does not allow for random selection or assignment of research participants to groups and often does not control for rival hypotheses.

Questionnaire-type scale   A type of measuring instrument in which multiple responses are usually combined to form a single overall score for a respondent.

Quota sampling   A nonprobability sampling procedure in which the relevant characteristics of the sample are identified, the proportion of these characteristics in the population is determined, and research participants are selected from each category until the predetermined proportion (quota) has been achieved.

Race   A variable based on physical attributes that can be subdivided into the Caucasoid, Negroid, and Mongoloid races.

Random assignment   The process of assigning individuals to experimental or control groups so that the groups are equivalent; also referred to as randomization.

Random error   Variable error in measurement; error due to unknown or uncontrolled factors that affect the variable being measured and the process of measurement in an inconsistent fashion.

Randomized cross-sectional survey design   A descriptive research design in which there is only one group, the dependent variable is measured only once, the research participants are randomly selected from the population, and there is no independent variable.

Randomized longitudinal survey design   A descriptive research design in which there is only one group, the dependent variable is measured more than once, and research participants are randomly selected from the population before each treatment.

Randomized one-group posttest-only design   A descriptive research design in which there is only one group, the dependent variable is measured only once, and research participants are randomly selected from the population.

Randomized posttest-only control group design   An explanatory research design in which there are two or more randomly assigned groups, the control group does not receive treatment, and the experimental groups receive different treatments.

Random numbers table   A computer-generated or published table of numbers in which each number has an equal chance of appearing in each position in the table.

Random sampling   An unbiased selection process conducted so that all members of a population have an equal chance of being selected to participate in a research study.

Rank-order scale   A comparative rating scale in which the rater is asked to rank specific individuals in relation to one another on some characteristic.

Rating scale   A type of measuring instrument in which responses are rated on a continuum or in an ordered set of categories, with numerical values assigned to each point or category.

Ratio level of measurement   The level of measurement that has a nonarbitrary, fixed zero point and classifies the values of a variable on an equally spaced continuum.

Raw scores   Scores derived from administration of a measuring instrument to research participants or groups.

Reactive effect   (1) An effect on outcome measures due to the research participants' awareness that they are being observed or interviewed; a threat to external and internal validity; (2) Alteration of the variables being measured or the respondents' performance on the measuring instrument due to administration of the instrument.

Reactivity   The belief that things being observed or measured are affected by the fact that they are being observed or measured; one of the four main limitations of the quantitative research approach.

Reassessment   A step in qualitative data analysis in which the researcher interrupts the data analysis process to reaffirm the rules used to decide which meaning units are placed within different categories.

Recoding   Developing and applying new variable value labels to a variable that has previously been coded; usually, recoding is done to make variables from one or more data sets comparable.

Reductionism   In the quantitative research approach, the operationalization of concepts by reducing them to common measurable variables; one of the four main limitations of the quantitative research approach.

Relevancy   One of the four criteria for evaluating research problem areas *and* formulating research questions out of the problem areas.

Reliability   (1) The degree of accuracy, precision, or consistency in results of a measuring instrument, including the ability to produce the same results when the same variable is measured more than once or repeated applications of the same test on the same individual produce the same measurement; (2) The degree to which individual differences on scores or in data are due either to true differences or to errors in measurement.

Replication Repetition of the same research procedures by a second researcher for the purpose of determining if earlier results can be confirmed.

Researchability The extent to which a research problem is in fact researchable and the problem can be resolved through the consideration of data derived from a research study; one of the four criteria for evaluating research problem areas *and* formulating research questions out of the problem areas.

Research attitude A way that we view the world. It is an attitude that highly values craftsmanship, with pride in creativity, high-quality standards, and hard work.

Research consumer A social work role reflecting the ethical obligation to base interventions on the most up-to-date research knowledge available.

Research design The entire plan of a quantitative and/or qualitative research study from problem conceptualization to the dissemination of findings.

Researcher bias The tendency of researchers to find results they expect to find; a threat to external validity.

Research hypothesis A statement about a study's research question that predicts the existence of a particular relationship between the independent and dependent variables; can be used in both the quantitative and qualitative approaches to research.

Research method The use of quantitative and qualitative research approaches to find out what is true; one of the six ways of knowing.

Research participants People utilized in research studies; also called subjects or cases.

Research question A specific research question that is formulated directly out of the general research problem area; answered by the qualitative and/or quantitative research approach; not to be confused with problem area.

Resources The costs associated with collecting data in any given research study; includes materials and supplies, equipment rental, transportation, training staff, and staff time; a criterion for selecting a data collection method.

Response categories Possible responses assigned to each question in a standardized measuring instrument, with a lower value generally indicating a low level of the variable being measured and a larger value indicating a higher level.

Response rate The total number of responses obtained from potential research participants to a measuring instrument divided by the total number of responses requested, usually expressed in the form of a percentage.

Response set Personal style; the tendency of research participants to respond to a measuring instrument in a particular way, regardless of the questions asked, or the tendency of observers or interviewers to react in certain ways; a source of constant error.

Review of the literature (1) A search of the professional literature to provide background knowledge of what has already been examined or tested in a specific problem area; (2) Use of any information source, such as a computerized data base, to locate existing data or information on a research problem, question, or hypothesis.

Rival hypothesis A hypothesis that is a plausible alternative to the research hypothesis and might explain the results as well or better; a hypothesis involving extraneous or intervening variables other than the independent variable in the research hypothesis;

also referred to as an alternative hypothesis.

Rules of correspondence   A characteristic of measurement stipulating that numerals or symbols are assigned to properties of individuals, objects, or events according to specified rules.

Sample   A subset of a population of individuals, objects, or events chosen to participate in or to be considered in a research study.

Sampling error   (1) The degree of difference that can be expected between the sample and the population from which it was drawn; (2) A mistake in a research study's results that is due to sampling procedures.

Sampling frame   A listing of units (people, objects, or events) in a population from which a sample is drawn.

Sampling plan   A method of selecting members of a population for inclusion in a research study, using procedures that make it possible to draw inferences about the population from the sample statistics.

Sampling theory   The logic of using methods to ensure that a sample and a population are similar in all relevant characteristics.

Scale   A measuring instrument composed of several items that are logically or empirically structured to measure a construct.

Scattergram   A graphic representation of the relationship between two interval- or ratio-level variables.

Science   Knowledge that has been obtained and tested through use of quantitative and qualitative research studies.

Scientific community   A group that shares the same general norms for both research activity and acceptance of scientific findings and explanations.

Scientific determinism   See Determinism.

Scientific method   A generic method with specified steps for solving problems; the principles and procedures used in the systematic pursuit of knowledge.

Scope of a study   The extent to which a problem area is covered in a single research study; a criterion for selecting a data collection method.

Score   A numerical value assigned to an observation; also called data.

Search statement   A preliminary search statement developed by the researcher prior to a literature search and which contains terms that can be combined to elicit specific data.

Secondary analysis   An unobtrusive data collection method in which available data that predate the formulation of a research study are used to answer the research question or test the hypothesis.

Secondary data   Data that predate the formulation of the research study and which are used to answer the research question or test the hypothesis.

Secondary data sources   A data source that provides nonoriginal, secondhand data.

Secondary reference source   A source related to a primary source or sources, such as a critique of a particular source item or a literature review, bibliography, or commentary on several items.

Secondhand data   Data obtained from people who are indirectly connected to the problem being studied.

Selection-treatment interaction   The relationship between the manner of selecting research participants and their response to the independent variable; a threat to external validity.

Self-anchored scales   A rating scale in which research participants rate themselves on a continuum of values, according to their own referents for each point.

Self-disclosure Shared communication about oneself, including one's behaviors, beliefs, and attitudes.

Semantic differential scale A modified measurement scale in which research participants rate their perceptions of the variable under study along three dimensions—evaluation, potency, and activity.

Sequential triangulation When two distinct and separate phases of a research study are conducted and the results of the first phase are considered essential for planning the second phase; research questions in Phase 1 are answered before research questions in Phase 2 are formulated.

Service recipients People who use human services—individuals, couples, families, groups, organizations, and communities; also known as clients or consumers; a stakeholder group in evaluation.

Simple random sampling A one-stage probability sampling procedure in which members of a population are selected one at a time, without a chance of being selected again, until the desired sample size is obtained.

Simultaneous triangulation When the results of a quantitative and qualitative research question are answered at the same time; results to the qualitative research questions, for example, are reported separately and do not necessarily relate to, or confirm, the results from the quantitative phase.

Situationalists Researchers who assert that certain research approaches (qualitative or quantitative) are appropriate for specific situations.

Situation-specific variable A variable that may be observable only in certain environments and under certain circumstances, or with particular people.

Size of a study The number of people, places, or systems that are included in a single research study; a criterion for selecting a data collection method.

Snowball sampling A nonprobability sampling procedure in which individuals selected for inclusion in a sample are asked to identify other individuals from the population who might be included; useful to locate people with divergent points of view.

Social desirability (1) A response set in which research participants tend to answer questions in a way that they perceive as giving favorable impressions of themselves; (2) The inclination of data providers to report data that present a socially desirable impression of themselves or their reference groups. Also referred to as impression management.

Socially acceptable response Bias in an answer that comes from research participants trying to answer questions as they think a "good" person should, rather than in a way that reveals what they actually believe or feel.

Social work research Scientific inquiry in which qualitative and quantitative research approaches are used to answer research questions and create new, generally applicable knowledge in the field of social work.

Socioeconomic variables Any one of several measures of social rank, usually including income, education, and occupational prestige; abbreviated "SES."

Solomon four-group design An explanatory research design with four randomly assigned groups, two experimental and two control; the dependent variable is measured before and after treatment for one experimental and one control group, but only after treatment for the other two groups, and only experimental groups receive the treatment.

Specificity One of the four criteria for evaluating research hypotheses.

Split-half method A method for establishing the reliability of a measuring instrument by dividing it into comparable halves and comparing the scores between the two halves.

Spot-check recording A method of data collection that involves direct observation of the target problem at specified intervals rather than continuously.

Stakeholder A person or group of people having a direct or indirect interest in the results of an evaluation.

Stakeholder service evaluation model Proponents of this evaluation model believe that program evaluations will be more likely to be utilized, and thus have a greater impact on social problems, when they are tailored to the needs of stakeholders; in this model, the purpose of program evaluation is not to generalize findings to other sites, but rather to restrict the evaluation effort to a particular program.

Standardized measuring instrument A professionally developed measuring instrument that provides for uniform administration and scoring and generates normative data against which later results can be evaluated.

Statistics The branch of mathematics concerned with the collection and analysis of data using statistical techniques.

Stratified random sampling A one-stage probability sampling procedure in which a population is divided into two or more strata to be sampled separately, using simple random or systematic random sampling techniques.

Structured interview schedule A complete list of questions to be asked and spaces for recording the answers; the interview schedule is used by interviewers when questioning respondents.

Structured observation A data collection method in which people are observed in their natural environments using specified methods and measurement procedures. See Direct observation.

Subscale A component of a scale that measures some part or aspect of a major construct; also composed of several items that are logically or empirically structured.

Summated scale A questionnaire-type scale in which research participants are asked to indicate the degree of their agreement or disagreement with a series of questions.

Summative evaluation A type of evaluation that examines the ultimate success of a program and assists with decisions about whether a program should be continued or chosen in the first place among alternative program options.

Survey research A data collection method that uses survey-type data collection measuring instruments to obtain opinions or answers from a population or sample of research participants in order to describe or study them as a group.

Synthesis Undertaking the search for meaning in our sources of information at every step of the research process; combining parts such as data, concepts, and theories to arrive at a higher level of understanding.

Systematic To arrange the steps of a research study in a methodical way.

Systematic random sampling A one-stage probability sampling procedure in which every person at a designated interval in a specific population is selected to be included in a research study's sample.

Systematic error Measurement error that is consistent, not random.

Target population The group about which a researcher wants to draw conclusions; another term for a population about which one aims to make inferences.

Target problem (1) In case-level evaluation designs, the problems social workers seek to solve for their clients; (2) A measurable behavior, feeling, or cognition that is either a problem in itself or symptomatic of some other problem.

Temporal research design A research study that includes time as a major variable; the purpose of this design is to investigate change in the distribution of a variable or in relationships among variables over time; there are three types of temporal research designs: cohort, panel, and trend.

Temporal stability Consistency of responses to a measuring instrument over time; reliability of an instrument across forms and across administrations.

Testing effect The effect that taking a pretest might have on posttest scores; a threat to internal validity.

Test-retest reliability Reliability of a measuring instrument established through repeated administration to the same group of individuals.

Thematic notes In observational research, thematic notes are a record of emerging ideas, hypotheses, theories, and conjectures; thematic notes provide a place for the researcher to speculate and identify themes, make linkages between ideas and events, and articulate thoughts as they emerge in the field setting.

Theme In qualitative data analysis, a concept or idea that describes a single category or a grouping of categories; an abstract interpretation of qualitative data.

Theoretical framework A frame of reference that serves to guide a research study and is developed from theories, findings from a variety of other studies, and the researcher's personal experiences.

Theoretical sampling See Purposive sampling.

Theory A reasoned set of propositions, derived from and supported by established data, which serves to explain a group of phenomena; a conjectural explanation that may, or may not, be supported by data generated from qualitative and quantitative research studies.

Time orientation An important cultural factor that considers whether one is future-, present-, or past-oriented; for instance, individuals who are "present-oriented" would not be as preoccupied with advance planning as those who are "future-oriented."

Time-series design See Interrupted time-series design.

Tradition Traditional cultural beliefs that we accept—without question—as true; one of the six ways of knowing.

Transcript A written, printed, or typed copy of interview data or any other written material that have been gathered for a qualitative research study.

Transition statements Sentences used to indicate a change in direction or focus of questions in a measuring instrument.

Treatment group See Experimental group.

Trend study A longitudinal study design in which data from surveys carried out at periodic intervals on samples drawn from a particular population are used to reveal trends over time.

Triangulation The idea of combining different research methods in all steps associated with a single research study; assumes that any bias inherent in one particular method will be neutralized when used in conjunction with other research methods; seeks convergence of a study's results; using more than one research method and source of data to study the same phenomena and to enhance validity; there are several types of triangulation, but the essence of the term is that multiple perspectives are compared; it can involve multiple data sources or multiple data analyzers; the hope is that the different perspectives will confirm each other, adding weight to the credibility and dependability of qualitative data analysis.

Triangulation of analysts Using multiple data analyzers to code a single segment of transcript and comparing the amount of agreement between analyzers; a method used to verify coding of qualitative data.

Two-phase research model   A model combining qualitative and quantitative research approaches in a single study where each approach is conducted as a separate and distinct phase of the study.

Two-tailed hypotheses   Statements that *do not* predict specific relationships between independent and dependent variables.

Unit of analysis   A specific research participant (person, object, or event) or the sample or population relevant to the research question; the persons or things being studied; units of analysis in research are often persons, but may be groups, political parties, newspaper editorials, unions, hospitals, schools, etc.; a particular unit of analysis from which data are gathered is called a case.

Univariate   A hypothesis or research design involving a single variable.

Universe   See Population.

Unobtrusive methods   Data collection methods that do not influence the variable under study or the responses of research participants; methods that avoid reactive effects.

Unstructured interviews   A series of questions that allow flexibility for both the research participant and the interviewer to make changes during the process.

Validity   (1) The extent to which a measuring instrument measures the variable it is supposed to measure and measures it accurately; (2) The degree to which an instrument is able to do what it is intended to do, in terms of both experimental procedures and measuring instruments (internal validity) and generalizability of results (external validity); (3) The degree to which scores on a measuring instrument correlate with measures of performance on some other criterion.

Variable   A concept with characteristics that can take on different values.

Verbatim recording   Recording interview data word-for-word and including significant gestures, pauses, and expressions of persons in the interview.

Wideband measuring instrument   Measuring instruments that measure more than one variable.

Within-methods research approach   Triangulation by using different research methods available in *either* the qualitative *or* the quantitative research approaches in a single research study.

Words   The basic data unit of analysis used in qualitative research studies.

Worker cooperation   The actions and attitudes of program personnel when carrying out a research study within an existing social service program; a criterion for selecting a data collection method.

Working hypothesis   An assertion about a relationship between two or more variables that may not be true but is plausible and worth examining.

References and
Further Readings

Allen, M.J. (1995). *Introduction to psychological research.* Itasca, IL: F.E. Peacock.

Austin, M.J., & Crowell, J. (1985). Survey research. In R.M. Grinnell, Jr. (Ed.), *Social work research and evaluation* (2nd ed., pp. 275–305). Itasca, IL: F.E. Peacock.

Badgley, R. (Chairman). (1984). *Sexual offenses against children. Volume 1: Report of the committee on sexual offenses against children and youths.* Ottawa, Canada: Ministry of Supply and Services.

Baumeister, R.F. (1988). Should we stop studiying sex differences altogether? *American Psychologist, 43,* 1092–1095.

Berg, B.L. (1994). *Qualitative research methods for the social sciences* (2nd ed.). Boston: Allyn & Bacon.

Beveridge, W.I.B. (1957). *The art of scientific investigation* (3rd ed.). London: Heinemann.

Bisno, H., & Borowski, A. (1985). The social and psychological contexts of research. In R.M. Grinnell, Jr. (Ed.), *Social work research and evaluation* (2nd ed., pp. 83–100). Itasca, IL: F.E. Peacock.

Blase, K., Fixsen, D., & Phillips, E. (1984). Residential treatment for troubled children: Developing service delivery systems. In S.C. Paine, G.T. Bellamy, & B. Wilcox (Eds.), *Human services that work: From innovation to standard practice.* Baltimore: Paul H. Brookes.

Bloom, M., Fischer, J., & Orme, J. (1994). *Evaluating practice: Guidelines for the accountable professional* (2nd ed.). Englewood Cliffs, NJ: Prentice-Hall.

Borowski, A. (1988). Social dimensions of research. In R.M. Grinnell, Jr. (Ed.), *Social work research and evaluation* (3rd ed., pp. 42–64). Itasca, IL: F.E. Peacock.

Bouey, E., & Rogers, G. (1993). Retrieving information. In R.M. Grinnell, Jr. (Ed.), *Social work research and evaluation* (4th ed., pp. 388–401). Itasca, IL: F.E. Peacock.

Calgary Herald: "Show ignores Native stereotype," September 6, 1991a, Section B, p. 6.

Calgary Herald: "Another kidnap bid has parents nervous," September 6, 1991b, p. 1.

Campbell, P.B. (1983). The impact of societal biases on research methods. In B.L. Richardson & J. Wirtenberg (Eds.), *Sex role research* (pp. 197–213). New York: Praeger Publishers.

Campbell, D., & Stanley, J. (1963). *Experimental and quasi-experimental designs for research.* Chicago: Rand McNally.

Carley, M. (1981). *Social measurement and social indicators.* London: Allen & Unwin.

Ceci, S.J., Peters, D., & Plotkin, J. (1985). Human subjects review, personal values, and the regulation of social science research. *American Psychologist, 40,* 994–1002.

Coleman, H., Collins, D., & Polster, R.A. (1997). Structured observation. In R.M. Grinnell, Jr. (Ed.), *Social work research and evaluation: Quantitative and qualitative approaches* (5th ed., pp. 315–332). Itasca, IL: F.E. Peacock.

Committee on the Status of Women in Sociology (1985–86). *The status of women in sociology.* New York: American Sociological Association.

Corcoran, K.J. (1988). Selecting a measuring instrument. In R.M. Grinnell, Jr. (Ed.), *Social work research and evaluation* (3rd ed., pp. 137–155). Itasca, IL: F.E. Peacock.

Cresswell, J.W. (1997). Using both research approaches in a single study. In R.M. Grinnell, Jr. (Ed.), *Social work research and evaluation: Quantitative and qualitative approaches* (5th ed., pp. 141–158). Itasca, IL: F.E. Peacock.

Denmark, R., Russo, N.F., Frieze, I.H., & Sechzer, J.A. (1988). Guidelines for avoiding sexism in research: A report of the Ad Hoc Committee on Nonsexist Research. *American Pyschologist, 43,* 582-585.

Denzin, N., & Lincoln, Y.S. (Eds.). (1994). *Handbook of qualitative research.* Newbury Park, CA: Sage.

Diamond, J. (1987). Soft sciences are harder than hard sciences. *Discover, 8* (August), 34–39.

Dillman, D.A. (1978). *Mail and telephone surveys: The total design method.* New York: Wiley.

Doyle, C. (1901/1955). *A treasury of Sherlock Holmes.* Garden City, NY: Hanover House.

Duehn, W.D. (1985). Practice and research. In R.M. Grinnell, Jr. (Ed.), *Social work research and evaluation* (2nd ed., pp. 19-48). Itasca, IL: F.E. Peacock.

Eagly, A.H. (1987). Reporting sex differences. *American Psychologist, 42,* 756–757.

Eichler, M. (1988). *Nonsexist research methods.* Boston: Allen & Unwin.

Epstein, I. (1988). Quantitative and qualitative methods. In R.M. Grinnell, Jr. (Ed.), *Social work research and evaluation* (3rd ed., pp. 185–198). Itasca, IL: F.E. Peacock.

Finkelhor, D. (1984). *Child sexual abuse: New theory and research.* New York: Free Press.

Fischer, J. (1993). Evaluating positivistic research reports. In R.M. Grinnell, Jr. (Ed.), *Social work research and evaluation* (4th ed., pp. 347–366). Itasca, IL: F.E. Peacock.

Franklin, C., & Jordan, C. (1997). Qualitative approaches to the generation of knowledge. In R.M. Grinnell, Jr. (Ed.), *Social work research and evaluation: Quantitative and qualitative approaches* (5th ed., pp. 106–140). Itasca, IL: F.E. Peacock.

Gabor, P.A., & Grinnell, R.M., Jr. (1994). *Evaluation and quality improvement in the human services.* Boston: Allyn & Bacon.

Gabor, P., & Ing, C. (1997). Sampling. In R.M. Grinnell, Jr. (Ed.), *Social work research and evaluation: Quantitative and qualitative approaches* (5th ed., pp. 237–258). Itasca, IL: F.E. Peacock.

Gabor, P.A., Unrau, Y.A., & Grinnell, R.M., Jr. (1998). *Evaluation for social workers: A quality improvement approach for the social services* (2nd ed.). Boston: Allyn & Bacon.

Garvin, C.D. (1981). Research-related roles for social workers. In R.M. Grinnell, Jr. (Ed.), *Social work research and evaluation* (pp. 547–552). Itasca, IL: F.E. Peacock.

Gilgun, J. (1997). Case designs. In R.M. Grinnell, Jr. (Ed.), *Social work research and evaluation: Quantitative and qualitative approaches* (5th ed., pp. 298–312). Itasca, IL: F.E. Peacock.

Gochros, H.L. (1988). Research interviewing. In R.M. Grinnell, Jr. (Ed.), *Social work research and evaluation* (3rd ed., pp. 267–299). Itasca, IL: F.E. Peacock.

Green, G.R., & Wright, J.E. (1979). The retrospective approach to collecting baseline data. *Social Work Research and Abstracts, 15,* 25–30.

Greenwald, R.A., Ryan, M.K., & Mulvihill, J.E. (1982). *Human subjects research.* New York: Plenum Press.

Grinnell, F. (1987). *The scientific attitude.* Boulder, CO: Westview.

Grinnell, R.M., Jr. (1981a). Becoming a knowledge-based social worker. In R.M. Grinnell, Jr. (Ed.), *Social work research and evaluation* (pp. 1–8). Itasca, IL: F.E. Peacock.

Grinnell, R.M., Jr. (Ed.). (1981b). *Social work research and evaluation.* Itasca, IL: F.E. Peacock.

Grinnell, R.M., Jr. (1985a). Becoming a practitioner/researcher. In R.M. Grinnell, Jr. (Ed.), *Social work research and evaluation* (2nd ed., pp. 1–15). Itasca, IL: F.E. Peacock.

Grinnell, R.M., Jr. (Ed.). (1985b). *Social work research and evaluation* (2nd ed.). Itasca, IL: F.E. Peacock.

Grinnell, R.M., Jr. (Ed.). (1988). *Social work research and evaluation* (3rd ed.). Itasca, IL: F.E. Peacock.

Grinnell, R.M., Jr. (1993a). Group research designs. In R.M. Grinnell, Jr. (Ed.), *Social work research and evaluation* (4th ed., pp. 118–153). Itasca, IL: F.E. Peacock.

Grinnell, R.M., Jr. (Ed.). (1993b). *Social work research and evaluation* (4th ed.). Itasca, IL: F.E. Peacock.

Grinnell, R.M., Jr. (1997a). The generation of knowledge. In R.M. Grinnell, Jr. (Ed.), *Social work research and evaluation: Quantitative and qualitative approaches* (5th ed., pp. 3–24). Itasca, IL: F.E. Peacock.

Grinnell, R.M., Jr. (1997b). Preface. In R.M. Grinnell, Jr. (Ed.), *Social work research and evaluation: Quantitative and qualitative approaches* (5th ed., pp. xvii–xxvi). Itasca, IL: F.E. Peacock.

Grinnell, R.M., Jr. (Ed.). (1997c). *Social work research and evaluation: Quantitative and qualitative approaches* (5th ed.). Itasca, IL: F.E. Peacock.

Grinnell, R.M., Jr., Rothery, M., & Thomlison, R.J. (1993). Research in social work. In R.M. Grinnell, Jr. (Ed.), *Social work research and evaluation* (4th ed., pp. 2–16). Itasca, IL: F.E. Peacock.

Grinnell, R.M., Jr., & Siegel, D.H. (1988). The place of research in social work. In R.M. Grinnell, Jr. (Ed.), *Social work research and evaluation* (3rd ed., pp. 9–24). Itasca, IL: F.E. Peacock.

Grinnell, R.M., Jr., & Unrau, Y. (1997). Group designs. In R.M. Grinnell, Jr. (Ed.), *Social work research and evaluation: Quantitative and qualitative approaches* (5th ed., pp. 259–297). Itasca, IL: F.E. Peacock.

Grinnell, R.M., Jr., & Williams, M. (1990). *Research in social work: A primer.* Itasca, IL: F.E. Peacock.

Grinnell, R.M., Jr., Williams, M., & Tutty, L.M. (1997). Case-level evaluation. In R.M. Grinnell, Jr. (Ed.), *Social work research and evaluation: Quantitative and qualitative approaches* (5th ed., pp. 529–559). Itasca, IL: F.E. Peacock.

Guba, E.G., & Lincoln, Y.S. (1981). *Effective evaluation.* San Francisco: Jossey-Bass.

Hanson, J. (1989). *The experience of families of people with a severe mental illness: An ethnographic view.* Unpublished doctoral dissertation, University of Kansas.

Hempel, C.G. (1966). *Philosophy of natural science.* Englewood Cliffs, NJ: Prentice-Hall.

Herek, G.M., Kimmel, D.C., Amaro, H., & Melton, G.G. (1991). Avoiding heterosexist bias in psychological research. *American Psychologist, 31,* 858–867.

Hoffart, I., & Krysik, J. (1993). Glossary. In R.M. Grinnell, Jr. (Ed.), *Social work research and evaluation* (4th ed., pp. 439–450). Itasca, IL: F.E. Peacock.

Hornick, J.P., & Burrows, B. (1988). Program evaluation. In R.M. Grinnell, Jr. (Ed.), *Social work research and evaluation* (3rd ed., pp. 400–420). Itasca, IL: F.E. Peacock.

Hoshino, G., & Lynch, M.M. (1985). Secondary analyses. In R.M. Grinnell, Jr. (Ed.), *Social work research and evaluation* (2nd ed., pp. 370–380). Itasca, IL: F.E. Peacock.

Huck, S.W., & Sandler, H.M. (1979). *Rival hypotheses: Alternative interpretations of data-based conclusions.* New York: Harper & Row.

Hudson, J., & Grinnell, R.M., Jr. (1989). Program evaluation. In B. Compton & B. Galaway (Eds.), *Social work processes* (4th ed., pp. 691–711). Belmont, CA: Wadsworth.

Hyde, J.S. (1991). *Half the human experience: The psychology of women* (4th ed.). Lexington, MA: Heath.

Ihilevich, D., & Gleser, G.C. (1982). *Evaluating mental health programs.* Lexington, MA: Lexington Books.

Jackson, G.B. (1980). Methods for integrative reviews. *Review of Educational Research, 50,* 438–460.

Jordan, C., & Franklin, C. (1995). *Clinical assessment for social workers: Quantitative and qualitative methods.* Chicago: Lyceum Books, Inc.

Jordan, C., Franklin, C., & Corcoran, K.J. (1997). Measuring instruments. In R.M. Grinnell, Jr. (Ed.), *Social work research and evaluation: Quantitative and qualitative approaches* (5th ed., pp. 184–211). Itasca, IL: F.E. Peacock.

Jorgensen, D.L. (1989). *Participant observation: A methodology for human studies.* Newbury Park, CA: Sage.

Krueger, R.A. (1997). *Focus groups: A practical guide for applied research.* Thousand Oaks, CA: Sage.

Krysik, J. (1997). Secondary analysis. In R.M. Grinnell, Jr. (Ed.), *Social work research and evaluation: Quantitative and qualitative approaches* (5th ed., pp. 391–406). Itasca, IL: F.E. Peacock.

Krysik, J., & Grinnell, R.M., Jr. (1997). Quantitative approaches to the generation of knowledge. In R.M. Grinnell, Jr. (Ed.), *Social work research and evaluation: Quantitative and qualitative approaches* (5th ed., pp. 67–105). Itasca, IL: F.E. Peacock.

Krysik, J.L., Hoffart, I., & Grinnell, R.M., Jr. (1993). *Student study guide for the fourth edition of Social Work Research and Evaluation.* Itasca, IL: F.E.

Kyte, N.S., & Bostwick, G.J., Jr. (1997). Measuring variables. In R.M. Grinnell, Jr. (Ed.), *Social work research and evaluation: Quantitative and qualitative approaches* (5th ed., pp. 161–183). Itasca, IL: F.E. Peacock.

Lavrakas, P.J. (1987). *Telephone survey methods: Sampling, selection, and supervision.* Thousand Oaks, CA: Sage.

LeCroy, C.W., & Solomon, G. (1997). Content analysis. In R.M. Grinnell, Jr. (Ed.), *Social work research and evaluation: Quantitative and qualitative approaches* (5th ed., pp. 427–441). Itasca, IL: F.E. Peacock.

Lincoln, Y., & Guba, E. (1985). *Naturalistic inquiry.* Thousand Oaks, CA: Sage.

McClelland, R.W., & Austin, C.D. (1996). Part four: Writing your report. In L.M. Tutty, M.A. Rothery, & R.M. Grinnell, Jr. (Eds.), *Qualitative research for social workers: Phases, steps, and tasks* (pp. 120–150). Boston: Allyn & Bacon.

McMurtry, S.L. (1997). Survey research. In R.M. Grinnell, Jr. (Ed.), *Social work research and evaluation: Quantitative and qualitative approaches* (5th ed., pp. 333–367). Itasca, IL: F.E. Peacock.

Milgram, S. (1963). Behavioral study of obedience. *Journal of Abnormal and Applied Social Psychology, 67,* 371–378.

Milgram, S. (1974). *Obedience to authority: An experimental view.* New York: Harper & Row.

Mindel, C.H. (1997). Designing measuring instruments. In R.M. Grinnell, Jr. (Ed.), *Social work research and evaluation: Quantitative and qualitative approaches* (5th ed., pp. 212–234). Itasca, IL: F.E. Peacock.

Mindel, C.H., & McDonald, L. (1988). Survey research. In R.M. Grinnell, Jr. (Ed.), *Social work research and evaluation* (3rd ed., pp. 300–322). Itasca, IL: F.E. Peacock.

Mook, D.G. (1983). In defense of external invalidity. *American Psychologist, 38,* 379–387.

Morgan, D. (1988). *Focus groups as qualitative research.* Thousand Oaks, CA: Sage.

National Association of Social Workers (1980). *National Association of Social Workers code of ethics.* Silver Spring, MD: Author.

Neuman, W.L. (1997). *Social research methods: Qualitative and quantitative approaches* (3rd ed.). Boston: Allyn & Bacon.

Nurius, P.S., & Hudson, W.W. (1993). *Human services: Practice, evaluation, and computers.* Pacific Grove, CA: Brooks/Cole.

Palys, T. (1997). *Research decisions: Quantitative and qualitative perspectives.* Toronto: Harcourt Brace.

Papell, C.P., & Skolnik, L. (1992). The reflective practitioner: A contemporary paradigm's relevance for social work education. *Journal of Social Work Education, 28,* 18–26.

Reid, P.N., & Gundlach, J.H. (1983). A scale for the measurement of consumer satisfaction with social services. *Journal of Social Service Research, 7,* 37–54.

Reid, W.J. (1993). Writing research reports. In R.M. Grinnell, Jr. (Ed.), *Social work research and evaluation* (4th ed., pp. 332–346). Itasca, IL: F.E. Peacock.

Reid, W.J., & Smith, A.D. (1989). *Research in social work* (2nd ed.). New York: Columbia University Press.

Reinharz, S. (1992). Feminist survey research and other statistical research formats. In S. Reinharz (Ed.), *Feminist methods in social research* (pp. 76–94). New York: Oxford University Press.

Roethlisberger, F.J., & Dickson, W.J. (1939). *Management and the worker: An account of a research program conducted by the Western Electric Co. Hawthorne Works, Chicago.* Cambridge, MA: Harvard University Press.

Rogers, G., & Bouey, E. (1993). Reviewing the literature. In R.M. Grinnell, Jr. (Ed.), *Social work research and evaluation* (4th ed., pp. 388–401). Itasca, IL: F.E. Peacock.

Rogers, G., & Bouey, E. (1996). Part two: Collecting your data. In L.M. Tutty, M.A. Rothery, & R.M. Grinnell, Jr. (Eds.), *Qualitative research for social workers: Phases, steps, and tasks* (pp. 50–87). Boston: Allyn & Bacon.

Rogers, G., & Bouey, E. (1997). Participant observation. In R.M. Grinnell, Jr. (Ed.), *Social work research and evaluation: Quantitative and qualitative approaches* (5th ed., pp. 368–387). Itasca, IL: F.E. Peacock.

Rossi, P.H., & Freeman, H.E. (1993). *Evaluation: A systematic approach* (5th ed.). Thousand Oaks, CA: Sage.

Rothery, M.A. (1993a). The positivistic research approach. In R.M. Grinnell, Jr. (Ed.), *Social work research and evaluation* (4th ed., pp. 38–52). Itasca, IL: F.E. Peacock.

Rothery, M.A. (1993b). Problems, questions, and hypotheses. In R.M. Grinnell, Jr. (Ed.), *Social work research and evaluation* (4th ed., pp. 17–37). Itasca, IL: F.E. Peacock.

Rothery, M.A., Tutty, L.M., & Grinnell, R.M., Jr. (1996). Part one: Planning your study. In L.M. Tutty, M.A. Rothery, & R.M. Grinnell, Jr. (Eds.), *Qualitative research for social workers: Phases, steps, and tasks* (pp. 24–49). Boston: Allyn & Bacon.

Rubin, A. (1993). Secondary analysis. In R.M. Grinnell, Jr. (Ed.), *Social work research and evaluation* (4th ed., pp. 290–303). Itasca, IL: F.E. Peacock.

Rubin, A., & Babbie, E. (1993). *Research methods for social work* (2nd ed.). Pacific Grove, CA: Wadsworth.

Rubin, A., & Babbie, E. (1997a). Program-level evaluation. In R.M. Grinnell, Jr. (Ed.), *Social work research and evaluation: Quantitative and qualitative approaches* (5th ed., pp. 560–587). Itasca, IL: F.E. Peacock.

Rubin, A., & Babbie, E. (1997b). *Research methods for social work* (3rd ed.). Pacific Grove, CA: Wadsworth.

Russell, D. (1984). *Sexual exploitation: Rape, child sexual abuse, and workplace harassment.* Newbury Park, CA: Sage.

Scarr, S. (1988). Race and gender as psychological variables: Social and ethical issues. *American Psychologist, 43,* 56–59.

Schinke, S.P., & Gilchrist, L.D. (1993). Ethics in research. In R.M. Grinnell, Jr. (Ed.), *Social work research and evaluation* (4th ed., pp. 79–90). Itasca, IL: F.E. Peacock.

Seaberg, J.R. (1988). Utilizing sampling procedures. In R.M.

Grinnell, Jr. (Ed.), *Social work research and evaluation* (3rd ed., pp. 240–257). Itasca, IL: F.E. Peacock.

Siegel, D.H. (1988). Integrating data-gathering techniques and practice activities. In R.M. Grinnell, Jr. (Ed.), *Social work research and evaluation* (3rd ed., pp. 465–482). Itasca, IL: F.E. Peacock.

Siegel, D.H., & Reamer, F.G. (1988). Integrating research findings, concepts, and logic into practice. In R.M. Grinnell, Jr. (Ed.), *Social work research and evaluation* (3rd ed., pp. 483–502). Itasca, IL: F.E. Peacock.

Sieppert, J.D., McMurtry, S.L., & McClelland, R.W. (1997). Utilizing existing statistics. In R.M. Grinnell, Jr. (Ed.), *Social work research and evaluation: Quantitative and qualitative approaches* (5th ed., pp. 407–426). Itasca, IL: F.E. Peacock.

Singleton, R.A., Jr., Straits, B.C., & Miller Straits, M. (1993). *Approaches to social research* (2nd ed.). New York: Oxford.

Smith, N.J. (1988). Formulating research goals and problems. In R.M. Grinnell, Jr. (Ed.), *Social work research and evaluation* (3rd ed., pp. 89–110). Itasca, IL: F.E. Peacock.

Sperry, R.W. (1968). Hemisphere deconnection and unity in conscious awareness. *American Psychologist, 23,* 723–733.

Straus, M.A., & Gelles, R. (1986). Societal change and change in family violence from 1975 to 1985 as revealed by two national surveys. *Journal of Marriage and the Family, 48,* 465–479.

Strauss, M.A., Gelles, R., & Steinmetz, S. (1980). *Behind closed doors: Violence in the American family.* Garden City, NY: Anchor Books.

Stuart, P. (1997). Historical research. In R.M. Grinnell, Jr. (Ed.), *Social* work research and evaluation: Quantitative and qualitative approaches (5th ed., pp. 442–457). Itasca, IL: F.E. Peacock.

Taylor, J. (1993). The naturalistic research approach. In R.M. Grinnell, Jr. (Ed.), *Social work research and evaluation* (4th ed., pp. 53–78). Itasca, IL: F.E. Peacock.

Taylor, S., & Bogdan, R. (1984). *Introduction to qualitative research methods: The search for meanings.* New York: Wiley.

Thyer, B.A. (1993). Single-system research designs. In R.M. Grinnell, Jr. (Ed.), *Social work research and evaluation* (4th ed., pp. 94–117). Itasca, IL: F.E. Peacock.

Toseland, R.W. (1993). Choosing a data collection method. In R.M. Grinnell, Jr. (Ed.), *Social work research and evaluation* (4th ed., pp. 317–328). Itasca, IL: F.E. Peacock.

Tripodi, T. (1985). Research designs. In R.M. Grinnell, Jr. (Ed.), *Social work research and evaluation* (2nd ed., pp. 231–259). Itasca, IL: F.E. Peacock.

Tutty, L.M., Grinnell, R.M., Jr., & Williams, M. (1997). Research problems and questions. In R.M. Grinnell, Jr. (Ed.), *Social work research and evaluation: Quantitative and qualitative approaches* (5th ed., pp. 49–66). Itasca, IL: F.E. Peacock.

Tutty, L.M., Rothery, M.L., & Grinnell, R.M., Jr. (Eds.). (1996). *Qualitative research for social workers: Phases, steps, and tasks.* Boston: Allyn & Bacon.

Unrau, Y.A. (1993). A program logic model approach to conceptualizing social service programs. *The Canadian Journal of Program Evaluation, 8,* 33–42.

Unrau, Y.A. (1994). Glossary. In P.A. Gabor & R.M. Grinnell, Jr. *Evaluation and quality improvement in the human services* (pp. 399–406). Boston: Allyn & Bacon.

Unrau, Y.A. (1997a). Implementing evaluations. In R.M. Grinnell, Jr. (Ed.), *Social work research and evaluation: Quantitative and qualitative approaches* (5th ed., pp. 588–604). Itasca, IL: F.E. Peacock.

Unrau, Y.A. (1997b). Selecting a data collection method and data source. In R.M. Grinnell, Jr. (Ed.), *Social work research and evaluation: Quantitative and qualitative approaches* (5th ed., pp. 458–472). Itasca, IL: F.E. Peacock.

Unrau, Y.A., & Coleman, H. (1997). Qualitative data analysis. In R.M. Grinnell, Jr. (Ed.), *Social work research and evaluation: Quantitative and qualitative approaches* (5th ed., pp. 501–472). Itasca, IL: F.E. Peacock.

Unrau, Y.A., & Gabor, P.A. (1997). Implementing evaluations. In R.M. Grinnell, Jr. (Ed.), *Social work research and evaluation: Quantitative and qualitative approaches* (5th ed., pp. 588–604). Itasca, IL: F.E. Peacock.

Unrau, Y.A., Krysik, J.L., & Grinnell, R.M., Jr. (1997). *Student study guide for the fifth edition of Social Work Research and Evaluation: Quantitative and Qualitative Approaches.* Itasca, IL: F.E. Peacock.

Van Maanen, J. (1988). *Tales of the field: On writing ethnography.* Chicago: University of Chicago Press.

Walker, L. (1979). *The battered woman*. New York: Harper & Row.

Watts, T.D. (1985). Ethnomethodology. In R.M. Grinnell, Jr. (Ed.), *Social work research and evaluation* (2nd ed., pp. 357–369). Itasca, IL: F.E. Peacock.

Webb, E., Campbell, D., Schwartz, R., & Sechrest, L. (1966). *Unobtrusive measures: Nonreactive research in the social sciences*. Chicago: Rand McNally.

Weinbach, R.W. (1988). Agency and professional contexts of research. In R.M. Grinnell, Jr. (Ed.), *Social work research and evaluation* (3rd ed., pp. 25–41). Itasca, IL: F.E. Peacock.

Weinbach, R.W., & Grinnell, R.M., Jr. (1987). *Statistics for social workers*. White Plains, NY: Longman.

Weinbach, R.W., & Grinnell, R.M., Jr. (1991). *Statistics for social workers* (2nd ed.). White Plains, NY: Longman.

Weinbach, R.W., & Grinnell, R.M., Jr. (1995a). *Applying research knowledge: A workbook for social work students*. Boston: Allyn & Bacon.

Weinbach, R.W., & Grinnell, R.M., Jr. (1995b). *Statistics for social workers* (3rd ed.). White Plains, NY: Longman.

Weinbach, R.W., & Grinnell, R.M., Jr. (1996). *Applying research knowledge: A workbook for social work students.* (2nd ed.). Boston: Allyn & Bacon.

Weinbach, R.W., & Grinnell, R.M., Jr. (1998). *Statistics for social workers* (4th ed.). White Plains, NY: Longman.

Weinbach, R.W., Grinnell, R.M., Jr., Unrau, Y.A., & Taylor, L. (in press). *Applying research knowledge: A workbook for social work students* (3rd ed.). Boston: Allyn & Bacon.

Wilkinson, W.K., & McNeil, K. (1997). Cultural factors related to research. In R.M. Grinnell, Jr. (Ed.), *Social work research and evaluation: Quantitative and qualitative approaches* (5th ed., pp. 605–630). Itasca, IL: F.E. Peacock.

Williams, M., Grinnell, R.M., Jr., & Tutty, L.M. (1997). Research contexts. In R.M. Grinnell, Jr. (Ed.), *Social work research and evaluation: Quantitative and qualitative approaches* (5th ed., pp. 25–46). Itasca, IL: F.E. Peacock.

Williams, M., Tutty, L.M., & Grinnell, R.M., Jr. (1995). *Research in social work: An introduction* (2nd ed.). Itasca, IL: F.E. Peacock.

Yllo, K. (1988). Political and methodological debates in wife abuse research. In K. Yllo & M. Bograd (Eds.), *Feminist perspectives on wife abuse* (pp. 28–49). Newbury Park, CA: Sage.

Zuckerman, M. (1990). Some dubious premises in research and theory on racial differences. *American Pyschologist, 45,* 1297–1303.

Credits

M. Grinnell, Jr. Copyright © 1995 by F.E. Peacock Publishers; *Statistics for social workers* (1st, 2nd, 3rd, 4th eds.), by Robert W. Weinbach and Richard M. Grinnell, Jr. Copyright © 1987, 1991, 1995, 1998 by Longman Publishing Company; *Applying research knowledge: A workbook for social work students* (1st, 2nd eds.), by Robert W. Weinbach and Richard M. Grinnell, Jr. Copyright © 1995, 1996 by Allyn & Bacon; and *Applying research knowledge: A workbook for social work students* (3rd ed.), by Robert W. Weinbach, Richard M. Grinnell, Jr., Yvonne A. Unrau, and Lynne Taylor. Copyright © in press, by Allyn & Bacon.

Glossary: Some of the terms in the glossary may have been adapted and modified from: *Evaluation and quality improvement in the human services*, by Peter A. Gabor and Richard M. Grinnell, Jr. Copyright © 1994 by Allyn & Bacon; *Evaluation for social workers: A quality improvement approach for the social services* (2nd

ed.), by Peter A. Gabor, Yvonne A. Unrau, and Richard M. Grinnell, Jr. © 1998 by Allyn & Bacon; *Research in social work: A primer*, by Richard M. Grinnell, Jr. and Margaret Williams. Copyright © 1990 by F.E. Peacock Publishers; *Student study guide for the fourth edition of Social Work Research and Evaluation*, by Judy Krysik, Irene Hoffart, and Richard M. Grinnell, Jr. Copyright © 1993 by F.E. Peacock Publishers; *Student study guide for the fifth edition of Social Work Research and Evaluation: Quantitative and qualitative approaches*, by Yvonne A. Unrau, Judy Krysik, and Richard M. Grinnell, Jr. © 1997 by F.E. Peacock Publishers; *Research in social work: An introduction* (2nd ed.), by Margaret Williams, Leslie M. Tutty, and Richard M. Grinnell, Jr. Copyright © 1995 by F.E. Peacock Publishers; and *Statistics for social workers* (1st, 2nd, 3rd, 4th eds.), by Robert W. Weinbach and Richard M. Grinnell, Jr. Copyright © 1987, 1991, 1995, in press, by Longman Publishing Company.

Index

INTRODUCTION TO SOCIAL WORK RESEARCH
Edited by John Beasley
Production supervision by Kim Vander Steen
Cover design by Lesiak/Crampton Design, Inc., Park Ridge, Illinois
Line drawings by Donna Gaylord
Internal design and composition by Grinnell, Inc., Dallas, Texas
Paper, Finch Opaque
Printed and bound by McNaughton & Gunn, Inc., Saline, Michigan